THE AMERICAN RELIGIOUS EXPERIENCE

Other books by John K. Roth:

FREEDOM AND THE MORAL LIFE:
The Ethics of William James

PROBLEMS OF THE PHILOSOPHY OF RELIGION

Other books by Frederick Sontag:

DIVINE PERFECTION:
Possible Ideas of God

THE EXISTENTIALIST PROLEGOMENA:
To a Future Metaphysics

THE FUTURE OF THEOLOGY:
*A Philosophical Basis
for Contemporary Protestant Thought*

THE PROBLEMS OF METAPHYSICS

THE CRISIS OF FAITH:
A Protestant Witness in Rome

GOD, WHY DID YOU DO THAT?

THE GOD OF EVIL:
An Argument from the Existence of the Devil

HOW PHILOSOPHY SHAPES THEOLOGY:
Problems in the Philosophy of Religion

UNDERSTANDING UNDERSTANDING:
The Philosophy of Philosophy (Forthcoming)

THE SOUND OF SILENCE:
The Context for God (Forthcoming)

THE
AMERICAN
RELIGIOUS
EXPERIENCE

THE ROOTS, TRENDS, AND

FUTURE OF AMERICAN THEOLOGY

By FREDERICK SONTAG and JOHN K. ROTH

HARPER & ROW, PUBLISHERS

NEW YORK, EVANSTON

SAN FRANCISCO

1817 LONDON

FIRST EDITION

LIBRARY OF CONGRESS CATALOG CARD NUMBER: 73-163164

For

all who venture

on the spiritual odyssey

•

"Why dost thou stand afar off,
O Lord?
Why dost thou hide thyself in
times of trouble?"
—Psalm 10:1 (RSV)

CONTENTS

PREFACE

This book explores the thesis that every American is living through a crisis of identity and that his future will be different from—although drawn out of—his past. In his own way, each of us must struggle with the question: What has it meant, and what should it mean in the future, to be an American? Many approaches may be taken to answer that question, but in this volume we consider it from a religious perspective.

The formation and development of this nation cannot be adequately understood apart from a grasp of the theological thinking that has permeated the American bloodstream from colonial days to the present. Thus, it is important to decide whether religion's role will be different in the future. By exploring the roots, trends, and future of American theology, we hope this book may provide for men of varied backgrounds and persuasions an outlook helpful for understanding both themselves and their future. We need to see how theological reflection might make a difference to the quality of life ahead of us.

Our intention has been neither to write a detailed history of religion and philosophy in America nor to produce a systematic statement of theological doctrine. Instead, we wanted to present a creative and forward-looking interpretation of the contributions made by the major theologians and philosophers out of our own background, as well as others who contribute to the "American tradition." We have gone about this by concentrating on the following issues: What is distinctive about the American theological and philosophical tradition? Can this really help us to resolve the am-

biguity presently attached to being an "American"? Does this tradition provide any useful insights for a future understanding of
the nature and action of God? Did Americans in the past consider
themselves related to God in any special ways, and can they see
themselves as related to him in any distinctive ways in the future?

One of the important themes of the book is that the variety
of contributions free individuals make can be made compatible
one with another, and can actually encourage and support each
other. That principle is a historic part of the "American ideal," and
it also became a reality for the two of us as we wrote this book.
As our work and writing blended together, we found something
emerging that was both different from and better than anything
either of us could have produced alone.

We have not tried to reach an absolute consensus on every point.
Thus, there are some places where our interpretations and suggestions simply will not fit together smoothly. In spirit, however,
we believe we have reached a common perspective, even though
our agreement on detail may not be exact. We did work to eliminate any serious points of conflict, but we have not aimed to obscure the fact that the book was written by two men who sometimes see things differently.

Primary responsibility for drafting Chapters II, V, VI, IX, and
X is Frederick Sontag's, while John Roth did the major outlining
on Chapters III, IV, VII, and VIII. Each of us, however, contributed something to every chapter. In fact, by this time it is very
difficult to delineate which portions of Chapter I, for instance, each
of us first developed.

One further point about the writing of the book is worth mentioning. We began this project while we were both in Claremont,
California. Soon, however, John Roth left Claremont for a year
at Harvard University. If the physical separation sometimes made
communication difficult and time-consuming, our thinking was en-
larged by the difference in location and numerous travel experiences in America.

This land is both huge and varied. It wears many different aspects. A farm in Vermont is about as far away from New York
City as you can get, and the quadrangle at Pomona College is a
scene very different from Harvard Square. We are diverse, and

yet we are also one—but not perhaps to the degree that we can and should be. We have our problems, it is true, and they may even swallow us up in violence. But there is still much that is amazing, exciting, and beautiful about America—even as she now stands with many centers in decay. Americans still have will power, and we may even learn to cooperate again. Skyscrapers, superhighways, town meetings, schools, libraries, factories, colleges, and churches —the list could go on and on—all testify to these possibilities.

If we could find a source to renew and sustain our will, and if we could convince ourselves of the urgent need to cooperate in order to solve our problems, America could regain and extend an identity she is now perhaps in the process of losing: namely, to stand as a land of promise and hope for all who come and live here. Reflection on our theological heritage will enlighten us in this crucial task—that is our premise.

We received support from many persons as we worked on this book. A grant from the Intercollegiate Research Committee of the Claremont Colleges helped to support the final preparation of the manuscript, and John Roth's leave of absence from Claremont Men's College was made possible by a Graves Award in the Humanities, administered by Pomona College. Donald R. Cutler encouraged us to write a book like this, and it bears some of his imprint. Clayton E. Carlson of Harper & Row provided the editorial guidance that carried it into final form. Mrs. Ariel Strombotne typed most of the rough draft of the manuscript, and then Mrs. Harriet King put the manuscript in final form for us. We are grateful to all these friends, but especially to our wives and children, who contended with all our worries, met all our needs, and loved us all the way.

As we hope the reader will discover, this is an amazing time to explore and appraise the documents that record the scope of our past. And it is even more exciting to try to draw the future out of this. That is why we elect to dedicate the book to all who will risk such a venture.

F. E. S. J. K. R.

Pomona College *Claremont Men's College*
Claremont, California *Claremont, California*

I

SECULARISM AS
A RELIGIOUS CONTEXT:
AMERICA COME OF AGE

A. American Theology and Our Search for Identity

Beneath the contemporary criticisms of our national life a furious searching goes on to uncover what it does and can mean to be an American. Whether young or old, Americans live in a time of identity crisis—both as individuals and as a nation. Puzzlement about the present is exceeded only by uncertainty as to what the future holds. Even the past is not totally secure. Although we may know what events took place, their *meaning* for us is incomplete, because that depends partly on what we do today and tomorrow. This is not to say, however, that we are absolutely at loose ends. Americans have always been a vigorous, goal-oriented people. We continue to develop projects and to muster the energy to carry them out. No society has had a greater quantity of long-range planning, and some of our decisions still show genuine self-understanding.

There are even those among us who appear blessed with a special clarity of vision. On the one hand, some Americans are perfectly certain of the total depravity of our nation's life. They are convinced that a purification by violence and destruction must occur as a prelude to any restoration of society. Some of the younger generation are persuaded that the political and social situation is so hopeless that the only viable move is to withdraw and to establish an individualistic or communal life-style apart from the masses. At the same time other men, glossing over or failing to sense the dimensions of the staggering problems and dangers that threaten our existence, take the basic goodness of American life as a truth which ought to be self-evident to everyone.

The commitment and apparent confidence of men with such certainty lead them to think they have escaped the crisis of identity which most Americans must face. Firm commitment, clarity of vision, self-control, and self-understanding do frequently accompany each other. Nevertheless, we also know that both commitment and a display of confidence sometimes become most intense where real clarity is lacking. This is particularly true when one feels his vulnerability to threats from without or disintegration from within. Intense commitment to a belief, cause, or goal can be a cover-up for fragmentation, uncertainty, and a deep-seated insecurity about one's place in life. We are often offered a choice between uncritical allegiance to the goodness of American life and radical commitment to purge America of her sin by fire and brimstone. Must we give up our country as lost by withdrawing from its mainstream?

Like most things in this world, America herself is an ambiguous blend of good and evil, beauty and ugliness, purity and pollution, clarity and blindness. Whether we like it or not, we are all residents of an impure middle ground. Moreover, most of us recognize this pervasive ambiguity and know that such uncertainty forces us to reflect on our identity as Americans. We can scan the Atlantic from Plymouth Rock and give thanks for the determination and faith that brought the Pilgrims to America. Yet we know that one result of the immigration from Europe was the destruction of Indian life all the way to the Pacific. We can stand on Concord Bridge and experience the joy of being part of a revolution launched in the name of human freedom and integrity. At the same time, we know that all revolutions—even our own—proceed from mixed motives and can be romanticized beyond truth.

The ideals we first fought for are still not honored as they should be. We can walk the battlefields at Gettysburg and feel awe at the courage and sacrifice of the men from North and South caught in that internal struggle. Yet we know that slavery tore us apart then and leaves us divided now. We can absorb the unrivaled beauty of American national parks or feel proud over achievements of commerce and technology. At the same time, we see nature blighted and human life dragged through urban dirt. We also know we were the first people to drop atomic bombs on human beings, and now we must live with My Lai as well.

To be an American today is both invigorating and profoundly disturbing. Moreover, we are at a point of no return. Our day of youthful innocence as a nation—if it ever existed—is now part of an irretrievable past. We also know that, in these perilous times, "innocence" cannot be a quality in any individual's life for very long. Each new generation now grows up very fast. In addition, it is neither possible nor desirable for us to continue in the position we now occupy. Time itself will move us on somewhere else, and even a combination of invigorating and disturbing new experiences will leave us short of achieving health. We are truly a people "come of age." To say this, however, raises more issues than it solves, for we are left with a puzzling dilemma: What have we become, and can we make our individual and national life more worthwhile in the future?

Some of our forefathers participated in the birth of a nation. Our need and task is to bring about a rebirth at every level of American life, and rejuvenation is more difficult to achieve than first formation. Whether an age of ambiguity such as ours can produce this transformation—this is unclear. Yet, as far as we are concerned, no other starting point is available. Some of us are more hopeful than others,[1] but one thing is clear: unless many turn their minds and wills to this task with seriousness and determination, national demise will occur. We may fail anyway, since our situation is at best extremely precarious and difficult. Traditionally, however, Americans have welcomed stiff challenges. Where life itself is the prize, we must be bold.

American religious life and theology—their past, present, and future—these are the subjects of this book. But why, it may be asked, is it important to think about these things now? Many of us are struggling simply to find our identity, and some are trying desperately to get away from being "American." The answer is this: our nation is not only one of the few in history whose origin was the result of self-conscious thought, but it is also both important and true that the thought that produced her was to a large extent religiously and theologically oriented. If, therefore, Americans are to understand themselves and what they can become, attention must be given to the religious and theological frameworks that shaped the common past. These archaic vestiges still influence the present and contribute to the total context out of which we must structure the future. We may react to them in a plurality of ways. Whatever our response, however, understanding these origins is essential just because they are part of what we are.

Our hope is that, by examining our theological and philosophical heritage, we can recover and reformulate insights helpful in bringing about a rebirth of American life. Such a renewal will not come by any simple reinstatement of past views. Theories of previous eras always are to some degree inadequate for present problems, and certainly they cannot determine future action. By measuring our reactions to the past, by seeing where we agree and differ with the theological spokesman who helped to build our particular intellectual climate, we may clarify who we are, where we are headed, and perhaps the direction in which we can and ought to be moving.

At this point we should note that "theology" and "society" have a multifaceted relationship. They can, for example, criticize, support, and reflect each other. The relationship of reflection is of special interest because, if we face an identity crisis in American life, certainly one also exists in contemporary American theology. In fact, theologians in America may be worse off than other intellectuals today. Not only do they face an identity crisis as Americans, but there is widespread uncertainty over the present status of theology and as to whether it can ever have a healthy future in an American setting.

This is an intriguing phenomenon to observe in a nation which, in spite of its emphasis on the separation of church and state, has to a large degree understood its history, ideals, and destiny in religious categories. The secularity of our age may lead us to forget this, but it is historically true nonetheless. It is impossible to measure the exact degree to which social change has produced uncertainty about the tasks and possibilities for theology. It is hard to quantify the extent to which theological work itself has contributed to our secularity and uncertainty about who we are. But it will be profitable to examine whatever connection may exist between a rebirth among the American people and the revival of American theology.

In this book, to speak of a revival of American theology involves certain assumptions. First, we assume that there has been and is a genuine strain of "American philosophy" whose doctrines affect other areas of intellectual and practical life. Second, something which it is legitimate to designate as "American theology" already exists and has grown up in this context. Third, this American theology has important insights for us as we face the future, even though it is presently in some ways defective and in need of transformation.

We will argue that all three of these points are true. What we offer, therefore, is first a broad-scale analysis—both sympathetic and critical—of what those thinkers said who by their words shaped the context of American philosophy and theology from its beginnings down to the present day. Second, we will try to extract from this heritage what seems to be its unique aspects and assemble them to point out the way in which they open the possibility for a theological rebirth shaped by distinctively American contributions, which in turn may make possible a rebirth of America herself.

Having stated these general intentions and goals, we should consider in a little more detail how and why this study might open doors for a rebirth of theology in America which would also reshape American life. Consider two objections that might be raised against our basic thesis.

In the first place, it could be argued that the history of American theology to date is simply an extension of Continental thought. If so, it is so little connected with anything specifically American that a unique theology cannot emerge out of it even in the future. In the second place, it could be argued that our problems now are "international" in character and scope. If this were true, even if we found something unique in the American religious experience, it might be of no particular help in shaping either a new theology or a national consciousness adequate to the future.

We will attempt to answer the first question by outlining what the distinctive American strands in theology are. Of course, not every concept we stress is either characteristically American in content or unique to our thought alone. A great deal in any theology is unassociated with any specific country or people. On the other hand, no theology appears in a social and cultural vacuum. Each is rooted to some extent in the experiences of particular men in times and places that are unique, and the marks of this fact are found in the thought itself.

To the extent that any theology is particular, it has some weaknesses. The range of its impact is restricted because time moves on and circumstances change. On the other hand, particularity can be a strength, because the illumination of specific problems and situations is indispensable to human fulfillment. A similar analysis holds with respect to the universality of theology. Universality increases breadth and shows us what is common to existence irrespective of date and place. At the same time, the universality of doctrine enables us to illumine specific details of our lives at best only partially. All the men we study here recognize the tension between the universal and the particular in theology.

Now consider briefly this question: What form does the relationship between the universal and the particular take in the theological positions we examine? Our first response is that there are many possibilities, and that any particular form will depend largely on the interests and decisions of the individual theologian. Beyond that, however, we can suggest that universality will emerge in the themes and problems selected for consideration. The particularity, then, of American theology will stem more from the context and the ways in which the problems and themes are answered and developed.

Americans are not different from other men in seeking some intelligible way to understand the sources that structure human existence, the nature of good and evil, and the significance of man's abilities to think, choose, love, feel responsibility, and hope. Yet we want to treat these problems and themes within the geographical, historical, political, economic, and religious setting we share, and ask: Do we appropriate this as something different from that of non-Americans? Much of this book will be devoted to making these generalizations concrete.

The second issue—that our problems are now "international," and that even if there is something unique in the American theological experience it would be of no particular help to us in shaping a theology and a national consciousness adequate to the future—all this is closely related to the first question. The issue of the "relevance" of our past depends upon whether religion and theology require a concreteness and a community of particular experience for their claims about God to become meaningful and believable. If our answer to this is Yes, then we cannot recreate a satisfactory religious life and ritual, or shape a future theology, unless we can capture and build upon what has been and is most real and vital in our own experience as a union of divergent states.

Religion and theology can be neither exclusively contemporary nor purely an individualistic matter. Both involve recapturing a past beginning and participating in events not part of our own immediate culture and intellectual time. However, in order for this past to live again, it must assimilate indigenous forms of experience which enable the ancient events to have new life and forcefulness in a present age. Any study of the church fathers, of medieval theology, or of Reformation developments shows this to have been true of every creative era since the close of Christianity's founding age. The church fathers had to struggle with Hellenistic thought forms. Medieval and Reformation theology are not understandable unless we consider the development of the hierarchical church and an aristocratic society, plus the deficiencies which both revealed.

The situation the reformers faced in Europe is not the same as the context of Protestantism in America, either now or in our early formative years. What, then, is so characteristic and powerful in our own experience as a people that it can serve as an intellectual context of sufficient strength to structure an effective theology? We must discover for ourselves what thoughts are so much a part of our heritage that we tend either to overlook them or to take them for granted. Upon principles which are so fundamental, an effective religious life can be built and a theology developed strong enough to help us in the future.

In our present mood, dominated as it is by a spirit of criticism, uncertainty, rebellion, and even revolution, we cannot afford to take anything about our past for granted. If we do, it probably will be destroyed before our eyes. We must become intellectually self-conscious as Americans; not just economically and socially aggressive, as we have been. If we do not, the violence of the day will make it impossible for us to save what is crucial to preserve in our inheritance. Thus the way into the future for America—theologically and nationally—lies first through recovering our past. Can we discover in retrospect who we are, as distinct from the myriads of other men who have walked the face of the earth?

B. The Distinctive Marks of American Theology

What, then, are the unique hallmarks of American theology? Many could be mentioned, but one approach to this question is to cite three recurring themes in American thought and practice of religion and then to point toward another characteristic which overarches all three. An examination of American theology and religion indicates constant concern over the following issues: (1) the source, nature, and ultimate power of evil in the world, (2) the characteristics and significance of freedom, and (3) man's possibilities for finding fulfillment and meaning in the individual and communal dimensions of life.

Notice that the bare statement of these themes contains no direct reference to God or even to religion. In a book about American theology, this fact requires some explanation. If the statement of our themes is "secularized," it is because the thrust of this book is to illuminate contemporary life and future possibilities. We live in a time when many of us find that traditional theological language and religious practices no longer speak effectively. Thus, one thing is clear: If theology is to have a future in America, and if it is to illuminate either individual or corporate life, it must start where people live in late twentieth-century America.

Not every man is religious, but few men can avoid facing at some point the issues listed above. Life thrusts them on us. Every man faces his share of tragedy. All of us suffer, and we look with suspicion on the man who claims never to have done wrong or to have felt moral guilt. By the same token, every attempt at self-understanding raises problems about freedom. As we try to make something of our lives, questions about the nature and value of freedom become existential dilemmas, not abstract problems remote from everyday living.

Finally, the deepest question of all confronts us: What does it, can it, and ought it mean to exist? Every man who has "come of age" knows that he will die and that nations have no guaranteed eternal life. But if men die and nations wax and wane, we are also beings who hope. Life is not always congenial to hope, but it is our nature to try to make sense of existence in a way that renders each life meaningful. We may be divided about the extent of fulfillment possible, but we are unified in longing to replace the specter of absurdity and despair with lasting meaning.

Theology and religion have always made contact with precisely these issues. Any theological and religious treatment of such themes —either past or present—may use language and categories (e. g., sin, predestination, justification by faith, grace, etc.) which have lost their power and are neither very much in vogue nor widely understood today. Nevertheless, the basic issues dealt with in those formulations are largely the same ones that confront any man, however secularized he may have become. Whenever different languages are spoken, men appear to be worlds apart. Yet they still share something fundamental in facing the questions that life thrusts at them. Communication between men is difficult, but it is not impossible just because many of the fundamental questions about life are universal in the impact they make upon us.

It is not enough, however, to point out that a widespread alienation from the use of traditional theological discourse does not change the issues. An effort must be made in the following chapters to show, not only that the concerns of a secular age are not unlike those of a time when religious categories were more obvious in their influence, but also that renewed theological reflection can reinforce these themes in ways that will speak to contemporary men with power. We have to start where we live, but our health cannot be sustained by remaining at that point.

Thus we are faced by the question, "Why should any American—especially those who consider themselves secularized—be concerned about his theological and religious heritage and about the possibility of developing an American theology for the future?" Our answer is that by recovering and transforming a theological and religious understanding of our existence, we may achieve an awareness which can renew every sphere of American life. This is an extremely large order. It is also a worthwhile goal.

Earlier we stated that one characteristic in American religious experience overarches the three themes outlined. This can be stated as follows: Although American theology did not begin with such a goal in mind, *"pluralism" has emerged as its first principle.* What is the significance of this assertion? Obviously, it suggests that American theology contains a wide variety of possible positions. The problems and themes may be largely the same, but we recognize that a variety of approaches and treatments are open for adoption. More important and distinctive, this claim implies that such plurality is not only possible but desirable. No single theological theory ought to demand or expect the allegiance of every man, if this is the case.

To a considerable extent, what we know as American life had its origin in a desire to escape religious intolerance and discrimination. It was not, however, the intention of the early Puritans to establish a society of freethinkers. The unique American achievement—the establishment of a society and government which would extol, at least as an ideal, the fundamental value of liberty and pluralism—this emerged only through struggle, compromise, and hard work.

The "American experience" of our forefathers—which usually had its religious dimensions—was a changing experience. What they learned was this: A society which allows real freedom of thought, belief, and action is not only possible but also desirable. Thus, if toleration of religious differences in America began as the result of an unresolved struggle, there is a sense in which the outcome yielded a culture that did more than tolerate pluralism. We moved on to encourage it, in the belief that unity and variety in life-style are both compatible and mutually enriching.

The fact that this lesson was learned once, however, does not make it secure for all time. We live in an age when the fruitful tension between unity and pluralism hammered out by our forefathers is in danger of being fragmented by movements toward both a dissolution of communal life and a repression of freedom. Perhaps reflection on our religious and theological heritage can convince us of the importance of pressing for a balanced, if precarious, middle ground.

Still another point about pluralism in American thought is worth noting. An atmosphere of theological difference, such as America eventually fostered, ought to lend itself to speculative boldness in theological work and creativity in religious life. The American continent should provide an environment for theological and religious opportunity, as well as for economic and political openness. No American should feel hemmed in by the theological theories and religious practices of others. His heritage urges him, instead, to seek and to create something viable for himself which perhaps others might enjoy too. If theology and religion do not have a future in America, they are unlikely to have one elsewhere. Every option is open here, if men are willing to do the hard work necessary to make them come alive.

On the other hand, American life has never guaranteed success to everyone who tries. Failure is one of the harsh facts of life. In our American system, this harshness may even be somewhat escalated. Opportunity is available to any who will seize it, but freedom, if given to so many, can have the effect of thwarting us or forcing us to draw back before our project is off the ground. Constructive theological work and religious faith are, therefore, both easy and difficult within an American culture. They are easy because so many options are open, but difficult because support for any idea or practice is not guaranteed. Thus, in a secular society such as ours, theology and religion can leave their mark and perhaps initiate rebirth, but theologians and churches will have to have their wits about them if they hope to gain a hearing.

Consider one final point about the relation between pluralism and theology in America. If our experiences of freedom and evil and our search for fulfillment join to create issues which demand a continued religious interpretation, American theologians may do well to add the phenomenon of pluralism to their list of topics needing clarification. One interesting way to approach this issue theologically would be to ask what hypotheses can answer the following question: What kind of God would create a world in which such a plurality of theological views is possible? In particular, how can he relate to a society which consciously fosters this plurality, thus often making religious life more difficult? If pluralism is a distinctive mark of the American religious experience, it ought to be interpreted theologically, and American thinkers may find that this approach opens a provocative access to new thought about God.

C. American Experience and Its Distinctive Theological Marks

Having discovered some central marks of traditional American theology, let us explore in a little more detail (1) how these dominant features have manifested themselves in our heritage, and (2) what further implications such an analysis may reveal with respect to the task of building a "theology for our common future." In Chapters II–IX, we shall explore these issues as they relate specifically to American theologians and philosophers. For the present, however, let us take a brief look at some basic features of our nation's history.

Any account of the religious and philosophical origins of America must recognize at least three facts. First, no one group with a single outlook originally settled America. The Puritans were among the first arrivals, and they did try to establish a theocracy antithetical to the notion of religious tolerance. Nevertheless, the early settlements of Roman Catholics in Maryland and Quakers in Pennsylvania indicate that religious pluralism characterized the beginnings of this nation. Second, the separation of church and state and religious tolerance were not principles unanimously agreed upon from the outset. Some colonies would have united secular government with religious motives and fastened down a required religious orthodoxy. This may have been based on different principles, but it was still no less tight than that from which they had fled. Separation of church and state and religious tolerance, it is clear, both arose as matters of political expediency. They became necessities only if diverse colonies were to find a viable basis for political and economic union.

Third, American thought was not, at least at its origin, set in the context of a "United States." The early colonies were not revolutionary in their thinking. Instead, the new settlers reflected the variety of backgrounds from which they had come and the mixed purposes for which they sailed the Atlantic. Independence and union may eventually have become powerful goals, but they were not strong attractions for the original settlement of the land. In fact, independence and union became dominant issues in American thought precisely because the variety in our views and the heterogeneity of our backgrounds in themselves forced freedom upon our thinking. We had to be led gradually to see that, despite our diversity, we shared many interests in common.

Plural at birth and at odds in both life-style and conviction, when our split from European origins became a forced option and union became indispensable for the success of the Revolution, we found tolerance and separation of church and state the only practical means to achieve this goal. Born out of plurality and opposition, independence and union were achieved in spite of this, as necessities but not as originally agreed aims.

Unity with emphasis on pluralism and freedom of individual determination, plus restrictions against either political support or interference in religious matters—these are very different from Reformation ideals, and they mark America as being not just a "Protestant country." We became something beyond Calvin's goal of a controlled Geneva. We developed into a country religiously open to all, including the nonreligious. Theology in this setting ought to be somewhat differently oriented, since it lacks the entanglements of a state religion. Because the state supports no religion here, each brand must develop its appeal among the people or be refused continued status. Thus, if organized religion finds itself rejected today, it must reattract its followers or go out of business, for the state cannot enforce religious belief. This drives theology into the market place; but perhaps—for Americans—that is not a bad arena in which to ask religion to prove itself.

In spite of the qualification stated above, it is hard to talk about the origins of an American theology without implying that these are so dominantly Protestant that any Roman Catholic theology is shut out from such a base. It is true that almost all the early determining figures in this country were either Protestant or oriented in that direction. For a long time it seemed that Protestants and Catholics could find little in common, at least on specifically

American ground. However, given the reexamination of Catholic doctrine going on so intensely all around us, Roman Catholics today may suddenly find a basis for their own revised contemporary theology in the American story of a struggle for pluralism and religious tolerance.

American democracy makes everyone into a civilian—even those in special religious dress—and any early anti-Catholic feelings that cropped up in our history were sparked partly by Rome's overtly imperial trappings. Today, as Catholicism sheds much of its inherited regal pomp, it actually comes much more into line with the American tradition. In this country we have always wanted to maintain civilian control over the military, and in religious affairs our tendency has been toward strong lay participation in church governance. This is an American, not a Reformation, ideal. A careful balance of power is spelled out clearly in our Constitution precisely to prevent the rise to absolute power of any one man. This inclines us, when we turn to religion, to allow no man single authority in that sphere either. Thus the current movement in Roman circles toward "collegiality" fits much more easily into our American heritage.

Diversity is primary and ultimate. No single religious group embraced all the American people at the beginning or seems likely ever to do so. If the Puritans in New England wanted to try the "holy experiment" of a union of church and civil government, their own internal disagreements soon made this impossible. Furthermore, no such notion ever characterized the outlook of all the colonies, and so it could never form the basis for union. The new states could not identify with a single church because there never was one church to identify with. Roger Williams denied that the state had the right to force the conscience of any man, and his dissenting view ultimately prevailed. The union of the individual colonies would have been impossible without the agreed separation of church and state. If a union was to be achieved, freedom of religious practice and belief had to be constitutionally guaranteed.

From our earliest days, the Quakers provided a refuge against every attempt within the colonies to impose religious conformity. Their very existence made impossible a uniform or militant theological orthodoxy. Thus, the Quaker presence in Pennsylvania actually provided the opening which brought representatives from nearly every Protestant tradition to America, and this thwarted any potential Anglican dominance stemming from the Church of England. The battle of conformity vs. dissent was indigenous, even before our nation's official birth. We are neither completely free-thinkers nor strictly orthodox. Instead, we are a strange mixture—and thus a perpetual clash—of both tendencies. As a people we were born in an argument over slavery and freedom. We may have changed the specific issues, but the original battle has never ceased.

Bishops were as much a target as kings when the struggle for independence mounted and was finally thrust upon the thirteen colonies. If we felt strongly that the economic and political affairs of men in the new land were not to be determined from a distance without appeal or participation, neither were we about to allow religious leaders to dictate from afar. The principles of self-determination became as fixed in religion as in government, which explains the long-standing suspicion that haunted Roman Catholics, as if they were still under allegiance to a "foreign power." All churches in America were forced in the direction of religious liberty, even though some never favored it and would have had it otherwise if they could. Our forms of religious life were born out of forced compromise, and out of the impossibility for any one group to have its own way exclusively. If this is a good situation, it is indigenously American.

Perhaps no nation ever does, but America certainly did not begin religiously in any Garden of Eden with all its citizens in peaceful agreement. Pluralism and controversy did not develop only after some tempting snake seduced us; they were with us from the start. We came here because we labored under religious persecution and discrimination, but the freedom we found never provided absolute unity or resulted in any dominant form which could become a state religion. The original tensions between the colonies over diversity in religion and a variety of individual attempts to enforce orthodoxy—all this is still with us. Are we able to recognize that religion is always born in controversy and is perhaps healthiest in pluralism, where no one can dominate? If we can see that a rigid and unopposed orthodoxy always verges on persecution and self-righteousness (that original sin of all religious life), we may be better oriented toward what is possible in our future.

Like the thirteen colonies, the churches of America also had to find a way to establish their independence from European ties after the successful Revolution. Pluralism and independence were bound to be our religious keynote, but this prevents spiritual ties from uniting all Christians. If we are to find a union of spirit, it cannot depend on national ties or legal and hierarchical control. This fact always allows Americans to see religion in purely local terms, but our inherent tendency to religious provincialism at the same time carries with it the strength of providing native roots from which the religious spirit can grow. If we lack an established church and comfortable state sanctions for religion, at least that leaves religion free to express the community concerns of the congregation's location.

William Penn stands as a model for our now constant opposition to all state support for religion, a position which finally prevailed against centers in both North and South which gladly would have linked religion to state auspices. Not without opposition, Virginia established full religious liberty by law in 1785. Nevertheless, the avowed friendliness of our government toward religion was always affirmed (e. g., by institutional tax exemption), and this still remains an item of contention.

When the movement to settle the frontier began, two qualities came to characterize American religion: (1) its missionary spirit of following the people wherever they settled, and (2) the continual phenomenon of religious revivalism. Such a religious life is bound to be direct, personal, highly emotional, and immediate; these qualities also go hand in hand with religious liberty and pluralism.

If the chief features of the early American dream were shaped by religious concern, it may be true that its fruits are to be found in the secular society we have today.[2] In spite of the religious motivation of some of the early colonists, secular interests were probably equally fundamental in forming American society from the beginning. Yet today even the most original and basic religious goals have been largely secularized. Lacking state coercion, there is no need now for anyone to recognize the claims of religion if he does not want to. At least this is true once religious affiliation no longer plays a large role in economic, social, or political success.

If religion has striven to build a certain quality of life in America, we cannot understand our country today without assessing the effect of these ideals. Furthermore, if the place of religion in American life has changed, the effect of this shift on our ideals of life will be significant. Since theology builds on the context of the church's cultural setting and life, theology too will have a different future just to the extent that religion's place in our national life is changed. For instance, the early goal of religion was to mold American life in certain ways—for example, by the vast effort to found church-related colleges. If these aims have now been dropped and religion no longer has this formal influence, then to the extent that these goals are fully secular, theology will have to find a new function.

Religion in the early years shaped this country's goals, or at least played a heavy part in doing so. Even if the theocratic ideal of the Puritans was rejected in favor of Protestant pluralism coupled with a Roman Catholic immigrant wave, still the churches as plural bodies individually exercised profound influence on American national life. Consider the YMCA and Salvation Army movements, without which it seems impossible to understand the era only just now closed. The goals of American religion (e. g., education open to all and care for the poor) are now by and large secular responsibilities. If these aims have been achieved, their very success demands a new role for theology. Religion in America often dreamed of a society open to all. To an extent this aim has been widely accepted, and thus no longer is a specifically religious goal.

In this country we hoped to promote novelty, and we also encouraged it when we saw it as a religious ideal. Creativity is our byword. This factor is still operative in American religious life today, but it is hardly any longer considered to be specifically religious in its inspiration. A "covenant theology" originally inspired nationalism as one means to provide cohesion among the early settlers. Today the bonds that bind us as a nation are hardly religious.

We may cite secular goals as our common cause, but now we are at odds over some of them—e. g., our welfare programs. Thus theology, in the days ahead, cannot expect either to provide a simple basis for national unity (as in the founding era) or even necessarily to profit from whatever national goals we agree upon. The unity of the nation can no longer be religiously guaranteed, and the unity of religious groups will likely receive little help from the dominant forces in our national life.

There is no question but that the early settlers and pioneers— to some extent at least—thought of America as "God's country." Thus it had a religious mission to perform. We literally considered ourselves to be a "new Israel." Secular, political, and economic aims were equally important, but religious goals and zeal were no small motivating force in the founding era. If this situation has now changed, what does it say about America's future and the altered role of theology? For one thing, the aims of religion cannot be tied to national success. They must be disentangled from any demand for an approval of American policy. Theology has always been culture's critic, but now that religion plays a smaller social role, any theology of the future may be forced still further into a contrasting position.

To a considerable extent, America has been ahistorical or non-historical. This is largely because its own history did not really go back beyond the colonies, and because the Revolution made us anxious to break our European ties and start afresh. Many early immigrants made a conscious effort to forget their homeland. The Bible has always served as our basic religious norm, although its normative function has been variously interpreted. We were too busy creating a future to build our theology on a foundation of an extensive historical study of European and classical sources. Such historical theology as is now in use is an imported product. If revivalism made us feel that we were close to Christianity's origin, this was experienced as an immediate relation and not as the result of any historical or evolutionary pattern of development. Politically we shunned entangling alliances, and theologically we looked for a fresh start. Now, however, we have lived long enough to record our own history as a nation, and our emergence as a world power has made us painfully conscious that we no longer are an isolated, pioneering land.

D. The Shape of the Future Given by the Past

In the late twentieth century we have been shaken loose from simple identification with our founding ideals, a feat which the Vietnam war perhaps accomplished. What kind of theology can be built from the awareness of our own history, when powerful forces have detached us from our original idea of a national purpose? Once we have been made aware of our own sin, perhaps a less self-righteous and less self-satisfied theology can be ours. For decades we contrasted ourselves with Europe (the Old vs. the New World). Today we feel old and battle-scarred as a nation ourselves, so that theology here should be more mature and less immediate in its goals. Now in this country we can at last feel our own power less and the necessity for God's power more.

Religious life as it developed in America could not of itself unify the country, in spite of the attraction of the religious goal of creating a utopia and a land which would fulfill God's promise. This was because religious life in America was diverse from the beginning, never unified in a single church. Thus the direction of religion on these shores has been toward plurality of structure, not unity. If either our religious or our national goals are ever to be achieved, a way must be found without demanding uniformity of belief or opinion as a condition. If religion in America cultivates pluralism, can we still be brought together by some unifying loyalty? Nationally, it will have to be subject to constant variation. Religiously, it can never demand institutional unity and individual conformity or adherence to a single creed.

Religious pluralism became the hallmark of the American way of doing things, and its unique result is a free church spirit and tradition. Any theology raised upon this foundation cannot be "church theology" in a narrow sense, since we have no institution here capable of providing that unifying force. This fact gives some Continental theology a strange sound when it is read here. "Church" in this land means only one of many. Thus every formal structure remains open to challenge and constantly needs to justify itself against its competitors. If our free enterprise system has limitations as a social policy, still this is a healthy pattern for theology, since it forces every religious form constantly to justify itself and prove its worth. *There cannot, then, be only one "American theology"; that is a contradiction in terms as we understand America. However, there can be several "free theologies"—ones which never seek justification by their institutional or historical connections alone.*

In opposition to this thesis, as an individual one may argue that he is a member of one church, in virtue of which he has a theology—or at least a theological tradition—given him. Still, although any person can say this, he can never argue along this line simply on the basis of being an American. By that fact alone he has no specific theology provided for him—except a free theology, which means a theology open to individual assessment against its counterparts and constantly in need of justification. Today our society gives us no religion simply by virtue of being a member of it; the dream of the Puritan theocracy was overcome by the facts of religious pluralism and diversity. If this account of the future for American theology sounds "too Protestant" in its features, actually it is not far from Roman Catholic self-understanding since Vatican II.

America began with a Puritanism which wanted to restore the simplicity and purity of first-century Christianity; it is interesting to note how strong the yearning is today—in both Roman Catholic and Protestant circles—for a return to the original, and thus less complicated, religious forms. At the founding of our country, it was European ecclesiastical and princely complexity and degeneration that drew our opposition. Today it is our own evolution that has brought us so rapidly to the place where we must either reform or perish. Once we felt the weight of the mistakes of others; now it is our own sins from which we need to be freed. *Any theology of the future will need to be built around a theme of the need for national—and thus individual—rebirth.* Our religious goals today form a counterpart to the original objections we made against the decadent Europe from which we fled, except that now these protests are transferred to our own past.

Though Anglicanism was established in Virginia as an officially supported religion, one result of the union of the states was the compromise necessitated over religion. (The same was true of slavery, except that the results of compromise were better in the case of religion.) If this country were not a union of states, as opposed to being the result of the successful conquest by a single power, religion might not have been held separate from the state. We Americans blundered into our advantageous religious position. It occurred not because we did not make an effort to impose our religion on everyone else, as others before us had done, but because simple political expediency dictated toleration as a condition for the union of autonomous states.

It is odd to consider that, in spite of our pride in religious toleration and freedom of conscience, this was by no means a part of the belief of either the immigrating Puritans, Anglicans, or Roman Catholics. Puritans banned all diversity and gave magistrates certain powers in religion. The Anglican divine was not geared to tolerate opposition in religious matters. However, the economic and political dissent in this country gradually forced upon the colonies in reaction to English repression carried along with it an implicit openness to all beliefs. The protection of the natural rights of the individual became the uniting concern of the colonies, and in the course of events this had to embrace religion too.

If Roger Williams championed freedom of conscience in 1644, he was unique for his time. The best reforms often are practical necessities and not born as original ideals. As every sect and denomination poured into America, all hope for a religious conformity and purity was lost. Henceforth each religious form in America either made it on its own in a rough-and-tumble world, or not at all. Since our early failure to establish a pure religious state, religion has been either justified pragmatically in this country or else dismissed. It would seem that *all religion in the future of America must at the same time fill a spiritual need and serve a social purpose, or its theology will not be found compelling.*

The wellsprings of religious fervor in America have dried up many times, only to be renewed again. We never seem to learn that the direction prevailing at any given moment may not continue in force, but may swing all the way around once more. When religious interest runs high, we plot our course as if this pace could only increase. When great numbers turn away from the churches, we panic and act as if that signaled the end of all formal religious institutional life. Actually, the fluctuation of power in religious life is more capricious than any fixed cycle. Our nation was clearly in many ways religiously founded, yet the evidence of moral indifference was not long in appearing. When debauchery reaches its peak, reformation may be at hand—as well as total degeneration. This is clear in our national past in the time of what we call the "Great Awakening."

In 1714 religion was thought to be on the wane, but within twenty-five years a vast revival was sweeping the country.[3] Although it may have begun as a rural or village phenomenon, this wave quickly spread to the cities. The results were mixed, but an upsurge of humanitarian impulses did occur, education being one of the chief beneficiaries. In the same period, deistic religion increased its influence among intellectuals. Deism indulged the emotions less than revivalism, but its philosophical foundations enabled it to become an important source of spiritual and intellectual release. Liberal movements are as characteristic of our life as conservative theology, even in the pre-Revolutionary era before the Union was formed. A profound horror of uniformity existed even then, and this worked to tear down any proposal for unification based on religious conformity.

Protest against state-supported religion arrived simultaneously with the Revolution. Backing for the adoption of the Constitution came to depend on assurance of the abolition of any religious establishment. Religion was not to be discouraged, but enforced conformity, persecution, and intolerance were. We have never been antireligious as a country. We support religion by political and economic favors, but—it is important to note—this never centers on one religious form in preference to others. It took a long time for a Roman Catholic to be elected President or for a priest to be elected to Congress, but that was more a matter of the political facts of life than the result of religious suppression.

E. The Religious Sources of a New American Dream

Today, when things American are under challenge, we are also haunted by the suspicion that—just perhaps—one of our problems lies in not having understood exactly what it means to stand in the "American tradition." As Plato pointed out in his Dialogues, you must be sure you understand the true nature of something before you can be safe in rejecting it.

One of the first things every schoolboy learns (and some theologians are inclined to forget) is that the founding of America was deeply involved with a serious struggle to obtain "freedom" of religious belief. Not all who sailed to these shores were religiously driven. Many were either economically motivated or simply adventuresome. Nevertheless, the evils of religious persecution were very much in the minds of those who first came, although probably it was a matter of money and political oppression that eventually brought about the separation of the colonies from England. The important point to note is that our religious heritage began with a principle of strict separation of church and state, and this notion was not the original premise of any European country. "Religion without political alliance" is an idea we should not overlook in our attempt to shape a future theology for ourselves, and this applies equally to the social liberal and the economic conservative.

Anticlericalism has never been strong in this country because, except for one early experiment, the church never gained a national dominance which allowed it the luxury of oppression. The church in this land claimed no official tie to the nation's artistic or cultural life. Sometimes this results sadly in a church which aesthetically is merely imitative. If artists see no reason to give the church any particular loyalty, as they might in a church-dominated culture, our lack of creativeness in religious art does give religion in America a clear-cut distinction from being simply another form of the aesthetic life. Unlike our way of thinking about the medieval church, we ought not to confuse our appreciation for art with a love of religion. If capitalism is sometimes tied to Protestantism in Europe, and if Marxism is antireligious on economic grounds, the church in America has never officially been identified with economic privilege, and our required separation of church and state has kept Protestantism here from being connected publicly or officially with our economic policy. Of course, on an individual and local level where immediate concerns are expressed, the situation could be—and often is—quite different. However, the whole of the American scene is our concern here.

In Europe there is a strong tendency to identify Christianity with Western culture, because for so long the two were intimately connected. American "culture" (such as it is) has no such religious identification. Or at least any influence of religion on aesthetic production flows along more individual and less formal lines. Many important thinkers in America's formative years were personally very religious men, as will be seen clearly when we examine their thought. But the life of religion in the New World is not much intertwined with our artistic and cultural heritage. Ministers were the educators in the first decades of this country, and churches were the major founders of colleges. Still, we have never had anything here that compares to the role of religion in public life so characteristic of the Middle Ages.

Since religious groups (particularly the Quakers and the Puritans) set about establishing schools very early, religion from its beginning in this country was associated with learning and with rational thought. Thus theology here has always been closely allied with philosophy and therefore open to its influence, as has not been the case with every religious development. In our South, however, democratic education for the masses was not originally an accepted principle. Thus a parallel strain of religion developed, less associated with schools and more with folkways. Just as America has never been without internal strife over the problem of slavery, so intellectually oriented religion in America has never been without a healthy infusion of emotionally based, antisophisticated religious fervor.

We must distinguish sharply what we want to distill in this volume from any inquiry into *the history of the churches* in America.[4] To be sure, we are arguing that economic and social and political conditions in America eventually worked to give our theological and philosophical thought a unique cast. However, it is one thing to chronicle the growth and life of the various institutional church structures and another to try to assess the potential vitality of the ideas generated by that process. Yet a study of the churches' development does reveal a tendency in this country toward constant free experimentation, while at the same time there is a maintenance of the Bible as a basic norm for belief. Thus "freedom" and "fundamentalism" are both equally bedrock in American religious life, and they set the stage for constant tension. To learn to live in the midst of that struggle—both creative and destructive in its results—is an important theological task for the future.

If Emerson could say, "Europe extends to the Alleghenies, while America lies beyond"—this has been somewhat characteristic of American religion, too. The Midwest, the West, and the South have consistently been sources both of strength and of a religious life built solidly on the folkways of the country. If this long-established national pattern is now changing and all sections are becoming more alike with no area any longer isolated, it is still true that a great deal of the continued strength of religion in America comes from the West and South. If it were not for the pioneering and settling of the West, we could never have developed and sustained the idea of creating "the kingdom of God in America." And if today we are disillusioned about our ability to realize that dream for everyone equally, still only that original western expansion could have made us think it possible at all.

Out on the frontier, evangelism had to try to be convincing to people who had not come to this country for religious purposes in the first place. The theology of the revival reflected the new spirit of democracy in the country, but it is also true that both a revivalist spirit and a democratic theory of the church tend to give a distinctive tone to American theology. We ought not to be averse to the expression of emotion in religion; it is too solidly built into our origins. The expansion of the country dictated a missionary and an evangelical orientation for American religious life which we can abandon only by being false to ourselves. On the other hand, all the various churches entered into the business of education, founding colleges with fantastic vigor. This work was often done as much for missionary purposes as for love of the intellectual life. Nevertheless, "intellectualism" is a dimension of America's religious heritage too—however surprising that may seem.

Calvinism, with its strong sense of sin and determinism, was imported to this country. Yet as new theologies developed here, they took a more optimistic view of man and his possibilities. Such a change in outlook was natural and appropriate in a land with open frontiers and rich resources, and it surely has been an important factor in our pioneering endeavors—from the settlement of the West to the exploration of space. No theology can be distinctively American which does not place a strong emphasis both on man's freedom and on his potential worth and creative possibilities.

At the same time, in a precarious pioneer setting there is always the practical problem of survival under frontier conditions. When we think of the Hebrew tribes in the wilderness, it does not seem so strange that a sense of God might become most real under the threat to survival that was common experience in the American West. Cowboys and Indians and missionaries and stagecoach robbers all have a place in an open American theology. We ought to emphasize that man's existence is not only free and full of options, but also that God placed us—and may come to meet us—in a framework of harsh wilderness conditions which test us to the core.

Slavery divided the colonies, and it ruptured the union of states so badly that we have never fully recovered. It is one of the bitter ironies of human history that men came to American shores seeking freedom and yet failed to avoid the tragedy of human slavery. But if religion shares the guilt for perpetrating this evil, and for failing to hasten the reconciliation so much needed, it is also true that efforts to free the slaves and to achieve justice often received their strongest impetus and support from American religious sources. This suggests that any theology which seeks to be distinctively American by being true to what is best in our tradition ought to side with the suppressed and the downtrodden in the name of freedom. Freedom has always been at the heart of the American experience, and it has returned to dominate our thinking of late. The concept is so crucial now that no American theology can avoid giving it a determinative role. To do so also involves a need to reassess the nature of evil and its relation to God.

Americans have sometimes thought that their nation was divinely chosen for a world mission. This form of alliance between religion and the state has as many advantages for our sense of moral commitment to the world scene as it has drawbacks in encouraging a too provincial outlook. Precisely at this point, it should be noted that the traditional social and religious emphases of Judaism are also very deeply ingrained in our national social consciousness.

The existence on both our coasts of one of the largest Jewish populations in the world contributes to make America "Christian" in only a formal sense. The famous qualities of Jewish spirituality (coupled always with raw secularity) have been influential in shaping our national consciousness. The crucial point, however, is this: the closeness—without identity—of religion to our national destiny should make us feel that any reassessment of national goals must have its theological counterpart. Similarly, as churches change their roles the religious impetus behind nationalism is bound to be affected at the same time.

For Americans, to become thoroughly secular is to lose something valuable in our cultural heritage. Theology in this land has never had the power to control national policy, but the religious spirit has been, and still is, a major factor in developing American self-understanding and in producing our best moral insight. The influence which religion has, or can hope to exercise, is not a legal one. Now, as always in our past, its power depends on moral persuasion. Any "American theology" will have to remain politically independent but morally oriented.

The pattern of flight from the evils of religious persecution, political inequality, and social injustice has repeated itself again and again in our history. The nation was born in rebellion against tyranny and suppression, obsessed with the vision of a society that would extend the opportunity for human fulfillment beyond any existing limits.

Our history is a mixture of success and failure in achieving these goals. The very evils against which our forefathers rebelled in fleeing Europe have cropped out among our own people time after time. On the other hand, it is hard to see that any other society has done as much to extend freedom and to give men a chance to use it fruitfully. Our task is to pull a theology forward from this accomplishment by a fresh understanding of how even this much of a miracle came to be.

NOTES

1. For the most positive statement of optimism, see Charles A. Reich, *The Greening of America* (New York: Bantam Books, 1971). For our critical response to this, see Chapter IX.

2. See William A. Clebsch, *From Sacred to Profane America* (New York: Harper & Row, 1968).

3. See Clifton E. Olmstead, *History of Religion in the United States* (Englewood Cliffs, N.J.: Prentice-Hall, 1960).

4. See, for example, Jerald C. Brauer, *Protestantism in America* (Philadelphia: Westminster Press, 1953).

II

THE ORIGINS OF
A NATIONAL SPIRIT

A. From the Many, One

The variety of churches now present in this country was not split apart from some original perfect union. We began as broken, separate, and structurally different religious entities. No one form of faith—not even Christianity—has ever had total dominance in America. Our early political union brought together widely differing political states, but it never even occurred to the early colonists that a union of all churches was something to be desired. In fact, the opposite is the case: our political union would never have been consummated if it had depended upon a prior religious unification, or if it had even carried this implication with it. Religious pluralism became a primary condition for our political unification.

Whatever we try to accomplish religiously in America, we will have to do as cooperating diverse structures. Whatever unity of spiritual purpose we achieve, it will have to come from a deeper level than simply the direction of a single church hierarchy. However we celebrate and serve God, it can never be through one form—barring a religious war. Even if ritual plays a part in our political life, this never has been and never will be of any single type. Thus the simple holiday intrusion of religious ritual into public life (e. g., Christmas) is not to be feared. No one faith can dominate and exclude all others here. Rather, our heritage is to allow the celebration of all rituals to the exclusion of none. If any man is to make his personal identification amid this variety, he will have to do so by individual selection and personal tenacity. No external force will guide him to any one religious form.

The Puritans gave us an original respect for intellectual training in the ministry, and this resulted in our characteristic widespread emphasis on a college education, which was even endorsed by those who did not go themselves. At the same time, anti-intellectual and individualistic interpretations of religion were an ever-present threat to an educated leadership, just as they still are today. Thus the religious and the political life of this country cross and diverge. Before the colonies were united into states, theology was independent and confined primarily to separate groups and their particular tradition. Once political union was consummated, we faced the question of how to reconcile the diverse religious traditions within one land.

Nevertheless, the setting we must grasp if we want to understand our early religious life (as well as its reflection in theology) is that of the political debate, first as carried out with Europe and then amongst ourselves. Alexis de Tocqueville (1805–1859), for instance, tells his readers that if they want to understand a nation they must study its social conditions.[1] In the case of America, these are "eminently democratic" (p. 2). Today we take this so much for granted that we are likely to forget it, and yet for decades the rest of the world looked on us as the stronghold of democracy. If presently this is our weakness as well as our strength, it is still true that democracy provided an original environment within which a unique development of religious thought took place.

Whether intellectual or otherwise, Americans respect native talent and accomplishment, or so Tocqueville is convinced. The germ of aristocracy was never allowed to grow here. Because of this, we have a different notion of "property." It does not represent simply the family, since property accumulated in this country does not stay intact as such. It is too individually connected. Thus we have no aristocratic support for transmitting the pursuit of knowledge as a pleasure for its own sake. Men, and likewise churches and religions, are more to be judged on their own than for external or traditional reasons. The doctrine of the sovereignty of the people took possession of our state as it formed, and created an ethos which built religion on that same principle. In America, God must be a democrat or else not rule at all.

Aristocracy, at least in theory, trains the best to hold the highest office. Tocqueville claims to have been surprised to find so little distinguished talent among the governing group here. This is because, with a democratic thrust, both administrative and official office is less likely to be regarded as of prime importance. We neglect them at our peril, of course. Still, "the people" are more apt to be the focus of attention, and they—it is more usually thought—are where power and ultimate value lie. No bishops, palaces, or state centers for religion are likely to be built in such circumstances. Both theology and our religious life are a community affair. We are inclined to see theology either as coming from the people or as of no value.

When we ponder the formation of the Union, now so distant from our time, we tend to think of it as having been "smooth" and "natural." In point of fact, disintegration threatened our first tenuous united existence even as it formed. And to face that threat again today is to experience once more the pain of national birth, together with the uncertainties of its future success.

If, then, we were not all certain in advance of the wisdom of our original rebellion against English rule, when once we were separated, anxiety continued to pervade the discussion of union. Finally welded together, we think of our bonds as having been inevitable. To know uncertainty in our national purpose now is to pass over the sheltered adolescent years and to realize once again, in later life, how nearly we failed at the start. After our rupture from Britain, we were not sure whether the locus of authority should be in one central government, or split up among us all, and we are hardly more sure of it today.

Sometimes we forget that to operate under a constitution is a special kind of government and that it probably has been the least prevalent form of government in our earth's history. If we accepted a constitutional mode of government, that fact in itself is distinctive. Churches were usually formed on other bases, but ours tend to show both the strengths and weaknesses of operation by constitution. Theologically speaking, we are likely to have to determine our collective religious direction through meetings modeled on a constitutional convention, and surely this is a form of religious governance unknown in much of the world's past. How does (or should) theology differ in such a democratic setting?

When Edmund Burke (1729–1797) considered the "errors" of the French Revolution, he was convinced that the mistake was to start by destroying the old state. They should have built something new by using the foundations left them, he thought.[2] Religiously, we had no indigenous foundations when we came here, but we brought whole traditions with us from Europe. Just as politically we did not destroy what we inherited from pre-Revolutionary times, so religiously our traditions suffered no great dislocation in their reorganization into independence.

Lack of unity and preservation of diversity Burke saw as a good (p. 40). It forces compromise, and this art prevents destruction. It teaches respect for one's forefathers and thus for ourselves. We had to compromise in our origins because of it. Only now does a lack of total unity seem likely to become unacceptable and thus destructive, both religiously and politically. Today, compromise is often unpopular, regarded by some as a sign of weakness and by others as immoral. If such inflexibility dominates, political and religious chaos will surely increase.

Once the union of originally independent states has been achieved, it is difficult to recall that both the size and form of government of the projected United States itself was originally an item of great debate. Anyone who reads the *Federalist Papers,* for instance, will be reminded of the various options suggested at the time and of our original lack of agreement as to whether a republican form of government for a United States was in fact the best solution. Did these arguments then—or do they now—affect the religious life and the kind of theology formed in America? As we shall see shortly, for men living then the political debate seemed to have few religious implications. However, obvious consequences did develop later and are more evident now.

Alexander Hamilton (1757–1804), for instance, is convinced that the American people are called on to make an important decision regarding the viability of democratic forms of government.[3] Can good government really be established by reflection and choice rather than by accident and force? The crisis that arose in that early time forced the colonies to make a decision. This decision to adopt a conscious form of republican government was ultimately reflected in our notions of church rule too. Moreover, it eventually informed American theology and gave us a new notion of God, deriving from our more democratic view of man's relationship to the divine and our right to share even in his governance. As our notion of a ruler changes, so eventually will our idea of God and of the way in which man ought to serve him in a democracy.

The original choice among the colonies, as John Jay (1745–1829) argued (p. 5), concerned whether to have one nation under federal government or a division into separate confederacies. We did opt—although not without eventual civil war—for federal government, but designed a form of it which still offered wide areas for local rule and individual decision. Likewise in our religious notions, we may still find ways to acknowledge divine authority—although only when coupled with individual responsibility. Our adopted form of government sought to distribute power, not to concentrate it; and to do this by using a system of checks and balances. God in America stayed on in a monarchical image for a time. However, political experience in America is ultimately such as to lead us to demand a distribution of divine power too.

Perhaps the greatest original impetus to the union of the separate states, then and now, was the avoidance or control of the violence threatened by division. However, we did not opt for repression, with its demand for uniformity of opinion as the price of union. Instead, as James Madison (1751–1836) pointed out (pp. 10 ff.), we agreed to preserve individual liberty, which meant both that fallible reason could err and that a variety of opinions would be formed. We did not try to remove all faction, but only to control it. "The *causes* of faction cannot be removed, and . . . relief is only to be sought in the means of controlling its *effects*" (pp. 14–15). Equally important, in a democratic form we did not want even a majority to be able to move to carry out any scheme of oppression against a dissenting minority.

These fundamental political notions are not reflected in the theology of their time, although acknowledged in the acceptance of a variety of religious forms within the new republic, and by the early moves to guarantee religious freedom. Eventually our political fore-fathers said much about the latitude an individual should have in determining his own belief and the toleration we must develop in order to accept religious disagreement and even individual error. *Uniformity, a condition so often thought essential to the survival of religion, now is seen as antithetical to its health in a political union such as we have formed.* Even God's nature must be such, we eventually will realize, as to allow him to express himself in a variety of forms.

We hold diversity to be a political advantage, because it allows no single faction to inflame a whole people. If we consider this as a good, it must rest on an assumption that truth is sufficiently complex and multiple so that no one man can be wholly right. In this case, diversity is itself a means to truth and to the good, whereas uniformity is not. Madison was afraid of any religious sect becoming politically dominant, and a variety of religious forms is the best safeguard against such a danger. Yet strong religious control can only be considered a danger if we are convinced that no one source can be wholly right, and that truth is grasped most fully by allowing a variety of voices to achieve balance within a stable framework. The moderate path we have chosen, one between anarchy and violence on the one hand and authoritarian control on the other, is not at all easy or clear. And variety in religious life and theological expression equally requires us to maintain a precarious balance. Such a delicate condition is always threatened, but it is the necessary means to a richer life for a greater number of individuals.

As we read again the lengthy and complex debate behind the formation and final adoption of the Constitution, a basic fact stands out: We tried to form a union by constitutional means and not by war and conquest. Other empires have been formed as the result of victory in war. If we chose a peaceful means of debate and compromise as a way to unite independent territories and peoples, then religious wars are equally outlawed here, and compromise with circumstance becomes a religious mode too.

John Adams (1735–1826) recognizes that most governments are founded on "fear," but is convinced that Americans will reject any such basis.[4] This is a complex idea and equally difficult to ex-

tend to religion and to square with political reality. It is obvious
that the "fear of God" has been prominent in the history of most
religions. It can even be argued that fear continues to be a legitimate passion in the religious sphere. Moreover, fear is not excluded
from our understanding of government. But Adams still points toward a fundamental truth: Fear cannot be the dominant experience
in any political or religious life that is authentically American, although some principle or passion in the mind of the people is the
foundation of every government.

One important American principle is that no one body ought
ever to govern absolutely. Adams is sure that "a people cannot be
long free, nor ever happy, whose government is in one assembly"
(p. 87). Thus, no individual should be supreme in church governance, nor ought any single rule dominate the individual religious
life. Heterodoxy and complexity characterize our difficult road.
This is not because we can do no other, but because we think this
complex path best avoids the vices to which men are prone.

We accept these features in spite of the lack of stability that
goes with such nonuniformity. Along with this principle goes the
obligation to rotate all top administrative offices. Lifetime tenure,
in a republican form, is always a threat to freedom and an invitation to the abuse of liberty and openness. Religiously, it has taken
us a long time to get these messages translated into our church
forms, but it is never too late to renew and extend the principles
of a democratic spirit.

As Americans what we tend to forget politically is "how few of
the human race have ever enjoyed an opportunity of making an
election of government" (p. 92). Religiously it is also hard for us
to remember how few people have ever had an option (at least
publicly) in either the selection or the rejection of their religion.
This holds true, in a negative sense, even in officially atheistic lands,
where genuine religious options cannot even be presented. The majority of the peoples of the world have their religious options fixed
for them.

The ability to choose a religious life freely from a wide variety
of approaches—such a freedom is not easily achieved. Religion is
no less subject to a constant tendency to repression than political
government. In both areas we suffer from the laxness which comes

when a variety of options is taken for granted, as it tends to be. Too often no option is exercised and no choice is vigorously affirmed.

Now, as we turn to consider the religious and philosophical atmosphere of the era surrounding the formation of the Union, it is amazing to see how *unreflective* it is of the novelty and excitement involved in the discovery of new political forms and possibilities. By nature religion begins more from its past and is slow to appropriate its present. Perhaps rightly, it does not break easily with its own traditions and previous modes of thought. As we have said, the original Protestant Reformation did not at all base itself on what was to become the American political model of pluralism. Perhaps it is the American Revolution, as politically reflected, that only recently launched the second Protestant Reformation, and then later emerged in Roman Catholicism too.

B. Cotton Mather and the Pressure for Orthodoxy

We have learned by now not to treat the Puritans in too simplistic a manner, and we realize that many competing forces were present at the origin of this country and not just one. Yet in some sectors it is clear that the early years in America were characterized by a pressure to achieve religious orthodoxy. If our most important political discovery lay in a decision to reject all uniformity and to create quite consciously a system to foster plurality, it is still important religiously to understand this early urge to theological orthodoxy. The Puritan mind certainly looked on the new church and the new commonwealth which they hoped to create as forming one entity.[5] Without question, the clergy were prominent in shaping ideas about what this country's moral and social climate should be, and clergy do not always have such a dominant hand in political events.

They hoped to form here the "Holy Commonwealth" which they had failed to do in England. Political participation and church membership were linked. "Theocracy was . . . synonymous with the democracy of the elect" (p. 29). Yet, as Cotton Mather described it, such notions were not easy to enforce, but instead were themselves the cause of dissension. The church again became a battlefield. Since Quakers, Anglicans, and other sects in this country did not share the ideal of the Holy Commonwealth, theocracy was bound to meet with religious opposition and could not go unopposed. Laws aimed at forcing church attendance and support failed; the pressure for orthodoxy produced variety instead.

As Robert Baird has remarked, "If oneness of origin be essential to the formation of national character, it is clear that the people of the United States can make no pretension to it."[6] We are wrong if we consider our origins as uniquely Puritan, and yet Puritan thought, by virtue of its hold on New England, perhaps did have a more than proportionate influence on us. There the affairs of church "were conducted with the same system and order that marked their civil economy" (p. 33). Whatever else may be true of the rest of the colonies, it is the case that the principle of uniformity was taught and practiced by the leaders of Massachusetts. "Orthodoxy" was a word used to cover the actions of their colonial magistrates and ministers as they moved to suppress dissent.

In point of fact, this country was not born already linked to a notion of total freedom. Actually, our history involves a constant tension between orthodoxy and suppression vs. liberty and dissent. Each is original, and together they lead to the constant conflict we experience and find baffling—no less today than before.

The term Puritan has been used as a comprehensive sneer against every tendency in American civilization held reprehensible—sexual restriction, censorship, Prohibition, theological fundamentalism, and political hypocrisy. Puritanism was a more complex phenomenon than that, but its support of orthodoxy was unmistakable. In its Puritan form, Protestantism then had not yet undergone its second reformation in order to escape such a need for final and absolute authority.

Puritanism was never unopposed here. It was indeed only one way among many in colonial America.[7] Alongside it we find the rational liberalism of Jeffersonian democracy, the Hamiltonian conception of conservatism and government, the Southern theory of racial aristocracy, plus the rugged notion of frontier individualism. But Puritanism was at first the most conspicuous, the most sustained, and the most fecund influence in early American national history. "The force of Puritanism, furthermore, has been accentuated because it was the first of these traditions to be fully articulated" (p. 1). When we consider the influence of Puritan thought as against its heterodox setting, it becomes evident that any idea can dominate temporarily if it is strongly and intelligently voiced, unless other strains in the legitimate American past are given new and forceful articulation opposing it.

The modern usage of the word Puritan (implying frigidity, abstinence, and rigid morality) does not quite correspond with the facts. It is true that Puritan thought did involve an avoidance of excess in all action, but their notion of religion was far from fundamentalist. They stressed and began an intellectual approach to the ministry, and their clergy considered religion to be a highly complex and subtle affair. However, Puritanism was not only a form of thought but a way of life which involved man's emotions as much as his intellect. We tend today to think of it as narrow. However true this appraisal may be, there is a sense in which the scope of Puritanism was broad. As an outlook it included every aspect of man's existence—artistic, literary, and political—with a degree of unity hardly equaled in any other American form. A Puritan knew what kind of man he wanted to be.

In their time, the Puritans were not unique or extreme in thinking that religion was the primary and all-engrossing business of man. Moreover, we must remember that religion was not narrowly conceived in that era. It brought together every aspect of man's existence—something it seldom does now (except perhaps among such groups as the Mormons). As such, a demand for reform in religion was bound to be important business, enough to force the Puritans to pull up stakes in England and migrate to the wilderness in search of a return to the "purity" of first-century Christianity. From the New Testament book of Acts they derived the notion that government of the minutest event was under the direct and immediate supervision of God. To be a Puritan meant to see the unity of life and to seek the political and economic conditions that allowed its expression.

Emotion in religion must be subservient to the intellect, for the Puritan. Thus colleges and schools to train scholars and writers were essential to Puritan religion and life. All raw expression of "enthusiasm" was to be avoided; this was a sophisticated religion and not a frontier faith. Puritanism was autocratic, hierarchical, and authoritarian. Command was to be only in the hands of the properly qualified. They were humanists and believers in classical education, but any notion of "pure democracy" is far from their thought. They believed in the immutable essences of Plato and in man's conformity to them. Rationality is implicit in man and inherent in the order of the universe. Puritanism was Renaissance humanism embodied in a system of Christian belief.

In opposition to the Anglican love of solemn ritual, the Puritan upheld a veneration for the Bible as the sole approach to spiritual life, and he resorted to it for guidance on the smallest detail. The high seriousness and intensity of the Puritan code demanded strenuous self-analysis and a never-ending search of conscience. Yet its Calvinist base also connects with a certain realism about the faults of man and a tough-mindedness that lent itself to shrewd bargaining in economic concerns. It involved a turn to plainness and directness that set it in opposition to every ornate and elaborate style. Although Puritanism may be lacking in warmth, still it set an original model for American thought we find hard to break away from even in this era of sensuous extremes.

If late nineteenth-century American thinking was to be dominated by professors and philosophers, the early thought of that century was born amid a mixture of preachers and individualistic thinkers and writers. However, in the seventeenth and eighteenth centuries it was still the political writer and the preacher-theologian who set our style. Cotton Mather (1663–1728) is the man to understand if we want to identify with this era. His ministry was a career of leadership, and he studied and wrote constantly. He was descended from the pioneers of New England Puritanism, and was inspired to make New England a place where purity of worship and righteousness of life should be valued above all else. He felt he could speak with authority, since his people had fled the depravity of Europe to establish a new purity of life.

In his *Magnalia Christi Americana* Mather wrote a history of the Protestants who had been driven from England to America in order to practice religion according to the light of their conscience.[8] They felt their age to be very much like the first era of Christianity—a golden age, the return to which makes a man a Puritan (p.

7). Looking back on what we now think of as a rather rigid orthodoxy, it is hard to remember that Puritans thought of themselves as reformers, as men who sought a return to a simpler and more primitive and perfect period of Christian practice. A true latter-day Puritan, it follows, should constantly seek reform and the dissolution of any obstructing practices that obscure simple ways.

When we think of Cotton Mather, then, as the original representative of the continual pressure for orthodoxy in America, we should remember that his zeal did not spring from a desire to oppress. Rather, respecting always the rule of reason, "orthodoxy" meant to search for a primitive purity of life-style and belief. When Mather praises William Bradford as the Governor of the Plymouth Colony, he points out his similarity to Moses leading his people in the wilderness. Religion needs heroic men of sound practical judgment as well as thinkers. Under such circumstances, it is easier to see how religion becomes a matter embracing all facets of life. In unsettled days, then and now, it cannot afford the luxury of being merely a matter of intellectual and individual inner debate.

If everything is seen through the eyes of religion, it does not seem so strange that liberty should be held subservient to the authority of a magistrate. If "the whole world is indeed a temple of God," as Cotton Mather describes it in *The Christian Philosopher* (*ibid.*, p. 287), every facet of life will be considered in that light. Even the volcanoes and the mountains will testify to it. "Magnetism is in this like to Gravity, that it leads us to God, and brings us very near to Him" (p. 314). What we need in order to understand Puritanism at this point is a comparison to medieval mysticism, for this is very similar to the way every avenue of nature leads to God, for instance, in St. Bonaventure's *The Mind's Road to God*.

Atheism, Mather is convinced, has now forever been driven from the face of the globe by irresistible logic. There are dark things in God's providence, to be sure, but creation testifies so strongly to his work as a creator that we need not search out his understanding in every aspect. Thus the return to atheism and secularism we find today would seem irrational to Cotton Mather, an evidence of our sin and our tendency to return to cannibalism when God is forgotten. If reason so clearly leads us to God, as Mather is sure it does, it is no wonder that religion should inform every sphere of life and that preachers actually served as the intellectual source for the early community. As in a monastic order, the whole style of life and work was meant to reflect the overarching sense of God's presence in every aspect of existence.

Yet if Cotton Mather represents a pressure for orthodoxy which is continually present in America, it is interesting to note that his zeal was against the grain of his own time. The ideal of Puritanism was already waning. From the shared vision of an ideal life, it drifted toward dogmatism and excessive statement in the face of the reality of declining religious fervor among the people. The church officials of the day were as much involved in politics and educational leadership as in church affairs. When you begin with the goal of holding so many aspects of society together in one vision, variation on any front will seem like religious apostasy.

It is sometimes hard to remember that the separation of church and state was not a Puritan ideal. It is also hard to remember, especially in an age given to complete license in individual belief, that *a thrust toward orthodoxy is the only way we can achieve such a vision of the integration of all aspects of life.* Orthodoxy never became the political bedrock of the union of these states, and thus the theocratic dream ended. But orthodoxy, and a pressure for return to pure and simple religious beginnings, are so central in the formative days of the country that they always have their place in any notion of "American." Orthodoxy tends to be unhappy unless it has exclusive adherence. Can we make it one among a plural set of religious forms and still not lose its purifying and energizing zeal—a power so crucial in our early years?

C. Jonathan Edwards and Systematic American Theology

It is hard to say that Puritanism is not "systematic." Yet it is generally agreed that Jonathan Edwards (1703–1758) is America's first systematic theologian. It may be useful to draw a distinction here and say that Puritanism was more a dogmatically developed religious view than a technical theology. Once we reach Jonathan Edwards, however, we find the first full-scale treatment of the philosophical and theoretical issues involved in a theology.

There is nothing in Puritan thought, for instance, like Edwards' treatise, *Freedom of the Will*. The early Puritans had a specific and well-developed religious belief, but they did not analyze it philosophically. They argued it out polemically.

As we have already pointed out, Puritanism was not the only religious doctrine of early America. Yet, perhaps because of its close tie with education and classical learning, it seems to have generated the first full-scale systematic theology. In later circumstances, in spite of their vitality and their approach to numerical dominance, evangelical and conservative religious groups have not produced a theology anywhere near the quality of those connected with the English and Continental schools. Now the question arises as to whether the American religious experience has matured enough to produce a theology primarily from its own sources. Jonathan Edwards offers a good case study of the degree to which our earliest systematic theology was at all "American" at its base or in its sources.

Edwards was also a philosopher who wrote on moral theory.[9] It was perhaps this philosophical side (lacking in Cotton Mather) that gave him the framework for a more analytical theology. Edwards follows in the Calvinist tradition, but he wants his ethical theory to rest on rational and empirical grounds. It takes a while in the maturing of a country before its religious thinkers pay much attention to modes of philosophical justification, but when they do, systematic theology is born. Edwards' tendency to Platonism is clear, particularly when we find that he defines virtue as a certain species of beauty, namely, beauty of the heart that involves a love of God (p. 14). God's goodness, as Edwards sees it, is derived from his love for himself (p. 23).

In this definition of love as originating primarily in self-love, which then is extended to objects important to our use (p. 50), we also see Edwards' kinship to Spinoza. A moral sense is natural to mankind and is the same as natural conscience, he feels. This kind of blending of philosophical elements to form the context for theology seems to begin in America with Jonathan Edwards. Self-love alone is not true virtue. Love of God, as it develops from this, is. Edwards' goal is very much like Spinoza's "intellectual love of God." Reading this treatise, one finds himself a long way from the practical implementation of a specific religious view, such as absorbed the early Puritans. In Edwards, we begin with philosophical reflection and then move on to elaborate a technical theology from that basis.

In the Calvinistic tradition, Edwards is perhaps remembered for a less philosophical doctrine, namely, the absolute sovereignty of God. Interestingly enough, he tells us that he at first objected strenuously to the notion that God accepted and rejected whom he pleased for eternal life. This idea became the focus of his attention, however, and eventually he came to think of it as both just and reasonable. He even ends by calling such a view of salvation and damnation "pleasant, bright, and sweet."[10] God's excellence, wisdom, purity, and love seemed to appear in everything as Edwards' sense of divine things gradually increased. We perhaps remember this doctrine most vividly as expressed in his famous sermon, "Sinners in the Hands of an Angry God" (pp. 155–172).

It is important to note that Edwards' text for this sermon is from the Old Testament. He begins by recalling God's vengeance on the wicked and unbelieving Israelites, rather than by pointing to the Christian notion of God's love expressed in Christ. He then proceeds to draw a terrifying picture in order to awaken those who are unconcerned. Wicked men are kept from falling into hell for the moment by the mere pleasure of God. Natural men are held in the hand of God over the pit of hell. He is under no obligation to keep them out of hell at any moment. "There is nothing between you and hell but the air; it is only the power and mere pleasure of God that holds you up" (p. 162).

Edwards paints God as being angry and wrathful, and it is interesting to contrast this almost violent sermon with his careful and detailed theological analysis, say, in his volume, *Freedom of the Will*. "A man never, in any instance, wills anything contrary to his desires, or desires anything contrary to his will," Edwards is sure.[11] "The will always is as the greatest apparent good is" (p. 142). The world and men appear rather neat and simple on Edwards' view. The will is determined by the strongest motive, and merely follows the last dictate of the understanding. He argues at length against the Arminian notion that the will determines action by its own free motions, because, he thinks, this would involve the notion of something coming to be without any cause. His elaborate arguments aim to show that all assertions of the freedom of the will involve this absurdity. Of course, this argument fits neatly into Edwards' religious idea of God's absolute sovereignty, since to allow human freedom in self-determination would involve compromising God's own full determination.

Edwards has already decided, on metaphysical grounds, that God's nature cannot contain any indeterminacy. Since freedom of the will would require this, he is forced to rule it out. "Cause" for Edwards implies necessity, and thus whatever is caused cannot involve any contingency whatsoever (p. 213). He does see that such completely determined foreknowledge on God's part involves the difficulty of deciding whether God also determines sin (p. 300). In quite traditional fashion he says that God's knowledge only "permits" sin; it does not "produce" it. God permits sin only to achieve a great good, never for its own sake. Edwards does not shy from making God responsible for sin in this case, but he joins Leibniz in happily viewing ours as the best of all possible creations.

Jonathan Edwards agrees with Aristotle in using "necessity" to prove God's existence. To admit real contingency in events, he feels, would be to render proof of God impossible. It is interesting to note that he is more rigid here and less modern than Thomas Aquinas, who adds a proof from contingency to the other traditional proofs. Yet Edwards goes beyond Augustine in viewing sin as good insofar as it is a necessary part of God's plan. Since God orders his own conduct, he necessarily and designedly orders all things (p. 432). As in Spinoza's doctrine, no being is self-determining except God, and "liberty" in moral agents does not involve self-determining powers.

It is impossible that God should pursue any other design than he has. By this view Edwards binds his God to the most rigid necessity. Nothing is new to God in any respect (pp. 434–435). He thinks it reflects modesty to leave every genuine decision to God rather than to the discernment of men. Edwards truly writes a systematic theology, but it has little to do with any growing American sense of the freedom of self-determination in a new land.

However, in a manner of speaking that glowing ideal is an ideology which only grows as the country matures. It simply was not a part of the Puritan's imported religious beliefs. If Puritanism alone had shaped America's religious and theological context, we would never have broken from a rigidly deterministic Calvinism. If American thought was to go on to discover man's freedom, as well as God's, the experience in which to ground this awareness had to come from a different source.

There is another and almost more characteristic aspect of Puritan religious thought which leads in a different direction. In fact, it almost anticipates William James's *Varieties of Religious Experience*. Every Puritan had to struggle with the question of how the presence of the divine spirit can be discerned. In the effort to establish the criteria needed to distinguish genuine from spurious piety, the Puritans opened a whole new approach to religion through the analysis of psychological states. It is as if every era discovers for the first time the difficulty of distinguishing true religion from false. Rather than being rigidly rational, as he is about freedom and indeterminacy, Edwards finds it "mysterious" that there should be so much good and so much that is bad mixed together in the church of God.[12]

He sees that much was spoiled in the results of the Reformation and understands that his hopes for religious purity have been thwarted by the failure to instill the New England theocratic ideal. Even in a revival of religion, the false is mixed with the true, and so all religious health lies in our ability to learn to distinguish these two strains as they appear in what purports to be genuine religious emotion. When dissension breaks out, the middle path of moderation is neglected, so that our problem is to restore a balance to religious affections. However, such trials and testing are an important ingredient in the life of religion. Oppression is part and parcel of what we can expect to find in all religious experience (p. 93).

The affections (e. g., love and joy) are more a part of religion than the understanding is. Religion takes hold of men only insofar as it affects them. Thus, more than reason, it is the affections that we must understand if we want to be able to discriminate among things religious. Zeal and love are close to the heart of true religion, and they give us one test of its presence. But since there are false affections, simply to be moved by emotion is not good, unless the hearts of men are in fact moved to do good (p. 120). Here is the beginning of a pragmatic view of truth and its stress upon practical results as the test for the validity of a theory.

A high degree of affection proves religion neither true nor false. Nor is a great amount of talk any guarantee of religion's good intent, particularly if the person speaks too much of his own experience (p. 137). Mere boldness provides no test either, since false affections move more quickly to declare themselves than do the true. Even love can be counterfeited, and so the show of love offers no certainty of true religion. It requires more testing to distinguish true love. For example, it should not be momentary but should endure to the end. Terrors and fears may accompany God's presence, and yet even their impact is no guarantee of his appearance. God's spirit cannot be held to any particular plan, and Edwards thinks that being "born of the Spirit" can be "mysterious" and "unsearchable" (p. 161). This idea is a far cry from the Edwards who is so certain that man's will cannot be free, because if it were it would defy his notion of reason.

He endorses St. Augustine's theory of "two cities," one oriented to God, another with love only for man. On this earth the true saints and the false are strangely intermixed, and they will never be separated into the purely true and the clearly false (p. 181). We simply must learn to live with the uncertainty of not knowing conclusively by any surface sign who is the hypocrite and who the saint. Then, like the medieval manuals on the steps of humility, Edwards sets out to give us a list of signs which can guide the individual. We can learn to determine which religious affections are the true ones in the public mixture, although no test in itself can ever be certain. First we must look to see if the influences on the heart are "spiritual," "supernatural," and "divine" (p. 197). This, of course, involves Edwards in a detailed analysis of what spirit means, and it turns out that the Third Person of the Trinity is the most important factor for the religious life. The "natural man" and the "spiritual man" are different, and a new kind of exercise of the understanding is involved in moving from one life to the other.

The second crucial sign involves a change in the direction of love, one which is away from self-love. The hypocrite takes himself as his own ground; the saint sees that his love is not his own but antecedently God's (p. 247). The joy of hypocrites is really in themselves and has its source in self-love. Moral excellence is a third sign, and the fourth is that the mind is enlightened in order to understand divine things—that is, things obscure to the natural man. A certainty regarding divine things, plus humiliation in one's own utter insufficiency, form two additional tests. An alteration of nature is required, so that anyone not changed by what appears to be religious affection is, at least so far, not genuinely affected. An actual shift in conduct and outlook is a very practical and important matter, then, in addition to the experience of things spiritual.

A spirit of love and forgiveness points out what is genuine in religion, whereas quarrelsomeness tells us what is not. Tenderness of spirit should be the result. When this does not follow, we ought to doubt the genuineness of religious emotion. Beauty should show through, but false saints will be satisfied with themselves and cease struggling. Good fruit must come out in actual practice or the sentiment is not to be trusted.

With these outlines of the tests of genuine religious sentiment, plus Edwards' certainty that no religious group should ever expect to attain purity, he has both drawn on medieval spirituality and transformed it by placing it in an American setting. Emotion now plays a decisive role in religion, with reason as its instrument of discernment. The criterion for the validity of religious experience becomes much more practical and action-oriented than in some earlier manuals on spiritual exercise. Contemplation of God, interestingly enough, is nowhere mentioned as either a test or a goal. Our aim is not simply to produce enlightenment but to change men, and this can be judged by the direction of their affections and the actual results of their activities. Here is an account of religion at once intensely spiritual and yet still evaluated primarily in terms of its concrete results.

If in some aspects Jonathan Edwards appears to be the most severe transplant of the deterministic theology of the Continent, his account of religious emotion is both subtle and sensitive to the importance of practical consequences as providing religion's crucial test. However, he does not have either a God or a picture of the rational process to go with this important doctrine. His personal experience is less severe and more compassionate than his rationalism, but he does not yet see the possibility of elaborating the former into an account of an "American God" whose nature would match this insight. Not that a provincial God is desirable; yet, if Edwards found something solid in American religious affection as he knew it, then all he lacked was a more flexible metaphysics to enable him to elaborate a new vision of God. As it is, his both rigid and capricious God stands in stark contrast to his own discovery of the subtlety, freedom, and strange paradox present in religious affections. Edwards' true God remained unborn in his time.

D. The Formative Era in Political Thought

The Age of Reason by Thomas Paine (1737–1809) is a small but influential book which has implications for both religion and political theory. Insofar as our religious life comes to be tied up to such doctrines, these political ideas raise grave questions for the future of religion. Like many "liberal" theologies, this one proposes reason as an absolute base and a means to win back those who would reject God on any other grounds. Perhaps youth is always optimistic about what it can accomplish by means of reason alone and thus reluctant to accept any other grounds for religion. However, if today we have reached maturity as a people, then such an exclusive assumption may have to be modified.

Of course, a period of revivalism soon swept America, just as such movements have done at intervals since, and this put an end to any thought of rationalism as religion's only basis in this country. Nevertheless, Paine believed reason to be a "weapon against errors,"[13] and it is true that wherever emotion rules some mistakes will be made. The issue is whether religion can remain alive without taking such risks. Paine rejects all religion that is drawn along purely national lines, and correctly sees that, in such cases, political revolution will also breed changes in religion. What he is unable to see, in good empirical tradition he rejects as unreliable. Universal proof is demanded. Belief should not rest merely on special or privileged experience. His God becomes a kind of magnification of his principle of reason. "Demythologizing" is not a new motion; Paine advocated its use in religion long ago.

If God is as rational as Thomas Paine, everything should

eventually work out nicely. If he is not—as some have suggested—then Paine's scheme is frustrated. His "deism" is a hard doctrine to follow, since he makes reason the only path to God, whereas we tend to see this as a less conclusive argument. His ideas found sympathy among the Quakers, which once again tells us that no single origin can claim to be the exclusive religious base for America. He is convinced that "truth never envelops *itself* in mystery" (p. 52). He denies a God who would do this—but how has Paine become so certain about God's purely rational ways? This itself is a mystery. He thinks that belief in God is universal; it might shake his trust in reason if he found no such uniform conviction today.

In *Common Sense,* Paine calls the cause of America "the cause of all mankind"[14] and so we have tended to think of it—until a new generation called this conceit into question. Thus, if we are in serious doubt over America's role today, this indicates a similar uncertainty about what goal we seek as men. Paine takes a romantic view of the native goodness of man and the unavoidable evil of government. "Freedom" and "security" are the only justifiable ends of government (p. 6). Someone who adopts this principle in political theory is not likely to accept a church as anything other than a free association of individuals. His theory of the church will be tied to the political function he assigns to the state. He will reject a church monarchy, just as he rejects any guidance in religious questions which comes from outside the individual, unless it be as from God.

A political theory which promotes such freedom is bound to breed a "free church." Benjamin Franklin (1706–1790) is likewise a "freethinker" and a follower of the Enlightenment, so that *this strain is clearly just as original in our national political and religious life as are the more rigid theocratic notions of the Puritans.* We have never been of one mind on religion, and this important fact prevented any state church from gaining a foothold and forced a pluralistic practice upon us.

Franklin is perhaps one of the first important representatives in this country of religion developed on the basis of rather simple moral notions. He was not a churchman. Thus he heads a long line of Americans who reject the institutionalization of religion but still seek to support it individually by a shared moral code of life. He acknowledges "divine providence," but its consequences are more an individual affair than any justification for a church.

Benjamin Franklin, of course, is against persecution for any reason, and he is just as strongly for religious tolerance. Since we are not to coerce anyone, no church should be supported by general taxation.[15] He opposes slavery, but sees clearly the difficulties that flow from abandoning it and then thrusting slaves into unaccustomed freedom.

Franklin approves of a "general happy mediocrity" (p. 194) and—somewhat ironically—does not see extremes of wealth and poverty as ever being an American problem. We are not interested in status or right of birth but respect simple skills (p. 195), he thinks. America is a land of labor. The youth know no bad examples; religion is respected and atheism unknown (p. 201), he seems sure. His picture is appealing, but *if such an age of economic and political innocence is gone today, so is all hope of individual simplicity in religion.*

The political creed of Thomas Jefferson (1743–1826) centered on human freedom and man's capability for self-government, and the Jeffersonian heritage in religion will certainly feature the lack of all central control or coercion. If Jefferson is hostile to every form of tyranny over the mind of man, no religion can be compatible with this ideal unless it gives free reign to individual growth. "Liberty" should be a byword as much in the church as in the political state. Religion must be prevented from restricting liberty and is to be accepted only when its result is to free the person. It is God himself who endows us with unalienable rights, according to Jefferson's statement in the Declaration of Independence,[16] and this is rather high authority for personal freedom.

The Declaration itself states that it is the right of man not to put up with corrupt government, and such a right should apply to the church as well as to the state. Since self-government is our aim, a split in the power of control (checks and balances) is the most effective way to achieve it. Thus it is hard to see how any centralization can be tolerated in religion either. (Ironic that today we promote such unification as a good.) "Self-government" is by no means religion's aim in every land. Indeed, if it becomes so here, a unique religious setting results.

Jefferson opposes slavery on one hand and proclaims liberty of religious opinion on the other (p. 15). Since tyranny of all forms is Jefferson's enemy, only a free spirit can hope to find a commensurable religion. Fear is rejected in political dealings and is little likely to be acceptable as an attitude toward God (p. 32). *If the mind is created free, the only true religion is one that keeps it free.*

It is easy to see that differences of opinion will be an advantage in religion (p. 37), whereas the aim of most religious spokesmen has usually been to remove all lack of unity. Religious disputes can be ignored politically, since it is not important to the nation whether they are settled one way or another. *America should consider itself unique because we banished religious intolerance, which so long caused men to bleed and suffer.* (Ironic if some of us have developed an intolerance of religion itself that tries to banish it from public view.) Political and religious toleration are linked together as indigenous to this country. But whether in church or in state, can a republican form of government be strong, or does strength lie only in totalitarian forms? To achieve strength in republican circumstances, *a uniform willingness to abide by the will of the majority is crucial.* Otherwise, each individual attempts to impose his own will.

It is amazing to see how many times Jefferson lists "freedom of religion" as one of the essentials of a free government. One wonders, then, if the decline of religion, as well as its appearance in intolerant forms, will have a damaging effect on political freedom. Religious belief, even on an individual and unprescribed basis, does involve the individual in some basic commitment. *Without this, perhaps our commitment to free government weakens too.* Jefferson remarks that a rich country cannot be free (p. 63). He does not consider America in this class. Yet, if it has become so, an accumulation of wealth, coupled with the decline of religious commitment, will work toward enslavement rather than the liberation we imagined affluence would produce.

If "a little rebellion now and then is a good thing" (p. 67), there is no reason to exclude the potential rebel from the religious ranks either, and the health of religion may depend just as much on him as on our adherence to orthodoxy. (We must realize how

different this is from other views which stress the primacy of orthodox adherence.)

Universal education, of course, is a prerequisite to the constructive use of both types of potential rebellion. This links our churches
closely to the drive to educate rather than restrict the power of
independent thought. Jefferson sees America in expansive terms,
with few inhibiting problems and with room enough for everyone to
come and to succeed. As this original pioneering mood comes to an
end in our time, the current limits set on physical expansion are
likely to change our attitude toward religion as well as toward
democracy. Success may follow less automatically in both areas.

Jefferson thought we could stay out of wars and simply preserve
peace around us in this hemisphere. If that isolation now is gone
forever, so is our hope of achieving our goals in separation from
the rest of mankind. In spite of our national achievements and distinctive differences, if we are now linked to the success or failure,
peace or war, of mankind as a whole, then our religious situation
has changed quite decisively from the way we have understood it
since our beginnings.

The whole weight of the past comes to bear on us now, and we
can neither solve our own problems without solving every man's,
nor discover religion without coming to terms with its whole history of evils and abuses. Our experience, finally, is no longer separate, as we once hoped it could be. The answers we once achieved
—so brilliantly if so temporarily—by isolation and special circumstances are no longer viable. Americans have passed a "point
of no return" religiously as well as politically.

Thomas Jefferson rejects all artificial aristocracies, including
those which place the clergy in a special position. On the other
hand, a natural aristocracy, one based on virtue and talent, is
another matter, and this he thinks very necessary to the cause of
freedom. Still, no single political or religious group can control our
destiny. The way must be left open to encourage new leadership
democratically chosen on the basis of merit. In any case, religious
structure should be left open to modification, and its control must
never become the prerogative of the few, or be used to defend the
status quo. This should give religion in America a different role
than has sometimes been envisaged for it in other lands. True,

it opens our religious life to mistakes, but only as the price of maintaining its vitality and freedom.

John Adams is convinced that most governments have been founded on fear, but he is sure Americans will reject any political institution so based.[17] Probably this is still true. If so, religion in America will have to reevaluate its dependence on the fear of God as a source of religious feeling. For a while, of course, the traditional fear of God is likely to remain. However, any religion which takes its cue from an American form of democracy will find that God must be reconceived to modify and reassess the aspect of fear involved. Also, just as Adams is persuaded that freedom requires a split in the governing powers between various groups (p. 87), so church structure cannot become autocratic or be left to the domination of any one group.

Rotation of office and the necessity to mediate between various groups and the executive power—these notions indicate at once a different style of church life and a new notion of God and of how he may rule. It is easier in our political tradition to conceive of God as sharing his power or control, and it is also less difficult to see that men now might bargain with God over their shared responsibility. If all offices are to be rotated politically, in a democratic religious life God might even agree to let man assume the powers of God from time to time. In other words, we might shape our own future.

The necessity for omniscience in a monarch is also lessened, since the American model of "executive control" is less absolute than such a traditional picture. Thus our God can be subject to greater contingency and variation. Moreover, by its very notion, democracy must fail from time to time, just as a God conceived of along these lines might be open to defeat too, while still accepting this situation as his best available system of control. Thus failure in church community is to be expected frequently, and it must be constantly overcome.

Since liberal education is tied to the notion of the success of democracy, theology must become a lay concern and ought never to be left exlusively to the professionals or to a church hierarchy. *Lay opinion is the ultimate court of appeal for a democratic theology.* Excellence cannot be widespread; such theology on a mass scale will be less rigorous than might satisfy Continental experts or fulfill their scholarly and professional desires.

Nevertheless, theology must subject itself to mass evaluation and judgment in its American setting. The norm in theological construction thus can no longer be a strictly technical affair, but must be gone about with an eye on its usefulness to the wider number. It must, so to speak, stand constantly for reelection. A final and fixed theology is impossible, just as one unalterable political balance is unacceptable, although for both variation is possible only within some constitutional framework.

If Americans have tried the experiment of establishing a government by choice and reflection, as Hamilton says,[18] we may come to see the church not as divinely given or constituted but as being constructed by men only after an analysis of their needs and goals in religion. This view of church origins fits a democracy consciously conceived. We had the choice of uniting separate confederacies in one pluralistic nation or remaining disunited. We chose a loose form of federal union. The early Americans felt they had made wholly new discoveries concerning modern forms of government— forms which least restrict the individual, yet still control violence on a group level. Instability and confusion are constant threats, it is true, but we accept this as the price of minimum individual restriction. However, we are always prepared to stop short of self- or community destruction.

Liberty inevitably allows factions to develop. Thus, when liberty is our prize, we must accept a form of union which is never free from the threat of disagreement and division. Only an authoritarian exercise of power could successfully suppress this danger, and the American experience of democracy tends to say that even God is willing to pay the necessary price of liberty's defects. A free God cannot be a "perfect" God, in the classical sense, but one who must constantly renew his loose form of control. We remain ultimately divided into various parties without the unity of a single religious body because, as Madison says, we have "a zeal for different opinions concerning religion" (p. 13). In such a situation, strict unity of institutional structure is neither possible nor desirable.

Democracy does not always place the best talent at the pinnacles of power; using this model, it is easy to see why we are constantly threatened with dominance by the powers of evil. A democratic God does not give every good unchallenged control. The causes of faction cannot be removed in a pluralistic structure. We can only move to control their effects by a constant alert, both human and divine.

In order to make an unwieldy democracy work, the majority must be prevented from effecting any scheme of oppression, even though this means allowing the constant possibility of division and thus violence. A God-of-democracy must, by his nature, be willing to take the more venturesome path—in spite of its potential for destruction. This is why America always lives so precariously close to violence and the outbreak of evil.

A variety of religious sects is most advantageous to a republican form of representative democracy, Madison thinks (p. 19), because one uniform religious body is too capable of exerting an unbalancing and thus coercive political pressure. It turns out, then, that *a God drawn on this model will not demand or want a single church organizational structure.* Such a unified religious instrument could become politically oppressive and upset the very balance of power on which democracy rests.

A "republican God" will treat the importance of church structure always as a secondary consideration. He will refuse to identify with any one institution and remain open to many. Any government which operates by constitution rejects the location of power in a single center. A "constitutional" God will even refuse to centralize all power in himself. He will decentralize it, in spite of all the accompanying risks both to himself and to man.

As pointed out earlier, when Edmund Burke reflected on the errors in the revolution in France, the main fault he uncovered was that the French revolutionaries attempted to destroy the old foundations of the state rather than build on them.[19] American democracy was born in revolution but changed relatively few of the forms it inherited. Rather, it created a framework to federate the existing pluralities. Contemporary revolutionaries, whether political or religious, might consider this example from American political history and its successes.

Some Christians have been and are revolutionaries. According to an American notion, however, revolutionaries should never be merely destructive—whether Christian or not. They should seek to find a way to make diversity move together for a common good. A God who would operate in this way must be very patient with error. He should be restrained in his use of both his resident power and his ability to give direct orders.

If freedom is to maintain dignity, it cannot begin with destruction, even though it might be easier simply to do away with old and inhibiting structures. A lack of unity is good, but only if it makes all change subject to the check of compromise. A God who would consent to operate in this fashion must neither have a single good in mind nor be determined to have his way unmodified. He must be capable of a constant revision in his plans. Democracy, furthermore, does not require a pure and unified religious setting, based as it is on the value of pluralism. Total destruction is not necessary along such a precarious path. The past can be respected, preserved and yet subjected to change.

When Tocqueville looks at American democracy, he finds it largely unaristocratic, although respect for intellect is high.[20] A humble God, not a proud one, it would seem, might choose to relate to such a society as his modern instrument. Uniformity of condition, rather than spots of bright excellence, need not be all bad. Intellect is no longer associated with the leisure class but with the means essential to create improvement.

A democracy which struggles for the rise of the common man can neither be essentially contemplative in style nor reach its goals by such isolation from activity. The medieval goal of unity with God by way of contemplation is no longer acceptable. Equality belongs in the political world, and it characterizes even man's relation to God. An "American God" treats man as an equal and expects to be treated so in return. God is to be discovered on a level with man and not by directing our thoughts "above" or by turning away from human tasks, no matter how vast God's powers may be.

If democracy is as Tocqueville notes—such that it rarely places the most able men at the head of affairs, but keeps the most distinguished talent among the subjects—then one will not look for God's representatives necessarily in church hierarchies or in high public office. Rather, they are found among the men in the pew—

or wherever humble acts of mercy are performed. The bishop does not necessarily represent God's presence among us, but only an expedient form of nonautocratic governance. *God must be such as not to have his nature revealed by rank and hierarchies,* in spite of Augustine and Anselm. Scales of rank must be simply interesting structures of convenience; they cannot be the true reflection of a democratic God, one who is more to be found among the masses.

Tocqueville notes that our young democracy shows a passion for equality (p. 83). In this case, *God might be discovered more in a leveling process than in an exalting action.* Freedom has many forms, but Americans seek it through equality. If we as a people are to be entirely equal as a condition for being perfectly free (p. 84), then God might be disclosed best at that moment when all distinctions are torn down and everything is laid low. As a matter of fact, excessive structuring will work against revealing an American-made God. Since equality more than freedom distinguishes a democratic era from other ages, God is not necessarily disclosed when freedom is at its zenith but rather when maximum equality among men is achieved. Freedom, we must learn again and again, if allowed to go unchecked can produce inequality where equality should be the dominant criterion.

If "individualism" is of democratic origin, a God-of-democracy must be a self who is both conscious of being an individual and ready to meet men as such. Each individual, in like fashion, must know himself before he can consciously relate to God. Yet the bond of human affection is at the same time extended, and in a democracy man cannot love God until he has either learned or tried to love all men. God cannot be singled out for special and solitary affection, as he has sometimes been said to demand. If Americans have been capable of making "great and real sacrifices to the public welfare" (p. 96), this is because they think God is located only if men reach out.

Finally, Tocqueville finds "religious insanity" to be very common in the United States (p. 102). This is to be expected when our paths to God spread out and open up in such limitless ways. Only strict unity and tight orthodoxy could prevent the mental imbalance we democratic men inherit from the God-of-democracy. He is one who knows both the risks he takes and those to which he exposes us.

E. The Origins of Our Experience Viewed in Retrospect

If religious pluralism lies behind our national political union and is one of its premises, the decline of religion as a fundamental aspect of American life may have adverse political consequences. That is, if the initial pluralism of religious views originally forced upon us the toleration of different ideas and promoted political pluralism of power, then as religious influence declines, a pressure toward conformity and centralization of political power may result. On the other hand, any American theology should be nonexclusive in its claims and so constructed as to be open both to change and to the necessity of compromise with competing forms.

If we have had to remove all political sanctions supporting religion in order to get agreement on our proposed political union, then religion in America will have an inescapable personal orientation. "The individual"—Kierkegaard's favorite category—becomes our prominent term too. Strictly speaking, no American inherits his religion. He must take the initiative and discover one for himself. Since being American by birth determines nothing for us religiously, any religious form, to be continued, must give evidence of its power to provide hope and accomplish personal transformation. If in a plural society the majority is the important political group, any religious form must continue to receive the majority vote of its constituency or face extinction. Nothing else can keep it alive. However, the necessity to preserve the right of the minority to pursue its own way is equally crucial for any view which abides by majority decision.

Although forced religious conformity was ruled out when diverse traditions were joined in political union, the preservation of diversity and the right to dissent are both crucial. Originally we had to be forced to discover the benefits of religious pluralism; now we must protect and insure its survival. The unique social condition which this country provides is "democracy," and our religious life is bound to reflect that circumstance. This need not mean that all notions of authority are out of place in American religion, but it does mean that authority in our religious life never goes without the check of a democratic appeal. Theology in such a setting cannot really be "dogmatic" but must be more "pragmatic." That is, it is based on an appraisal of its utility to the people, although simple momentary popularity need not be the criterion.

Our developed notion of the sovereignty of the people means that any American notion of God's sovereignty ought to have some important qualifications. God can "rule" religiously in this country, but like Plato's statesman he must govern always, not for his own benefit, but with a concern for the good health of the majority of the people. Such a God can never require any action that is personally destructive. Moreover, theology must come from the people, and if in a democracy the highest offices are not necessarily held by the best people, theology can never be a matter for church officials to dictate on their own. We follow distinguished individuals, not church titles, and such men may arise outside the official church hierarchy quite as often as within it.

If our original union was uncertain, and remains so still today, no theology in such a setting can escape uncertainty and the need to reestablish its bonds again and again. To build an American theology (or political structure) is to ask over and over, "Why are we together as one group?" and, "What gives us our grounds for unity when we admit our basic diversity of background?" If our theology must have a constitutional base vs. an autocratic one, this does not mean that it obeys no rules. It does mean that the rules of theological construction are man-devised and not God-given. Such a theology is more directly accountable to man than to God, though its function is to present a fruitful conception of God.

If we did not begin by destroying the religious traditions we imported with us, this means that any authentic American religious revolutionary will not destroy old forms, but accept the compromise of allowing both the ancient and the new to live together and to blend. If we began by thinking that at least our notion of God could remain the same as it had been in our European origins, one result of attempting to mold our government by conscious choice is that we find theologies also subject to reflective construction, using principles of our own choosing. God must embody the option of plurality and be concerned to keep every avenue open, rather than restrict our approach to him to one means. All approaches are not equally good, but the discovery of the best route to God is subject to human variation.

If politically we seek constantly to distribute power rather than to concentrate it, even God must be willing to disperse rather than guard his own power. Decentralized power means allowing areas of individual control, and such a God is forced to compromise, much as we are. He knows that the course will be precarious, not that it will automatically succeed or necessarily fail. Just as we seek to avoid the violence of faction and division by preserving our union, God contains the destruction of violence in his nature and seeks to surround factions so that they do not destroy the structure itself (that is, our universe). A democratic God is never repressive, but preserves the right of dissent even against himself. He supports his critics as well as his advocates—an ideal of openness men attain only for rare moments.

Precarious balance is the political path we have chosen, and in this setting theology will always have to be a dangerous enterprise. It is so because no one solution can remain stable, and every doctrine needs to be constantly revised if we are to assure its power to maintain stability. If force is outlawed as a political instrument, God also coerces no one, and this leaves us always free to turn away from him. If our form of religious expression is elected and not given, God must be such as not to wish to determine a single mode of approach for us. If we rejected the early demand to impose religious orthodoxy, we must implicitly have guessed that God is not identified with any one ritual path to him. In not allowing Puritan orthodoxy to triumph, we also cast our lot for a less rigid concept of God.

Only if orthodoxy is our aim should churches become a battlefield where one group attempts to force conformity on others. In an American spirit, churches should avoid narrow militancy and yet work for righteous peace. However we attempt to promote religious values, we cannot force acceptance. A God who would adopt plurality as his expression is not coercive. Conflict will, however, mark such a relationship—both of God to himself and of God to man. God rejects the role of the single and absolute authority, since his nature involves plurality and thus plural means of approach. In this situation, with no single dictated path, education becomes closely linked to religious life. An ability to hold to one choice among many requires intellectual skill as well as emotional tenacity. Any religion in this context must involve intensive schooling.

If religion is stern when the country demands strong leadership, and mild (that is, uncaring about orthodoxy) when life is easy, we abandon strict religious practices at our peril in time of national distress. Or at least we must realize the important role religion first played in strengthening an inherently weak nation. If we no longer have the sense of God's presence in all aspects of life, as the Puritans originally did, our blatant secularism and pagan revels testify to our new use of "reason." If our vision of a unified goal for the country has been lost, at least we should remember that religion first served this function of a unifying purpose. Even if those original goals are now realized in a secular fashion, their achievement may become meaningless if we have abandoned the source of their inspiration. The drive behind the goal may be more important to us than its actual fulfillment—we have learned that in spiritless affluence.

If Cotton Mather reflects the early American push toward religious purity and primitivism, and Jonathan Edwards the original transplant of rigorous Protestant orthodoxy, neither yet shows in his systematic thought the ethos of the early American experience. However, there are two important exceptions to this fact, significant because they offer hope for a changed future. Mather's veneration of the early pioneering spirit adds a note of rigorous yet ruggedly individual religious thought that is still missionary and constructive in its intent. Edwards' analysis of religious emotion offers the opening wedge of an American pragmatic base, one that judges truth by action and validity of intent by its actual results—not its verbalization.

From Edwards' test of religion via the validity of affection and the actual changes it produces, we move all the way to Thomas Paine's exclusive emphasis on reason as religion's base and its only standard. Neither man thinks he is building a national religion. What each advocates for this land should be open to all but forced on none. It is clear that, by background, we are driven neither to pure reason nor to emotion as a sole basis for religion.

Since as a nation we see ourselves as a free association of individuals, it will be hard to treat the church in any other manner, however we may allow doctrine to be determined. Balancing the "free church" spirit against the equally primitive Puritan theocratic ideal, we seem to have been destined from the beginning to live in between, and to have no uniform agreement about the locus of authority in religion. Thus authority is not ruled out as a factor, but uniformity in our conception of it is.

Lacking uniformity, we are destined to structural mediocrity. No church aristocracy can be produced, a fact which blocks out the possible good results along with the bad. If Americans thought liberty or freedom was God's gift, religion too must reflect this goal of individual growth. Of course, these terms may have slightly special meanings in relation to God. They need not represent individual autonomy and license.

Yet, even if freedom is subject to God, and liberty involves respect for one's neighbor, still the expansion of individual talents and powers must be a central thrust of American religion. Such powers perhaps ought to be employed in God's humanitarian service and held back from destruction. Maximum growth for all is still an American religious aim. The notion of majority rule in religion casts God in a very different light, although this is not at all to say that every majority decision is right. It simply means that *God may agree to put up with error to avoid repression.*

Wealth and power are today the greatest religious enemies we face, perhaps the only dangerously corrosive forces which the founding fathers could not foresee. But if we support the idea of lay judgment in theology, any church must reflect all the people and not just one class. If it can do this, the local church may become our last democratic refuge in a country rapidly threatening to split apart along economic lines. The function the town meeting once served, the church may still provide—but only if it can bring together rich and poor alike and represent moral power as a check on the use of force.

Americans may have to rediscover a God who is not afraid to take the precarious path of compromise. His goal is still an equality among men, to which freedom is an uncertain means and never an end in itself. This means that any freedom that demands the lifting of every external restraint, while it may be fascinating, is not God's carefree way. He cannot be so easy on us or on himself. Compromise involves a more tortuous way to equality, since it does not demand the removal of every distinction of quality.

NOTES

1. Alexis de Tocqueville, *Democracy in America* (selections), trans. Henry Reeve (Chicago: Henry Regnery Company, 1951), p. 1.

2. Edmund Burke, *Reflections on the Revolution in France,* ed. Thomas H. D. Mahoney (New York: Liberal Arts Press, 1955), p. 39.

3. Ralph H. Gabriel, ed. *Hamilton, Madison and Jay on the Constitution: Selections from the Federalist Papers* (New York: Liberal Arts Press, 1954), p. 3.

4. John Adams, *The Political Writings of John Adams,* ed. George A. Peek, Jr. (New York: Liberal Arts Press, 1954), p. 85.

5. See Herbert W. Schneider, *The Puritan Mind* (Ann Arbor: University of Michigan Press, 1958).

6. Robert Baird, *Religion in America* (New York: Harper & Row, 1970), p. 21.

7. See Perry Miller and Thomas H. Johnson, eds., *The Puritans: A Source Book of Their Writings,* 2 vols. (New York: Harper & Row, 1963).

8. See Cotton Mather, *Selections,* ed. Kenneth B. Murdock (New York: Hafner Publishing Company, 1926), pp. 1–283.

9. See Jonathan Edwards, *The Nature of True Virtue* (Ann Arbor: University of Michigan Press, 1960).

10. Jonathan Edwards, "Personal Narrative," in *Selections,* ed. Clarence H. Faust and Thomas H. Johnson (New York: American Book Company, 1935), p. 59.

11. Jonathan Edwards, *Freedom of the Will,* ed. Paul Ramsey (New Haven: Yale University Press, 1957), p. 139.

12. Jonathan Edwards, *Religious Affections,* ed. John E. Smith (New Haven: Yale University Press, 1959), p. 85.

13. Thomas Paine, *The Age of Reason,* ed. Alburey Castell (New York: Liberal Arts Press, 1948), p. 3.

14. Thomas Paine, *Common Sense and Other Political Writings,* ed. Nelson F. Adkins (New York: Liberal Arts Press, 1953), p. 3.

15. Benjamin Franklin, *The Autobiography and Selections,* ed. Herbert W. Schneider (New York: Liberal Arts Press, 1952), p. 181.

16. Thomas Jefferson, *The Political Writings of Thomas Jefferson,* ed. Edward Dumbauld (New York: Liberal Arts Press, 1955), p. 3.

17. Adams, *op. cit.,* p. 85.

18. Gabriel, ed., *op. cit.,* p. 3.

19. See Burke, *op. cit.,* p. 39.

20. Tocqueville, *op. cit.,* p. 2.

III

LIBERAL THEOLOGY

AND TRANSCENDENTALISM

A. The Liberal Theologians and Their Context

The Revolution that established the American nation and the Civil War that tested it so severely are both pivotal points in our intellectual history. What of the years in between? Although the events between 1800 and 1860 are less dramatic, yet in that period it did become clear that our struggle for identity had not been completed by the Revolution, but only just begun. The basic framework for the national spirit was set, yet only as we lived through the nineteenth century did we comprehend either what we had created or how the established framework still allowed for a plurality of paths.

The period from 1800 to 1860 was one of exploration, expansion, and the settlement of the middle and western regions of the land. It was also a time of conflict and compromise over slavery. New states were added to the Union, and almost every addition raised the slavery question again. When slavery is the issue, compromise has its limitations. As the Union grew in size, the potential for violent fragmentation increased. We had to learn that everything is subject to compromise except the basic principles of the nation: equality and opportunity for all.

All the problems, however, were not internal. Two wars were fought during these years—one with England and one with Mexico. If the former was a vindication of our power to stand free and demand respect from other nations, the latter caused a substantial division of opinion among citizens concerning the use of military power and our relations with other countries. In this period Americans experienced with new force the ambiguity of military conflict.

To support America right or wrong may have been the watchword for some, as it still is today. However, events between the Revolution and the Civil War were sufficient to convince many not only that our policies and actions could be misguided, but also that dissent against the nation itself is often indispensable if it is to be true to its ideals. For others, active political dissent seemed less desirable than partial withdrawal from American life for the purpose of establishing small utopian communities. In times of extreme stress, withdrawal and separation from common life is always a tendency. American idealism helped to foster these efforts in the first place, but their existence also testifies to the fact that—by word and deed—social and political criticism in the name of moral ideals has long been a part of America's heritage.

Once more today our capacity to accept criticism and dissent from within is being tried in new ways, but the basic phenomenon is far from novel. Founded on dissent and criticism, America is a test case to see whether men can live together fruitfully without uniformity of opinion. More importantly, we experiment to see whether radical difference of opinion may even be desirable in forming a community which maximizes creativity and fulfillment. This issue has not yet been settled, but it was an important concern in the first half of the nineteenth century. If it was not then handled with complete success, the issue was at least kept alive so that other generations could confront it.

American life from 1800 to 1860 was characterized by the exploration and settlement of new geographical areas, an increasing tension over the existence of slavery, and the realization that a new nation must cope with self-criticism and internal dissent as well as with the pressure of foreign powers. Similar elements may be found in the development of American theology. In fact, the theological outlook described in this chapter played a significant role in the development of the problems and characteristics just outlined.

After 1800, our theology became more distinctively American than it had been before. An imported Calvinism was the main theological foundation of colonial America, and its influence remained throughout the eighteenth century. There were modifications, it is true, and Deism emerged as a trend quite antithetical to Calvinism. But the modifications rarely went beyond the basic Calvinistic framework, and Deism was an outlook largely imported from Europe too. Theology never seems to break completely away from the past, but as the nineteenth century developed, certain theologians in America attacked the serious defects in both Calvinism and Deism and sought to correct them by shaping theologies that were both new and more indigenous.

These efforts neither escaped the influence of the perspectives they sought to reject nor were they formed without appropriating new European sources (e. g., metaphysical idealism). Nevertheless, religious trends began to respond more directly to the "American experience." Men came to America in the seventeenth century to make a fresh start, and attempted in the eighteenth century to establish a new nation. Some of their nineteenth-century successors moved out to complete the task by developing new theological perspectives. They sought an intellectual framework which would more adequately interpret the tasks ahead for the American people and inspire men to fulfill them.

Who was most influential in bringing about this theological shift? We will focus on five thinkers. Two of them—Ralph Waldo Emerson (1803–1882) and Henry David Thoreau (1817–1862)— are known to most Americans at least by name. The other three— William Ellery Channing (1780–1842), Theodore Parker (1810– 1860), and Horace Bushnell (1802–1876)—are complete strangers to the average man. Each made a contribution to American life through his religious and theological efforts. None of them accomplished or desired a total break with either Europe or the past, but all sensed that the uniqueness of the American experience called for a fresh approach to both religious life and its theological statement. Not one of them provides a perspective which can be fully adequate now, yet each helps us understand who we are and what we may become—both theologically and nationally—because they are examples of how we arrived where we are.

How shall we represent the religious and theological insights of these men? In the first chapter we suggested that American theology could be characterized by a concern about at least three main themes—evil, freedom, and human fulfillment. These in turn are overarched by an emerging principle: the possibility and desirability of pluralism. Can we show the treatment of these themes, and how these writers illustrate the presence and emergence of pluralism in American theology?

B. The Rejection of Calvinism and an Analysis of Man's Religious Awareness

Theodore Parker was the descendant of a Lexington Minuteman, a Harvard graduate, a fiery preacher, and an abolitionist. He was so radical in some of his views that his fellow Unitarian clergymen attempted, without success, to prevent him from holding a pastorate in Boston. He produced the most succinct, scathing, and possibly one-sided criticism ever launched against Calvinism. Castigating the theology of Calvin and Edwards as "the greatest evil of our times,"[1] Parker claimed that it made man a worm, religion a curse, immortality a torment, and God a devil (pp. 124–191).

Channing, Emerson, and Thoreau might use milder language, but they would not disagree. Although Bushnell differed from the others in being trained at Yale rather than Harvard, and by his ability to see that Calvinism had some merits, he too would have found considerable truth in Parker's charge. Parker's estimate is that Calvinism misinterprets the nature of both God and man, so that creation becomes a tragedy without even comic relief. Depraved human sinners, set in a deterministic context and confronting a God whose righteous anger slackens only enough to elect a few for salvation—this is the outlook against which the opposition of the more liberal theologies (Unitarianism and Transcendentalism) was formed.

If the American nation grew out of rebellion against a tyrannical king, it is not surprising that Channing attracted a following when he announced his major religious principle: "We cannot bow before a being, however great and powerful, who governs tyran-nically."[2] Like our political revolution, this theological rebellion occurred not merely as a protest but in the name of a vision of life—divine and human—that seemed to offer something better. What was the content and source of this new vision? The answer varies with each theologian, but the emerging theological outlook is characterized by: (1) an emphasis on the beauty, goodness, and justice in all creation and in human life in particular; and (2) an interpretation of God's perfection which stresses his inti-mate connection with, and universal love for, his creation. The source of these insights and their development rest on an ex-panded understanding of man's capacity for religious awareness.

An approach such as this emphasizes a reliance on *intuition*. It works against a restrictive empiricism, which stood at the roots of Deism. It also opposes a narrow doctrine of revelation and a fixed interpretation of scripture, such as characterized much of Calvinism. "Sense experience" is not the only source of knowledge and insight. Revelation occurs through personal feelings, imagina-tion, emotion, instinctive hopes, and moral inclinations just as much as through theological doctrine and scripture.

Established theological doctrines have no privileged access to truth—not even if they are regarded as authoritative. The validity of any doctrine is certified only by its power to illuminate the lives of individual men and not by its status as an official pronounce-ment. Scripture has an important role to play, but only after it has been subjected to rational analysis and creative interpretation by feeling, imagination, emotion, hope, and moral inclination. These factors in combination produce an intuitive grasp of reality which can be trusted.

The appeal to intuition is basic here. It makes use of scripture in order to discern truth, but it interprets scripture in terms of what we might call *reasoned feeling*. Nevertheless, within this gen-eral formula a variety of positions become possible, and the the-ologians under study here are diverse in detail, although perhaps unified in general outlook. In his famous sermon on "Unitarian Christianity" (1819), Channing lays down his guideline: "Our leading principle in interpreting Scripture is this, that the Bible is a book written for men, in the language of men, and that its meaning is to be sought in the same manner as that of other books" (p. 4).

For Channing, this means subjecting the Bible to the most rigorous logical and textual criticism that can be produced. Claims which are clearly contradictory or even conflicting should be eliminated or reinterpreted so that the conflict is removed. This approach to scripture is not, however, divorced from positive religious feelings and motives. On the contrary, the entire purpose of the critical investigation is to facilitate the clarification, communication, and apprehension of basic truths about God and man. These are set deeply within us but await discovery.

Thus, if reason disallows the doctrine of the Trinity, Channing's theology will still emphasize the fatherhood and moral perfection of God: "To give our views of God in one word, we believe in his parental character" (p. 23). This suggests that belief in miracles can be rational. God ordains natural laws as *means,* not as ends in themselves. Thus, if these means are sometimes insufficient for accomplishing the ends that God does intend, he may intervene and depart from nature's established laws in startling and surprising ways. As for Jesus, his uniqueness is stressed, but it consists in what he does—teach, heal—and this serves as a norm for human excellence. It requires no paradoxical claims about his being fully man and fully God at the same time. Human sin is not denied. It is simply viewed in a context that stresses the essential goodness of man and his possibility for improvement through renewed effort stimulated by the example of Jesus.

Emerson and Thoreau give us a more marked emphasis on intuition. The result is an elaboration of philosophical and theological themes that are at best only latent in Channing's view. Emerson's interpretation of scripture was one factor in his decision to leave the Unitarian ministry. He could not find scriptural justification for the continued practice of the Lord's Supper. His proposal to drop the practice from his church was not favorably received, however. Emerson subsequently resigned, never again to resume his pastoral role in a church. Nevertheless, his writings make clear that his personal feelings about the lack of meaning in the ritual of the Lord's Supper were more influential than biblical criticism in spurring his decision. Questions about the proper interpretation of scripture are of less concern to Emerson than to Channing. True, scripture does give us a view of Jesus, who is to be accepted as the great moral example. Still, Emerson's philosophy suggests that an awareness of the life of Jesus is not necessary for a man to be genuinely and fully religious.

Emerson was a transcendentalist. He believed that the combined powers of man's reason, feeling, and imagination—in short, intuition—could move him beyond the appearances of sense experience to an apprehension of the essential unity, spirituality, beauty, and goodness of all existence. All authentic religious life should be characterized by moral awareness and sensitivity. These qualities are rooted in the individual's reverent attempt to use his own thoughts and feelings in order to perceive the basic structures of nature and human life. The world exists for our education, and "life is our dictionary."[3] When a man consults life with reasoned feeling, Emerson believes, he will recognize that he inhabits a world which is not only the creation of God but one in which God is also present in every thing and event.

All that exists is a manifestation of God; the world is a sacred unity in which all things influence and participate in each other. Moreover, as God manifests himself in nature, the result is a moral process in which virtuous action is compensated and evil incurs retribution. An emphasis on the unity of being is coupled with a stress on the need for each man to discover his own nature and to be self-reliant and self-sufficient. Each person is to develop his skills in a unique and disciplined manner, one which does not permit him to be swallowed up in mediocre social conformity. Unity is the goal, then, but only with each being cultivating and realizing his own uniqueness. This idea is fully American, and the striving toward it is at the core of Emerson's understanding of genuine religious life.

In 1836 Emerson said, "In the woods, we return to reason and faith."[4] In 1845, Thoreau began to test those words at Walden Pond. If his writings make few references to scripture, God, or religion, it is nonetheless true that his experience as recorded there contains religious insights. Emerson's transcendentalism had been significantly influenced by philosophical idealism. That is, he rejected the view that our world is composed of independently existing material objects, and believed that all existence is both grounded in an overarching Mind and of the nature of thought and will throughout. Thoreau was more a naturalist and less a metaphysical idealist. While he was not as inclined to subsume all being under the categories of thought and will, he nevertheless agreed with Emerson on the interrelatedness of all things.

Everything is connected by virtue of the fact that "there is nothing inorganic."[5] Moreover, "our whole life is startlingly moral. There is never an instant's truce between virtue and vice. Goodness is the only investment that never fails" (p. 465). Nature interpreted through reasoned feeling—that is Thoreau's source of religious insight. Existence is a blend of wildness, novelty, beauty, and justice, although not with as clear a sense of retribution and compensation as Emerson suggests. Man's task in this worldly setting is to cultivate the moral qualities that make him unique—sincerity, the ability to see and strive for the right, and the capacity to recognize the unity, goodness, beauty, and morality of existence in spite of appearances to the contrary.

To achieve this level of manhood, solitude—although not necessarily total isolation from other men—is required. As it exists, human society distracts men and fragments the self with trivial concerns. Most men lead lives of quiet desperation; they seek to find themselves but so often look in the wrong places. The secret is to simplify one's existence, to learn to live with and rely on oneself. We need to practice an ascetic life-style which puts us in communion with nature and enables us, in quietness, to become teachable.

Emerson paid his taxes; on some occasions Thoreau did not. They agreed on the importance of self-reliance, but Thoreau stressed the idea of noncooperation with evil and added a view of civil disobedience. "It is not desirable to cultivate a respect for the law, so much as for the right. The only obligation which I have a right to assume is to do at any time what I think right."[6] In Thoreau's understanding a genuine sense of duty, plus the decisions arising from it, can never be the results of immediate and subjective whims. Critical thought is necessary all along the way.

Thoreau knew—and no doubt intended—that this view of

obligation would often put an individual at odds with his immediate community and nation. However, to fail to act on one's sense of the right is not only to fall short of self-reliance but also to fail other men. The greatest contribution one man can make to another's life—or to his community or nation—is to provide an example by taking a stand when his conscience speaks and demands action.

Thoreau sees that human existence contains harsh elements, but the self-reliant man has confidence and conviction. He knows that he has strength sufficient to cope with the negative forces of existence, for his life is rooted in an apprehension of the basic structures of reality. These are wildness, variety, and novelty, each held within an ultimate context of beauty, goodness, and justice. Such a religious outlook is not nature worship, but it does consist less in a God-oriented faith than in a comprehension of the rhythm and transcendental significance of natural processes and man's actions within them. Still, Thoreau would not disagree with the basic premise of liberal theology, namely, that the goodness and fatherhood of God ought to be stressed and that the highest function of religion is to invigorate the human spirit. We need this to give us a vision of our own participation in divinity and to encourage us to strive for excellence in this life.

Although Thoreau did not emphasize these themes directly, they lie at the heart of Theodore Parker's message. The center of his activity was neither a New England village nor the solitude of a rural setting. Parker worked in the city of Boston and within the Unitarian church. Outspoken and controversial, he was also one of the most powerful and influential preachers America has produced. We have already noted his critique of New England Calvinism, whose intensity derived from the fact that Parker had a positive vision of man and God to which Calvinism was directly antithetical. He believed that it is man's nature to be religious and that his religious concern will persist in spite of bad theology. Poor theology, on the other hand, can be a definite hindrance to the growth of man's religious life. When this happens, it should be removed in favor of an outlook that encourages genuine religious development.

When Parker says that men are religious by nature, he means

something like this: Human consciousness has a dimension—he sometimes speaks of it as a faculty—which enables us to apprehend both the existence and the basic nature of God and our relationship to him. This intuitive perception of God, which for Parker is perhaps more direct and immediate than for Channing, Emerson, or Thoreau, yields results which are eternally valid.

Such insights, and their implementation in human life, constitute what Parker calls *absolute religion*. The following are its basic characteristics: (1) God's existence is apprehended as infinitely perfect, which in turn implies that God has created from a perfect motive (love) and produced the best of all possible worlds. (2) God transcends nature, and all of nature is dependent on him for existence. At the same time, God is immanent in the world, moving it toward completion and fulfillment. Creation and providence go together. (3) Man himself participates in divine perfection. This is shown by his awareness of moral law and the assurance of immortality that intuition provides. (4) Man's privilege and duty are to live a life inspired and informed by all this knowledge, with particular emphasis on the correction of moral evil. The church's task is to liberate men, both by holding this vision before them and by acting in the world as a community of love and justice.

Notice that this description of absolute religion contains explicit reference neither to Christianity nor to Jesus. Parker sees himself clearly enough as part of the Christian tradition. But his thrust is to argue that it is important to ferret out what is permanent and essential in Christianity. We must dispense with everything else in the tradition which no longer helps in delineating what is eternally and essentially true. A variety of religious practices and theological statements can be useful in communicating the truth of absolute religion. This, of course, is Christianity rightly understood. However, care must be exercised to see that the permanent and the transient are not confused.

Parker is radical in his conception of the difference between the permanent and the transient in Christianity and in his emphasis on the power of human consciousness to grasp religious truth. This is demonstrated in the following claim: "So if it could be proved— as it cannot—in opposition to the greatest amount of historical evidence ever collected on any similar point, that the gospels were the fabrication of designing and artful men, that Jesus of Nazareth had never lived, still Christianity would stand firm, and fear no evil."[7] The point is this: the Christian faith contains insights that are eternally valid. The four characteristics of absolute religion mentioned above provide examples of this, but their validity does not depend alone on the truth of particular events in history. Religious truth can be and is mediated through concrete happenings, but every man has a more direct access by way of "intuition." This involves a reasoned feeling whose content stands firm even in the face of the most serious doubts concerning what has transpired in the past.

Such a position led Parker into serious disagreement with Unitarian orthodoxy. Parker was critical of traditional Unitarianism because, in the first place, he found its outlook dominated by the negative approach of trying to refute the errors of Trinitarian Christianity. Even in its positive stress on Jesus as providing a moral example for men, Parker felt that Unitarianism often fell short. It gave attention to Jesus as a moral example at the expense of cultivating direct religious apprehension by individual men. References to Jesus were of vital importance so long as they were means to this end. Whenever their function did not aim clearly in this direction, Parker would eliminate them.

Parker's message to the people of Boston was a combination of philosophical theology and social gospel. His meditations on the perfection of God and the goodness intended by God in creation were coupled with repeated and constructive attacks on the five great evils he saw in American life: war, wicked government, slavery, selfish antagonism in society, and degradation of women. He argued that the church was in a state of decay, owing both to its preoccupation with Calvinistic theology and its reluctance to face serious moral issues. However, he had a great vision of what an American church could become: "The church of America, the church of freedom, of absolute religion, the church of mankind, where Truth, Goodness, Piety, form one trinity of beauty, strength, and grace—when shall it come? Soon as we will. It is yours to help it come."[8]

To the southwest of Boston at Hartford, Connecticut, another clergyman, Horace Bushnell, shared Parker's hopes for the American church, but in a rather different theological context. Bushnell was a Congregationalist. In spite of his persistent quarrel with Calvinistic orthodoxy, he was a staunch Trinitarian with a good dose of Calvinism informing his thought. His theology is interesting because it attempts to be both more comprehensive and more mystical than either traditional Calvinism or Unitarianism.

As to comprehensiveness, Bushnell believed first of all that "language will be ever trying to mend its own deficiencies, by multiplying its forms of representations."[9] Thus, a plurality of theological theories is not only possible but helpful in moving us toward an adequate understanding of God. This is even true when theories are in conflict, especially if the valid insights of the parties involved can be drawn out and restated in a more adequate way. The role of theological mediator was the one Bushnell chose for himself. His efforts, however, did not aim at an eclectic compromise of previous theologies. Rather, he worked to produce a new statement which would hold together truths that had not been adequately stated in any previous theory.

Bushnell was convinced that the goal of theology should be to produce an intuitive, mystical apprehension of God and human existence. "Man is designed, in his very nature, to be a partially mystic being; the world to be looked upon as a mystic world" (p. 104). He certainly did not believe that the first principle of all theology should be to avoid emphasis on paradox, mystery, or even outright conflict of statement. Language can, after all, only point toward the reality it intends to reveal. Sometimes the richness and vastness of reality can best be grasped by means of paradox and through opposition of statements. Thus, while Emerson asserted that a foolish consistency was the hobgoblin of little minds, Bushnell suggested that even contradiction in theological statement might on occasion provide us with important insights about God.

It is not surprising that Bushnell should have criticized traditional Calvinism and Unitarianism for being too "rationalistic." The flaw in Calvinism was that it combined a narrow view of revelation and a too literalistic interpretation of scripture with a harsh view of God that essentially denied man's fundamental feelings and hopes about God's universal love and our ultimate salvation. Unitarianism, on the other hand, erred by removing the traditional and admittedly paradoxical doctrines of the Incarnation and the Trinity. In Bushnell's eyes, these doctrines contained the vital insight necessary for an adequate and fully meaningful theological statement. Bushnell never played with paradox or mystery for its own sake. But his understanding of language was such that he thought something valuable would be lost if we follow exclusively conventional criteria for clarity, avoiding paradox and every conflicting meaning.

Bushnell rejects the extreme Calvinistic doctrines of the depravity of man and the harshness of God, but by the same token finds the Unitarian concepts of man and God imperfect too. They lack a profound awareness of human sin and thus miscalculate the way in which judgment and love are intertwined in God's relations to men. Bushnell believes that one of the first and most fundamental affirmations of a sound theology is that all men are caught in a web of sin. This is not to say they are without worth, but it does point up one basic fact: that men have failed by their own volition to achieve what God has expected. Thus they have put human existence in jeopardy.

Sin puts us in a fix. It sets an obstacle between us and God which we cannot remove by ourselves. No amount of Unitarian talk about Jesus' role as a moral teacher who spurs us on to new and wonderful acts can remove the fact that our past exists and leaves us guilty. A man who knows he is guilty may have the hope of doing good things in the future, but he also knows that this does not erase the fact of his guilt before God. Once defiled in this manner, his existence can be radically transformed only when a power from the outside—God himself—intervenes.

The Christian concept of the Incarnation proclaims that such a transformation occurs, but it does not do so by interpreting Jesus exclusively as our moral teacher. Instead, the Incarnation testifies that, in Jesus, God becomes man primarily to show us that, in a context of divine judgment, God's love is still present to restore us and set us free. Bushnell's God is both moral judge and loving father, and each side is fundamental to his nature. God places demands on men, and these demands can never be merely dropped away. God's love is not that simple. Instead, the demands hold, but God, suffering with us in our inability to fulfill them, comes to us in Christ.

Christ not only lives a perfect human life, thereby providing an example for us. He also experiences and reveals the destructiveness of our sin. Christ convicts us, but at the same time bears man's sin for the purpose of revealing a crucial fact: God's love does not remove his high expectations, but it does forgive the sin that fragments and kills human life, and it does ultimately restore us to health. Faith in Christ, therefore, is man's salvation. It liberates him to face the future as a new being, and it persuades him that death can be transcended by everlasting life.

Bushnell's account of the Incarnation is not a theory produced in an experiential vacuum. He is convinced that his interpretation comes closest to illuminating the facts of life adequately and provides the hope we need. Men do not always confess their sin openly. Yet within the human spirit there is an awareness of guilt before God and of man's inability to remove it by his own efforts. Moreover, there is also an awareness that both the judgment and the love of God are irreducible qualities of his nature. The doctrine of the Incarnation captures these experiences clearly and puts them into a context of hope. It is true that we may not be able to explain fully how Christ is both divine and human, but the idea has its instrumental function. If the doctrine were not already part of our tradition, we might well have to invent it to be able to present the truth of religious experience in a graphic form.

The doctrine of the Trinity can be regarded in like manner. Bushnell is convinced of its instrumental value. It is a provocative vehicle for the truth that God is creator and judge, both loving savior and sustaining spirit. "Every human soul that will adequately work itself in religion, needs this trinity as the instrument of its working; for without this, it is neither possible to preserve the warmth, nor to ascend into the true greatness of God" (p. 192). Recognizing, however, that an instrumental function requires an ontological grounding, Bushnell goes on to defend the view that the doctrine of the Trinity is not merely a useful metaphor but also a genuine revelation of God's nature.

The doctrine affirms both the unity of God and the conviction that he is three persons—Father, Son, and Holy Spirit. Strictly speaking, although our experience and language make person-discourse the most fruitful way of speaking about God, it is somewhat inadequate to say that God is a person at all. Strictly on that score, the Unitarian view that God is one person is no better than the Trinitarian formula. Nevertheless, Bushnell is convinced that the doctrine of the Trinity conveys a vital theological truth: God is a being not only absolute but also relational. He is so in "datelessly and eternally becoming three" in order to be apprehended by finite beings in his work of creation.[10]

Bushnell would be the first to admit that this interpretation does not solve every problem. Nevertheless, he regards it as provocative and capable of stimulating reflection that may lead us to feel God's reality more adequately. "Through a certain feeling of multiplicity and vagueness, we are able to realize God dynamically, as we could through no definite conception of him."[11] As with the Incarnation, to give up the traditional doctrine of the Trinity in the name of logic and clarity is to sacrifice the very form of expression which is rich enough to direct our hearts and minds toward God.

Bushnell tried to be a creative and liberating mediator. Taking positive insights from both Calvinistic and Unitarian theologies, dropping or transforming the inadequacies he discovered in each, he wanted to develop a new statement that would overcome divisions. He surely knew that mediators are not always welcomed with open arms, yet it must have been disappointing to him when few Unitarians were persuaded, and some of the conservative Congregational districts in Connecticut worked to have him condemned for heresy and removed from his church. Like Parker, however, Bushnell was attractive to many people, and the efforts to prevent him from being heard in Hartford did not succeed.

C. Evil, Freedom, Human Fulfillment, and Pluralism

It is clear that Channing, Emerson, Thoreau, Parker, and Bushnell all share several strong convictions: (1) that man often falls short of what he ought to be, (2) that freedom both contributes to our downfall yet is indispensable to our highest achievements, and

(3) that human fulfillment is lacking if we are unable to perceive our relation to the powers that are the ground of existence and to discover that this relation brings hope and positive meaning into life. At the same time, each man offers many variations on these themes.

We can begin to see their insights and differences by considering this question: What is the context in which man's freedom operates and evil occurs? For each of these writers the immediate context is nature, which includes both other men and a world environment. "Nature," however, does not exhaust reality. In the end the context must be broadened out to include God and his intentions toward us and the world. All these aspects of reality must be interpreted in order to answer the original question.

Channing's position is probably the simplest but the least provocative and illuminating for our present situation. His emphasis is on the goodness and love of God toward men and the moves toward perfection that men can make by following the pattern provided by Jesus. Sin does exist in Channing's world. It is widespread and must be overcome, but its destructiveness can be avoided. It is true that we live in a natural order and a human community which contain suffering and violence and may tempt us toward wrongdoing, but these circumstances were placed there to test and perfect us. God has given us the resources to meet these trials— which are really goods in disguise—and in utilizing them we move toward full humanity. The tests are not such as to break us ultimately if we are honestly trying to do well. If failure does occur, it is met by God's forgiveness and love, which in the end assure us of a blessed immortality.

Contemporary men may rebel at much in Channing's view. It lacks an adequate grasp of the depth and power of negative forces in existence. Some men do meet tests successfully. Others who make a genuine effort are broken by forces which seem demonic and pervasive. We do have our own resources, but sometimes they are woefully inadequate. Moreover, when we think of God we are led to ask whether God is, after all, "good," or at least we are puzzled by what we can mean when we make such an affirmation. Our view is more that many worlds are possible and that this one seems to contain a setting for human life more threatening than it needs to be. Channing's idea is that some evil is necessary in order to test and perfect us, and that where freedom is present failure can occur. Such a view may be true as far as it goes, but it is still the case that the circumstances and resulting waste seem neither to have been imposed on God as necessities in creation nor to have been as favorable a setting and outcome as might have been provided for our struggles.

A further difficulty lurks in Channing's conception of the relation between God and human freedom. Whereas Channing's conception entails not only God's absolute goodness and infinite power but also his eternally complete grasp of all being, our conception of freedom demands that our lives be genuinely open-ended and indeterminate. It is not clear that these two points of view can be held together in a believable manner. If God's perspective is from eternity, the absolute completeness of his knowledge necessitates that a man's life be fixed in its course before he lives it. That result is opposed to a contemporary understanding of man's indeterminism in freedom.

Channing rebelled against the Calvinistic doctrine of man's total depravity and God's intense anger, but his theology is not radical enough to escape the feeling of theological predestination. The result is not only that our understanding of freedom is threatened, but also that Channing must now face the charge that—contrary to his professed position—God is extensively responsible for evil and sin. God may well be more involved in the causes of evil and sin than traditional theology has wanted to admit, but the point here is that Channing wants to emphasize God's goodness while maintaining his knowledge of existence as complete from eternity. Nothing acts apart from God's knowledge. In fact, although God's knowledge may shape existence, reality seems to reveal the presence of negative forces more extensive than Channing allows. Thus his theology may hold God more responsible for evil and make God less obviously good than he would want to acknowledge.

Channing makes a more positive contact with the twentieth century in his affirmation of the value of human life, his belief that men can improve themselves and their environment, and his conviction that our existence is ultimately surrounded by the love of God. These at least are ideals and hopes that many can still share.

On the other hand, America is older and perhaps a little wiser than in Channing's time. Americans today will not find it so easy to accept his view as fact. Present estimates of life's worth and possibilities are permeated by a more profound sense of the negative factors in existence. If we are to affirm that we live in a world surrounded by God's love, this conclusion will be reached only after much questioning of ourselves and God. It cannot be apprehended as something plain to see.

Emerson and Thoreau sense the presence of the negative in existence to a greater degree than Channing, but their interpretation of its significance remains within a total framework that is much the same. Emerson had a vision of freedom which emphasizes self-reliance, but at the same time he affirms: "There is a crack in every thing God has made."[12] Nature is beautiful and men may be virtuous and discover truth, but existence has its flaws as well. Nature often is destructive, cruel, and wasteful, and men can turn on each other and even destroy themselves from within. But if God is responsible for these properties of nature, as well as for the negative potentials of human life, it may still be true that his creation of them is part of a broader moral design.

"The world exists for the education of each man."[13] The lesson we are taught is this: Evil does not triumph but always is justly punished. Virtuous action, on the other hand, may bring new trials of its own. Yet it rewards a man by causing him to see that his existence is a dimension of a divine life characterized by truth, beauty, and goodness. "Benefit is the end of nature."[14] Rightly apprehended and courageously faced, our tribulations convince us of this fact and even help to assure us of our everlasting participation in the life of God.

Nothing could be more American than to envision life as an illuminating and ultimately successful struggle against severe difficulties, especially if a strong emphasis on man's freedom, responsibility, and need for self-reliance is added in for good measure. Emerson agrees with Channing that the presence of evil and suffering is part of a moral plan, but he is more perceptive about the extent of these negative qualities, and is bolder about making God share responsibility for them. On the other hand, in spite of his emphasis on freedom and self-reliance, Emerson's

views about the relation of freedom and God are not without difficulties.

His transcendentalism entails the immanence of God in
human life and in the world, all of which may be hard to discern in a destructive age. Moreover, Emerson retains the traditional idea that God's existence is an omniscient unity. Thus
his mysticism and idealism leave us without a clear account of
human individuality and also with the uneasy sense that our freedom is really swallowed up in the completeness of God. Emerson pictures nature and human life as "fluid and volatile,"[15] but
his view of the completeness of God's knowledge compromises
human freedom. Thus his theology seems less than adequate for a
contemporary estimate of life.

Thoreau's perspective on evil is at once less theological and
more romantic than Emerson's. Like Emerson, Thoreau emphasizes the novelty, variety, and beauty of nature, but he goes beyond
his friend by reveling in the *wildness* of the natural order.

I love to see that Nature is so rife with life that myriads can be
afforded to be sacrificed and suffered to prey on one another; that
tender organizations can be so serenely squashed out of existence like
pulp—tadpoles which herons gobble up, and tortoises and toads run
over in the road; and that sometimes it has rained flesh and blood![16]

This is not Thoreau's confession of a morbid interest in suffering
and destruction but rather his way of expressing wonder and awe
at the power and ongoing quality of life. Nature is Thoreau's
teacher, and what he learns is that the individual participates in a
living, organic process which is inexhaustible and one. If we can
learn to look at existence in this way, we see that its seemingly
negative features actually are aspects which contribute to an un-
surpassed beauty and goodness.

A romantic outlook toward evil is possible from the perspective
of Walden Pond. Such a perspective may even have been widely
available to nineteenth-century Americans, but it is not the dominant one for us. We require something beyond Thoreau's view.
Interestingly enough, however, Thoreau asks the very question
that might lead us to a clearer understanding: "Why do precisely
these objects which we behold make a world? Why has man just

these species of animals for his neighbors; as if nothing but a mouse could have filled this crevice?" (p. 471).

Why this world and not some other? That question is full of theological implications, and it is one which many are asking today, often in protest and rebellion over the magnitude of evil in our world. Unfortunately, Thoreau leaves the question largely unanswered. By implication, however, his view is that God creates this world because it is beautiful and good. This answer is tantalizing in its simplicity, but perhaps generates more problems than it solves.

Man's possession, use, and cultivation of freedom are essential factors in the beauty and goodness of life which Thoreau extols. Every man is free and unique, and his task is to avoid being swallowed up by social conformity and to "be very careful to find out and pursue *his own* way" (p. 325). The man who honestly moves in this direction will not be disappointed. The goodness and beauty of life will vindicate themselves, and he will find new strength and meaning in his existence.

Thoreau's outlook has religious overtones, but he did not consider himself a theologian and there is no developed conception of God in his writings. This opens him less to direct theological criticism than Channing or Emerson where the interpretation of freedom is concerned, but it also leaves his view of freedom incomplete. The reality of freedom raises theological questions, just as the presence of evil does. Until these have been directly addressed, it is unlikely that the significance of freedom can be adequately understood—a possibility which every American might ponder with profit.

Parker's theology stresses the perfection of God and the view that he has created the best of all possible worlds. (In this context, "world" includes the totality of created existence.) The result is an interpretation of freedom and evil which makes him an American Leibniz. Parker believes that evil is real in the world, but how is this compatible with the claim that God has created the best of all possible worlds? The analysis of this question begins with two sets of distinctions. First, there are two *kinds* of evil that are logically possible—partial and absolute. Parker rejects the option that the best of all possible worlds can be one in which evil is absolute. Therefore, assuming that this is the best of all possible worlds, the evil it contains must be partial. That is, retribution for evil done, as well as compensation for suffering and misery experienced, always transcends the negative forces in existence. However, it is true that such retribution and compensation may not always be immediately apparent to us.

Second, evil exists in two *modes:* (1) pain, misery, and destruction which occur apart from any voluntary transgression of God's moral law, and (2) sin, which is a voluntary and conscious violation of a known law of God. Evil in the first category is an indispensable and perfectly balanced part of the best of all possible worlds. It exists to educate and bring us to greater perfection. Thus, the misery that men experience "is all along remedial, is never excessive for its work and function. God achieves the maximum of effect with the minimum of means; the maximum of welfare with the minimum of misery."[17]

Sin is more difficult to account for, especially when we fill in Parker's ideas about God and freedom. He not only affirms the reality of human freedom, but also takes it to be a crucial factor in making this the best of all possible worlds. At the same time, however, he affirms two points relative to freedom which complicate the interpretation of sin. First, freedom seems to increase vastly the amount of misery in the world. Parker's estimate is that if you could quantify the amount of freedom in reality and square it, the resulting figure would correspond to the amount of misery for which freedom is responsible. Second, Parker conceives God to possess complete knowledge of all creation.

If there be freedom, then God, as the perfect cause thereof, must have perfectly understood the powers of that freedom; and understanding perfectly the powers, He knew perfectly all the actions, movements, and history thereof, at the moment of creation as well as today. (p. 209)

Now this question must be asked: Sin is a result of freedom, but on Parker's view who bears the responsibility for it, and how can sin be a part of the best of all possible worlds? Following the line of criticism brought against Channing and Emerson, it would seem that Parker's God is more responsible for sin than man, since he creates and knows the outcome of freedom "at the moment of creation as well as today." Although Parker would prefer to hold

God accountable only for the creation of freedom as a good, his theological perspective makes it difficult to avoid extending God's responsibility further than that.

Parker, in fact, does place some responsibility for sin on God. In order to maintain that sin has a place in the best of all possible worlds, Parker moves toward a Leibnizian solution. The best world involves freedom, but where freedom is present sin may occur. Therefore, if freedom exists, sin must be permitted. "Permitting" sin, however, is different from creating it directly. God is responsible for sin, but only to a degree and only indirectly. Moreover, the effects of sin are never absolute. If sin is permitted, God also provides for its correction and transformation into good. In fact, as sin is overcome, both the perfection of God and the goodness of existence are made all the more evident.

Is such a solution satisfactory? Only if we make at least the following assumptions: (1) that God's nature must entail a complete and unchanging knowledge of all reality, (2) that genuine human freedom is compatible with such knowledge, and (3) that God's options in creating are actually quite limited. Our previous analysis questioned the compatibility of genuine human freedom and the completeness of God's knowledge of reality. Further, as we will point out in later chapters, it is possible to develop a viable concept of God without the extreme emphasis on completeness of knowledge that Parker's theology requires. Nevertheless, consider the third assumption now in more detail.

The traditional doctrine of the best of all possible worlds assumes that there is a single, fixed hierarchy of values which delineates the good, one which God knows and in terms of which he creates. Moreover, there is only one set of circumstances which fits those norms absolutely. For postmodern men, both assumptions are suspect. Our outlook—permeated with freedom—tends to be that no single value combination can be absolutely the best. Many combinations are both possible and desirable. Absolute priority for any one form of the world is not decided exclusively by reference to knowledge and reason but depends partly on choice, feeling, and emotion. Furthermore, even given a priority for a particular combination of values, our tendency is still to think that plural sets of circumstances are compatible with this goal.

Again, choice, feeling, and emotion will enter into any final determination of circumstances. The issue as to which will or should exist is not one that can be settled by rational analysis and knowledge alone.

It is unlikely that we will agree that the world is the result of creation by a God who is bound so firmly to the assumptions of Parker's theology. In fact, a theology which is viable for us will very likely need to dispense altogether with the rationalistic doctrine of the best of all possible worlds. All that we may be able to affirm is that God creates a world—one out of a plurality of possibilities—which he finds to be desirable given his choice of certain value priorities. If combined with a theological view that stresses the open-endedness and incompleteness included in God's nature, a world of genuine freedom becomes more intelligible. In addition, although men may be accountable for much of the evil in the world, the task of assigning God his share of the responsibility becomes less apologetic and labored in a theology free of Parker's rationalistic assumptions.

If Parker's theology is too rationalistic, does Bushnell's more mystical outlook provide a better way where freedom and evil are concerned? The answer must be largely negative, because Bushnell retains the traditional idea that God has created the best of all possible worlds and that God's knowledge is absolutely complete from a perspective of eternity.

But if we go above the actual to contemplate God, before the foundation of the world, as dealing with intelligibles, or possibles, perusing systems of possibles, foreknowing them and their contents, not as actual, or historical, but as intelligible; then instituting, or by a fiat of will actualizing the best and wisest, we shall see that, in putting that best system on foot, he has made it certain that all the contents of the system will emerge, historically, in due time.[18]

At the same time, however, Bushnell's theology contains considerable possibilities for a novel interpretation of what God might take to be the best of all possible worlds. He constantly emphasizes that we are dealing with a God who does not take the most obvious routes in dealing with men. Language and reason can take us far in understanding how God operates, but the best they can do is to point us in a fruitful direction. Theology helps to interpret God's actions, and it aids us in seeing that his ways really are best. Yet Bushnell never ignores the possibility that God's ways are also hidden and partly obscured in paradox. He may communicate wisdom through foolishness and reveal strength through weakness.

Bushnell, the creative mediator, had the potential to be the most radical theologian of his day. His God—who is characterized by the comprehensiveness and equilibrium with which he holds antagonistic forces together for a good end—could have broken free from the rationalistic tendencies of both Calvinism and Unitarianism. Bushnell saw himself striving to fulfill this task. However, in the end the traditional qualities prevail in his theology too. This is especially true in certain aspects of his analysis of sin.

God's knowledge of human freedom and action is complete, but he desires no sin. He only permits it and does not regard it as a good in disguise. Bushnell discounts the possibility that God's exhaustive knowledge makes sin a necessary factor in our lives, but he does admit that man's existential circumstances are such that sin is unavoidable in practice. There is a "privative" quality in men which involves—but does not cause, produce, necessitate, etc.—"their certain lapse into evil."[19] "Liberty we know is not annihilated. And yet we say, looking on the state of man made perilous, in this manner, by liberty, that we can not expect him to stand" (p. 236).

Now why is sin tolerated by God, seeing that he does not desire it? God accepts it partly because it is the price of freedom and partly because he wills to triumph over it. Coupled with Bushnell's emphasis on the way in which the deck is stacked so as to make sin unavoidable in practice, this last suggestion—that God wishes to overcome evil—goes far in the direction of implying some sense in which God *desires* sin. But Bushnell refuses to hold God so directly responsible. On the contrary, he pushes the responsibility for any evil as far away from God as he can. For example, he argues that man is accountable for the violence and destructiveness in natural processes which exist prior to man's appearance on earth.

Bushnell finds traces of the demonic in nature more readily than the other writers we have discussed in this chapter, but negative forces appear in nature as an anticipation and perpetual reminder of the havoc created by man's sinfulness. Nature helps reveal our faults to us, but we are responsible for the defects in the first place—not only in ourselves but in nature as well. A more man-centered and fantastic interpretation of evil can hardly be imagined.

We have been interpreting and reacting to insights about freedom and evil developed by Channing, Emerson, Thoreau, Parker, and Bushnell. Now, more briefly, we turn to their suggestions about human fulfillment and to some of the ways in which their thought manifests the principle of pluralism which is at the heart of American theology. All these men agree on two points. First, religious insight is necessary to maximize the meaningfulness of human life. Second, if human life is restricted to the finite time we spend in this present world, it will never transcend the qualities of fragmentation and destruction which tend to make life empty and absurd.

The first point is a corollary of the conviction that man is by nature a religious being. Some members of this group do not go as far as Parker in speaking about a special religious faculty in man, but each one does affirm that human consciousness is tuned to God's vibrations. With effort, we can clarify their significance and discover a source of strength and hope. When this is done, we perceive that every man is a center of unique possibilities, placed in a rich, varied, and sometimes violent natural order for the purpose of seeing what he can make of himself and his world. In this condition, man is not without guidance from God. Nature is our teacher. Virtuous action is rewarded by increased insight and greater appreciation of the world's goodness. Sin yields punishment, but always for the purpose of our edification. Ultimately, the human drama occurs against the backdrop of God's love. If he places heavy demands upon us, he is also ready to forgive our failures and to transform evil into good.

The latter point is crucial and is interpreted as having implications that point beyond man's finite existence in this world. If these writers think that God has created the best of all possible worlds, this conviction exists only because they hold that there is more to human existence than our earthly life affords. Not all share Channing's straightforward doctrine of immortality. Each hopes, however, for some continuation of life beyond death, since reward for moral accomplishment and recompense for evil are far from being immediate; in some instances it is hard to detect any compensation at all in our present existence. They affirm that our lives reach fulfilling completion, but only because God's love transforms and extends them beyond the fluctuations of good and evil we experience now.

These men live in no secular city. On the other hand, their orientation is not otherworldly. It would be hard to imagine five theologians or philosophers more active and concerned about the quality of life in this world. They were spokesmen against slavery and repressive government; advocates of improved education, better conditions for laborers, women's liberation, preservation of nature, and individual self-reliance. Each tried to awaken America to high ideals, and each made effective contributions to this task.

One cannot read the writings of these men without concluding that their efforts were largely religiously motivated. In contrast, we tend to assume now that moral energy does not necessarily spring from religious sources, and to a large extent our secular culture demonstrates the validity of this view. Our problems have never been greater, but it is also true that genuine moral concern has rarely been as widespread, and that this occurs precisely when the impact of religion on our nation's life is far less apparent than it once was.

Theodore Parker was convinced that atheism results in destructive selfishness, but more recent American theologians (see Chapter VII) have suggested that atheism actually frees us for genuine moral concern. No simple resolution is possible where such divergence of opinion exists, but American self-understanding might be improved by considering again the connection between moral life-styles, theological reflection, and religious practice. This would require us to reflect also on the extent to which human fulfillment is possible in this present life.

The thought of the five men we have been considering shows certain similarities, but we have seen differences as well, which testify to the pluralistic quality of American theology. In addition, there are further traits which accentuate pluralism. The writings of these men sometimes have a rationalistic flavor, but attempts are rare to claim that anything has been proved universally. More than one of them emphasizes the certainty that comes with intuitional approaches to philosophy and theology. However, usually they stress both the personal nature of the convictions and the need for other persons to test the claims in their own experience. All five are rebels against religious authority. No man has a privileged position that entitles him to speak finally for another in religious matters. Self-reliance and finding one's own way— these are watchwords for this group of American thinkers.

At the same time, the efforts and ideals of these men were not always gladly received. If each was a rebel and an independent thinker in religious and theological matters, all had difficulties with the religious establishment of the day. Their efforts were viewed by many as a threat to truth and community. Far from regarding their own work as such a threat, this group became convinced that free, open, and radical inquiry was indispensable in achieving the religious vitality needed to develop a community in which men could grow as individuals while lending support to each other too.

Channing, Emerson, Thoreau, Parker, and Bushnell were the winners in the battles they fought. The importance and desirability of establishing and maintaining a community which not only allows but nurtures pluralism—in all areas of life, not just in theology— this becomes clear in their struggles. Their vision, of course, was not of a pluralism that would be uncritical or anarchistic. What they extolled was a thoughtful approach to life, which might manifest itself in a variety of ways but would also uncover common, unifying values. To encourage such an outlook toward life is risky business. The middle ground of a fruitfully pluralistic community is never easy to maintain against destructive tendencies that push toward either repressive conformity or chaotic individualism. But risks are worth taking in order to achieve this American ideal.

D. The Present Challenge to Romantic Optimism

Theology develops by bringing present unsettling experience, plus hope for the future, in touch with a religious and theological tradition. The development of individual men and nations may follow a similar pattern. Very rarely, however, do past theological statements speak adequately in the present, any more than past dimensions of our individual and national lives are sufficient to pull us through every crisis we shall yet face. Sometimes we are even forced to break sharply with the past in order to confront circumstances with a fresh vision capable of success. On the other hand, no man can cut the past either out of his life or out of theology. To attempt to do so is to invite a fragmentation and a rootlessness which thwart positive growth. What is to be hoped is that a man's relation to his past can be such that necessary critical reaction to it does not produce either severe alienation or the desire to substitute an entirely different heritage.

Where Channing, Emerson, Thoreau, Parker, and Bushnell are concerned, our relation to the theological past will not be free of serious criticism and disagreement, but neither must it produce a radical break. These men fostered a healthy pluralism. Thus, even a person who considers himself nonreligious can appreciate their efforts and affirm their right to inquire about God and to have religious faith. These men helped to further the American ideal of putting religion and theology in an open market where diverse ideas are free to compete for the conscious allegiance of men. No idea should be imposed from the outside or simply assumed as a part of an inherited culture.

Such an ideal was not the result of timid withdrawal from the conviction that religion and theology make a significant contribution to the health of the nation. Rather, these moves toward pluralism and toward placing religion and theology in open debate were a manifestation of the belief that the best contribution they could make to American life would come only if they were not equated with the "establishment." Only if they help to bring men to new levels of self-consciousness, by encouraging each to seek and choose critically his own forms of commitment, are religious ritual and theological doctrine to be encouraged.

Channing, Emerson, Thoreau, Parker, and Bushnell believed that free inquiry would result in religious commitment because they assumed that man is by nature a religious being whose consciousness is ultimately attuned to God. We do not seem safe in making that assumption today, however. It may be that man's existence is structured so that theological questions arise; yet there is a difference between finding questions before us and affirming that inquiry into them will result in positive religious faith. Moreover, even if such commitment does result from inquiry, it is unlikely to find an adequate basis in a traditional theology which emphasizes the completeness and the absoluteness of God's being and knowledge. How can we include process, change, and open-endedness in the divine nature? Can we speak of the perfection and goodness of God without acknowledging his heavy responsibility for evil? These are crucial theological questions now.

The men accounted for in this chapter rebelled against their forefathers, but they maintained continuity with the past through an essentially classical concept of God. In our world—where the experiences of freedom and evil are central and radical—such a theology produces a clash which seriously threatens the possibility of maintaining a religious faith continuous with our tradition. This fact manifests itself in the increasing American interest in Oriental religions.

In a pluralistic America, non-Western explorations should be welcomed, but not at the expense of losing what is more uniquely ours. We may have to reject much in a particular theological heritage, but an effort at theological reconstruction, utilizing our own resources wherever possible, ought to be a part of any American theology of the future. True identity for an American, or for any human being, comes as one faces his past and builds on it—making radical changes wherever necessary while preserving continuity whenever possible.

Romantic optimism is always alive somewhere, and it exists in America today. Still, the view of God common in early nineteenth-century America seems at least partly out of place in the late twentieth century. This is not so much because we must abandon the traditional American ideal of fulfillment of human life for all. It is rather that, if we are still to hold to the ideal of individual fulfillment in the present world, we will have to do so recognizing both that the world makes this less easy and more subject to failure than we thought and that God is not quite so overtly favorable and supporting as we had hoped. The early nineteenth century seems to have been an age of optimism. If we are still to retain that hope, it will have to be against discouraging odds.

Individualism seems to have been at its height in the nineteenth century. We still stress today the primacy of individual concerns, but also realize more clearly just how this can lead to destructive conflict, and how great the community assistance must be if some individuals are to have even an initial chance. God seems to leave us much more on our own in the struggle for human development than once we hoped. We may still find God in this process, but today he seems more aloof from immediate concrete assistance, and capable of absorbing larger dimensions of defeat. We are less romantic in our appraisal of the value that destructive evil can provide. The forces that work against the possibility of fulfillment need more accounting for than the intentions of a simple, all-good God can provide.

We are no longer overly optimistic about the possibility of achieving good merely by individual human effort. The very structures we build to help us can turn and restrict us and resist our efforts to alter them. We may not have lost the notion that every man is capable of fulfillment and ought to be offered the chance; but we see more clearly that he may refuse the chance, resist it, or even be so disoriented as not to recognize or know how to pursue it.

Some early nineteenth-century writers seem to have experienced quite deeply the power of freedom, and felt free to revise their theological heritage when it was inadequate to their new experience. But their protest against the inhibiting power of evil was not equally strong. They launched a revolt against determinism, although they failed to extend this release to God. Our contemporary revolt is more against the thwarting presence of destructive evil, and in this battle God cannot remain the same.

The philosophers and theologians of this age were men who saw their role as independent social critics. But we can hardly escape the feeling that they lived in an age no longer real, an age of innocence where good intentions and right feelings were easy to locate and simple to follow. A sense of basically conflicting values and possible general disorientation was less real for them than it is for us. When our experience shifts its basic direction in this present century, destruction and conflict demand a new theological resolution. If we face a frustrating presence of moral ambiguity and the threatening force of evil, our concepts of God—if we are to have any at all—must take us beyond a romantic view of existence.

NOTES

1. Theodore Parker, *Theism, Atheism and the Popular Theology*, ed. Charles W. Wendte (Boston: American Unitarian Associatoin, 1907), p. 187. Hereafter referred to as *Theism*.

2. William Ellery Channing, "Unitarian Christianity," in *Unitarian Christianity and Other Essays*, ed. Irving H. Bartlett (Indianapolis: Bobbs-Merrill Company, 1957), p. 22.

3. Ralph Waldo Emerson, "The American Scholar," in *The Selected Writings of Ralph Waldo Emerson*, ed. Brooks Atkinson (New York: Modern Library, 1950), p. 54. All Emerson references are to the volume edited by Atkinson, hereafter referred to as *Selected Writings*.

4. *Nature*, in *Selected Writings*, p. 6.

5. Henry David Thoreau, *Walden*, in *The Portable Thoreau*, ed. Carl Bode (New York: Viking Press, 1964), p. 548.

6. "Civil Disobedience," in *The Portable Thoreau*, p. 111.

7. Theodore Parker, "The Transient and Permanent in Christianity," in *Theodore Parker: An Anthology*, ed. Henry Steele Commager (Boston: Beacon Press, 1960), p. 51. Hereafter referred to as *Anthology*.

8. "The Power of the Merchant Class," in *Anthology*, p. 153.

9. Horace Bushnell, *God in Christ*, in *Horace Bushnell*, ed. H. Shelton Smith (New York: Oxford University Press, 1965), p. 93. All Bushnell references are to the volume edited by Smith, hereafter referred to as *Bushnell*.

10. "The Christian Trinity a Practical Truth," in *Bushnell*, p. 215.

11. *God in Christ*, in *Bushnell*, p. 193.

12. "Compensation," in *Selected Writings*, p. 178.

13. "History," in *Selected Writings*, p. 126.

14. "Compensation," in *Selected Writings*, p. 181.

15. "Circles," in *Selected Writings*, p. 279.

16. *Walden*, in *The Portable Thoreau*, pp. 557–558.

17. *Theism*, p. 374.

18. "Christian Comprehensiveness," in *Bushnell*, p. 120.

19. *Nature and the Supernatural*, in *Bushnell*, p. 222.

IV

THE GOLDEN AGE
OF AMERICAN PHILOSOPHY

A. Five Philosophers and Their Context

Ask a person what American philosophy's most distinctive theory is, and if he can say anything the response is likely to be *pragmatism*. If you ask next about the content of pragmatism, any reply will probably emphasize the notion that our thought and action ought to be oriented practically and concerned with hard-headed estimates of what will or won't "work." Inquire about the men who developed these ideas, and the names mentioned are likely to be William James and John Dewey. At this point, however, the replies are almost sure to end. Further questions as to who these men were, what they did, and what they wrote and thought will rarely elicit much more information or interest.

No one escapes the American public school without knowing something of his intellectual foundations. Many even pick up some acquaintance with pragmatism, if only by reading newspaper accounts which tell us that our President is a "pragmatic" man. Most citizens have at least heard of James or Dewey, particularly since the latter's name is often mentioned in attacks on the "permissiveness" of our culture and our lax educational systems. At the same time, however, most Americans have little understanding of, or interest in, their philosophical heritage. The average citizen is too worried over today's problems and tomorrow's possibilities to be very concerned about yesterday's ideas—especially when they are merely philosophical. Current questions and future opportunities are "where the action is," and any nation or person who lives chiefly in the past will not be around as a power for long. On the other hand, it is difficult to have the confidence that success requires unless your own past is something you can appreciate and in which you can find a secure footing.

Scholars say that there has been a golden age of American philosophy, and that pragmatists such as James and Dewey were part of it. Most of us will not be surprised by the suggestion—only indifferent. But the fact remains that there is a provocative, if not exciting, story of developments that took place in American philosophy between 1870 and 1935. They relate to our future prospects for religious life, theology, and national renewal.

William James believed that the most interesting and important thing about a man is the philosophical perspective he holds. Certainly the philosophical views developed by James and others of his period have done much to shape our contemporary outlook. We have affinities with earlier thinkers, but the ideas of the men considered in this chapter are now in the marrow of our bones. By either acceptance or rejection of their thought—or some position in between—our present and future life-style is still being influenced by these philosophers.

If the philosophies men hold are indeed the most interesting and important thing about them, then the developments of the period between 1870 and 1935 ought to be relevant to us even now. To illustrate, let us look at the insights produced by five men, paying special attention to their implications for religion and theology. James (1842–1910) and Dewey (1859–1952) have already been mentioned. The other three are Charles Peirce (1839–1914), Josiah Royce (1855–1916), and George Santayana (1863–1952).

What are some of the major themes these men articulate? Out of what context do they emerge to produce a golden age of American philosophy? When you consider the period from 1870 to 1935, it is World War I, our national experiment with Prohibition, and the Great Depression that are sure to stand out. But only Dewey experienced these events at first hand from an American perspective. Peirce, Royce, and James had died before the end of World War I, and Santayana had left for Europe. However, in two earlier events—one intellectual and scientific, the other social and political—we obtain a glimpse of the backdrop for the philosophies developed by this group. They are: (1) the emergence of the biological theory of evolution, symbolized by Darwin's *Origin of Species* (1859), and (2) the American Civil War.

One might suppose that the Civil War would have a direct influence on American philosophy, but actually evolutionary theory is the more dominant. Philosophers feel the effects of war—sometimes perhaps as profoundly as the combatants themselves—and this group of American thinkers is no exception. However, their response is subtle. Their theories offer few references to the war itself, but are full of concern about a problem that war—civil war in particular—always involves, namely, that of *community*. To see how this issue is handled, let us first examine the impact of evolutionary theory on American culture and philosophy.

Although we may still be far from recognizing all the philosophical implications of Darwin's discoveries, evolutionary theory today is old-hat. It was not always so. Americans often appreciate and study nature, but to conceive of the emergence of man from surprising and primitive forms of life and from the depths of almost unimaginable spans of time was a mind-blowing experience for many in the nineteenth century. Nevertheless, if these suggestions were a shock to the foundations of self-understanding, for some they were also a stimulus to fresh thought. They even became a welcome sign of man's release from the traditional theological view that placed him in an eternally fixed position within an essentially finished creation.

All the philosophers we have named worked in an environment shaped by evolutionary views. Fundamentally, this implied that man was in and of the world—a natural creature. His home was a world in process, and man himself was a creature in flux. Man and world, both shaped and shaping, were moving in time. Their ultimate origin and their destination were unknown—perhaps unknowable. In such a setting it became possible, even necessary, for men to turn their inquiries away from absolute truths and supposed certainties—religious, philosophical, or scientific—and move toward fresh empirical studies of life and experience.

If temporal existence involves us in an ambiguous flux, the only way to shape and control it for human ends is to understand it on its own terms. Thus, along with renewed efforts to extend and improve education, empirical science and technology came into their own in the United States. Americans have always tried to understand nature. Edwards examined spiders; Franklin performed scientific experiments; and no one has exceeded Thoreau's care in penetrating nature's mysteries. But we became a scientific and technologically oriented people only in comparatively recent times, and largely through the impetus provided by evolutionary theories.

Philosophy in America both helped to produce and has been shaped by scientific concerns. With the possible exception of Emerson's work, it is difficult to separate philosophy from theology, political theory, or natural history before the Civil War. For better or worse, this situation began to change rapidly. After the war, a new group of thinkers appeared with an outlook subtly but substantially altered, largely by the influence of scientific advances and evolutionary thought. Old desires to understand man's place in nature were retained, and allegiance to democratic political principles continued to run deep, but both were transformed by new views concerning methods of inquiry, knowledge, and truth itself. Traditional preoccupation with moral values and religious faith remained, but a shift in conviction set in as to their status and significance. The interpretation of the relation of religion to established institutions changed.

Part of the new mood may be summarized by noting that James, Royce, Santayana, and Dewey spent a large part of their lives teaching in universities. Peirce would have done so too had greater opportunities been available to him. America arose out of philosophical principles, but the life of the university professor spending his time pursuing philosophical questions was something new in this culture. As with most things in American society, the results of this phenomenon have been mixed. The advantage is an increase of self-criticism and self-understanding in many dimensions of life. Disadvantages have accrued in overspecialization and narrowness of outlook, which frequently remove the philosopher's attention from problems most pressing and worthy of concern. If Peirce, Royce, James, Santayana, and Dewey are part of a golden age of American philosophy, it is because they helped to produce genuine self-awareness in America without lapsing into the stifling technicalities of narrow interests.

Philosophical efforts in America before this era lacked the unique combination of originality, depth of critical analysis, and breadth of constructive concern that characterize this period. And it is difficult to follow such a brilliant performance as these men offered; their successors, unfortunately, have seldom matched them. In recent times, the originality inspired by reflection on American life and goals has been replaced by attention to European sources, while breadth of constructive effort has been largely sacrificed to descriptive and analytic concerns.

As a result, numerous philosophers in America are perhaps in greater difficulty than our theologians. Contemporary theologians may not know what they can or should say, but at least they seem to have a faithful audience waiting for them to decide, hoping that their efforts will produce light and warmth by which to live. Many philosophers, on the other hand, while they seem more confident in pursuing their historical, analytical, and phenomenological investigations, may find before long that few Americans—except their patient colleagues—are listening. Philosophers are not immune to the identity crisis the American people as a whole now face. The outcome could be a new golden age in American philosophy. But we are not in such a period now, and to arrive there will require a considerable shift in the problems to which philosophers give top priority.

The impact of evolutionary theory on our consciousness not only directed attention toward nature in new ways, but also created a crisis in America's religious life. For many the gulf was absolute. If science meant evolution, one could not be both a scientific and a religious man. In some quarters, science and religion still eye each other uneasily. However, except where there is real ignorance or rigidity, some sense of accommodation and even mutual support has been achieved. If this is true, such reconciliation is due in no small part to the efforts of the men discussed in this chapter. Their concern with man's scientific and technological advances was not without critical moments. Whenever science was equated with a narrow and deterministic empiricism which ignored the moral and religious dimensions of life, they rebelled.

As a part of their protest, they called attention to the fact that intolerance, dogmatism, and an inhumane leveling of life can masquerade as scientific. They argued that the genius and value of science lie in its emphasis on open-ended inquiry, tolerance of novel hypotheses, empirical testing, and vast potential for humanizing life. When technology consumed rather than served men, their anger was aroused. At the turn of the century, our economy and industrial power were expanding and our international influence increasing. Americans often spoke of national growth and progress. But these philosophers reminded us that quantitative increases may be misleading measures of society's health. The *quality* of its life determines whether a nation is really growing and making "progress."

It was, moreover, precisely in helping us understand what is genuinely valuable in life, and the goals toward which our scientific knowledge and technology ought to be applied, that these men saw an indispensable role for *religious* insight. However, this must be elaborated to avoid confusion. In many ways each man was a harsh critic of established religion, ecclesiastical institutions, and theological doctrines. None was interested in a repetition of the Great Awakening or a revival of romantic transcendentalism.

What did concern them was the renewal—or perhaps even the initial birth—of a sense of *community* in American life. They took their model more from scientific associations than from the institutional church, but understood the ideal of community to be essentially religious in character. We shall see these claims illustrated in discussing the various figures individually; the point to be made here is that each of these men was a creative mediator who sought and found a way for man to be both scientific *and* religious. All believed that both dimensions were essential for a humane communal life.

What about the second factor which formed the background for American philosophy in the period 1870–1935? Democracy in America means that we will always be struggling to achieve

a viable sense of community and common purpose. In a pluralistic society people can go in many different directions. That
is what the democratic promise allows. Not every combination,
however, is conducive to unity. Some compromises become intolerable because they violate principles basic to our common life;
bitter conflicts may occur which leave us at odds long after their
superficial resolution. The Civil War is a case in point.

Every analysis of this event leaves something out and thus is
oversimplified. Nevertheless, there is no escaping these facts: the
institution of slavery, and our compromises in the face of it, shattered national unity. The war that resulted had consequences
which leave us divided in ways that might still lead to a national
demise. No American today can talk seriously about "community"
without confronting the old, forward-thrown shadows of slavery
and civil war. It does not seem likely that the situation was much
different for Peirce, Royce, James, Santayana, or Dewey.

Although these men did not write much about the causes and
effects of the Civil War, the specter of it could not have been very
far removed from their awareness. Men often speak most pas-
sionately about just those qualities that are missing from their lives
or societies. If the theme of community is central to the concerns
of these writers, the fact is understandable when we consider the
Civil War as the background for their thought. It may have preserved the Union, but it did not create a community.

These philosophers agree in feeling the need for an awakening
of communal concern and spirit. Philosophers cannot make a nation move, but they can help a people understand themselves and
clarify their goals. In a country dedicated to the ideal of liberty,
the value of community looms large, since it is only as men respect
and cooperate with each other that real freedom is possible. In a
nation committed to individual freedom and fulfillment but marred
by slavery, civil war, and racial hatred, the need for community
is extreme. Without it national life may come apart at the seams
all over again.

The Civil War had another effect on American life which ought
not to be ignored and which plays a part in the interpretations
of religious life as explored by this group of philosophers. It may
be true that there are no atheists in foxholes, but wars frequently

have a divisive effect on churches. We have seen this at first hand in the Vietnam experience, and it was certainly true a century ago —slavery and the Civil War split the American churches. Moreover, these divisions, when combined with the controversies of evolutionary theory, produced tensions beyond endurance.

These factors compounded our religious pluralism in undesirable ways. Conflict that was fragmenting and heated—but hardly heartwarming—dominated much of the ecclesiastical scene. Thus, if we take pluralism always to be a virtue, it becomes clear that the *quality* of the pluralism is absolutely crucial. Unless it is genuinely *humane,* it can destroy community.

Amid such institutional chaos, it would not be surprising to see philosophers discard the religious life altogether. But Peirce, Royce, James, Santayana, and Dewey saw man's spiritual element as too important to be drowned in church quarrels. The scientific community provided their model, but into it they poured the spiritual and moral values for which religion at its best has stood. What once were religious goals now appeared in more secular form.

B. The Pragmatic Challenge to Idealism: Peirce, Royce, and James

In the 1870's a group of American intellectuals—among them Chauncey Wright, John Fiske, Oliver Wendell Holmes, Jr., and William James—organized a philosophical discussion group in Cambridge, Massachusetts. The group became known as the Metaphysical Club. Another of the participants was Charles Peirce. In this setting, largely unnoticed, Peirce shared and developed the ideas that made him the father of American pragmatism.

Peirce's training was in science and mathematics, but these interests developed into philosophical concerns as to methods of inquiry and the nature of belief. His study of science led him to conclude that legitimate scientific investigations employed a method of inquiry vastly different from and superior to the approaches that characterized philosophy and theology. Intrigued by these realizations, Peirce published "The Fixation of Belief" (1877). In it he described the fundamental context for inquiry and then outlined and analyzed four ways of forming beliefs.

As to context: to believe something is to be prepared to act in some specifiable way and to expect some specifiable set of experiences to result. Beliefs are reinforced as long as we get expected results. When there is a breakdown, we have to stop and reconsider. Inquiry begins when beliefs break down. The opposite of belief, then, is not disbelief, which actually is a form of belief, but *doubt*. Doubt is the state of uneasiness in which we find ourselves when beliefs have broken down. In such a state, we do not possess either a firm course of action or a clear set of expectations. We have to find our way anew. Doubt leads to inquiry. "Hence, the sole object of inquiry is the settlement of opinion."[1]

The fundamental question is this: What are the available ways for settling opinion, and which course is most worthwhile? Peirce discusses four options. Three of them—the methods of tenacity, authority, and a priori appeals to reason—have a long history and have exerted great influence, but they also have some deficiencies. The method of tenacity fixes belief by individual choice—often arbitrary—and by subjective liking. This approach ignores the communal dimension of knowledge. It leaves no option for handling error, except by another tenacious affirmation of belief. The method of authority is more communally oriented. Yet it, too, ultimately falls back on a single group or person and involves all the dangers of subjectivism that haunt the method of tenacity.

The a priori appeal to reason is little better. Here Peirce's special target is Descartes' view that genuine knowledge and certainty are ours when—after being subjected to radical doubt and rigorous criticism—our ideas emerge as "clear and distinct." This approach involves a more extensive use of reason than the method of tenacity; it requires the individual to free himself from authoritarian dogma. Yet a dangerous subjectivism still lurks in the a priori approach. The fact that some idea or claim appears to be clear and distinct—even after extensive rational criticism—is no absolute guarantee of its truth. Appeals to "clarity and distinctness" still leave us with the possibility of error. Using this approach to the fixation of belief, error comes as a nasty surprise which can only be dealt with by refixing belief through another a priori appeal to reason. However, no a priori appeal to reason is sufficient to prevent experience from boiling over and annihilating supposed certainties.

It is not difficult to apply Peirce's analysis to religion and theology. To claim certainty for religious beliefs or theological doctrines on the basis of either personal feeling, appeals to authority, or rational intuitions is unsound and in the long run detrimental to religious life. This critique touches the nerve of many a Calvinist and transcendentalist. There is little certainty in Peirce's world. No groups or individuals have special access to truth. The possibility of error is permanent and pervasive. Even a man's introspective judgments are not immune from doubt.

To have knowledge entails making claims and judgments about experience, and where claims and judgments are made, *interpretation* takes place. Interpretations of experience—religious or otherwise—are always fallible. We are warranted in holding any given interpretation so long as critically sifted, empirically and publicly grounded evidence bears it out. Yet even fulfillment of these conditions gives us no absolute guarantee of knowledge and truth.

The method of science incorporates an accurate understanding of the predicament men face in inquiry and provides the most fruitful approach for the fixation of belief. Scientific method recognizes that human claims are fallible. It insists, therefore, upon regarding our claims as hypothetical and in need of testing by a community of investigators. To put it another way, this method of inquiry is *self-corrective* in ways unavailable to the other three. Faced with error, the previous methods can respond only by a fresh act of tenacious affirmation or by appeals to authority, "clarity and distinctness," or self-evidence. The scientific method, however, escapes the embarrassing and often disastrous consequences of pronouncing a claim to be certain only to have it directly contradicted by later experience.

The method of science, since it places a premium on the permanent possibility of error, shies away from absolute assertion. It tests the claims made, actively hunting for mistakes. As experience unfolds, judgments and facts, expectations and consequences, are kept in close contact and these relationships are examined critically. Where the meeting is harmonious, confidence in our possession of truth is increased, but it is never made absolute. Where the meeting is disruptive, experience is reappraised, creative inquiry occurs, and new hypotheses are formed and tested with the hope that they will be more adequate. Peirce's scientific man has come of age. He gives up a simple trust in his own capacity to discern the truth and faces the fact that existence is a precarious and risk-filled adventure. He decides to live with fallible probabilities instead of fixed certainties.

In this setting Peirce lays down some additional points which form the core of his pragmatism. The publication of "The Fixation of Belief" was followed by another essay: "How to Make Our Ideas Clear" (1878). The motive behind this paper is simple. Peirce believes that the scientific method can be used in many areas of life, including philosophy. However, in order to work well it must be supplemented by a method that helps us to be clear about the *meaning* of our ideas, claims, and theories. That is, before we can know how to proceed in testing a hypothesis, we need to be as clear as possible about what it entails. We have to determine what sorts of experiences it leads us to expect and what kinds of results ought to occur if it is true.

"Our idea of anything *is* our idea of its sensible effects. . . ."[2] That proposition is crucial to Peirce's pragmatism, which is essentially a method for determining the meaning of ideas, claims, and theories. He summarizes the central aspects of his view in the following statement: ". . . Consider what effects, which might conceivably have practical bearings, we conceive the object of our conception to have. Then, our conception of these effects is the whole of our conception of the object" (p. 124). Peirce's summary is complicated, and that should tip us off to the fact that the specification of meaning can be a complex task. Our thoughts are often richer and more ambiguous and interrelated than we realize, and the application of Peirce's pragmatic maxim will not render things instantly clear.

However, to the extent that we can translate our concepts into experiences, we will facilitate the testing of hypotheses and also be able to recognize bogus problems or meaningless concepts. Bogus problems will be uncovered whenever we are unable to point to any possible differences in the experiences entailed by views that seem to be in conflict. Furthermore, if we find that a concept prompts no specifiable expectations or points to no possible experiences at all, we can regard it as meaningless.

The goal of Peirce's pragmatic approach to meaning is to enrich human life by providing a method of inquiry that increases communal understanding and knowledge. But what is the broader metaphysical context in which Peirce places these methodological suggestions, and does it contain a positive interpretation of religion? Peirce was not only a skilled logician and philosopher of science, but also developed some broad and provocative metaphysical hypotheses. His appreciation for lawful regularities in nature was accompanied by wonder and delight in the experience of *novelty*.

To him the world seemed to be a place where genuinely new things occur. Peirce believed that real novelty was incompatible with deterministic or necessitarian views which regard events and experiences as the fixed effects of some primordial cause or law. Such views were held by some as indispensable for the support of scientific inquiry. For Peirce, they were merely assumptions, unnecessary in fact to scientific work and contrary to the sense of our own experiences of freedom.

Lawful regularities exist, but in Peirce's view they are set within a broad evolutionary context of novelty. Our world is in process. Probably it is emerging out of a primordial chaos, and possibly it is moving toward higher degrees of order and harmony. Spontaneity and structure mingle together at every moment. Neither is ever absent entirely. Thus, if the process of existence moves toward greater order and harmony, spontaneity and freedom will not be missing but will function to assure freshness and beauty.

Peirce is a man of science, but he does not forsake entirely the romantic warmth of American transcendentalism. The world is moving somewhere. This movement and its outcomes reveal a growth and magnificence which suggest that existence is not merely the play and result of blind forces. It may be grounded in a divine and perpetually creating power which lures the world on in love. Such a view has religious qualities, but Peirce never developed these theological implications very far. Some further insights, however, may be obtained by noting his discussion of what he called the "neglected argument" for God's reality.

One aspect of human life which held special interest for Peirce was the fact that men are often successful in forming hypotheses about experience and nature which really do illumine and explain. The possibilities for error are vast. Yet the human mind functions almost instinctively in hitting on hypotheses initially plausible and often eventually corroborated. Man and nature seem to be in tune with each other. Peirce was not opposed, then, to having men trust their intuitions. If a hunch felt right, it might be true; the trick was to avoid mistaking the intuitive feeling for the mark of truth itself. The presence of truth could be confirmed only after critical testing.

The significance of this analysis for religious insight is that Peirce was willing to trust his intuitions in metaphysics and religion as well as in science—but only so far. He was struck by the fact that, when one contemplates the beauty and vastness of nature and allows his mind to play freely, reflection about God may occur.

. . . The idea of God's Reality will be sure sooner or later to be found an attractive fancy, which the Muser will develop in various ways. The more he ponders it, the more it will find response in every part of his mind, for its beauty, for its supplying an ideal of life, and for its thoroughly satisfactory explanation of his whole threefold environment.[3]

"Musement" produces no clear and distinct theory of God, but it leads to the concept of a divine power who grounds and sustains existence in love, and such a concept has an intellectual, moral, and aesthetic appeal that is tantalizing. It provides a reason for existence, and it points to a moral ideal with its intimations of love and reasoned growth in existence. This provides an account for the reality of beauty which itself is beautiful, and our aesthetic sensibility is touched. The instinctive appearance of the idea of God in the context that Peirce assumes, together with its natural appeal as we reflect on it further in this context, commend the hypothesis of God to us. Yet, even if it speaks to us religiously, the question still remains as to its validity and truth.

Truth is discovered only through empirical testing, but how can a hypothesis about God fit this model? Peirce recognizes that the vagueness of the hypothesis prohibits testing it in terms of precise expectations or experiences. He suggests, however, that there may be another way in which the hypothesis about God can be empirically tested. We might judge its validity and truth in terms of "its value in the self-controlled growth of man's conduct of life" (p. 375). What does that imply?

Peirce seems to have the following factors in mind. At times, the hypothesis of God has a strong appeal to our search for intelligibility and to our moral and aesthetic sensibilities. *Prima facie* the hypothesis helps to render human existence reasonable and meaningful. If the hypothesis about God is true, commitment to it ought to have the effect of further extending intelligibility, moral value, and beauty in the world.

Peirce now turned to an appraisal of religious life, the place where the hypothesis is taken seriously. But if the concept of God produced in musement was vague, the outcome of his appraisal left things ambiguous. The religious life he observed was a mixture. It did not always produce an extension of meaning, value, and beauty in the world. Its effects were often quite the contrary. Nevertheless, he thought the emphasis on *love* in religion was not only a hopeful sign but also important evidence in favor of the God-hypothesis.

Love entails understanding, concern for freedom, growth, fulfillment, and sensitivity to beauty. It is indispensable to "the self-controlled growth of man's conduct of life." Religion can become bogged down in doctrine and forget the centrality of love. Even religious men who speak of love often fail to practice it. Still, Peirce believed that lives of love motivated and nourished by faith in God remain a compelling, if still only partial, evidence for the truth of the God-hypothesis.

From a theological perspective, it is easy to criticize Peirce. His concept of God is only a sketch. It involves no clear statement about the relation between God and human freedom. It seems to give little attention to the problem of evil, which is always a major obstacle to religious faith. In spite of these shortcomings and Peirce's suspicion of theology because of its tendency to dwell on doctrine instead of love, his philosophy contains valuable insights for constructive work in American theology. Peirce gives us a vision of a world in process where genuinely novel events take place. We may not share his feeling that the process is moving in the direction of increasing harmony and beauty, but his emphasis on change and development does fit the experience of freedom.

Peirce's statements about God make love divinity's most striking characteristic. This may not seem obvious to us in a world we tend to see as equally full of evil and suffering. But although he has little to say about the problem of evil, Peirce does offer a provocative suggestion. If God is characterized by love, his love will not be merely self-love. It will extend even to that which is hateful, evil, and destructive in order to control and shape such forces so that they eventually become productive of positive value. "Love, recognizing germs of loveliness in the hateful, gradually warms it into life, and makes it lovely."[4] This idea suggests the possibility that it may be precisely a God of love who creates a world with elements of destructiveness and negativity for the purpose of transforming them, finally, into means toward a good end. Could God's love be like that? Peirce does not help us decide finally, but he raises an important question.

Peirce's chief significance, however, in our analysis of the possibilities for religious life and its role in our future may lie in still another area. Two things stand out. First, he stresses the need for hardheaded criticism and empirical investigation, but he does so from a perspective that emphasizes human fallibility and the indispensability of love if we are to achieve humane communal relationships. Second, he sees that love can be sustained and enriched by religious commitment. Belief in God always remains plausible—at least initially—because it touches and sustains intellectual, moral, and aesthetic needs.

None of the serious obstacles to an intelligible theology or a lasting religious faith are removed by pointing out these things, but Peirce has his fingers on some fundamental facts about human life. He is a scientific man, but he has not lost the sense of wonder and appreciation in which the idea of God comes to life for men and in which the impetus to love is felt. If error is a permanent possibility, so are faith and love. But just as the former is difficult to escape, so the latter are not easily achieved and extended.

The views that Peirce developed in the nineteenth century did not take the country by storm—even in philosophical circles. German philosophy and American transcendentalism exerted much greater influence in late nineteenth-century America. Philosophically, *absolute idealism* dominated the intellectual scene. Peirce's empirical and pragmatic views were partly a reaction to the excesses of idealistic metaphysics, and in the hands of William James pragmatism was to mount a full-scale attack on idealism. Still, in this period absolute idealism represented the mainstream, and Josiah Royce was its major American spokesman.

Royce was born and raised in California, but he spent his career teaching and writing at Harvard, where he was a friend and colleague of James for many years. His philosophical stimulation came primarily from German sources—Schelling, Schopenhauer, Lotze, and Hegel—but his basic philosophical outlook will be familiar to those who know the American transcendentalists. Royce believed that man can grasp the basic structures of his existence and that a philosophical system can be developed which describes them and demonstrates their reality. He held, moreover, that reality is an Eternal and Absolute Mind and Will—Royce sometimes speaks of it as God. This manifests itself in—but is not exhausted by—a vastly rich temporal universe of individuals who are organically and socially related.

The Absolute's awareness is eternally complete. It unifies and knows all these manifestations as a totality which is fully good and meaningful. In particular, human existence is a manifestation of the Absolute, and every person's life is ultimately assured of fulfilling, positive significance because it is essential to the universal community known and willed by the Absolute. Like transcendentalism, Royce's philosophy is full of religious and theological implications. He differs from his transcendental predecessors in arguing dialectically for the existence of the Absolute rather than appealing so strongly to intuition. However, let us concentrate on the themes of evil, freedom, and fulfillment which are at the core of his work.

Royce's philosophy argues that God's knowledge is eternally complete and that the totality of existence is good and fully meaningful. In fact, as we shall see shortly, he believes that our lives dissipate into meaninglessness and absurdity unless we are participants in the life of the Absolute. On the other hand, if we are such participants, each man receives a full share of completion and meaning. But there are problems. In a world of absolute goodness, why are there evil and suffering? If the Absolute sees existence from a perspective of eternity which entails completeness, how is freedom possible?

Faced by the problem of evil, Royce tries to defend the view that evil and suffering have a place in a world of absolute goodness without glossing over their power and negativity. One of his most penetrating discussions of these themes is found in "The Problem of Job." This essay argues that the perfection of the universe is not compatible with the reality of evil and suffering if they are simply produced by our freedom or inflicted on us by external forces—divine or otherwise.

This incompatibility, however, can be overcome if our encounters with evil and suffering are themselves experienced by God as necessary conditions for his own perfecttion, and hence for the perfection of existence as a whole. Royce maintains that this is precisely what his idealism asserts.

The answer to Job is: God is not in ultimate essence another being than yourself. He is the Absolute Being. You truly are one with God, part of his life. He is the very soul of your soul. And so, here is the first truth: When you suffer, *your sufferings are God's sufferings,* not his external work, not his external penalty, not the fruit of his neglect, but identically his own personal woe. In you God himself suffers, precisely as you do, and has all your concern in overcoming this grief.[5]

Royce's idealism assures us that God overcomes evil. God's knowledge is absolute. He knows what is desirable, and what God knows is the case. But God suffers because such experience is necessary for perfection. The greatest goodness does not exist where evil is absent altogether, but where it is experienced and overcome. Our world—the best of all possible worlds—*must,* therefore, contain evil. Royce emphasizes that evil is neither illusory nor simply good disguised. If perfection involves overcoming it, evil is just as real as it can be. At the same time he stresses that, if men do evil and suffer in the world, they can also be agents for transcending these negativities. Through atoning action and the realization that every human life is ultimately a fulfilled component in the Absolute's perfection, positive meaning and joy triumph over wrongdoing, tragedy, death, and sorrow.

In a later work, *The World and the Individual,* Royce addresses himself more fully to the nature of man's existence and freedom. A human life is a center of purpose and striving. Every man is a moving moral agent, not a thing or a static substance. He is a temporal process of experiencing, willing, and choosing, which is both an active aspect of the moral order willed by the Absolute and a questing for unity, understanding, and fulfillment of his own. As temporal beings, we are always trying to find ourselves, but Royce believes that we never have full self-comprehension at any single moment of time. We are *becoming* ourselves. We are self-determining free beings who do not know in advance what the detailed outcomes of our searching and striving will be. As long as we live in time, we experience a basic incompleteness in self-understanding.

Incompleteness, however, does not have the final word. If it did, Royce would agree with those who appraise existence as finally devoid of fulfilling meaning and ultimately absurd. Idealism enables Royce to hold that we share in a perspective which knows us as persons who are completed and fulfilled. We are, after all, manifestations of the Absolute, and we participate in its eternal perspective from which all being is comprehended as possessing these qualities.

Does such a theory constitute a theological determinism which makes one's life complete before he lives it and makes inescapable the evil men do and the suffering they experience? Royce replies that the Absolute's eternal knowledge is not the same as temporal foreknowing. Eternal knowledge grasps the whole of the temporal order and comprehends our freedom in all its aspects, but it neither eliminates our freedom nor makes it illusory. From eternity God knows our acts as free, but his knowledge does not determine or cause them.

As for evil and suffering, Royce continues to point out that the limits and incompleteness of temporal existence breed frustration and conflict. But to suffer and to struggle with evil are necessary conditions for absolute goodness and perfection. Moreover, in overcoming these obstacles in our finite manner and achieving success wherever we can, we experience fulfillment in time. Yet, if evil and suffering are necessary for perfection, Royce holds that the particular instances of evildoing and suffering that result from our freedom are not.

To assert the necessity of every negative event would undercut freedom, and Royce does not want to move in that direction. God experiences evil events and knows them fully in all their pathos from his eternal perspective, but our deeds and their consequences are not determined by him. God does, however, ultimately overcome every instance of evil and suffering so that the perfection of all being is assured. In the final analysis, this means that even the negativity of death will be transcended.

Late in his life, Royce addressed himself specifically to the relations between idealism and the Christian faith. The basic issue motivating his book *The Problem of Christianity* is: "In what sense can the modern man consistently be, in creed, a Christian?"[6] The answer to his question involves an attempt to demythologize Christianity in order to let its central message stand out clearly. His goal is to see whether this message can speak with power to men of an increasingly critical, scientific, and secular outlook.

The core of the Christian faith does not reside exclusively in particular beliefs about who Jesus was or in his moral teachings. Instead, Royce believes, the essence of Christianity revolves around the rich, but often neglected, concept of the Holy Spirit. It points toward the fundamental claim that all being and human life in particular are created and intended to be a community of love and loyalty. As Royce understands this idea, it does not gloss over the pervasiveness of man's sin and his need of a release from guilt which he cannot provide by himself. God's establishment of a community of love and loyalty through atoning action in the face of sin and evil—this is what the doctrine of the Holy Spirit is all about.

Royce takes this doctrine to be one that both squares with his idealistic metaphysics and meets human needs. A reflective man can readily understand that his own well-being and that of nature and the human community at large are inextricably related. In particular, love and loyalty are indispensable for drawing out the best in us. A thoughtful man can also see that, if his existence is to be ultimately significant—not swallowed up in sin, guilt, evil, and death—there must be a communal dimension to reality. This must be such as to transcend these negative qualities and allow for greater self-understanding and fulfillment than our present temporal existence makes possible. Both idealism and Christianity point toward the existence of such a redeeming dimension, and they are one in affirming that "we are saved through and in the community" (II, 390).

The initial reaction to Royce's metaphysics is likely to be negative today. In spite of his attempts at reconciliation, it is difficult for us to see that real freedom is compatible with the existence of his Absolute Knower. Moreover, it is unlikely that we will be immediately convinced that evil is a necessary condition for full goodness and the perfection of existence. Our intuitions will be correct regarding the question of freedom. The completeness that characterizes Royce's Absolute Knower does conflict seriously with our experience of freedom, and no distinction between eternal knowledge and temporal foreknowing will be sufficient to eliminate the opposition. On the problem of evil, however, we may do well to think twice before committing his views to the flames.

Royce is more straightforward than most thinkers in making God bear responsibility for evil. He does not merely say that God permits it. God actively chooses a world with evil in it for the reason that the best of all possible worlds is one in which evil has its day but is overcome. The best world is not one of innocence but one of triumph over negation. Royce's God is rather daring. He is willing to let destruction and brutal forces into the world, since he is confident that in the end—and even in the temporal process—love, loyalty, and fulfillment will win out. Peirce's insight about God's relation to evil seems to get elaborated in Royce's idealism.

We can comprehend the notion that a world of innocence may be less desirable than one in which evil appears but is transcended. In offering us a God who shares direct responsibility for evil, Royce may touch contemporary experience at a crucial point. Still, there are problems. Royce's philosophy gives no clear accounting of the *degree* of evil that exists, and yet he clings to the idea that this is the best of all possible worlds. Our intuitions tell us that this is not the best of all possible worlds. Without a more specific account of the reasons for the degree of evil in existence, we are not likely to be convinced otherwise.

Royce's rationalism traps him at this point and leaves his view ultimately vulnerable. He puts some important missing pieces into the theological puzzle, but ironically the totality of his view is incomplete in its ability to cope with the breadth of experience. What is needed is a greater emphasis on freedom—both God's and man's—so that the doctrine of the best of all possible worlds is eliminated altogether. Then we need only hold God responsible for creating a "good" world. We recognize that more than one standard of goodness is available, and we hope that the one employed by God does not lead to results which run roughshod over our own human desires.

We are not the first to point out difficulties and inadequacies in Royce's philosophy. Idealism may have been dominant in the late nineteenth century, but rebellion was under way even then. In American philosophy, this struggle is most vividly portrayed in the controversy between Royce and William James. Royce was younger than James, and it was largely through the latter's influence that he received the opportunity to teach at Harvard. Yet when Royce had settled down to the task of developing his idealism, James was still in a process of intellectual transition.

James's training and early teaching at Harvard were in physiology. His interests, however, included psychology, an area in which he did fundamental work culminating in the publication of his two-volume *Principles of Psychology* in 1890. In addition, philosophical concerns were never far from his attention. Prior to the publication of his psychology text, James had given courses in philosophy and written essays on moral and religious themes. Indeed, *The Principles of Psychology* itself is full of philosophical insights. In the last twenty years of his life, philosophy held James's full attention, and much of his energy was devoted to developing and refining an alternative to the idealism Royce represented.

James and Royce held many ideas in common, but they were

fundamentally at odds on at least three issues. They differed, first, in their basic convictions about the power of human reason. Royce was inclined to believe that men could comprehend the basic nature of reality with certainty. Rational analysis could deliver clear and final conclusions about the forces and structures that produce, explain, and fulfill human life. James, however, took his cue from Peirce. He stressed the tentativeness of every philosophical claim. Haunted by the permanent possibility of error, he believed that our philosophical and theological theories are primarily options for risk-filled belief, not propositions whose truth or falsity can be known with finality.

Still, James had his own convictions about reality, and two of them conflicted directly with his colleague's idealism. Royce labored to develop the view that our experience of declaring propositions to be true or false is intelligible only if an Absolute Knower exists whose awareness constitutes the ultimate standard required to make these declarations meaningful. This idea was at the core of Royce's efforts to demonstrate the existence of the Absolute. James's famous pragmatic theory of truth, on the other hand, was formed in the teeth of this idealistic thesis. In place of Royce's view, James took over Peirce's pragmatic method for determining the meaning of concepts and extended it—not without Peirce's dissent—into a view of truth which is more empirically grounded.

Idealism holds that the truth or falsity of our claims depends on their agreement or disagreement with the Absolute's awareness. James argues that a pragmatic analysis leads to different conclusions: If a claim is pronounced true, all this means is that it leads us to have particular expectations which, upon critical testing, are fulfilled. Similarly, if a claim is pronounced false, what we mean is that it leads us to have particular expectations which, upon critical testing, are not fulfilled.

Reference to an Absolute Knower is in no way required to make our declarations of truth and falsity intelligible. Our own experience provides an adequate grounding. Of course, many of our beliefs and propositions lead us to specific expectations which we have not tested or are not yet able to test. On James's account, these claims *become* true or false as proper analysis occurs. This means that truth and falsity are not fixed and complete in an Eternal Mind. They are qualities our claims come to have as they are tested.

James remained true to his philosophical temperament. He neither offered his theory of truth as an absolutely final position nor claimed to have shown that Royce's view was impossible. He acknowledged that the Absolute Knower might exist and even that it had a positive religious function in its capacity to provide fulfillment for human hopes. Yet he failed to see the necessity of its existence. In spite of its religious function, he also found the Absolute to be an obstacle to adequate understanding of man's moral striving and freedom.

James felt that belief in the Absolute involved a theological determinism in which our lives are eternally complete, no matter how open-ended and free they may seem to us. Coupling this determinism with the implication that the supposedly perfect Absolute was also responsible for evil and suffering, James concluded that Royce's idealism was unsound. This was not only because of its speculative excesses and epistemological weaknesses, but because its ultimate effect on man's will and moral sensitivity was debilitating.

Both Peirce and Royce were aware that existence is temporal and changing and that it provides us with genuine instances of novelty. James pushed these themes even further. As his theory of truth suggests, existence is radically open-ended. We live in an ambiguous, moving world of freedom, and men are active forces in shaping it for good or evil. Our lives are indeterminate and incomplete, and we come to know who we are and where we are only as we think and act. Positive meaning for our lives is not secured in advance. We struggle to achieve it. The human condition leads neither to automatic optimism nor to inescapable pessimism. Life is a mixture of good and evil. It can be improved, but no guarantees are available. In a word, *meliorism*—the view that fulfillment and salvation are neither necessary nor impossible and that man's efforts make a difference in the final outcome—is James's creed.

James rejects any theological view which portrays God and the world as essentially complete and fixed. On the other hand, his meliorism is not atheistic. A world without God is likely to lack overarching purpose and moral intelligibility. It will probably be one in which the negativity of death has the final word. An atheistic perspective on existence is not likely to awaken and support the strenuous mood required for authentic existence in an indeterminate world. If the ultimate backdrop of existence is a cosmic indifference, this dissipates the significance of our striving and our intention to suffer and sacrifice for the well-being of others.

There is no systematic theology in James's thought. Like Peirce, he is suspicious of such efforts because of their tendency toward rationalism and their neglect of feeling and emotion in religious life. Nevertheless, his philosophy reserves an important place for God. His God retains the traditional function of holding men responsible for real concern for each other. God also provides hope that human finitude, evil, and death do not have the final word in our lives and that our best values and efforts may find support beyond themselves. On the other hand, God's nature differs considerably from what earlier theologies suggest. In one place, for example, James states that we might do well to think of him as "finite, either in power or in knowledge, or in both at once."[7]

This suggestion is not developed very far, but at least four ideas are implied. (1) The outcome of the world's process is not known beforehand in every detail by God. (2) Although God's existence is everlasting, he is himself in a process of development, rather than being static, complete, and essentially nontemporal. (3) A basic value for both God and man may be a creative use of freedom in the face of difficulties. (4) God is neither ultimately responsible for evil nor capable of eliminating it by himself. All these points are provocative, but the last is especially interesting and worth commenting on.

James is a radical thinker, but in one sense his concept of God is very conservative. He refuses to hold God responsible for producing evil knowingly. James's suggestion that God's knowledge may be limited leaves open the possibility that divine ignorance leads to evil, but he does not stress that option. Instead, the emphasis is on God's goodness and his battle to overcome evil. James's account neither implicates God directly in the existence of evil nor pictures him as constantly struggling to correct mistakes made in ignorance. At the same time, however, it is evident that God has not rooted out all the evil factors in the world. If God were fully good, omniscient, and omnipotent, these factors would be gone.

Having retained the idea that God's goodness is incompatible with direct responsibility for evil, and having sacrificed omniscience in the interest of freedom, James moves in the direction of restricting God's power as well. Consequently, he stresses the role that men must play in aiding God in the battle against evil. In making these suggestions, James claims that he is presenting a view very close to what the ordinary man *feels* in his religious experience.

"God," in the religious life of ordinary men, is the name not of the whole of things, heaven forbid, but only of the ideal tendency in things, believed in as a superhuman person who calls us to co-operate in his purposes, and who furthers ours if they are worthy. He works in an external environment, has limits, and has enemies. (p. 124)

In James's view, the elimination of idealism in favor of a world view which emphasizes process, a genuine plurality of individual beings and powers, meliorism, and a finite God radically alters our understanding of the problem of evil. "In any pluralistic metaphysic, the problems that evil presents are practical, not speculative. Not why evil should exist at all, but how we can lessen the actual amount of it, is the sole question we need there consider" (p. 124). James follows his own advice and offers no metaphysical theory to account for the presence of evil. His statement about *being* applies to evil as well: "The question of being is the darkest in all philosophy. . . . [Being] makes itself somehow, and our business is far more with its What than with its Whence or Why."[8]

James may be right, but it is not easy to escape the feeling that Royce's view is more profound at this point—at least in its willingness to try to provide some ultimate account of the existence of evil. Who can avoid asking a metaphysical "Why?" when faced by radical evil and tragedy? James may consider such metaphysical questions not very pragmatic, but in fact they are in this circumstance. No satisfactory answers may be forthcoming, but to try for one is surely as human as to strive for the elimination of evil. Moreover, James's own meliorism and interest in maximizing human fulfillment and meaning force the "speculative" problem back on the stage. What kind of fulfillment is really available to us? To comprehend our options, some attempt to understand evil metaphysically is needed in addition to our efforts to overcome it practically.

On the other hand, the radical sense of freedom and open-endedness that James's philosophy provides speaks to the late twentieth century more clearly than Royce's absolute idealism. Theologically, we need to be somewhere between the two. We require a theology that takes account of freedom and process without conflicting with our experience. Such a perspective is likely to find a prominent place for freedom, incompleteness, and temporality in God. At the same time, an account of evil that has Royce's metaphysical boldness is attractive. We seem to demand a view that stresses both God's responsibility for evil, freely chosen, and his ultimate capability and intention to control its power for a good end. This suggests that a finite God—at least in the Jamesian sense—will not be adequate to such a task.

C. Religious Experience Without God: Santayana and Dewey

If idealism was a dominant philosophical force in the late nineteenth century, there can be little doubt that the pragmatic perspectives of Peirce and James are better suited to fit the intellectual mood as we cross into the twentieth century. In a moving, growing, vibrating society James was correct: our business is more with the What of existence than with its Whence or Why. Thus, even in philosophical circles, idealism went into eclipse. Its influence remained, but a pragmatic-scientific orientation assumed philosophical leadership.

The dialectical argumentation and sweeping metaphysical boldness of Royce were supplanted by new attempts to understand human experience in its natural setting without the underpinnings of idealism. "Nature" replaced the "Absolute" as a fundamental subject of philosophical concern. This shift had significant consequences for interpretations of religion and theology. In some instances, the views of Peirce and James were victims of a trend they had helped to initiate. The philosophy of religion developed by George Santayana and John Dewey illustrates these points.

Philosophers may not be immortal, but some of them live a very long time. Santayana and Dewey are examples. They were not much younger than Peirce, Royce, and James, but their lives lasted far longer, extending into the second half of the twentieth century. Santayana was a student and colleague of both James and Royce. Dewey's philosophical career was in full swing while Peirce, James, and Royce were still alive. Yet in their interpretations of religion and theology the younger men were far more radical. They retained a place for religious experience, but only within an empirical and naturalistic framework that virtually excluded God.

Santayana was not a native American. He was born in Spain and came to the United States as a boy. At the age of fifty he left his teaching position at Harvard and returned to Europe. He adopted the naturalistic and fallibilistic orientations of pragmatism, although he was critical of it as well. Apart from Emerson, Santayana's writing is more poetic than that of any other American philosopher. Moreover, in his view poetry and religion have similar functions. Both lead us to crucial insights about life, but neither should be mistaken for literal statements of fact. Such confusions, unfortunately, have occurred all too frequently in the past. Thus, reason must intervene and clarify the function of religion. The result will not be the elimination of the religious dimension from human life, but a fresh and purified vision of its true power and significance.

Briefly, Santayana's estimate of the human condition is this: We are creatures of nature, products of evolutionary processes, both blessed and cursed with self-consciousness and reason. We thirst for meaning and value in a world that neither fully supports nor completely thwarts us. Man is a value-oriented being. He strives to make his existence intelligible and meaningful, and religion is one product of his effort. It is a human response to existence, a natural phenomenon prompted by a longing for and appreciation of meaning and value in life. Religion concentrates on ideals. It delights in their presence in life and seeks their appearance where they are absent.

Historically embodied religion, however, has created more problems than it has solved. The chief difficulty lies in the fact that

religious expression tends to interpret ideals and values as supernatural powers or persons. This would not be disastrous, if the
mythological and poetic function of such expression were understood, but our tendency is to take these expressions as literal statements of fact. Such inclinations are not restricted to our primitive
ancestors. They appear in modern times in sophisticated doctrines
of God or philosophical conceptions of the Absolute.

Most religious life, then, is an ambiguous mixture. It is headed
in a useful direction insofar as it extols ideals that enrich human
existence. Man is altogether a creature of nature, but "nature neither is nor can be man's ideal."[9] It is too wasteful, too indifferent
and insensitive. Human consciousness and reason are selective.
Men can move toward an understanding of nature and recognition
of the goods that make life meaningful.

To extol such goods, to honor them and strive in their service,
is to be fully human, and religious expression plays an indispensable role in all such activities. On the other hand, religious life
moves in an undesirable direction insofar as it leads us to think
that nature is transcended by supernatural beings or forces or idealistic Absolutes. Such claims divert attention from our natural existence and create bogus problems which rob our lives of the meaning presently available within the sphere of nature. The problem
of evil provides an example of this.

The insoluble problems of the origin of evil and of freedom, in a
world produced in its every fibre by omnipotent goodness, can never
be understood until we remember their origin. They are artificial
problems, unknown to philosophy before it betook itself to the literal
justification of fables in which the objects of rational endeavour were
represented as causes of natural existence. (p. 117)

So much for Royce's blood, sweat, and tears over the problem
of evil! As far as Santayana can see, we are so much a part of
nature that we are unable to fathom its depths in order to solve
questions of origin. "Everywhere is beauty and nowhere permanence, everywhere an incipient harmony nowhere an intention,
nor a responsibility, nor a plan."[10] That is the way nature strikes
Santayana. In such a setting, we are well advised to find and create
whatever meaning and value are possible within our natural lives.

Nothing, however, is gained by trying to escape into the supernatural or the Absolute. Nothing is accomplished if we attempt to make nature more rational than it is by developing complex metaphysical answers to inappropriate questions.

Santayana has a profound sense of the negative factors present in human life. "A note of failure and melancholy must always dominate in the struggle against natural death."[11] The most manly quality, however, leads us to face these negativities and still appreciate the goods we can really experience. Man's task is to become a naturalized citizen of the world. This involves living religiously but without God. Religion becomes primarily an aesthetic sense, an appreciation of essentially human spiritual values.

A similar view, although articulated less poetically, is offered by John Dewey. He believes that the concept of *religion* is too diffuse in its meaning to be helpful, and he has no particular interest in furthering the cause of any of the particular *religions* found in the world. He does, however, have an intense concern for the *religious* aspect of experience. Like Santayana, he wants to rescue this from the clutches of dogma, rationalistic metaphysics, and traditional theology.

Human life is a process within a moving natural order. Men are shaped by nature, but they also initiate change. In Dewey's view, man's activities have a religious quality when they are motivated by and in the direction of "inclusive ideal ends, which imagination presents to us and to which the human will responds as worthy of controlling our desires and choices."[12] The pursuit and extension of justice, freedom, and knowledge are primary examples of these ideal ends. They are especially effective in drawing out human energy, since striving for their achievement makes life worth living. But religious life must not be restricted to them alone. "Any activity pursued in behalf of an ideal end against obstacles and in spite of threats of personal loss because of conviction of its general and enduring value is religious in quality" (p. 27).

The term "imagination" is used by Dewey to designate the creative function of human intelligence as it appears in the communal and individual dimensions of life. Imagination—creative thinking—can pinpoint ideal ends. These present themselves as worthy of fulfillment and as capable of giving meaning that lasts. Dewey stresses, moreover, that these unifying ideals are not essentially related to forces, powers, or gods that are in any sense supernatural. Their source—imagination—is an organ of nature, and their actualization is a task and a process within nature. Experience of and dedication to them, however, are rightfully called "religious," because these ideals present themselves as being of ultimate worth.

Dewey retains the concept of God as a collective term which is useful to summarize all the inclusive ideal ends of life and the natural powers that work to implement them. He agrees with James that the concept of God ought to refer only to the ideal tendency in things. But Dewey's naturalism is more radical than James's, and "God" becomes a metaphor. It should appear as no surprise, therefore, that Dewey shares Santayana's opinion that an adequate religious perspective is incompatible with traditional theism. Dewey equates traditional theism with the view that God is an all-powerful creator and sustainer outside of the natural order, a notion unacceptable to him. In addition, although his interpretation of the individual's dependency on nature and his fellow men draws heavily from idealism, he has little sympathy for the Absolute either as a metaphysical principle or as a source of religious insight.

Although he does not give serious consideration to James's finite God one way or the other, Dewey has two main reasons for rejecting traditional and idealistic conceptions of God. First, he believes that such concepts do not fit with our best forms of inquiry. Scientific method—Dewey sometimes speaks of it as the "method of intelligence"—emphasizes empirical, open-ended, self-corrective testing that leads to communal agreement about matters of fact.

This method is relevant to every aspect of life, and Dewey regards it as "the final arbiter of all questions of fact, existence, and intellectual assent" (p. 31). It produces results that are not susceptible to the crucial weakness of traditional and idealistic claims about God. Their weakness is that they go beyond sound empirical verification and ultimately rely on a faith that, if not sectarian, still is too subjective.

Theological claims—as opposed to religious claims rightly understood—have little empirical grounding, but the second difficulty is perhaps more severe. Traditional theism and all concepts of the

Absolute threaten man's freedom and introduce a speculative problem of evil. Both results draw man's attention and energy away
from concrete problem-solving within the natural order. Dewey's
response to evil is not unlike Royce's: "We long, amid a troubled
world, for perfect being. We forget that what gives meaning to the
notion of perfection is the events that create longing, and that,
apart from them, a 'perfect' world would mean just an unchanging
brute existential thing."[13] Still, to spend time and energy interpreting the ultimate reasons for evil or attempting to make the
completeness of God compatible with the open-endedness of our
existence is to fail to put our energy to a higher use. Our proper
task is to seek to understand nature's processes and to relieve
human suffering. God and theology can stand in the way of human
betterment. Their elimination will be no serious loss if we concentrate on implementing in other ways the ideals that stand at the
center of religious life.

Dewey's philosophy of religion attempts to provide people with
a "common faith." This faith centers on the shared values indispensable for the establishment of a genuinely humane community.
Freed from the sectarian concerns and intellectual hang-ups that
traditional religions and theologies produce, men may achieve an
empirically grounded estimate of their place in nature and an up-
lifting religious vision of their possibilities for growth and advance-
ment. Like Santayana, Dewey tells us that humane life is religious
life—but without God.

Of the men discussed in this chapter, Santayana and Dewey provide an interpretation of religion and theology which may match
most closely the feelings of many contemporary Americans. This is
not to say that Dewey's "common faith" marks our culture. If it did,
our divisions and uncertainties about American goals might be less.
Yet for many existence certainly feels like a natural process from
which God is absent, if he exists at all. Our orientation is toward
the problems and goals of secular life, and thought about God—
let alone worship or prayer—is rarely at the center of a majority
of lives.

Nevertheless, Santayana and Dewey may underestimate the
power of existence to render us concerned about the metaphysical
and theological issues they have dismissed. When tragedy knocks

us down or life's goodness lifts us up, we may reflect on the significance of existence in ways that refuse to be contained in the naturalistic boundaries Santayana and Dewey have marked out. Attempts to discount such efforts to question and understand God, by pointing either to their incompatibility with the "method of intelligence" or to a failure to comprehend the myths we create, may not convince us that we have stepped "out of bounds." Peirce, Royce, and James may be better judges of how far human nature will and should go than Santayana and Dewey.

This is not to say that Santayana and Dewey are mistaken. Still, their emphasis on man's finitude and fallibility does leave us in an open market where other options may be displayed. They have a solid product which is both empirically based and realistic. On the other hand, it lacks some desirable extras which are of vital importance if life is to be as full as our deepest hopes would have it. Santayana is honest: a view such as his or Dewey's cannot silence an irreducible note of failure and melancholy. A world with God may not be able to do that either, but the possibility is greater, and we ought not to dismiss it too easily.

Philosophies and theologies are like goods for sale. They compete for attention. Moreover, if you are going to deliver a more adequate product than your competitors, the only course is to take account of what they have to offer and then be bold enough to try to create something that works better for a majority of men. In an atmosphere that stresses the permanent possibility of error, competition is invited and encouraged, although no one should expect to win every verdict.

As William James put it at the conclusion of his detailed study of religious experience: "No two of us have identical difficulties, nor should we be expected to work out identical solutions."[14] If, however, we think boldly, it may still turn out that our difficulties are best met by solutions that involve God. That option is closed only if we choose to make it so.

D. God in the Golden Age of American Philosophy

William Ernest Hocking (1873–1966) is the only major philosopher of this era whose views we have not mentioned. Perhaps to recognize the views he held and the sources he used may give us another useful perspective on what happened to God in this period. Hocking was a prolific writer and quite influential in his day in the field of philosophy of religion. His ideas clearly testify to the impact of evolutionary theory on all American thought, since he thinks earlier doctrines are inadequate and that Christianity must evolve into a new state. We can also see here the beginning of the notion that a world religion must eventually be evolved. Christianity must find its affinity with other religions of the world, and some universal faith will result.

Hocking takes the existence of a plurality of religions to be a "scandal,"[15] which indicates how far he has come from the original American acceptance of plurality as difficult but basically both necessary and good. The plurality of religions is an original and ultimate fact, so that only the acceptance of some evolutionary scheme could lead us to expect that things would or could ever be different. Are the religions of the world (and the nations) evolving and merging toward one basic framework? This is a hard question and one which, if we reject the evolutionary assumption behind it, leaves us now (both politically and religiously) in a situation very much like the one of stress and tension in which this country was first born.

However, Hocking thinks that there will be a next stage, and his evolutionary assumptions convince him that a universalized religious perspective is on its way (pp. 211–269). Perhaps, then, what we are living through today is the disillusionment that follows a clear factual failure of this thesis. If we thought our religious life must evolve to a new state, we could concentrate less on God without much danger. If the nature of our religious experience itself does not move beyond its original condition, and if in fact it fails to exhibit the expected evolutionary direction, then religion falters. That is, unless it has a concept of God strong enough to account for this disappointing experience.

William Ernest Hocking's long and perhaps most famous book is cast almost entirely in the tradition and ethos of Continental thought, particularly idealism.[16] He accepts the challenge of pragmatism (p. xv), but his own response is to assert the superiority of what is basically an idealistic philosophy. His analysis of experience is such that religion seems to have a natural ground in this country, and life obviously and essentially appears "religious" in some immediate way. If, in fact, life in America nowadays is not overtly religious in its quality—if it is indeed highly secular —then Hocking's idealistic framework can no longer provide a picture of either religion or God commensurable with our present mode of life.

Although two profoundly disturbing experiences of the latter half of the nineteenth century in America were the Civil War and the acceptance of a theory of evolution, we must admit that positive ideas of God in this era seem to have been only barely altered by these events. If theologians and philosophers did respond by stressing the idea of community as central, still they hardly even began to reconceive God in the light of it, as they well might have. In that sense, the Civil War may not have had its theological effect until the late twentieth century, when at last we see that our notion of God has changed too. Well, how should the experience of the Civil War have altered our notions about God? One answer: We must be dealing with a God who can suffer (this aspect did begin to become clear at the time), one who forces options on no one and who is even capable of intentional involvement in destruction.

Industrialization is another prominent factor of the late nineteenth century which seems to leave theology largely untouched. Of course, this is partly because, to a struggling people, industrialization at first seems like the very path to heaven on earth. Only in the present century, once again, have we begun to feel the full impact of the negative and destructive side of the technology and mechanization which for years we accepted as inherently positive. Thus, the God moving in the late nineteenth century really only comes to be recognized a century later—yet that may have been true of the power behind the exodus from Egypt too. We did then believe in evolutionary progress toward the good; it is only now that evolution seems not always to have a positive direction.

Charles Peirce began to discern a God of the genuinely new, but this insight remains theologically unelaborated. "Spontaneity" also comes to be an important factor, but the optimism of nineteenth-century Americans made them tend to treat this as always positive. A century later we realize its destructive side, although we should have discerned it in the seeds that produced civil war. If Josiah Royce stressed freedom, but retained classical solutions to theological problems, then the changes in our notion of God which freedom and destruction require were not made until a later century reflected on them. Now we know that freedom is not easy to achieve and usually involves destruction. What must God be like if these results are possible?

When we view our lives as being indeterminate and incomplete, a concept of freedom which involves these elements forces us to alter any classical notion of God. Systematic theology does not seem to result from these seminal experiences, and yet a notion of God as eternal, unchanging, and omniscient is incompatible with them. If the philosophical explorations of the golden age we have been surveying were not explicitly theological in their result, certainly they set the stage for new conclusions. The notion of a finite God begins to be suggested, it is true. However, this still leaves open the question of whether God might be unlimited by nature and still reflect some of the qualities which become so central in philosophical thought—for example, indeterminacy and incompleteness.

A great divorce appears to have taken place in American thought by the turn of the century. That is, the natural world no longer is accepted as a direct representation of God, nor does it give us in itself a blueprint of his future plans. If this is true, where are we to look for a clue to God's nature, and how can we discern the future if not from the past or the present? This leads us to the idea that emerges later of religion without God. We can concentrate almost exclusively on the religious qualities in human life, but theologically we do not seem equipped yet to discern God on other grounds, once our "natural" basis has been abandoned.

As far as technical thought goes, God seems to have become increasingly less important in the nineteenth century, except as he continues to be held in classical notions. However, these rapidly become out of harmony with what is distinctive in American experience. Some of our romantic ideas of America's automatic blissful future rapidly disappeared during the Civil War, yet we did not develop a concept of God to correspond to this metamorphosis. Undoubtedly this is partly due to the fact that we had not yet accepted pluralism in theology as we had in political life. A variety of approaches to and views of God's nature still seemed to go against our imported notions of orthodoxy.

In line with our own experience of the plurality and compromise necessary in democracy, can we surrender the demand for a single religious solution and then build a notion of God theologically which in itself accounts for this unavoidable diversity? If a variety of views remain open and are either pursued or else left idle depending on what men find workable in their situation, a God open to flexibility of this sort must be unique in his nature. To begin in this way need not, as might at first be supposed, open us to a charge of conceiving God in our own image. He need not be like man, even if he is discovered in our definitive and crucial experiences. However, it is true that his nature must be open to some variation and some influence by contingencies.

If pragmatism is one of American philosophy's unique contributions, it is still true that we have no systematic concept of God drawn along pragmatic lines. Pragmatism did lead to reappraisals of religious experience, but it seems clear that at the turn of the century American philosophers were not disposed to do much reconstitution of the divine, and theologians still followed a more or less classical line. Moreover, on all sides the nineteenth century appears to be an era of optimism over progress and man's ability to improve himself. In this case, God is not likely to get much direct attention, since he has little function to perform. Even if the notion of community occupied nineteenth-century thought, this need not involve God—as long as we are convinced that community is a human product and can be achieved by our conscious and voluntary effort.

Peirce's notion of existence as precarious and risk-filled now demands a complementary notion of God, even if he differs from man in power and in his ability to control. "Novelty" and "regularity" may be taken as features of the divine life, but it will require sustained effort to work out a conception of God along these lines. Royce, on the other hand, has a more fully developed notion of God, although more traditionally idealistic in its outlines. He does allow God to suffer, but this is still set within a rather romantic and positive notion of the good in suffering. James introduces us to the importance of a psychological approach to religion,[17] but he only begins to use it as a means to develop new notions about God. He would like us to think about God as neither complete nor fixed, but he barely starts to elaborate what such a God might be like on the basis of his psychological insights.

Santayana and Dewey seem close to the late twentieth century in their interpretation of experience. On the other hand, they have the least tendency to delineate a picture of God along these lines. We must reconstruct a view of God for them within this context, or God is likely to be rejected. If human existence is free and open-ended, God cannot be merely eternal and set in his knowledge from eternity, although he need not be finite to be true to our experience. He merely needs to be open to contingency. Probably the religious life of the late nineteenth and early twentieth century paid little attention to the philosophical rejection of God because it did not see the possibility of drawing God along these lines. Today cultivating that possibility seems the only alternative to losing God through a violent reaction against tradition.

In the life of theology, we find that we must constantly reexamine what we mean by Christianity—that unauthentic interpretations tend almost automatically to work themselves into popular acceptance. Then, some recent and perhaps questionable definitions are offered as obviously original and orthodox, when in fact they are late overlays on tradition. Similarly, every notion of what is American needs constant revision ("demythologizing"). The idea of what is fundamental and unique to the American experience becomes encrusted and overlaid. Such ideas are perhaps defensible in themselves but are not really primitive in origin. Thus they should stand on their own and not be justified in the name of orthodoxy.

The Puritans sought out American shores in order to be able to get back to a pure and primitive practice of Christianity, which they felt they could not do in an unyielding Europe. It is central to our particular experience as a people that we constantly struggle against distorted notions of what "American" may have come to mean, but only by a late transformation. The period of 1870–1935 is a strange mixture of philosophical developments that go far toward adequately interpreting fundamental American experiences, but combined with a continued return to Continental and British notions in theology. Such a conglomerate does not pick up and develop the new notions of God possible on this novel basis, and that failure forces us now to seek once again what can be a new American interpretation of both Christianity and God.

NOTES

1. Charles S. Peirce, "The Fixation of Belief," in *Charles S. Peirce: Selected Writings,* ed. Philip P. Wiener (New York: Dover Publications, 1966), p. 100. Hereafter references to this anthology are abbreviated *Selected Writings.*

2. "How to Make Our Ideas Clear," in *Selected Writings,* p. 124.

3. "A Neglected Argument for the Reality of God," in *Selected Writings,* p. 365.

4. Charles S. Peirce, "Evolutionary Love," in *Philosophical Writings of Peirce,* ed. Justus Buchler (New York: Dover Publications, 1955), p. 363.

5. Josiah Royce, "The Problem of Job," in *Studies of Good and Evil: A Series of Essays upon Life and Philosophy* (New York: Appleton, 1898), p. 14.

6. Josiah Royce, *The Problem of Christianity* (New York: Macmillan Company, 1913), I, 14.

7. William James, *A Pluralistic Universe* (New York: Longmans, Green & Company, 1909), p. 311.

8. William James, *Some Problems of Philosophy: A Beginning of an Introduction to Philosophy,* ed. Henry James, Jr. (New York: Longmans, Green & Company, 1911), p. 46.

9. George Santayana, *The Life of Reason,* Vol. 3, *Reason in Religion* (New York: Collier Books, 1962), p. 97.

10. George Santayana, "The Genteel Tradition in American Philosophy," in *The Genteel Tradition: Nine Essays by George Santayana,* ed. Douglas L. Wilson (Cambridge: Harvard University Press, 1967), p. 63.

11. *Reason in Religion,* p. 178.

12. John Dewey, *A Common Faith* (New Haven: Yale University Press, 1964), p. 33.

13. John Dewey, *Experience and Nature* (New York: Dover Publications, 1958), p. 63.

14. William James, *The Varieties of Religious Experience* (New York: Modern Library, 1955), p. 477.

15. William Ernest Hocking, *Living Religions and a World Faith* (London: George Allen & Unwin, 1940), p. 17.

16. See William Ernest Hocking, *The Meaning of God in Human Experience* (New Haven: Yale University Press, 1912).

17. See *The Varieties of Religious Experience.*

V

THE SOCIAL GOSPEL
AND INDUSTRIAL AMERICA

A. Theology for the Machine Age

If the late nineteenth century was the era for the development of classical American philosophy, the first quarter of the twentieth century witnessed the formation of a distinctive American theology. Walter Rauschenbusch (1861–1918) opened that new era with the "social gospel." It soon became—and still is—a dominant characteristic of American religious life. The two Niebuhrs next arrived to expand this strain and move it toward a more classical theological form in the second quarter of the century. Justice-in-the-social-order became a common theme throughout the period. America had been industrialized before the century began, but the growing problem of large cities, mass immigration, and the grime of industrial life only came into theological focus later.

Interestingly enough, the second set of three who characterize this era are all European-born and trained, but each (Tillich, Gilson, and Maritain) came to live in North America for extended periods and was influential in American philosophy and religion as well as being affected by it. By the opening of this century, everyone feels at some distance from the original rebellion and its resulting union of independent colonies. New England villages, with their classic white architecture and town greens, are now surrounded and transformed by hordes of immigrants and expanding factories. The center of agriculture has shifted westward, and America has largely achieved the physical shape she will have as a nation. Chicago supplants Boston as a key to the problems and excitement of twentieth-century America.

Once we turn the corner into this century, the shape of the future is clearly visible—if we have the eyes to see. Every problem and opportunity is exposed, and never again can anyone quite hold the ideal picture of life-in-isolated-America which the original settlers envisaged. This country now both attracts and repels. Whitehead and Tillich came to live and teach here at the same time that artists and writers became expatriates because they did not think they could create in this atmosphere. William James stayed here to write; his brother Henry was driven abroad. Many, however, still continued to believe that we were separate from Europe and free of her problems—but such an illusion stems from an adolescent absorption in watching only our own growth. In point of fact, by that time we had joined all large, powerful, and expanding nations in the problems and divisions that giants always face.

The future cannot look the same to a country that is bursting its limits as it does to colonists who are trying to tame the wilderness. Once we were divided over whether we should separate ourselves from England and form a new union; now disharmonies result from internal expansion and the fading of pioneer goals. When every effort is bent on getting things going, the situation differs from what it is when we must attend to the problems we have created for ourselves in the process of rapid expansion. Colonial goals and life are not necessarily gone forever, but certainly they now exist in a vastly more complicated and often hostile society, one in which as many must suffer from our system as benefit from it.

In this new era we face the question of what "theology" means and what "religious life" ought to be like. According to Rauschenbusch, both should assume new forms. His claims are not modest: he announces the pure, the primitive modes of Christianity's presence just as the Puritans first claimed they wanted to use America to restore its original purity of practice. Along with the pragmatists, the majority of Americans still have a slight distrust of metaphysics as a theological base, and it is perfectly clear that almost all classical theology is thought of as having "distorted" Christian doctrine. Just as John Dewey thinks we have finally reached a new and open stage, so Rauschenbusch is sure that Christianity has arrived at a time of liberation and free expression hardly experienced since its origin.

In both his life and his writing, Walter Rauschenbusch reflects the turbulent yet creative era in religion of the early 1900s. Classical theological beliefs came under question then, just as traditional philosophical doctrine had in the preceding era. Industrialism and the curse of growing cities perplexed politician and minister alike. The church seemed to become a source of insecurity rather than stability. The existence of widespread spiritual unrest indicated, then as now, that the traditional assumptions of American life were under question.

Religion and secular culture had fallen in league in the late nineteenth century in ways not dreamed of since the original separation of church and state was guaranteed in the Bill of Rights. The church in America had once been a vigorous source of judgment on society, but it became less so now. After the Civil War, American churches lost much of their prophetic power, and one can hardly deny that the acceptance of racial and industrial division sapped their source of independent strength. The religious revival, so popular and successful in the untamed frontier setting and in agrarian America, seemed unprepared for the problems of the industrially dominated, sprawling cities. The kind of evangelism appropriate in the countryside had little relevance for city people living on the verge of destitution. In this setting, Rauschenbusch tried to figure out how men could help bring God's purpose to a worldly realization. He found his message in the Old Testament prophets: men must strive for social justice.

His recourse was to the poor, who in some sense religiously are specially blessed, but he differed from Lenin in holding the more optimistic view that men could intervene creatively in the social process without resorting to illegality or violence. Rather than irretrievably pitting class against class, Rauschenbusch felt that appeals to charity could move the American middle class to enlist in a crusade that would usher in God's kingdom. His optimism about society, and about the ability of men under challenge to rise to cure their ills, was an offshoot of the great American dream and was widely shared by American pragmatists and progressives. He found Western civilization in crisis, but he was sure it could meet its mounting social problems successfully.

Perhaps one of the most striking features of his highly influential book, *Christianity and the Social Crisis,* was his assurance that "the Church" could itself become a potent force for social change, just as he believed it had been in the past. The issue, of course, is whether or not the religious spirit is as potent a factor in shaping history as Rauschenbusch thinks it is.[1] If not, this may explain why society seems to develop somewhat independently from the pleas of the churches. In effect he links the church to culture, no less than those who use it to resist change, when he assumes that religious faith has the ability to make social institutions plastic and thus open to new forms.

As one might suspect, Rauschenbusch interprets Jesus in the line of the Old Testament prophets, and his God becomes one who demands righteousness and nothing but righteousness (p. 4). He understood his day to be a time of revolution (p. 45)—just as we do—but admits that Jesus did not approach social reform from the same economic and historical point of view that he proposes (p. 47). Although Jesus' intent was primarily religious and moral, Rauschenbusch shares in the myth that somehow Jesus' message was essentially perverted in the course of institutionalization. Its emancipation was begun in the Protestant Reformation, but now it has a new chance to realize its full freedom and primitive purity here in an awakened and fully democratic America—if only men will arouse themselves to the task.

Rauschenbusch interprets the kingdom of God as aiming primarily at a regeneration and reconstitution of social life (p. 143). This, of course, links it to the American dream and sets it in opposition to European cynicism. Alien forces have penetrated Christianity in the intervening centuries, he is sure, and they have short-circuited its revolutionary moral power, which is inherently capable of reconstructing social life. Thus the problem is to free that original pure force from its cultural entanglements. Dogmatism, ceremonialism, sacramentalism, ascetic and monastic ideals, he is convinced, are dying out, and Christian leaders should rejoice over this as the power of religion flows out in the service of justice. Now, somehow, it can achieve the task it could not accomplish before—"the essential genius of Christianity is being set free" (p. 209).

Like both the idealist and the pragmatic philosophers just before him, Rauschenbusch is caught up in a notion of evolution, so much so that he is convinced that somehow man's situation has essentially changed. What before was not possible, now is. If true, this provides a marvelous source of optimism concerning our ability to achieve the ideal of maximum personal fulfillment for all. However, should religion be unable to perform this gigantic feat of social change, the basis of the whole doctrine falls under question. In a beautiful piece of dialogue (pp. 211–213), Rauschenbusch shows how the proud nineteenth century failed to achieve its high human goals and instead left men under the blight of industrialization. In spite of all this, he still feels that the twentieth century can overcome the failure.

He admits that "modern" life is a paradox, due to the extremes of wealth and poverty which an industrial economy produces (p. 217), but he links Christianity to socialism and thinks modern poverty can be overcome. Rauschenbusch voices the common cry that moral forces have failed to keep pace with intellectual and economic development—but now "the moral power generated by the Christian religion is available for the task of social regeneration" (p. 220). As we developed our land originally in America, an agrarian economy could offer equal opportunity. When the land runs out, industrial society basically discriminates against the poor. The American dream will fail unless socialism can restore equality to economic conditions, so Rauschenbusch argues.

The growth of city churches has brought American religion into a new era, and "the condition of the crowded and landless people ought long ago to have aroused the Church to examine the moral basis of our land system" (p. 291). Since Rauschenbusch is convinced that religion in America has its power base in the large middle class, "a social system which lifts a small minority into great wealth, and submerges a great number in poverty, is thus directly hostile to the interests of the Church" (p. 308). In proving this, as he thinks he has, he is hopeful that religion in America will awaken to see that its future lies in aligning with social reform. In this way it can restore to the Christian gospel its primitive thrust, and in effect realize the Christian dream by way of religiously inspired socialism.

The crisis of society, the struggle of the working class against the upper classes, is also the crisis of the church (p. 332). Of course, in a sense this has always been true of any religious life which is sensitive to the needs of its people, as it was for both Puritan and frontier life. What has changed is the locus of the problem in American society. Yet if its center is now the city, and industrial dislocation its source, probably here in that social crisis is where God must be found in the early twentieth century. Rauschenbusch thinks that the fate of religion is tied to the health of the society (p. 332), but he perhaps makes the identification too close. The financial and political influence of the institutional church may be tied to a society's vitality; still, religious life itself may be more independent of the ebb and flow of power than this would indicate.

Rauschenbusch wants to link prophetic vision with Christianity's power to reconstruct society (p. 338). While it is true that the prophet has usually been the judge of his society's wrongs, it is not so clear that authentic religious life has always been linked with the success of reform. A social crisis does offer an opportunity for the infusion of new life and power into religion (p. 340), but the question is whether this is as easily tied to progress and social improvement as Rauschenbusch hopes. He thinks that differences over dogma have divided us in the past and that common social concerns can unite us in religion. The issue, however, is whether these social aims may not be just as divisive as the fine points of theological subtlety.

Of course, there have been times when the religious response to social decay has been to start a withdrawal from secular life. What has changed is that Rauschenbusch is convinced that "ascetic departure from the world" is dead as a religious reaction to crisis in the modern day (p. 342). To say this, of course, is in line with much American religious thought since its origins. Only the circumstances, shaped by the new forces of industrialization, have changed. Puritanism was tied to the conduct of the New England colonies, just as evangelism was to the settling of a raw frontier. Rauschenbusch wants to reconstruct human life, and he sees this as the aim of Jesus and all prophetic religion. The issue is whether such a promised religious reconstruction can appear entirely within the present social context or is only linked to a future age.

Of course, Rauschenbusch specifically rejects the interpretation of Christianity that postpones social regeneration to a future era and the return of Christ (p. 345). He adopts the simple Protestant notion that the otherworldly stress of Christianity is a medieval distortion of an early Christian activism. Yet what happens to religion when it becomes too closely tied to a particular sociological doctrine of progress and reform? If these doctrines are rejected, or if the programs fail, religion itself may be jeopardized. Rauschenbusch is convinced that Christ can regenerate the present. This may be true, but the question is whether this power operates on a broad social level as well as in individual lives.

"Repentance" becomes linked to social ills, and "faith" is tied to the establishment of new social orders. Rauschenbusch thinks that preaching about social problems has always been indigenous to Christianity, except for a lapse into complacency in the nineteenth century (p. 358). Probably this is true, but the issue concerns whether the "gospel" is itself identical with present accomplishment of social reform or not quite so simply related to change. In a way now fascinating, he links the labor movement with the press toward socialism; ironically, one of the most conservative classes today comes from the economically successful and politically powerful labor unions. The moral to be learned is this: *Christianity should risk social action, but to link Christianity too simplistically with any one economic program is to encourage religious obsolescence when change eludes our control and takes unintended forms.*

The religious spirit has always shared the style of life and social setting of its time, so that the vast problems resulting from the creation of modern industrial centers are bound to precipitate a social crisis that will alter Christianity. It was not born in separation from the social conditions of the people at the time of its origin, and it is not likely to be free of them in any later time. Although the machine age does give religion a new setting, and serious challenges too. The problem is to translate both the message of Christianity and its forms of religious life into a contemporary idiom, avoiding at the same time such close identification with any particular theory so that its demise will actually jeopardize Christianity and block individual religious experience. The issue, in other words, is this: Conditions in the world change, and how can Christian life relate to all this without becoming tied to ideas never destined to be realized?

B. The Niebuhrs and the New Sophistication

As should be expected, American theology and philosophy in the early days of the Union tended to be a simple continuation of ideas imported with the settlers, gradually altered by their new experience. Pragmatism in philosophy and social gospel in theology, plus frontier revivalism, finally emerged as authentic American strains. However, as we discover with Rauschenbusch, they were a little too closely tied to an expanding American optimism. Thus, should America's social and political goals falter or change, her religious and philosophical life might fail too.

With the rise of the Niebuhr brothers, we reach a blend of European sophistication and tradition with the American trend toward optimism and activism. Reinhold Niebuhr (1892–1971) accepts fully the function that Rauschenbusch assigns to religion as a social critic. He is much less enchanted, however, by the American notions of optimism and progress as the basis for his projection of Christianity's role. It is a minor but interesting point that his *Interpretation of Christian Ethics* was first delivered as the Rauschenbusch Memorial Lectures.[2] Niebuhr continues the role of the theologian as social prophet and judge, but now the whole weight of orthodox Continental theology comes in to temper any optimism over an immediate or future establishment of God's kingdom in conjunction with American life. If Rauschenbusch discovered the ills of industrialization, Niebuhr added the traditional notion of the inescapably "broken" quality of all human social life.

Reinhold Niebuhr senses the impending disintegration of modern civilization, and for just that reason he will not tie Christianity to any particular social success. Rauschenbusch realized the ghastly problems that industrialization had produced economically and socially, but he still shared the modern arrogance of assuming that his age had, for the first time, reached a level where it possessed the power to transform these defects into a new utopia for all. Niebuhr rightly judges that this optimism over our ability to produce social change is linked to the same expansive capitalistic system Rauschenbusch criticizes as the source of our woes. To tie Christianity to the economic goals of capitalism is no better than to link religion to the modern confidence in man's powers to perfect himself by his own unaided effort (p. 3 ff.).

Niebuhr is convinced that Christian doctrine must divorce itself from the particular social assumptions of any age, but the question is, how is such detachment from local and temporal secular goals to be accomplished? He is positive that there is no way to escape the tension and conflict between these two poles. Christian morality is destined always to live torn between its goals (which transcend any particular age) and those aims that represent the particular social requirements of the time. The coming of a new social order cannot eliminate this dilemma, nor can it ever become Christianity fully embodied. Total purity of motive and goal and accomplishment is impossible. Realizing this at least can keep us from the simplistic sin of identifying Christian life with any one set of social aims.

Thus Reinhold Niebuhr provides a needed corrective to Rauschenbusch's social optimism over a man-produced, fully embodied Christian state. He also represents the beginning of the end for the American dream, crushed on the rocks of mounting social ills now seemingly beyond hope of ultimate eradication. Rauschenbusch protested the capitulation of the church to a medieval ideal of contemplation; Niebuhr protests the identification of Christianity with modern notions of social evolution. "Liberal religion" had arrived in Niebuhr's day, and he unmasked it as a too easy accommodation to modern culture which simply resulted in an unduly optimistic outlook. Quite probably, of course, it has always been easier to unite religion with some reigning secular ideology than to have to live constantly in the tension Niebuhr recommends as our Christian fate.

As this contrast between Niebuhr and Rauschenbusch would seem to indicate, each age is alive to the distortions of the preceding generation's questionable assumptions, yet often blind to its own identifications of the gospel with contemporary cultural moods. Perhaps then *the only theology to be afraid of is the one that claims to have the essence of Christianity in a pure or final form.* There is not—and probably never was—such a thing as a knowledge of God not colored (enhanced and also obscured) by its cultural setting; the cycle of regeneration and reform goes on, like prayer, without ceasing. This is an essential feature of the religious quest. So long as it is accepted as man's situation, it can incline the believer to both intellectual modesty and practical caution.

Europeans came to a virgin American land carrying with them an old sense of religious sin. They tended, however, to lose this mood in the inevitable optimism of the vital expansion of a new land and its raw powers, especially when these resulted in an age of massive industrialization and startling scientific advances. We might expect, therefore, to recover a sense of original sin when the very forces we have counted on, when released, to usher in a good life for all produce a plethora of problems as well as economic abundance. Only in the twentieth century, as the nineteenth-century dream of "new life for all" faded away, could we turn religion away from its link with modern social optimism. Now we may reflect on the impossibility of escaping from all error and human contamination.

The recovery of a sense of sin is central to Niebuhr's neo-orthodoxy, along with the rejection of liberal religion and its accommodation to secular notions of imminent success. Liberal Christianity had thought that human nature had the resources to fulfill the ethical demands of the gospel (p. 65). For all his consciousness of the massive problems of an industrial society, Rauschenbusch essentially shared this liberal optimism. Niebuhr sees all "higher" social orders that may be proposed as still capable of sin, and it is true that what we have lost in this century is our optimism about the possibility of producing an errorless society. Only a situation dominated by paradox can do justice to the relationship of human nature to evil (p. 72), and we are incapable of eradicating such a state of affairs.

What Niebuhr essentially does is to give a critique of the "modern mind" and announce its demise. This is hard for American thought to accept, since while this divorces Christianity from certain secular notions of evolution and progress, it makes clear for the first time that America may not escape from the problems that have held back the rest of the world—as we had hoped to do. We may be stopped more by our own limitations than we realized. If evil is at the very center of human personality,[3] this flaw may be beyond our ability to overcome and may restrict our success in social reform.

But if we must abandon the idea of inevitable progress in human affairs (p. 24), this may not strike so hard a blow at original American goals as it does at certain nineteenth-century overlays on them. That is, we originally thought we could provide a new and a healthy context here in which men could develop, but the early colonists neither saw anything inevitable in this nor felt in any way free from limitations and recurring difficulties. Not in the original eighteenth but only in the nineteenth century was the idea set forth that America might in fact offer unlimited possibilities to everyone. Nineteenth-century man came to hope for redemption, either through a program of social reorganization or by some scheme of education (e. g., Rauschenbusch). It is instructive to rediscover that the original American ideal had been less optimistic and expansive than its later version.

Changing the social structure will not eradicate evil, since man is its source and he defies radical alteration. The modern mind's "estimates of human virtue are too generous and optimistic to accord with the known facts of human history" (p. 123). Thus, Rauschenbusch's attractive call for the church to lead the way to a new society proves to be more a product of modern thought than of original Christian (or American) assumptions. Improvement is not impossible, but this can never be such that we cease to produce the source of our own trouble. Our pride in our ability to transcend our former nature itself becomes a source of sin and thus of our downfall (p. 195). Rather than having confidence that social schemes can inaugurate a new era, Niebuhr is sure that "sinful pride and idolatrous pretension are thus an inevitable concomitant of the cohesion of large political groups" (p. 210).

However, lest this return to orthodoxy be taken out of perspective, it must be remembered that Reinhold Niebuhr's name is practically a household word for the battle to promote social reform. It is just that his estimates of human nature are closer to those that informed most early American religious notions, Puritan and otherwise, and he signals an end to nineteenth-century ideas of a final transcendence of our limitations through reason and human effort. "The church, as well as the state, can become the vehicle of collective egotism" (p. 217), so that Rauschenbusch simply reflects man's pride now projected onto the notion of what the church can accomplish in human affairs. The biblical-Christian faith, in Niebuhr's view, has an appraisal of historical dynamism less optimistic than alternative modern ideas.

Reinhold Niebuhr continually speaks of the crisis in which he lives. This sounds strange to the ears of men who believe that they themselves live in the first time of severe crisis, or who think it possible to transcend the old sources of division. Although for a time America fell prey to the notion that we might eliminate disharmony once and for all, our original goal in coming here had been much more to design a kind of government best able to deal with the strain of constant crisis. Niebuhr seems to have managed to bring us back to the chaotic time of the compromises that produced a union out of essentially divergent states. He leads us away from the late-arriving notion that somehow our new abundance can overcome man's constant sin. Human transcendence of evil is abolished and our primitive origins are reaffirmed in his work.

There are answers to man's misery, but no human resolution can be permanent or escape the sin of pride in its own self-confidence. The church must be just as careful of its efforts to cure social ills as it is of falling into complacency. Niebuhr begins to write at the height of the American opulence and expansion of the twenties, but his substantial writings, rather significantly, span the era from the Great Depression to the start of World War II. In such a time, it is possible to be more conscious of the failure of human attempts at social restructuring and to discover that God alone transcends the human dilemma. The rise of the new orthodoxy on the Continent is said to have inspired Niebuhr, but his classic stress on the inescapability of human sin fits the American experience of the time precisely.

H. Richard Niebuhr (1894–1962), Reinhold's brother, gave a fresh interpretation of revelation, a doctrine somewhat neglected in the modern optimism over social progress. No human form of understanding can escape the historical relativism of its situation.[4] All understanding must be provisional. If "God and the history of selves in community belong together in inseparable union" (p. 80), it follows that God can be revealed to America only as we understand our communal experience and follow its development. If "revelation must be looked for in the events that have happened to us, which live in our memory" (p. 81), Americans will not find God in imported theologies but must look back to rediscover those forces which first brought us together.

Certain special occasions of our common life are going to provide the only focal point that can make American life intelligible (p. 109). Thus, if we neglect to seek out these signal happenings in our past, it will mean a failure of insight into our present religious (and social) situation. Religion informed our past, and the present may be opaque until earlier crucial events have been reappraised—and this must be done time and time again if the significance of the present is ever to be "revealed." Where are we to look for these revelatory moments in our shared past experience? This question becomes our key, both for discovering meaning in the present and for achieving success in the future, since neither will open to intelligibility on its own. What has happened to us as a people that now conditions all our thinking (p. 138)? Much depends upon our success in finding the answer to that question.

The clarity we achieve about ourselves stems largely from our grasp of crucial events in our past. Moreover, any future risks unintelligibility if it cuts itself off from past notions of itself. In what moments of our history do we see ourselves as known (p. 152)? This question is central for our understanding both of God and the kind of community we have formed on these shores. Leaving it unanswered, we risk the arrogance of taking our ideals for granted and of losing them by not understanding their fragility. We are less likely to recognize our own corruption today unless we discover ourselves first in the past. If God is to be disclosed in

the present and our faults recognized, we must first reexperience
those few events in our common past when his presence was felt.
The possibility of any "revelation" in religion depends on this.

H. Richard Niebuhr thinks that American Christianity has "its
center in the faith in the kingdom of God."[5] If so, it may be
necessary to discover in what sense we ever thought it possible to
build the kingdom of God in this land. What Niebuhr discovers
is that the notion America can become the kingdom of God on
earth is more associated with the nineteenth-century social gospel
than with indigenous Puritan and Quaker colonial thought. Americans have no national liturgy, no one movement, but only a whole
cluster of histories of religious movements. No one time, then, can
realize the full meaning of the movement toward the kingdom, but
only all times together (p. xv).

If Americans developed a faith in their national destiny, it must
be connected to their various understandings of the kingdom of
God (p. 9). Yet since our history includes a revolutionary and
creative strain, it is impossible to reduce these views to any fixed
form. Still, we have tended to interpret the kingdom as involving
dependence on divine initiative—or at least we did until the rise
of a theory of romantic evolution which sought to transform man's
status. An economically emancipated man might mistakenly equate
his social interests with the will of God, and this tended to happen
as optimism in our own powers of transformation grew. To rediscover the kingdom of God in America today, then, might mean to
break the hold of the idea that we have transformed ourselves
beyond the reach of sin and self-pollution.

Although the "new society" in America adapted the Christian
gospel for its own support—and even though this attractive union
was popular in the development of religion in this country for
some time—it still ignores the creative and revolutionary side to
American Christianity. For this reason, the notion of the kingdom
of God refuses to be reduced to any one social pattern. In times
of national stress it breaks out again to challenge the society as
much as to support it. In such eras, when the notion of God's
kingdom opposes itself to current society, many conventionally
religious people feel betrayed. They must learn all over again the
judgmental side of religion as well as its supportive qualities. Since

we did not link religion to the state in setting up the American Constitution, it is just as free at any time to oppose the society's actions as it is to bless them. We initiated this dilemma when we refused to (or could not) create a state church in America.

Protestantism always involves the notion of protest against the state as well as its support. "The prophetic or revolutionary strain demands rebirth rather than conservation" (p. 11). Thus America's notion that it represents the possibility for the coming of the kingdom on earth is a double-edged sword so far as relations between religion and the state are concerned. Even if we do see the American state as offering hope for life in a new kingdom under God, it is just as true that the same concept offers the constant possibility for religion to turn against the state's goals and actions and to denounce them in the name of the ideal kingdom. Insofar as the idea of God's kingdom involves judgment, it offers no rest in the struggle between religion and the state.

In Europe, Protestantism had been forced to be critical and defensive. Once it arrived in America, it could turn to experimentation in the construction of a new society. This seemed to work for some time; perhaps only in the late twentieth century have we returned to the situation from which the nation first came. That is, by the mid-twentieth century we had developed a large and now time-heavy bureaucracy which evolved its own peculiar patterns and resistance to change. Once this has happened, it no longer is easy either to mold the state or to attack its deficiencies. In this case, genuine religion cannot be in league with the state, as if together they could inaugurate God's kingdom. Now it must return to its original role of protest and judgment, but this is disturbing to those who have so long accepted religion's apparent union with our national goals.

If almost all the early American colonies—not just the Puritans —intended to found theocracies, still these were not like the utopias envisaged by the nineteenth century. In spite of their various theological backgrounds, the earliest settlers were all convinced of man's original tendency to sin. Thus they could not have joined the utopians in thinking that a change in social structure might produce an ideal society and a new man. As we draw back today once again from the idea of achieving a universal utopia for all, we actually come nearer to the colonial notion of God's kingdom in America. That is, we realize that the struggle against the natural drift to depravity must be constant and intense, and that the church must be continually alert to judge society's goals. Such an opposition of church and state is not easy to live with, since it shatters any romantic notions we had of our society's eventual harmony.

Yet the church in America, no less than the state, is unfortunately subject both to institutionalization and to a taming of its revolutionary goals. Niebuhr believes this happened within the early Puritan and Quaker generations (p. 169). Once formalized, a movement is preserved, but also it unavoidably loses some of its vitalizing power. What originally were novel and liberating trends transform themselves into the stiffness they were born to oppose— certainly an ironic fate for religion. Thus we need to make a perpetual effort to revive original reform movements, both religious and social, and to seek to release them from the ineffective patterns into which they fall from time to time.

While Walter Rauschenbusch thought religion could be awakened to fight the ills of industrialization, and envisioned new utopias on the horizon, both Niebuhrs seem deeply aware that religion is as much a conservative and inhibiting force as a revolutionary one. If the state can sink into lethargy and decadence, so can religious ideals pale and turn inward to promote only their own perpetuation. As against the optimism of Rauschenbusch, if we follow the Niebuhrs we come to the sober realization that, quite probably, we are in a situation whose basic features we cannot change. We will have to remain just as constantly suspicious of religious institutions as of political vested interests. Rauschenbusch was convinced of religion's power for good, and so ignored the fact that it never fully escapes a tie with evil, even as it seeks to reform society.

However, even if America does not itself represent the coming of the kingdom of God on earth, and even if it tends as much to turn against this goal as to promote it, still we have two unique distinctions. First, the original religious motivation present in forming the union of the states did give us an inevitable thrust toward the goal of establishing a kingdom of God. This is an ideal which Americans can never quite escape, just because it is too much a part of our origins. Second, our original plurality of religious forms, plus the enforced separation of church and state which this requires, prevents us from making religion a massive, unified political force for good causes—but it also prevents an established hierarchy from using a religious institution for repression. Yet we are always open to the possibility that independent churches and clergy will continually rediscover their role as prophets and critics of any society that forgets humane goals.

C. Paul Tillich and the New Immigration of Theology

Although Tillich (1886–1965) had been famous in Germany through his identification with Christian social movements, ironically the theology he transplanted to America is now noted for a quite different emphasis. Perhaps this is because the mystical and metaphysical side of theology had been left undeveloped here, while social reform as a focus for theology was a commonplace (e. g., the Niebuhrs). In spite of William James's *Varieties of Religious Experience,* systematic theology had been neglected by American pragmatism, and mysticism was avoided in favor of a more practical emphasis in religion. Idealism, it is true, had both its metaphysical and its mystical side, but on the whole it had been rejected, due to the constant pressure to expand the social gospel.

Despite the fact that he is completely German in background and training, Tillich's major works were actually written here, and many were published first in English. He freely acknowledges the effect an American setting had on his thought, but it is not our purpose to trace the lines of this influence. Rather, the question is: How did Tillich's theology fit an American need, and—if we can uncover them—what clues to the future can we learn from both its virtues and its deficiencies? Thomas Altizer acknowledges his debt to Tillich, so that we can already see the dawn of the "death of God" movement here. However, more than that, how did Tillich's work serve to "revive" philosophical theology? How did it work to turn American interests toward the speculative and the mystical and away from the practical? What made the years of

Tillich's residence here so receptive to the spread of a theology with such a different tone?

Of course, it is not true that everyone accepted Tillich's work. The mainstream of interest in his period centered around his colleague Reinhold Niebuhr's more culturally oriented thought; yet Tillich became the major systematic thinker. His important writing began to appear just as the twentieth century shifted into its second half. In many ways, Reinhold Niebuhr represents American religion in the first half of this century. Tillich characterizes the change over to the second half—which was to become more dramatic and decisive in its split with much of the past than we could have forecast. Partly this is because America after 1950 was destined to become more like Europe. That is, it became an old culture caught in the throes of consciously admitting the impossibility of its early dreams of isolation. It could not secure its freedom from the accumulated ills of mankind.

Reinhold Niebuhr is associated with Detroit ("Motortown") and the American immigrant wave. He comes, not from New England or even from the Atlantic seaboard, but from the industrial and agrarian and still-frontier Middle West, the American heartland. By his time, waves of immigration, industrialization, and the shift to large cities had transformed both the face of the land and its future. With Rauschenbusch, we sought to apply American social optimism to the solution of these problems. With Niebuhr, we realized our involvement in the network of human sin and abandoned the pragmatic confidence in our ability to solve these human problems by the mere application of thought. America had suddenly become old, not just middle-aged. It was ready to reflect on the sins of its youth and to yearn for mystical transcendent release.

Tillich tells us that his *Theology of Culture* refers back to his first published speech, and that the problem of the relation between religion and secular culture has always been at the center of his interest.[6] Americans had not been terribly conscious of having a culture of their own since the passing of the early colonial theocratic ideals. Thus it is a new idea for us to seek religion in culture or to understand it in that way. Reinhold Niebuhr, of course, had done this in terms of social and political issues, but Tillich's extension of this approach to art, literature, and philosophy added a new dimension to the accepted social context for religion. Tillich wants us not to begin by asking the question of God's existence but instead to consider religion first as "an aspect of the human spirit" (p. 5).

Now we are advised to treat it as feeling (vs. social action). Religion comes to mean "being ultimately concerned," faith is the state of "being grasped by an ultimate concern about that which is and should be our ultimate concern," and God means "the name for the content of the concern" (p. 40). Tillich has introduced an "existential" orientation into theology which focuses on man, yet neither in the pragmatic nor in the practical way earlier American thought had done. This is a more intellectualized treatment of man, more associated with the city's theaters and art galleries than with its social welfare projects. Tillich forecasts the disappearance of the gap between the sacred and the secular realm (p. 41), which sets the stage for the secular as the proper context for religion. Because it expresses concern, culture is taken as having a religious substance. Thus the whole religious emphasis centers on culture and not on God as distinct from it. Now we are prepared for the gospel of the *Secular City*.

If theology's task is to answer the question implied in man's existence (p. 49), it has no choice but to use the language of contemporary culture to interpret Christian symbols, since the church's very forms of life are created by culture. However, since the level of the "holy" transcends nonsymbolic expression, we are forced always to use religious symbols to point beyond themselves to a reality otherwise hidden (p. 59). Religion cannot be pure and clean under these circumstances. It is inevitably involved in an ambiguity which is both creative and destructive. Since the ground in which everything is rooted is at the same time an "abyss" and is not to be directly grasped or expressed, an ultimate mystical restriction on reason is unavoidable. Psychology, then, becomes a key theological approach, but this is not at all behavioral psychology. Its model is more the interior analysis of despair provided by Kierkegaard.

Tillich had thought at first that he could not continue theology anywhere outside of Germany, but America cured him of this provincialism, he says. To the cultured European, America may appear provincial. Instead, Tillich finds, Europe itself is often more isolated, whereas in America there still is a give and take "between traditions from all over the world" (p. 160). Both here and abroad, there had been a tendency to identify all theology with the history of German theology in the last four centuries. Tillich's new "Americanization" opposes the arrogance of nineteenth-century theology which thought that it, above all other times, had come close to the truth. In America there could be no such closed shop in theology —but what kind of theological setting does such a "wild" and "wide open" culture provide?

German philosophy and theology had a vision of the world as a whole. Consequently, it despised every philosophy which was less than this. But when Hitler appeared at the end of the road of German philosophy and theology, the intellectuals themselves suddenly realized that something must be wrong with this culture (p. 163). Theology was once more cast out into the streets without a warm and secure context for its development. The American pragmatic, experimental approach, so much disdained by Continental dialectical theologians, suddenly seemed to have some merit. Theology is not treated as royally in America as it is in Germany. Yet Tillich found this enforced secondary role both healthy and refreshing. Theology's unity with European high culture had made it too proud and paved the way for its sin.

If theology in America is and has been centered more around social and ethical problems, this changes both the notion of its task and the materials for its construction. "Nominalism" (the rejection of universals as ultimate) lies behind the American pragmatic approach (p. 171). To do theology in such an insecure situation gives American theology another distinctive trait: courage (p. 172). It is easier to communicate the gospel to primitive peoples in a missionary setting (p. 204), and in many ways this had been the context for religion in America prior to Tillich's arrival. It is more difficult to write theology for a developed nation and an educated people, so that Tillich's stress on the importance of "culture" in religious symbolism only raises the urgent question of what kind of culture we have developed, or whether we have produced anything here distinctive enough to deserve that name.

Americans have not been a "cultured" people, even if our new millionaires bought up and imported European art by the carload early in the century. We may be culture-seekers, but that does not root our basic approach to life in culture. Thus our crisis is that, if we can no longer accept frontier religion, we must discover the distinctive shape of our own new pattern of life before its symbols can be put to any religious use. Tillich, for instance, treats "love" as a matter of ontological understanding,[7] but Americans are not used to thinking of love in these terms. That is, since Jonathan Edwards was replaced by more immediately oriented thought, we have rarely had a firm basis of our own for ontological understanding. Tillich wants to see love, power, and justice as rooted in the nature of being-as-such, but this requires a prior analysis, one such that to speak of our "being" as a people has meaning.

It might be that Americans could develop such an understanding. If for Tillich love is the drive toward the unity of the separated—not the union of the strange but the reunion of the estranged (p. 25)—the racial tensions and divisions of the Civil War might be able to define our national being. The war in Southeast Asia could give us grounds to understand how such an ontology might relate to social ethics. If the greatest separation love must overcome is that of self from self, American history is one of a never-complete union of peoples and ideas. If power defines being, we might be ready now to understand such a metaphysics—since today power has been thrust upon us, and the control and the use of power is our greatest national problem. Where once "nonbeing" might have seemed an abstract concept, now the constant threat of destruction makes us realize that our being as a nation has power only as it holds out against such a threat.

Today we are living through the most self-destructive period in America since the Civil War. Perhaps this gives us the grounds needed to understand concretely what once would have seemed to be only abstract metaphysics: "Power is the possibility of self-affirmation in spite of internal and external negation" (p. 40). When Tillich asks, "How can power be united with love?" (p. 48), a now reluctantly powerful nation, one which always fancied itself as representing love embodied, finds the question not idly intellectual but urgently practical.

Our American experience has come abreast of Tillich's important insights more rapidly than we would have cared to imagine. We had thought to escape having negative elements in our structure, but now the destructive elements are becoming so strong as to appear inescapable and just as real as our optimistic dreams. The Union did not stay united. Separation and reunion (being taking nonbeing into itself) is the style of life we have fallen into. Tillich's metaphysics describes our present experience.

Recently, the younger age groups have aimed to create a "love generation," but we need Tillich's dialectical understanding to grasp what this means. We did not think love was related to power, and yet it is "the strange work of love to destroy what is against love" (p. 49). If the Civil War did not prepare us for the profundities of metaphysics, the Vietnam war and the rise of black power did. Now we are ready to believe that the basic structures of being do not have the simple relations we had hoped for. Tillich's God takes the risk of destruction on himself in creating (p. 55), and today we can see the threat of destruction in everything new we attempt to create, a possibility we had perhaps forgotten when our original Revolution and union proved successful. Today the threat of destruction returns.

Successful patterns of life, such as ours in the nineteenth century, breed a sense of safety, but "the price paid for the safety in the old form is paid in terms of injustice" (p. 58). Now in order to seek racial justice we must risk the destruction of old forms of life. But if love is not to become destructive too, it must include justice, which means that there is no safe path for romantic love—which had been our national hope. If every encounter is "a struggle of power with power" (p. 87), there is no way for a basically diverse and pluralistic people to live together without the constant risk of destruction, in spite of the calm periods of growth which lead us to hope otherwise. Contrary to our national dreams, love, power, and justice must be in conflict and constantly threatening to separate. Only in God do they become one. Thus it seems impossible that these American states should ever become completely one nation.

Tillich thinks it impossible to solve our problems except by seeing them in the light of "being-itself." As Americans, we had hoped to be more practical and to avoid such intellectual abstractions. Today the impossibility of escaping the problems of conflict (which we had hoped to leave behind) has made us open to consider whether life's basic structures limit us in what we can accomplish more than we had supposed. A practical and active nation is made ready for deep reflection when it begins to suspect that it is trapped in structures beyond its control. Courage once seemed to mean to be bold and daring and pioneering. Now we may be ready to understand a courage modeled on European existentialism (whose "negative thoughts" seemed so foreign) as an act of self-affirmation in spite of the structure around us.

Faith, according to American religious experience in the nineteenth century, had seemed to mean to celebrate and promote the good things in life. At first we were not quite prepared to accept courage as the way to understand faith, which Tillich suggests.[8] Having escaped the accumulated guilt of Europe, and assuming ourselves free of its contamination, it was hard to admit the need for courage in faith because we are required to accept our own guilt. True, Jonathan Edwards and most of the early divines preached on sin and guilt. However, with the expansion and optimism of the nineteenth and early twentieth centuries, we had escaped the national awareness needed if we are to see religious faith in such a light.

Tillich might think of life as "ambiguous" (p. 27), but few Americans were really prepared to see this as its ultimate quality. We had hoped to create better conditions here. Now the original mold of American life has shattered, revealing its primal lack of unity, and ambiguity surrounds us. Acquiring the courage to will life under these conditions does give religious faith new meaning. Once we had courage because of our ideals, but in the late twentieth century we have learned what affirmation "in-spite-of" means (p. 32). It was Tillich who pointed out the power of the demonic in the human soul, but Americans had little ground to admit it (conditions leading to the Civil War being repressed) until the recent upheaval in our life-style. With thoughts of expansion dominating our minds, we had not seriously considered our possible national nonbeing. Today anxiety, as an awareness of the possible failure of our dreams, is real.

Fear always has a definite object. Americans have had healthy fears and met them, both in the Wild West and in interior poverty. Now it is anxiety in the face of nonbeing that grips us, and the rupture from past American goals is all the more painful because it has no specific object, in spite of all our attempts to focus on one—whether the scapegoat be students, hippies, or Communists. We are simply experiencing our finitude as a nation for a second time, after the early uncertainty of the success of the Union. As the Civil War showed us once—and all our recent affluence has not dispelled the possibility—we really could cease to exist. That threat produces a national anxiety which even a focus on the specific problems of minority races does not seem to dispel.

"Despair is an ultimate or 'boundary-line' situation" (p. 54). But if individually we have reached that point many times, we have not often been stopped and limited as a nation. This experience today produces a generalized religious attitude and receptivity, but most organized religion in this country still retains an identification with a different, more positive and optimistic, concept of our culture. Yet perhaps never before have we been in a better position to accept Tillich's definition of life as being "a continuous attempt to avoid despair" (p. 56). If anxiety is indeed the awareness of unsolved conflicts between structural elements of the personality, our national consciousness has only recently discovered why anxiety has become so dominant. In such a situation, courage is the only alternative to despair, but it is achieved only by taking anxiety into itself (p. 66). Until recently, Americans had hoped for a more positive solution.

Today we are in a better position to understand "grace" because we have been unable to command courage to rise at our bidding, as we were able to do earlier in the face of specific enemies. One reaction, of course, to our inability as a nation to cope with internal anxiety has been the growth of a romantic individualism, which seeks to avoid the community's disproportion by concentrating on self-development. However, if as Tillich suggests, "man is estranged from what he essentially is" (p. 127), this exaltation of the individual must fail too. But it is still hard for Americans who have tasted the fruits of their physical expansion to realize how deeply rooted is the disproportion of the national soul.

Existentialism on the Continent was actually a minority intellectual revolt in a century whose basic optimism ran against it. For Europeans, Tillich thinks, the nineteenth century came to an end in 1914, and existentialism then "became the mirror of an experienced reality" (p. 137). An existential mood, however, was not widespread among Americans early in the twentieth century, and did not take hold extensively even during the global World War II. America's rise as an atomic power in the midst of fantastic technological accomplishments did little to change the basically optimistic national outlook. Only as the new industrialization seemed to produce cultural and physical pollution, and as the black rebellion made clear the continued presence of our original national defects, were Americans prepared to experience despair and to recognize the element of courage necessary in all faith. "Meaninglessness" emerged at the very height and heart of amazing American economic affluence—which made the contrast all the more startling and hard to accept.

Tillich suggests that the "God above God" is the ultimate source of courage and that the "God of theism" will disappear in the anxiety of doubt (p. 186). Now, for many, a God whose reality seemed obvious has disappeared, and the question is whether religion can persist and endure in this anxiety until a new God appears. This is not the original nor our developed American notion of either religion or God, but it has become the American experience in the late twentieth century more than any early celebrant of the role of religion in American life ever could have guessed. Actually, we have returned to the anxieties preceding the consummation of the Union, and have come abreast of the divisions which first tore the church in the Civil War. We had thought rational discussion might produce a basis for union, but the disappearance of God and the appearance of national anxiety makes us suspect a more fundamental rift in the basic structures of our being and the unsuitability of a simple God for such a precarious situation.

If Tillich's thought has finally struck a responsive chord in recent American experience, why can it not simply become a "national theology"? For all its influence, it does not seem to control the contemporary theological scene. In fact, the "death of God" theologians claim Tillich as their forerunner. Tillich's *Systematic Theology* had as its aim to reinterpret the truth of the Christian message to a new generation.[9] Did he capture the situation—or why did he fail?

One of theology's tasks is to "answer" the questions implied in the "situation" (p. 6). Tillich uses "ultimate concern" as his way of interpreting religious life and God. Is that, or has it been, the way Americans might experience God, or will God be overlooked if that is the only religious approach open to us? If *"the object of theology is what concerns us ultimately"* (p. 12), such a theology might miss our situation in America, since God has tended to have a more practical and immediate identification for us. He has had a variety of interpretations here, never one. Tillich refuses to make "what concerns us" into a special object. This holds true for God (p. 14), which means that our understanding of God can never be very specific. Thus, if our experience demands either a specific God or the availability of direct answers, Tillich's "ultimate concern" is not able to formulate that for us.

He cannot use the Bible as a privileged literal theological source, which puts his thought at odds with a great deal of evangelical religion. He takes instead "the inspiring presence of the Spirit" (p. 45) as the ultimate source of theology. Since we experience this as the New Being in Jesus as the Christ, theology is placed in a status almost dependent on the experience of individual conversion and renewal. Yet our spiritual life is admittedly in chaos which means that theology may not be able to lead the way to a new unified experience of God. The stimulus to experience waits on leadership, but leaders can only formulate the experience. Thus the churches drift. What is genuinely mysterious cannot be put into systematic form (p. 109), and Tillich is convinced that God cannot be removed from that situation. Reason is driven beyond itself to what "precedes" reason. In such a situation answers are increasingly difficult to obtain.

Tillich warns us against the demonic, that is, the elevation of something conditional to an unconditional status (p. 140). Thus, he pronounces a judgment on much of American church life, which often too closely identifies its church customs with God's ways.

Yet, if God is simply the religious word for "the ground of being" (p. 156), it is clear that such a God can provide little specific guidance in a time of crisis. It is true that Tillich has made God safe from human misrepresentation, but he is also aloof from interrogation. The depth of the divine life involves "abyss," which makes it always mysterious no matter how much is revealed. Tillich wants God to be "the answer to the question implied in being" (p. 163), and still he has not conceived of him in a way that makes him capable of much explicit speech. Thus, if our national turmoil calls for a direct word, Tillich's God cannot speak it.

Tillich will not bring his God into the subject-object structure (p. 172), and this makes it very difficult for us to relate to him in a time when such divine communication is crucial. For this reason Tillich speaks more about man's courage than about God. As long as God's existence can be assumed, such a theology can support religious institutions. When both the organizations and God are under attack, then both his defense and religious practice demand a more direct response than Tillich is willing to allow his God to give. God does not exist; he is being-itself beyond existence (p. 205). Tillich drives us to the question of God. Yet, if little is possible in the way of a direct answer, the continuance of religion is left to depend on the strength of each individual's courage. As long as we assume that the holy still concerns man ultimately, religious belief is safe, but it dies when there is no God to oppose secular dominance.

According to Tillich, almost nothing can be said about God that is not symbolic. This means that it is all but impossible for God to address man in time of crisis as specifically as the Old Testament prophets did or as directly as Jesus spoke in God's name. If direct expression is our need, Tillich's "ground of being" is not a source which can provide it, and any religious life that depends on it will atrophy. Tillich thinks "there is a mystery about divine names which makes them improper, self-transcending, symbolic" (p. 242). That is, his God is not a self and cannot be called a person (pp. 244–245). This means that God cannot be very directly related to us as once we had supposed. But even if Americans have come to taste a more complex and less optimistic form of experience than before, Tillich's God plays little part in our experience although another God might become more central.

Tillich's God can accept no restricting conditions (p. 248). If our experience is again and again one of limitations—external and self–imposed—this will be at odds with Tillich's God. The question of theodicy (evil) can find an "answer" for Tillich only in the mystery of the creative ground. Since this is not a direct answer at all, if evil pushes us to ask for a specific reply, Tillich's God will be mute. He does not stand in a private or parental relation to man, since he represents a universal order of being (p. 288). The traditional Christian notion of a direct personal relationship to God is ruled out. *The fundamental democracy of American life works to make any theology unacceptable if it is based on an inaccessible God who cannot relate to man.* Such a notion of God fails to take root on American soil. It cannot reach out to meet our crisis.

D. The Clash of the Old World with the New

We think of American religious thought as having been imported with the early colonists, and after that as having developed on native soil. But just as in reality the waves of human immigration have hardly ever stopped coming to these shores, so new theologians and trends have always come too. Tillich observed that dogmatism was hardly possible here because we were open to so many influences from so many places. This fact gives Americans difficulty when they try to find an indigenous base for their religious thinking, but it also has the advantage of keeping us always open to each new importation. Of course, the aim of this volume is not to examine every idea that has become influential here, but only those of men who actually came to live and work here. We want to discover, not what ideas came in from abroad and were discussed, but which ones may have grown up from at least partly indigenous sources.

Tillich struck a responsive chord with his analysis of religious experience, since American life has come to have an existential quality with a speed hardly predictable a few years ago. Yet if our account is correct, the view of God suggested by Tillich—one not unlike Eastern mysticism—seems hardly to fit the American experience or to be capable of filling the vacuum left as earlier ideas of God fade out of sight. Tillich does have a mystical God beyond all knowledge, but such a God is not able to meet the religious needs of the time; all of this makes Tillich a forerunner of the death-of-God movement. Karl Barth is a precursor too. His God is specific enough, but Barth still is not really attuned to the twentieth-century American religious experience. Generalized religious interest in the United States seems strong, and yet no vision of God comes which is able to capture it.

If we consider the work of Jacques Maritain and Etienne Gilson, the first thing to be noted is that both are philosophers, not traditional church theologians. Of course, both also are Frenchmen who came to work for a considerable period of their lives in North America. Both also are Roman Catholics, which leads us to reflect that not until this time do we begin to find a Roman Catholic in either philosophy or theology who becomes prominent and determinative of a wider pattern of thought. This is not because Catholicism has not always been with us. It came with the first colonies, but its mold was traditional and reflected very little of its presence in America as opposed to its European origins. Although we have never been exclusively Protestant, still Protestant-based thought dominated the intellectual scene for some time.

Of course, during the first two hundred years in America all Roman Catholic theology was tightly orthodox. Thus, it varied little and never intended to become native to its various locales. In the late nineteenth century, Rome encouraged a revival of the study of St. Thomas, in order to produce a bulwark of philosophical thought to protect Catholic doctrine against the rising tide of modernism. Ironically, this pressure launched creative philosophical work in the first half of the twentieth century which then became the source of the Catholic theological revolution that has burst out during the last twenty years. True, these philosophical efforts turned, not to American thought or any other current ideas, but largely back to revive the work of the Middle Ages. However, genuinely creative philosophical investigation has a way of sparking innovation, even when it is historically oriented.

Gilson and Maritain are not repetitious Thomists but "neo-Thomists," and this updating and introduction of new elements into Thomas's thought has the effect of opening a fixed tradition to new interpretation. Their aim, supposedly, is to rescue the thought of the Middle Ages from abuse and to prove that it has contemporary use. However, as creative twentieth-century philosophers reflect on the thirteenth-century theologians, it is hardly likely that they can refrain from novel and suggestive interpretations. Being laymen, Maritain and Gilson are more independent than clerical theologians could be in this period. As philosophers, their ideas spark changes even when that is not their intention. The effect of philosophy has always been to raise new questions rather than to settle old ones. Thus in some ways Gilson and Maritain stand as American symbols of the kind of philosophical thought that sparked the post-Vatican II Catholic theological revolution.

Maritain seems to agree with Thomas Aquinas that the intellect can be led to certitude about God's reality.[10] Yet when he speaks of the human existence on which this intuition of God rests, Maritain uses such terms as "fragile," "menaced," and "exposed," so that clearly he has introduced a much more existential base. This leads him to the idea of a God absolute and irrefragable (p. 19). Yet it may be that, if our experience must be characterized in such different terms from those St. Thomas used, the traditional categories for describing God will also have to be revised or else lose their meaning. For a time, however, Maritain seems able to tack twentieth-century experience on to support a notion of God which is very different in kind.

Stressing the modern experience of "nothingness," Maritain is able to leap (as he puts it, borrowing Kierkegaard's term) to a God who is Being-without-nothingness (p. 20). This is how God has traditionally been conceived, but under these circumstances his existence does little to explain an admittedly very prominent feature of our own life. Certainly the medieval God was not similarly out of harmony with the way men saw their own existence at the time. Maritain is aware that we are in a different, even novel position today. He plants the seeds for a reinterpretation of God, rather than simply transplanting a traditional notion. For instance, he supports Thomas's "five proofs" for God's existence and speaks in classical fashion of the need for "something necessary in things" (p. 48). Yet his own way of speaking of existence points to a newer approach to God, a "sixth way."

Maritain joins Heidegger and others in this new approach by asking, Why something rather than nothing at all, why my thought when there might be *nothing?* (pp. 69–76). *From the primacy given to contingency and nothingness in experience a God may come who is less necessary in his relationship to the world than even Maritain envisaged at this time.* Maritain involves poetry, beauty, and aesthetic experience in his approach to God (p. 80), and this opens up the mystical avenue to God by way of "unknowing," as opposed to Thomas's strictly rational method. Thus Maritain stresses "the way of the practical intellect" in thinking about God, and does so in a much more appealing manner than the traditional rational proofs which supposedly he aims to support. He offers a knowledge of God "superior to reason" and which is not due to reason (p. 100). Thus he opens the door to a less traditional view of God as well as of human nature.

In both his teaching and his writing, Maritain drew an enormous response in America, even when it was one of opposition. By bringing in new strains of Continental thought, he prepared the way for us to revise our merely imported dogmatic thought structures, since in reality these did not express either the experience of God or twentieth-century man's peculiar quest for him. Nineteenth-century religious life was perhaps rather complacent in its notions of God and its view of the role of religion in the life of the people. However, Maritain on one side opens the way, not for the rejection of tradition, but for a novel interpretation. In that sense he initiates further, and perhaps more radical, change—particularly since the idea of a fixed concept of God does not seem to fit the American experience.

Maritain agrees that the existential acceptance of atheism and the renunciation of grandeur are forceful ideas and that this changes the situation in which we must think of God.[11] True, he goes on to give a supposedly traditional Thomistic and Aristotelian account of knowledge, but his constant stress on existence as being "beyond the intelligible" (p. 18) is bound to add a revolutionary seed which in itself is more attractive to some readers than his conservative framework. His continual references to the "act of existing" (e. g., p. 31), do not quite allow themselves to be reduced to conventional terminology. Our way of describing God is bound to be affected. When the genuinely creative philosopher reaches back in history to recover a strain of thought he fears will be lost, the most likely effect will be to crystallize the novelty of his own thought, merely using tradition as a backdrop. The next generation may remove the ancient setting and take over what is new.

If the creative and vital thrust of philosophy in Roman Catholic circles in the first half of the twentieth century did in fact lead to the novelty of theological reinterpretation in the third quarter of the century, both Gilson and Maritain are actually the forerunners of a radical theological movement in America whose authorship they might prefer to deny. Maritain conforms and agrees with the traditional notion that nothing is future for God (p. 87), but his analysis of existence may lead to different conclusions when the necessity to conform to orthodoxy is withdrawn. Still, Maritain wants to remove genuine freedom and contingency from God's knowledge, and he also denies that God intends or causes evil directly (p. 109). He stresses the eternality and immutability of the divine plan, but all of these factors may be so at odds with contemporary American experience that this theology must either be changed or abandoned. Left as it is, Maritain's view of God can hardly expect to support religious faith in the post–modern temper.

Gilson quite properly sees that the issue we are left with is the metaphysical problem of God.[12] He then proposes to use the historical approach to solve this question, but the issue is whether this predetermines us to unacceptable solutions. The concentration upon history is not an original American methodology, and thus it could be self-defeating when imported as an approach to God.

Gilson acknowledges his debt to Henri Bergson, but his God is hardly built according to Bergson's patterns. However, it is interesting to note that, when Teilhard de Chardin revolutionizes God's nature, it is Bergson whose thought serves as his primary metaphysical base. Gilson, on the other hand, begins his analysis with the Greeks and finds their gods to be living powers, endowed with wills of their own and operating in human lives. Yet he seems to link this with the idea of "necessity," and thus he finds in Greek thought a uniformity which in fact may not be there, although such a uniformity did come to dominate the Christian theological tradition later on. The point is not to argue the correctness or incorrectness of Gilson's historical interpretation but to see how he builds his view of God by reading back into an earlier period an agreement which may or may not really have been there originally.

He thinks it universally true, for instance, that the Greeks did not know how to treat the concept of will in God. Plato, he thinks, could not get divergent principles (gods and ideas) together, but Aristotle at last joined together his God and his philosophical first principle. Plato's metaphysical principles admittedly are more plural than those of some philosophers, but to assume Aristotle's greater success is to prejudge the question of a unity vs. a plurality of first principles. Gilson goes on to picture Thomas Aquinas as somehow uniting two otherwise divergent strains of thought, the pure being of Plato's ideas and the existential qualities of the human Greek divinities. Again, the point is not to debate the correctness of Gilson's favorable interpretation of the genius of the Middle Ages. What we need to do is to question whether the God whom Americans might discover can emerge from any analysis of the historical development of certain concepts or be made to depend on the correctness of some particular intellectual history of ideas.

Is the historical debate, however absorbing, somehow beside the point as far as determining the shape of religion in the future is concerned? This question has nothing to do with the fact that any new idea must borrow some of its parts from past tradition. It depends on how the investigation should be carried out in order to determine the course of the future and what role historical appraisal can play in solving present religious problems. Gilson wants "a philosophical God who can also be the God of a religion" (p. 141), but the issue is whether such a God can be recovered from strict analysis of Greek or European notions alone. Gilson turns to William James,[13] but this move fails to figure very conclusively in his theory when it comes to determining our sources for thought about God.

Gilson accepts an existential notion of actual existence: it is such that it cannot be represented by, nor in, a concept (p. 4). Yet at the same time he rigidly identifies Christian theology with a particular metaphysics, in this case one which places "Being" as the first notion, and thus must reject any neo-Platonic or mystical transcendence of Being. To do this is, of course, to identify Christian thought with a particular historical strain of Western metaphysics.

However, it may be this very historical analysis that throws us off in the contemporary quest for God, since it gives undue weight to the reading of history in one direction. To interpret the metaphysical tradition in this way may be more harmful than helpful. Its apparent support for Christian conclusions will be illusory if the interpretation is artificial. It seems to authenticate one particular conclusion on the basis of historical evidence, when perhaps our need is to stay open to a wider set of alternative approaches to God.

Gilson carried out the historical inquiry and thus once more raised old solutions to become possible lines of thought. This is a very necessary prerequisite to basic change. Nevertheless, considered against the experience of the moment, any historical line of development seems far removed, and he does leave out almost all that is peculiar and indigenous to man's existence in North America. Historical analysis revives thought, but it does not in itself yield a viable path for the future, as Gilson evidently hoped it would. Americans are not as ready as Europeans to find the solution to present problems in an investigation of past sequences. Gilson's brilliant exposition of the various metaphysical principles used in theology by the major historical thinkers is itself enlightening, but it is simply not the same as pointing a viable way into the future.

Thus the adequacy of Gilson's analysis itself becomes the crucial item of debate. If we accept the accuracy of his historical interpretation, we seem committed to his particular solution. But our situation in the realm of thought is much less secure than that, unfortunately. It may be that the historical sequence can give us food for thought and also some guidance. It is just not sufficient to build a solution adequate to the present or the future. Perhaps Americans are not made to be determined by the history-of-ideas approach which so dominated Europe in the nineteenth century. Not that we need to reject all history, including our own. It is just that our way to shape an adequate theology and a successful religious life may be somewhat more independent of such historical determinations. This may be one conclusion of our own historical experience: that we are not determined by history or subject to its dictates. Our thought fights for its freedom, too, as our bodies have done before.

In many ways, as the heading of this section suggests, this period is a time of clash between the old world and the new. Walter Rauschenbusch is a distinctively American voice, although perhaps too traditionally optimistic in outlining what we can accomplish. However, the emergence of the Niebuhrs does temper such native optimism about the possibility of achieving dramatic social change, adding a little of the orthodox theological perspective. Balanced against this we have Tillich, Maritain, and Gilson. No one of them is a native American, and yet all three immigrated to work in America and to influence our religious thought. Still, they do not produce an American theology fully adequate to the future—or to the American past either.

Here, then, are various sets of materials in our immediate past, each of which offers temporary success but does not predict the shape of the future. The industrial age came upon us and changed the face of America, as well as our notions about achieving our young dreams—so much is sure. In a characteristic American way, ethical goals and sensitivities were kept to the forefront, but no attempt was made to build a basic theology, a metaphysic, which draws on native sources and indigenous experiences. Imported metaphysics and related notions of God seem not to take hold here. If the adequacy of our vision of God is under severe question, the future of religious life is under a cloud until a native way is found to present God which can take root in our experience. A technological sweep has driven out our transplanted ideas of God, and they have not yet been replaced for the future.

However, a point of some significance is the fact that the development of religion in an industrialized America did not follow Marxist predictions. It did not function as the opiate of an economically oppressed people. Rather, it became tied to our economic expansion and went hand in hand with the rising power of labor unions. Not that every church gave early support to the union movement; this is not so. Yet neither the workers nor the middle class rejected religion as they attained economic success. Instead, they identified their newly achieved social status with religion and made the latter into another support for middle-class styles and virtues. Of course, for blacks in this country, religion did take on a more Marxist cast. That is, it flourished as an escape valve for their burdened spirits, bent under physical and economic oppression.

NOTES

1. Walter Rauschenbusch, *Christianity and the Social Crisis,* ed. Robert D. Cross (New York: Harper & Row, 1964), p. xxii. Originally published in 1907.

2. Reinhold Niebuhr, *An Interpretation of Christian Ethics* (New York: Harper & Brothers, 1935), Preface.

3. Reinhold Niebuhr, *The Nature and Destiny of Man* (New York: Charles Scribner's Sons, 1947), I, 16.

4. H. Richard Niebuhr, *The Meaning of Revelation* (New York: Macmillan Company, 1946), p. 37.

5. H. Richard Niebuhr, *The Kingdom of God in America* (New York: Harper & Brothers, 1959), p. ix.

6. Paul Tillich, *Theology of Culture* (New York: Oxford University Press, 1959), p. v.

7. Paul Tillich, *Love, Power, and Justice* (New York: Oxford University Press, 1954), p. 2.

8. See Paul Tillich, *The Courage to Be* (New Haven: Yale University Press, 1952).

9. Paul Tillich, *Systematic Theology* (Chicago: University of Chicago Press, 1951), I, 3.

10. Jacques Maritain, *Approaches to God,* trans. Peter O'Reilly (New York: Collier Books, 1962), p. 17.

11. Jacques Maritain, *Existence and the Existent,* trans. Lewis Galantiere and Gerald B. Phelan (New York: Pantheon Books, 1948), pp. 1–9.

12. Etienne Gilson, *God and Philosophy* (New Haven: Yale University Press, 1941), p. ix.

13. Etienne Gilson, *Being and Some Philosophers* (Toronto: Pontifical Institute of Medieval Studies, 1949), Preface.

VI

PROCESS THEOLOGY
AND THE COMING REVOLUTION

A. God in the Making

For all its excitement and novelty, it is clear that the social gospel accepted a rather traditional notion of God and was on the whole disinterested in metaphysics and systematic theology. Although Tillich was an exception, Rauschenbusch, the Niebuhrs, Maritain, and Gilson each held to an orthodox view of God while introducing novelties in other areas. In spite of the practical and sometimes antimetaphysical American attitude, it was natural that the revolution should extend itself and suggest a different way to think about God. Once again, however, novelty was not introduced by a native son, but by an Englishman who came here to teach and write. Alfred North Whitehead (1861–1947) was noted in England primarily as a mathematician and logician, but he joined the golden age of philosophy at Harvard, and this seemed to launch the metaphysical side of his work. Most of his writings on theology and religion stem from this American period.

It is sometimes said that "process theology," stimulated by Whitehead's thought, first suggested the radical notion that God too was subject to change. This, of course, is not quite accurate. Plato's demiurge not only changes but is the source of change, and of course Hegel and the radical German theologians of the nineteenth century all either treated God on an evolutionary scheme or interpreted him primarily in human categories. It is true that Aristotle's unmoved mover tends to dominate most "orthodox" notions of God, but the possibility that God might change is not a new discovery.

Still, the orthodox Protestant views that formed the early theology of America, and the neoscholastic tradition that became dominant in Roman Catholicism, accepted a basically similar metaphysics. This perspective took immutability as God's central attribute and looked on change as a threat to his omnipotence. Thus any return to a more flexible notion of the divine nature was bound to seem like a radical revolution. The intuitive metaphysics of the common man may continue to think of God mainly as eternal—as being beyond time and not as undergoing basic changes of his own through his continual involvement in creation. Seeing and feeling the difficulties of our changing life and world, to the average churchgoer the changeless quality of Plato's forms is certain to have considerable appeal as his notion of perfection. An age which shuns metaphysics is fated to accept one kind of vision of God. It takes an acquired metaphysical skill to resist such a natural religious prejudice.

It is significant, then, that all the philosophers and theologians considered in this chapter are primarily interested either in metaphysical construction or in using it as an approach to theology. To be able to change our conception of God requires some sublety in comparing basic metaphysical principles. An age which will not speculate dooms itself either to a conservative notion of God or to the loss of that God if he begins to seem out of place in the time. Since any change in our notion of God is hard to achieve, it takes constant philosophical effort. Otherwise we drift back to instinctive theological assumptions, whether adequate or not. The revolution that process theologians propose is not so much "new" as it is against the traditional assumptions about what God must be like.

Whitehead, of course, is not specifically Christian in his approach to religion and does not intend to be. Along with David Hume, he has an interest in "natural" religion, and attempts to define religion's function as a general human phenomenon.[1] He sees it as a mode of life, rather than as knowledge to be used like arithmetic

(p. 15), and gives us his now famous definition: "Religion is what the individual does with his own solitariness" (p. 16). This makes it an art involving man's internal life, and it is easy to see that this moves it away from a specifically doctrinal or theological orientation. Whitehead is quite willing to admit that religion involves emotion, ritual, and belief, with the rationalization of this coming last of all. Thus, religion must be defined primarily as a human enterprise.

His evolutionary frame of reference is evident at this point, for Whitehead forecasts the emergence of a religious consciousness which is universal, as against the tribal or social (p. 47). This raises an important question because, if religion actually follows an evolutionary pattern, then what once was true may no longer be so. If religion does not follow such a pattern, then our essential situation has not changed. Accordingly, it seems to make all the difference in the world whether you place religion in an evolutionary pattern or not. Whitehead, for instance, is convinced that both Christianity and Buddhism are in decay and have lost their hold on the world (p. 44). Unless an irreversible evolutionary pattern is in force, this could be true, and yet any religion could still be reversed, restored, and revitalized.

Whitehead also is convinced that the modern world has lost God and is seeking him (p. 74). This seeking will have to take place on a world-wide basis now. It involves "the value of the diverse individuals of the world for each other" (p. 59). He rejects purely historical investigation as being unable to found adequate religious belief. On the other hand, he is convinced that religion requires a metaphysical backing.

Very much like the role assigned to Plato's demiurge or world soul, Whitehead seems to use God as only one (but still a necessary) element in the world's process. The world is a community of "epochal occasions," and the congealing of this process requires both "creativity," ideal forms (like Plato's), and an actual but nontemporal entity, which Whitehead calls God (pp. 90–91). This is not the personal and all-powerful God of traditional religion, but then Whitehead's evolutionary scheme would not require the continuance of any traditional notion as such. God is included in every creature. He has a role to play in process; without him no definite result would emerge. This makes God very real and very important, but simply as an ingredient in the natural process.

There is so much that is possible in the world, but no possibility can actualize itself. God is required to bring about a definite determination to events. He is an actual entity which enters into every creative phase, yet is above change in crucial ways. Since evil means destruction for Whitehead, his God is by definition exempt from direct responsibility for evil. He is the creative catalyst. God's purpose is the attainment of value in the temporal world (p. 100). Thus we see him operative wherever values are enhanced, secured, and actualized.

Whitehead is concerned to deny every doctrine of individual substances. No entity, not even God, requires nothing other than itself in order to exist (the definition of substance) (p. 108). The metaphysics which Whitehead suggests makes every entity in its essence social, and this means that it requires society in order to exist. Such a mutual dependence characterizes God's situation too, even if his function in the process is different. The society for each entity is the all-inclusive universe; no entity can exist alone. God is the "completed ideal harmony" (p. 120) and has an essential function to perform in the creative process. There is freedom and infinite possibility in the process, but without God's actualizing effect nothing would come of this. God is known as that without which no actual entity would come to be in an open, creative process. Unlimited possibility and abstract creativity produce nothing if left to themselves (p. 152).

"The power by which God sustains the world is the power of himself as the ideal. . . . The world lives by its incarnation of God in itself" (p. 156). However there are also ideal forms (very much like Plato's) existing eternally as a part of both God and the world. They belong no more to one than to the other, which makes God important but not supreme in the process. Such forms are a "given factor" in God's nature, known and used by him in shaping the world. God is the binding element in the world, and his function is to direct our purposes to ideal ends. But God's creative role is partly determined by the forms; his freedom is not absolute. He is not the world, but the valuation of the world. God is an impetus to future attainments. In an evolutionary process, whatever ceases to ascend fails to preserve itself and decays.

This vision of God, which we have come to associate with Whitehead, is attractive to a modern spirit. Its evolutionary thrust, its stress on freedom, its limitation of God's power to the gain of man's—all this suits the contemporary temper. The major question arises over its religious use. Can this God fit in with most traditional religious views? Or what revisions are necessary in Christian beliefs if this picture of God is accepted? Lacking new metaphysical construction, certain notions in religion can change, but not our notion of God. Whitehead begins the first major metaphysical construction on American soil in some time, and a new idea of God is bound to emerge. Now the question concerns whether other alternatives are also open to us, and how a theology emerges if it is revised by the use of this metaphysics and its God.

Whitehead's more extensive work, *Process and Reality,* has become for many perhaps the most attractive basis for contemporary theological reconstruction.[2] He tells us the book is "modern" in its inspiration, that it depends on the line of thought from Descartes to Hume. The importance of Plato in his thinking has already been mentioned, and he says that his "philosophy of organism" is a recurrence to pre-Kantian modes of thought. However, it is his debt to Bergson, Dewey, and William James that he specifically mentions. He stresses his disagreement with the idealistic thought of F. H. Bradley, which perhaps shows the influence of the pragmatists on him. Yet when he says that " 'relatedness' is dominant over 'quality' " (p. ix), this surely is a hallmark of idealism. He refuses to refer the essence of the universe beyond itself, however (as idealism is willing to do). Thus, we know that any God of his must be a part of the essence of the universe and not a transcendent principle. This surely is a form of naturalism in theology. Whitehead's theology is characterized by such naturalism, and he tells us that he will not violate rationality, which cuts off any form of mysticism in religion. His God is appealing to the rationalist, the naturalist, and the nonmystic.

Creativity is the ultimate factor in Whitehead's philosophy of organism (p. 11), and God is simply its fundamental exemplification. This God has a "primordial" and a "consequent" nature (p.

19). The primordial side is eternal and complete. The consequent nature grows out of God's relationship to an evolving world. Whitehead's foundational concepts include "actual entity," "prehension," and "nexus," which seems to make these (as also creativity) basic, while his notion of God is more derivative and less fundamental.

The primordial nature of Whitehead's God is very much like the classical conception of eternality and immutability. A multiplicity of "eternal objects" make this up, and these have much the same characteristics as Plato's forms (p. 46). But understanding of the world is not centered in a single concept, such as Aristotle's "actuality." God's consequent nature is in a sense his knowledge of, and relationship to, the actual entities of the world. Both God and the world are, and are to be understood by, a loose collection of a variety of principles, some eternal, some temporal, some changing, some unchanging. With Whitehead we return to the question of the pre-Socratics and Plotinus: that is, whether the principal cause of the world is one or many.

God's immanence in nature is represented by an urge to the future, and creativity becomes a basic force in the life of all things (p. 47). Like Plato's concept of participation, change is "the description of the adventures of eternal objects in the evolving universe of actual things" (p. 92). The world is a process of generation of individual actual entities (p. 94). This is the philosophy of organism, and the theological question is whether God somehow becomes just a name for this process when it is viewed as a whole. Does "God" designate only a certain—if perhaps important— part of it? Theologically, the issue is one of control. Is the process self-contained and self-directive, or can any being stand outside of it and assume full direction? Can God be transcendent, or must he be a fully immanent part of nature?

"God's existence is not generally different from that of other actual entities, except that he is 'primordial' " (p. 116). Whitehead's vision is of a pluralistic universe, not unlike that of William James. The world is a "society" or "community" (p. 123). In such a scheme, God has a role to carry out, but it cannot become too dominant. God's primordial nature has no past, and his consequent nature is "the physical prehension by God of the actualities of the evolving universe" (p. 134). In this sense, although God has his duties to discharge, the constitution of his nature is, finally, a process he observes without ultimate ability to control. This depends on the outcome of innumerable actual processes.

God does have a purpose in the creative advance. It is "the evocation of intensities" (p. 161). It is as if a cohesive spark would pass out of the world without God. The temporal world is conditioned but not determined by the initial subjective aim arising from the primordial nature of God (p. 164). Pure chaos is impossible because of the immanence of God (p. 169). He has the function of supplying the basic conditions for order. Whitehead develops a philosophy of organism in contrast to a philosophy of substance, which means a concentration on the nature of "process." This tells us that God's nature will be primarily determined by the role he is assigned in the developmental sequence. Process will be the fundamental principle and everything else, including God, will be defined in relation to it.

"Feeling" becomes a universal term and is applied throughout the actual world (p. 268). Thus, God will not be immune to feeling, and every process will be interpreted in relation to this subjective quality. Whitehead is quick to admit his complete acceptance of the "subjectivist bias of modern philosophy" (p. 253). Nothing is to be received into the philosophical scheme which is not discoverable as an element in subjective experience. Furthermore, feeling transforms entities otherwise alien into components of one complex (p. 322). Thus feeling is, in some real sense, the unifying principle of the world.

In fact, "all actual entities share with God this characteristic of self-causation" (p. 339). God, then, is not unique in nature but merely represents the process writ large. The universe is a creative advance into novelty, on Whitehead's view, and this makes it the center of all metaphysical attention, even if God is assigned an indispensable role. It is not wrong to view God as the creator of each temporal entity (p. 343), but what this means in fact is that no actual entity is entirely self-contained. The "derived" conceptual feeling which influences its formation and direction is like a small reproduction of the data and valuation of God's conceptual feeling. In this sense, God is a part of each segment of the world. Creativity really is the key concept for understanding our universe, and "God is the aboriginal instance of this creativity" (p. 344).

God and the world are linked together inseparably. There is "no meaning to 'God' apart from the creativity and the 'temporal creatures' " (p. 344)—but it is also true that creatures require creativity and God in order to be understood. God, then, is a principle of the process, so that the process cannot be explained without him, but he also has no function apart from his role in the process of nature. His immanence is clear. In what sense, if any, he might still transcend the world is unclear (and also unimportant) for Whitehead. It is enough for the world and God to be mutually dependent. The world depends on God for both order and novelty (p. 377). Apart from his activity, the world would lack both.

" 'God' is that actuality in the world, in virtue of which there is physical 'law' " (p. 434). The important function God performs is not so much that of the Plotinian One from whom all things flow as it is a combination of Plato's world maker and Aristotle's unmoved mover. That is, Plato's demiurge imposes order on what otherwise would remain chaos. He moves by persuasion. Aristotle's unmoved mover does not move himself, but he does cause motion by attraction and desire. Whitehead's God combines these two factors in his primordial and consequent nature, but in no sense is he to be considered the sole source of all things.

The world is alive. There is nothing that is an inert fact (p. 472). Every reality is there for feeling and promotes feeling. Thus we are presented with a beautiful vision of a growing and dynamic universe. But it is also a very romantic picture. Up to this point there is little account of evil or destruction. Theoretically, all forces work together for good, and yet in life it does not seem to be so. Whitehead's world does not need a transcendent God, because the process itself moves beyond the negation and destruction of any particular moment, preserving all that is worthwhile and capable of being saved. The process itself does not require radical reconstitution. What can be done for good, to promote purpose and value, is being done in the course of the world's development.

Although there are nontemporal guiding elements to this process, time does not need to be transcended because of the good that is achieved and preserved within it. This is not to say that Whitehead's world lacks evil. Its presence is obvious and rooted in the fact "that the past fades, that time is a 'perpetual perishing' . . . [and] that the characters of things are mutually obstructive" (p. 517). The process itself entails loss: the past cannot be preserved in its immediacy. The struggle with evil is a permanent part of the necessary selective process. The latter, however, builds a harmony that will utilize as much as possible. Thus the harsh impact of destructive or opposing forces ultimately is at least reduced if not fully overcome. Evil like that men can deal with.

Whitehead ends *Process and Reality,* significantly, with a chapter on "God and the World." As far as the use of Whitehead's thought for religious and theological purposes is concerned, certainly the crucial issue is God's relation to the world. Or, to put it in another way: Does God have any existence apart from the role he plays as an ingredient in the world's process—however important that may be? It would be wrong to label Whitehead a Christian. He is religious in about the same sense that Spinoza is. That is, he neither embraces nor exemplifies any particular doctrine or tradition in his technical thought. However, it is clear that God has a role to carry out, and that to adopt a "religious attitude" toward the world has meaning and support from Whitehead.

Whitehead's philosophy has the appealing endorsement of his work in mathematics and logic, plus his use of science. Yet in its appropriation for technical theological use, certain questions inevitably arise. His God has much the same status as Plato's. That is, for explanatory purposes he may be talked about separately, but in fact he does not exist independently of the world, and has his existence only in connection with the total process. Such a God may be "creative"—indeed this is a central function of God for Whitehead—but he is not *the* creator. He exerts an influence on the world's development, but is hardly in a position to end the present age or reshape things in any radical way. In this sense Whitehead's God is at odds with many religious assertions.

One prime issue, of course, is whether this is the only conceivable role we can assign to God in a modern age—whether he must either be part of the process or else have no function at all today. Whitehead has certain prejudices of the modern world in his favor.

Yet if a wider variety of functions for God again becomes conceivable, his nontranscendence of the process might inhibit his religious use. Whitehead interprets the core of the Christian message as the slow and quiet operation of love in the world (p. 520). Seen in this way, his God can be accommodated to Christian thought. But if Christianity ought to announce anything more radical than this, Whitehead's God will become less suitable for the purpose.

Whitehead is quite clear that God is not an exception to general metaphysical principles. "He is their chief exemplification" (p. 521). He is with creation rather than before it. His primordial nature is in a sense the world before actualization. He orders and directs primordial objects (Plato's forms) in the process of creation, and in that sense the world's order is impossible without him. The world reacts on God, and his derivative nature is consequent upon the creative advance of the world (p. 524). His primordial nature is conceptual; his consequent nature is conscious. He does not create the world—he saves it. "He is the poet of the world, with tender patience leading it by his vision of truth, beauty, and goodness" (p. 526).

This is a highly romantic role in which to cast God. The question is whether we see the world as showing the effects of the work of Whitehead's God, and whether this interpretation provides theological principles adequate to remedy the world's ills. "God and the world," for Whitehead, "are the contrasted opposites in terms of which Creativity achieves its supreme task of transforming disjointed multiplicity" (p. 528) into concrescent unity. Lacking God, the world falls into disarray. The issue is this: *Can God ever achieve a combination of order and novelty significantly better than that which we presently experience?*

The world derives its aspect of permanence from God. We cannot do without the principles he exemplifies. He is in that sense an extrapolation of one basic aspect operative in the world's structure. Salvation means: in every moment I achieve eternality, in the sense that I become part of God's nature. God's consequent nature is composed of the multiplicity of elements accomplished by individual self-realization. In that sense, everything achieved is preserved. "The kingdom of heaven is with us today" (p. 532).

God becomes "the great companion—the fellow-sufferer who understands" (p. 532). We perish and yet we live forevermore—as a memory of an occasion in the world's process. God is right in there with us in such a scheme.

The world as Whitehead describes it is truly a romantic setting and God an immediate, constructive friend. Every issue that remains centers around the acceptability of what essentially amounts to a very optimistic picture. If we feel the world to be a progressing, creating situation, we may celebrate it in religious terms with Whitehead's God. If the structure of the world appears less friendly, perhaps even oppressive and destructive, the work of Whitehead's God will turn out to be less than adequate. For the "naturalist" who wants to find his ultimate principles within nature, Whitehead provides a God without transcendence. However, first one must make the prior decision that the structure of nature is acceptable as it stands and that religiously it requires no radical reconstitution. If so, this God can do everything expected of him.

Whitehead fits into one era of American experience very nicely, and quite probably his own thinking has, as he indicates, been affected by his presence in America. His limited God evidences an acceptance of pragmatic principles, and these always have an optimistic flavor. Religiously, all we seem to need from God and from each other is a little more cooperative assistance. However, if the world is viewed more negatively and less favorably, religious worship demands more for its object or else its God will die. As long as nature and the world appear favorable to us, God as a principle of nature is accepted as required. When man feels more alone, as if left to face an alien nature and a hostile environment, then an immanent God becomes helpless and only a transcendent God can offer hope for survival.

B. A New Vision of God

God plays a crucial role in Whitehead's cosmology, but it is as a part of the system that he is important. In that sense, Whitehead is a metaphysician and not a theologian. That is, his direct intention centers not on God but on the structural principles he uses to account for the world's basic form, the nature of Being. Of course, such investigation logically must come first. Therefore it is not surprising to find Whitehead's thought stimulating a more direct theological reconstruction which uses the novel features of his philosophy. Charles Hartshorne acknowledges his debt to Whitehead without apology, and it is easy to trace the latter's influence on his new vision of God.[3]

The questions Hartshorne raises are derived from the position to which God is assigned in Whitehead's thought, although Hartshorne acknowledges his debt to C. I. Lewis, H. M. Shaffer, and Charles Peirce as well. The issue is this: as Whitehead describes God's function, is he in any sense supreme or perfect as he has traditionally been described? As these terms have usually been conceived, the answer clearly seems to be No. Whitehead's God is not the only basic principle in his world, and in fact it is possible that other principles are really more fundamental—e. g., creativity. Thus, to center on the problem of God following Whitehead's lead is naturally to be forced to recast the theological tradition or challenge it. A new vision of God is produced principally by assigning God a new role and giving him a new function.

Hartshorne is convinced that secular knowledge no longer can support orthodox theology. Then the conclusion seems automatic that "God" must be reconstructed so that secular knowledge is able to support him. However, Hartshorne's main contribution may be to show and stress that there are, logically, many possible ideas of God (p. x). If so, our major problem is to understand just what ideas are possible, and which ones are viable in the present circumstances. Following Whitehead's notion of the two natures of God, Hartshorne does not want to deny that God is in some sense immutable, complete, and perfect, but he also wants to stress that he is complex, changing, incomplete, and growing in value (p. xv).

Such a new vision, Hartshorne is convinced, makes the problem of evil "disappear" (an amazing notion), since we see that not even a perfect power could guarantee complete harmony. Divinity does not escape all sufferings, but shares in them all. As in Leibniz's "best of all possible worlds," we account for evil by arguing that no more perfect order is really possible. Hartshorne attributes to William Ernest Hocking the notion that God is not in every sense absolute. If true, this has the advantage of removing large quantities of responsibility from God's shoulders, although the problem is that at the same time it limits what God can ever be expected to accomplish. The medievals discussed the question of "what God cannot do," as every theologian has. However, now the proposal is to limit God's role more severely and thus relieve him of responsibility. Augustine had done this by making him unchanging; Hartshorne does it by making him a part of change.

Like many of this era, Hartshorne is convinced that the theistic question is taking on a new form today (p. 2). On an evolutionary scheme, the development of thought has moved us along to a place where classical notions no longer are acceptable. Primarily, it is the idea of perfection that must be reexamined, although he is willing to grant that God is superior to other entities in some sense (p. 6). It is clear that there are still several options as to what perfection means, but one widely accepted notion is that it must exclude all change and thus not be subject to time. Yet, if all values are not compossible, then no being—not even God—can represent the actualization of them all. God is limited by what can coexist harmoniously.

If God is not perfect in all respects, he still could be perfect in some respects (p. 33), but it is clear that Hartshorne wants to find God's value primarily in his various relations to the world and so must refuse to allow his being to be independently complete. God is not fulfilled as he stands. He can be surpassed, even if this is a possibility open only to himself (p. 46). Partly this is true because Hartshorne wants to stress love as God's primary perfection (p. 50), and this must allow for growth vs. immutability. Conflict can exist in God as well as harmony, and this of course does not fit the traditional notion of "necessity" in God. As Hartshorne interprets the tradition, its metaphysical side has been completely out of harmony with the religious experience of men.

If we follow Whitehead and see both a mutable and an immutable aspect in God, Hartshorne correctly sees that we will have to renounce the doctrine of "simplicity" (p. 111). Such a God may be perfect in a new sense, but he will be complex. As might be expected, Hartshorne is rather rigid in his interpretation of the theological tradition. He sees it as being uniform (which is rather amazing), and as not in itself offering a variety of options for thought about God. Thus some of the validity of his analysis of God rests upon the correctness of his understanding of the tradition. Should the tradition not be as uniform or rigid as he makes out, this does not deny the account of God he offers; it only makes the option less forced.

Hartshorne is convinced that, for God to have ethical import, he must exist at least partly in time. "The divine love is social awareness and action from social awareness" (p. 173). God is involved in evil, but he is not made directly responsible for it. He is "himself qualified by what is positive in evil, namely discord, whch is not mere absence of harmony, but positive clash" (p. 196). Interestingly enough, Hartshorne still wants God to be "entirely good" (p. 198), although he is willing to recognize him in other ways too. However, his goodness is near to love, and this makes God dependent on others for happiness. Like Spinoza's "Substance," Hartshorne's God has the world for a body (p. 200). Being optimistic by inclination, Hartshorne takes this to be a matter for the fullest enjoyment, not grief.

If one celebrates nature and sees it as basically good and enjoyable, God can be "the cosmic 'adventure' (Whitehead) integrating all real adventures as they occur" (p. 227). Yet in order to see God as perfect in this way, you must be fairly romantic in appraising the joys of nature. To see the natural world less optimistically is to make God less perfect. Even though Hartshorne writes just as World War II is breaking out, still it is a time when America is confident of her powers to extend the good life and the benefits of nature to all. Optimistically viewed, to tie God to nature is to save him, at least for those inclined to venerate the natural process. Should the outcome appear less optimistic, God could be lost by such close association with a world that repels us.

Change becomes the key, and also the most disputed, concept. Must change be allowed in God in his relations to the world, and if so can part of God's nature still be conceived as "unchanging"? Here Hartshorne leans heavily on Whitehead's distinction between the primordial and the consequent nature of God. If you can see God as including two sides, the issue can be reconciled. Of course, time will be introduced into the divine nature, but this leads to a

God thought of as the self-identity of process (p. 269), an idea which brings us close to Hegel's Absolute. God becomes "the eternal and omnipresent unity of space-time" (pp. 273–274), and this places his nature in very close proximity to the natural process as an ingredient. This "saves" God for us. That is, it does so as long as we are able to see the natural process as representing the divine.

Following Bergson and Peirce, Hartshorne wants to make time a central category, whereas earlier theologians sought to protect God from this. Of course, this reversal is not quite as dramatic as it seems, since it all depends on the metaphysical principles selected and involved. Time originally meant (e. g., for Plato and Aristotle) incompleteness, change, lack of control, and possible loss, all of which were considered less than perfect. Hartshorne's view of time, on the other hand, takes it as the way "in which things can have both necessity and freedom in relation to each other" (p. 286). A greater value is now given to freedom, so that if time is what allows these to go together, then it really ought to be linked with "good" attributes.

Traditionally, too, God's omniscience was jealously protected, since his ability to know all things simultaneously was connected with his power to create and to control. Hartshorne does not see why God should observe all moments of time past, present, and future as one implicative whole (p. 287), since future moments do not exist. Being indeterminate, they cannot be known, and since freedom now is a primary value, this indeterminacy is no longer bad but good—even where God is concerned. Moreover, Hartshorne is willing to follow Berdyaev and introduce the tragedy of unfulfilled desire into God (p. 294). God "suffers" and existence for him is "tragic." To hold that freedom is the primary goal for men seems to require that God's eternality be denied. A certain element of freedom and disorder, of surprise and novelty, becomes a principal value just as much as repetition and predictability.

Hartshorne's desire is to find a way to join attributes often regarded as incompatible. The Hegelian influence of a dialectic which reconciles opposites must be operative here. "Eternity is the element of integrity in the ever expanding variety which is time" (p. 350). Of course, Plato's notion of participation allowed what was eternal to be present in time, and the theological notion of the Holy Spirit was meant to represent the presence in human existence of a God whose nature is not like ours. The difference lies in Hartshorne's attempt to unite the two, and like Whitehead he admits that he ends up with two natures of God. It is easy to talk about either the primordial or the consequent nature of God separately. The difficulty is to see how they are united in one being.

In his Terry Lectures, Hartshorne tries again to show how these two apparently opposing sides can form one being. He uses the term "supremely-relative."[4] Somehow he thinks that the relative or changeable aspect of God can include within itself the nonrelative, immutable, independent, or absolute side of divinity. He maintains that contrary determinations can be in the same entity if there is a distinction of aspects, and he is forced to attempt this separation because a personal God is one who has social relations and hence is relative. God orders the world by taking into his own life all currents of feeling in existence (p. xv). He works with and in it.

Many theologians (e. g., Augustine and Aquinas) argue from God's necessity to the fact that we must think of the world as determined in all its aspects. Hartshorne is convinced of the presence of contingency in the world's process and sees that he must argue backward to find an aspect of nonnecessity in God's nature too (p. 14). God's perfection originally was thought to require his necessity, but Hartshorne wants to argue that a God who is both the perfect and the imperfect is superior to a being who is perfect alone (p. 19). This perhaps is his most crucial assumption, which if accepted brings God out as the "self-surpassing surpasser of all" (p. 20). He surpasses himself in a subsequent state. It is God's social character that demands this.

God is not beyond our influence. His perfection of immutability is reversed. "He who is most adequately influenced by all may most appropriately exert influence upon all" (p. 50). Thus every decision in our minds casts a vote which must be taken account of and will produce effects in the divine decisions (p. 51). Hartshorne rightly labels this "the metaphysics of democracy" (p. 50), and it surely takes an optimistic view of the general good intentions and actions of men to see this as an asset in divinity. An actual divine knowing cannot be exclusive of relations (p. 75). It is the notion of the "wholly absolute" that Hartshorne opposes; but it is a question how many traditional theologians have in fact isolated God from contact in such extreme fashion.

Hartshorne spots the central issue and admits with Bergson that the only way to restrain God's determining foreknowledge is to make time a central category and say that time is creation (p. 84). Events can exist neither eternally nor at all times but only from and after the time of their creation or occurrence. This idea places genuine novelty both at the heart of things and in God, and it makes future knowledge always imperfect, a restriction not even God should now want to overcome. God is as truly contingent and as capable of accretions as are creatures, and this fact represents freedom for both of them (p. 89). Time has a directional flow or irreversibility which cannot be overcome (p. 97). Indeed, for freedom's sake, we should not want to overcome it.

A full description of God, on this view, entails every genuine description applicable to the actual universe (p. 109). God and the world are mutually interlocked in their nature. Either God must be brought into time or human freedom is impossible—this is the assumption. God becomes partially man-dependent. "In knowing any actual thing, God himself is related and relativized with respect to that thing" (p. 122). The existence of any entity consists in its contribution to the divine awareness. "We influence God by our experiences but do not thereby deprive him of freedom in his response to us. . . . The radical difference between God and men implies that our influence upon him is slight, while his influence upon us is predominant" (p. 141).

When Hartshorne states that "it is by molding himself that God molds us" (p. 142), it becomes clear that the setting for this doctrine is a fairly enthusiastic estimate of the various processes of nature and of man's interaction with them. One can see God as his senior partner in this program—if your estimate of the general human scene is on the whole positive and optimistic. However, if we become romantics who are disillusioned about the progress of mankind and about nature's kindness, then God will disappear as the process seems less than directly divine. Although Hartshorne writes in the post–World War II years, he still reflects a classic

American optimism over our ability to use the benefits of nature for all. But when nature and the future seem less cooperative and more threatening, as they surely do now, the hand of Hartshorne's God in the process is bound to become less visible.

Through freedom, Hartshorne gives man a role in determining the content of the divine knowledge (p. 146). To see this as a good thing requires that we view man's achievements as on the whole constructive. If we celebrate man's progress and evolution, God gains by being subject to this partial control. But what if our actions give God undesirable content for his knowledge? Hartshorne allows for that option. It is just that the tone of his writing clearly indicates his confidence and optimism over man's deserving right to cooperate with God. It is clear that Hartshorne's God does not feel the necessity to intervene dramatically, nor does he seem to fear that man's power may run amuck and need radical correction or alteration. Hartshorne's God rests content with the progress of evolution as it is coming about with man's cooperation.

C. The Reconstruction of Christian Concepts

The issue we inherit from Charles Hartshorne is this: What happens if the process should go radically wrong? Do we have, or do we need, a God sufficiently disengaged from the world so that he can escape its losses and perhaps even have the power to intervene to restore them? The issue is not at all whether Hartshorne's God is possible. The question is what kind of role God is called upon to play and what powers and independence he might need in order to be successful. Hartshorne, as a philosopher and metaphysician, has focused his attention on the nature of God. Next the question becomes one of determining the compatibility of this God when placed within a specifically Christian framework of assertions. It is this attempt that is made by each of the three theologians considered in this section.

What is the appeal of the Whiteheadian God to this group of theologians, such that they turn to Whitehead for their theological base? As indicated before, Whitehead is associated with logic, mathematics, and science. Yet he is not a reductionist. He has a God, but a "naturalistic" one to which a modern mind can easily accommodate. This God does not transcend the process; he is a part of it. Thus, although it is hard to account for how the evil and destruction present in the system might be dealt with or countered, the problem of how a transcendent God created such an imperfect world is sidestepped. God did not create from outside. He works from within under conditions no less specified for him than for us, and yet—happy thought—he is "on our side."

In appraising these accounts, two points are crucial: (1) the adequacy of the account of evil, and (2) our ability to accept a "modern" framework vs. the question of whether or not we have now passed into the postmodern age. Evil or destruction—the horror over the waste of the system—is in one sense accounted for by limiting God's powers in such a way that he neither elects nor can prevent all such loss. This means, however, that God's ability to alter the system substantially at some future point is made nearly impossible. Radically new beginnings or transformations are almost ruled out. This brings us to the second question. Must we limit ourselves to the assumptions of the modern world, which reject any God who transcends nature? Or have we really passed into a postmodern age, where reason is not the absolute standard and where the transcendence of nature is opened up again as a possibility? The notion of a radical end and a transformation of time perhaps is no longer out of the question.

Whitehead's *Science and the Modern World* is one classic text for this issue. Here he traces the rise of modern science and the lure of mathematics as a standard of thought. In many ways, Whitehead represents a return to classical Greek notions. He states, for example, that no metaphysics can get much beyond Aristotle's use of the unmoved mover who assures completion to the analysis.[5] Aristotle required God as a prime mover; Whitehead needs him as "the Principle of Concretion" (p. 250).

Neither of these Gods transcends nature; both are principles within the process. Whitehead does not think a reason can be given for why God imposes just the limitation he does (p. 257). Theology can only describe his activity; it cannot explain why he acts in one way rather than in some other. Thus the question we are left with is whether we must accept such a limitation on inquiry into the divine or whether, as postmoderns, we need no longer accept "nature" as a given.

Daniel Day Williams is probably the leading theologian to come out of Chicago who follows the process thought of Whitehead and, more directly, Hartshorne. Love is a central Christian concept, and it is interesting to see how Williams relates this to the nature of God. He reports a revolution as having taken place, such that evolution and development must be incorporated in a Christian doctrine of God.[6] The eternal God is involved in the world's becoming.

"Love is spirit taking form in history" (p. 3), he says, in words reminiscent of Hegel. Such love has communion in freedom as its goal, but God's love involves his participation in the history of his creatures. Williams opposes Augustine's treatment of human love as reflecting the love of God and wants to relate it instead to a God "conceived in dynamic temporal terms" (p. 9). God must respond to what happens in the world.

If, as Williams asserts, "love is what God's spirit is in his action in history" (p. 11), the problem is that the assessment of God is tied to our positive evaluation of the favorable trend of history. We can agree with Williams that "we need a new metaphysical vision which embodies the conception of God as living, creative and responsive to his world" (p. 17), but this still leaves open the question of whether God moves only within the process or may also transcend it. Love has a capacity to take a variety of forms, and if so we cannot grasp God's love under a single form (p. 18). For instance, love and wrath are woven together in the divine character, a fact which makes God's love never simple. It can become suffering love in order to deal with the suffering of the world (p. 32). Love makes itself manifest in the form of personal communion in the midst of suffering.

Williams sees the Augustinian notion of love as involving a turning away from the world, and he favors a Franciscan interpretation in which "love sets itself free by renouncing the kinds of obligations which would prevent its direct exercise" (p. 69). Humility is essential to love, as opposed to the life of the intellect, since learning leads easily to pride. Williams introduces the Whiteheadian concept of a God within process and suggests that this perspective can only deal with evil by not making God the sole cause of every happening (p. 110). Other factors exercise freedom and thus share responsibility. Since there is no love without suffering, a God of love must be capable of change. The being of God must reflect the structures needed to describe love: individuality, freedom, action and suffering, causality, and impartiality (p. 123). Therefore a creative, temporal, and relational aspect is required in God's nature. As a consequence, however, God's power is restricted. He does not have absolute omnipotence (p. 137). Moreover, we cannot even attempt to answer the riddle of why things are as they are.

As far as the Incarnation is concerned, any interpretation must involve a faith that love "has created a new body for its life in the world" (p. 169). This ties us to a certain optimism about the world's progress. We should see all history in a new way (p. 191), but the issue is whether history, in point of fact, displays such newness, or whether only some radical alteration in the future can rescue it from a destructive course. Can such love now release "a new possibility in the self which is created for communion" (p. 210), as Williams suggests, or is the work of love frustrated as long as the present structure remains unbroken? What is it that such a God can accomplish, and does the natural order require a more upsetting transformation which could only break in from outside its limits?

John B. Cobb, Jr., and Shubert Ogden have in a variety of ways developed additional lines of "process theology." Cobb dedicates his *Christian Natural Theology* to Charles Hartshorne and bases it on Whitehead's philosophy. Cobb thinks that Whitehead provides a framework that can help to restore "God" to meaningful discourse in contemporary life.[7] Whitehead's scheme is naturalistic at its base, but Cobb finds that it offers many religious possibilities. Man does, for example, have a soul (p. 47). However, it is subject to the same conditions as all other natural entities. This will not allow us to make a very sharp distinction between animals and men, and Cobb admits that Whitehead's theory does "pose problems for any doctrine of life after death" (p. 71).

Cobb thinks that freedom is one of Whitehead's fundamental

metaphysical categories. It must dominate any description of God (or man). Using this base, "beauty" tends to be of more interest than goodness (p. 108). This is understandable in a naturalistic view, which must celebrate nature if it is to be religious in outlook. Whitehead's God, Cobb sees, is the principle of limitation or concretion (p. 142). God is an actual entity—like others in the natural world but also, Cobb emphasizes, of a very special type (p. 147). However, the underlying substantial activity in the process of nature is not traced exclusively to God but called "creativity" (p. 149). God organizes the process. The "initial aim" of each occasion is derived from God (p. 154), and he orders the eternal objects. The "timeless envisagement of possibilities constitutes God's primordial nature" and one of his major activities (p. 155).

As with all actual entities, Cobb points out, Whitehead's God also has an aim at intensity of feeling, which is related more to his consequent nature, or physical role. Every achievement of value is preserved everlastingly in God's consequent nature, and it is the sense of the preservation of values in God's memory that constitutes his chief religious importance (p. 162)—and man's only real possibility for immortality. Cobb acknowledges that the primary philosophical argument for God in Whitehead's thought is traditional: the natural universe requires a ground for its order (p. 169). The crucial difference, however, is that process is introduced into God, since his consequent nature is affected by what occurs in the world. "His experience grows by addition to the past, but loses nothing" (p. 191).

One corollary of these themes is to deny that God has sole responsibility for what happens (p. 205). The role of the creator is, like Plato's demiurge, to provide form for a reality given to him. Thus Cobb notes that Whitehead has to reject Heidegger's radical question of why there is something rather than nothing at all (p. 208). The natural framework must be assumed and taken for granted; the process is everlasting.

A beginning or a radical end to time is not conceivable within this theory. "God" becomes the urge to adventure and the quest for beauty within the world as given (p. 217). Values are worth achieving, whatever life's temporal outcome, because they are preserved (remembered) in God's consequent nature (p. 219). God is our great companion—a fellow sufferer who understands (p. 221). But the issue turns out to be whether such a vision is adequate to support religious hopes and sufficient to justify the balance of evils and goods in life.

Cobb interprets Whitehead's God as one whose guidance is often thwarted and whose purposes are frequently ineffective. Yet this God is not fully defeated, because he can adjust his aim so that new possibilities of achievement always lie ahead (p. 251). To accept this interpretation of God, however, once again requires a relatively optimistic outlook regarding progress in nature and the possibilities for improvement. A pessimistic view of history's ability to provide success renders such a God impotent. He does not have the option to change the outcome by radically revolutionizing the structure itself.

Of course, Whitehead's work is never organized primarily around the doctrine of God, whereas a theologian's should be. This means that the natural limitations placed on God become much more pronounced when he is transplanted to a predominantly theological context. The question is whether Whitehead's God—even as interpreted by Cobb—can support Christian claims or demands their revision in order to scale them down to fit his more limited role in nature.

A theological view is defined by its main strengths—by what its assumptions allow it best to account for—but equally by what it can explain least well. This is not to say that any perspective is unacceptable because it has weak elements. That would be to assume that some theological system was possible which was equally strong in every aspect and free from defects. This never seems to be the case. Instead, we are forced to choose between various interpretations according to their merits and inadequacies and the religious stress of the time. Whitehead and the process theology that results from his thought meet certain needs and moods quite well. The issue is whether new religious desires have appeared and whether another view might be stronger at the places where Whitehead's naturalism is most vulnerable.

Shubert M. Ogden is also a "process" theologian, although other influences appear to be equally strong (e. g., Bultmann) in the development of his thought. When any important new mode of theology develops, it is seldom ever purely represented except by its originator. In fact, one of the tests of the fruitfulness of a new theoretical line is that it can enter into and be used in combination with other views, so that it produces solutions and insights for a greater range of difficult problems. Ogden is convinced that "the reality of God has now become a central theological concern."[8] He attributes part of the rise of this problem to man's increasing secularization and his acceptance of a scientific picture of the world, all of which excludes most traditional notions of God as now unacceptable.

Ogden is convinced that we have failed to appreciate the emergence of a "neo-classical alternative" (p. 20) to classical metaphysics, which if adopted might relieve our problem. The question is, he thinks, whether our common secular experience offers us good ground today to discover the reality of God. He is not content to have belief held by a few. It must be valid for all. "Unless God is somehow real for every man, he is not genuinely real for any man" (p. 22). Thus Ogden shares the universalism of modern thought, the hope that we should be able to find a common denominator in experience which then can unite us in our conclusions—if experience is properly analyzed. As in Whitehead's theory, Ogden's God serves the purpose of being an objective ground in reality which gives us an "ineradicable confidence in the final worth of existence" (p. 37). Faith in God becomes "the necessary condition of our existence as selves" (p. 43).

If we follow Whitehead and Hartshorne, Ogden is convinced that "this new philosophy enables us so to conceive the reality of God that we may respect all that is legitimate in modern secularity, while also fully respecting the distinctive claims of Christian faith itself" (pp. 56–57). The issue, of course, is not this assertion but the appraisal of how Christian doctrines emerge from such reinterpretations. Further, perhaps the basic concept centers in his notion that the accepted norm is conformity to "modern secularity." Here Ogden joins modern philosophy in its assumptions that only what is acceptable universally, in theory at least, can be valid for any rational man. Where theology is concerned, this assumption may be the main issue up for our debate. Can the theologian not stand apart from the assumptions of his day?

God is to be understood as continually in the process of self-creation (p. 59). "He is universally immanent in both actuality and possibility" (p. 124). Following Heidegger, Ogden affirms God's temporality as "essentially related to a world of others in whose being he actively participates" (p. 150). Given this framework, it is easy to conceive of God as "the eminent *effect* of all things" (p. 223). Thus we reach his assertion of the "new notion of God," a celebration of its release from classical molds, and the confidence that it provides a more adequate interpretation of Christian doctrine. Our only problem at this point is that the task of a detailed, systematic restatement of theology remains to be done. The picture of God that follows Whitehead's lead is clear. Its modern and naturalistic assumptions are obvious. The success of its recasting of Christian doctrine is still to be tested.

D. The New Metaphysical Naturalism

As stated at the beginning of this chapter, the idea of God remained quite static during the excitement of the impact of the social gospel. With the acceptance of process philosophy, the theological revolution is on its way. Now the situation is reversed, and the focus is on metaphysics and the notion of God, although the implementation of the reform of Christian concepts remains to be carried out fully. The radical theologians (see Chapter VII) will also criticize traditional notions of God. They will move further, however, and find the compromise of process thought unacceptable. The issue then becomes how far the revolution extends. That is, have some of the assumptions which once made God unacceptable themselves in turn fallen under challenge, so that the religious situation itself has been revolutionized? This is a question for Chapter IX.

Henry Nelson Wieman in one way stands apart from the movement of process theology, and yet the program of theological reform he proposes has many similarities, even though he is not a follower of Whitehead. In *Man's Ultimate Commitment* he begins by saying that "creativity is the central theme of this book."[9] This, of course, is the same notion that Whitehead wants to stress, and it is a key to the reconception of the natural order in more optimistic terms. The result is to emphasize the openness of possibilities to man, if only he will exercise his freedom. The creative transformation of the individual in the wholeness of his being—this is Wieman's grand aim. Creativity expands the range of what the individual can know, evaluate, and control (p. 4).

Religion asks how man can be transformed so as to save him from the depths of evil and bring him to the greatest good (p. 10). How must man live to realize his own potentialities? What ultimate commitment will deliver him from a false and superficial level of life? The word "God" means only whatever operates to save man from evil and brings him to the greater good (p. 12). "This evil is the inner conflict by which the self is divided into parts which war against one another" (p. 13). Yet the religious problem is that men cannot always free themselves from every inner resistance and move to the commitment which would deliver them from the evil of inner conflict, meaninglessness, guilt, or loneliness.

"Creative interchange" is the answer Wieman proposes as the enabling change, and it takes place only between individuals. "The religion of creativity" (p. 20) releases the individual from conformity and commits him to what creates his own original experience in depth and fullness and vividness of quality. Obviously, this is a theology which uses psychological categories as its primary means of interpretation. "Revelation" means the "process of human life undergoing transformation in such a way that it saves man from evil and endows him with the greatest good" (p. 28). God interpreted in such terms is not primarily supernatural. Yet Wieman's "creative communication" is somewhat like God as traditionally conceived, since it (not really "he") provides peace, courage, consolation, and renewal of mind (p. 32). Commitment to creativity, which calls for religious faith, can save us from the dangers that threaten us today (p. 35).

Wieman identifies himself with "naturalism" and thus belongs with the group of theologians considered in this chapter, whether Whitehead-inspired or not. "There is," he asserts, "nothing in reality accessible to the human mind more basic than events and their qualities and relations."[10] We ought to have no recourse to any transcendental grounds, orders, causes, or purposes. Here, in fact, he is more rigidly naturalistic in his assumptions than Whitehead, who can be said to allow for some transcendental aspects. Wieman ignores the traditional Christian affirmation of a God who resides beyond history. "The only creative God we recognize is the creative event itself" (p. 7). The transcendental must be ignored, except as an imaginative construction of the human mind. What religion now means is to "look at several common ways of seeking the increase of human good" (p. 9).

Our faith is pinned on evolution and on the conviction that the future can by human effort be substantially transformed and improved over the past. "The hope of man lies in cumulative development through history" (p. 11). We must discover a universal principle for choosing our own good and pursue this in such a way that it will be constructive and not destructive of the unique good of other persons. Evil becomes anything that "drains the precious and limited supply of energy for life" (p. 107). Our hope is pinned on man's ability to bring more and more of subhuman nature and the process of history under his control, while not being overwhelmed by the scope of the task. This is a romantic and challenging and optimistic view of the great possibilities open to man if he uses his creative powers properly. This is our religion and this is our God.

Paul Weiss was actually Whitehead's student at Harvard, but he has followed the latter's primary metaphysical thrust rather than giving his ideas a strict theological development. Actually, this is truer to the Whiteheadian tradition, which makes room for a religious dimension in a naturalistic metaphysics but does not legitimatize a pure theological extension. Weiss is in that sense religious but not theological. His metaphysics gives meaning to "religious values," but it does not make a formal worshiper out of him, nor will it lend much support to institutional churches. Religion can be carried on institutionally, but it should emphasize an aesthetic dimension. It will be, essentially if not wholly, a human activity with "God" as the name for an important aspect of such a life at its highest creativity.

Man has a basic need to be perfected, and he produces sacramental works in the process, "art in the service of religion."[11] There are multiple human needs which must be taken care of before God can be faced. In that sense, God ought not to be man's first concern. Since creativity is our goal, and since art "expresses man at his most creative" (p. 5), art should refuse to be subordinated to religion.

In fact, given these premises, it appears that art is man's most basic activity, not religion. Indeed, what will awaken thought or interest in God may more likely be art than something religious (p. 14). Religious art, however, embodies and points to "Existence" as affected by God. "We struggle with that Existence in many ways" (p. 23), in the course of which art and religion become coordinate and interlocking modes of approach (p. 96).

When Weiss considers God directly, he denies that we can discover what God is by "adding the assertions of the various religions to one another."[12] Rather, we discover God by a natural process. He is "an undifferentiated part of an ultra-natural domain of which we become aware" when we look beyond the conventional world in which we daily live (p. 5). Yet he is a transcendent as well as immanent being, one with whom we can also make contact by the production of an adequate idea. We are concerned with God in privacy and in community, but a man is religious "only if he lives in terms of a final, loving, just (that is divine) assessment of all there is" (p. 9). "The idea of God is the idea of one who is the perfect unity of all meaning and value" (p. 84). "We forge an idea of God for ourselves" (p. 94).

Like Whitehead, Weiss refuses to reduce everything to the lowest common denominator of experience. There are new and untapped forms of experience, and religion belongs to this dimension, perhaps best labeled the "ultra–natural." (See his Chapter I.) Nature need not be hostile. "The religious affirmation that there is a God is one with the affirmation that all beings are loved for what they are, by a single, constant lover" (p. 240). A man is religious only if he accepts God as his lover, Weiss adds. Thus it is clear that religion's function and belief in God are both tied to one's celebration of the richness of nature's potential for human creation. Should one's estimate of man or of nature's friendliness change, God could not be reached as quite so romantic a figure.

In his major metaphysical work, Weiss takes up the proofs for God's existence,[13] based on a social theory of being ("each thing is directed towards and acts in terms of all the rest" [p. 9]). Yet "God" is only one of four distinct realities (Actuality, Ideality, Existence, and God [p. 13]), and again we find a naturalism not unlike that of Plato or Aristotle. This gives God his function in nature, as one among other basic principles, but there is no theological urge to derive all being with reference to one center. God has his place. He is that being who "makes a unity of what otherwise would be a detached set of occurrences" (p. 15). Actualities, the Ideal, and Existence each have a role to play; "God strives to make unity present everywhere" (p. 16). This is his contribution. He is not supreme. "Each mode of being needs the others to enable it to be itself" (p. 17).

"There are four co-ordinate, irreducible modes of being" (p. 277), and each mode of being needs the others, God included. Thus the process of the world itself offers testimony to the existence of such a God. Like Aristotle's unmoved mover, God is needed to explain the operation of natural processes. God does not create all out of nothing. New things occur, but "there is no coming to be of Ideality, Existence, or Actuality" (p. 345).

God has needs of his own which are "satisfied through the aid of other beings" (p. 349). We are dependent on him for certain functions, but it is a mutual interdependence. "As one only of the modes of being, God is inevitably limited by, and needs the help of the others" (p. 538). God makes a difference to what else exists, but his control must operate by cooperation.

Metaphysically speaking, all seven men considered in this chapter as process theologians are genuinely similar in their outlook. They would be proud of the fact that they do locate a God and that they do so only as one important principle in the explanation of the creativity latent in the natural process. They offer a unique contribution to American thought, although it shares its kinship with all naturalism since Lucretius. It is not insignificant that its great initial flowering in America comes prior to 1960. In this early portion of the twentieth century we celebrated man and our belief that at last he had unlocked—or can unlock—nature's true potential. In spite of two world wars, this philosophical outlook showed no dimming of its ardor or its confidence in man's ability to use God's assistance to make life more fruitful.

It is interesting to consider, as the next chapter explains, that the second half of the twentieth century witnesses the burst of "death of God" theology, a doctrine far less optimistic in its assessment of God's role. To say this is not to suggest that we should rule out process thought, but it is to hint that the effectiveness of process metaphysics is geared to the modern world's confidence in reason and its celebration of human potentiality. If our assessment of nature's creative side becomes dimmed, the world itself does not seem to display so divine a power working within it for our benefit. When existence appears hostile and man is a sometime devil, it is harder to discern God within the process, if that is where he must be discovered. A naturalistic theology, to be successful, requires us to find life inherently religious. If we do not, God must be located independently from the process or lost from sight.

NOTES

1. See A. N. Whitehead, *Religion in the Making* (New York: Macmillan Company, 1926).

2. See A. N. Whitehead, *Process and Reality* (New York: Social Science Bookstore, 1941).

3. See Charles Hartshorne, *Man's Vision of God* (New York: Harper & Brothers, 1941).

4. Charles Hartshorne, *The Divine Relativity* (New Haven: Yale University Press, 1948), p. vii.

5. See A. N. Whitehead, *Science and the Modern World* (New York: Macmillan Company, 1925), pp. 249–250.

6. Daniel Day Williams, *The Spirit and the Forms of Love* (New York: Harper & Row, 1968), p. vii.

7. John B. Cobb, Jr., *A Christian Natural Theology* (Philadelphia: Westminster Press, 1965), pp. 14–15.

8. Shubert M. Ogden, *The Reality of God* (New York: Harper & Row, 1966), p. 2.

9. Henry Nelson Wieman, *Man's Ultimate Commitment* (Carbondale, Ill.: Southern Illinois University Press, 1958), p. 3.

10. Henry Nelson Wieman, *The Source of Human Good* (Carbondale, Ill.: Southern Illinois University Press, 1946), p. 6.

11. Paul Weiss, *Religion and Art* (Milwaukee: Marquette University Press, 1963), p. 1.

12. Paul Weiss, *The God We Seek* (Carbondale, Ill.: Southern Illinois University Press, 1964), p. 5.

13. See Paul Weiss, *Modes of Being* (Carbondale, Ill.: Southern Illinois University Press, 1958).

VII

THE DEATH OF GOD
IN AMERICAN THEOLOGY

A. Radical Theology and the Search for Identity

The Pledge of Allegiance says that we are "one nation under God, indivisible, with liberty and justice for all." In the 1960's most Americans came to realize that this assertion is not a statement of fact, and many decided that it might be nothing more than an impossible dream. No religious consensus emerged in this nation in the decade just closed, and certainly unity was not its most distinctive characteristic. This was a period increasingly marked by divisions, demonstrations, confrontations, and violence. The issues between the people focused primarily on the fact that liberty and justice do not seem to be "for all." The outlook in the last half of the sixties was more gloomy than in the first. In fact, the early years contained some optimistic moments in which we seemed to move toward both unity and a significant extension of freedom and justice.

The election of John F. Kennedy to the presidency, for example, pointed toward growing trust and understanding between Catholics and Protestants. In addition, when Kennedy asked us to think less about what our country could do for us and more about what we could do for our country, many Americans responded enthusiastically. The mood of American youth, in particular, shifted in the early years of the sixties. The apathy of the "beat generation" was out, and in its place a new concern for political life and public service was born. The Peace Corps and the Civil Rights Movement were hopeful signs.

The space program brought the country together too, since everyone took pride in the first steps toward the moon. The aerospace industry bolstered the economy and testified to our technological superiority over Russia. On the international scene, many were still concerned about the spread of Communist control, but military activity was confined mainly to the arms race. The American role in Vietnam was at first largely "advisory." In short, we seemed to be a nation that had found new youth and energy; many sensed that the American dream might come true after all.

Far from becoming a reality, however, the dream had in many ways turned into a nightmare by the end of the sixties. The assassination of John F. Kennedy on November 22, 1963 was one symbol of the turning point downhill. For a moment the country stood together in grief, but that unity dissipated rapidly in the events of the years ahead. Our role in Vietnam escalated into a full-scale conflict, one which is likely to scar the American soul more deeply than any event since the Civil War. When the Civil Rights Movement lost Martin Luther King, Jr. to an assassin's gun in Memphis on April 4, 1968 the breach between whites and blacks was intensified. The concern and alienation of the college generation were acted out in the sights, smells, and vibrations of the "love-in." Strikes, gunfire, and bombs followed close behind.

The nation began to feel the "generation gap," and the "credibility gap" became a part of everyday experience. Moreover, when the depth of domestic problems became clear, especially the growing threat of environmental pollution, even the space program lost its charm. Most Americans watched the television coverage of the lunar landing of Apollo 11 on July 20, 1969, but many also wondered whether sending men to the moon at the expense of deterioration of our environment and human relations was the best use of resources. In a word, the latter half of the sixties was a "dark night" for the American soul, and that emptiness has not yet been lived through. Many of our national "trips" have been bad ones lately, and the result is disorientation and a new depth of uncertainty.

It is not so strange, then, that also in the sixties some American theologians began to tell us that God is dead. This was not news to the many Americans who were already thoroughly secularized, but still "radical theology" produced its share of headlines. Just because religious concerns have always been influential in American public life, to have theologians proclaim God's death sparked interest and concern.

The theological interpretation and development of the concept that "God is dead" both clarify and contribute to the American crisis of identity. Radical theology is helpful because it highlights varied moods that permeate the present and the recent past. At the same time, these theological efforts threaten American identity by undermining the hope that human existence will not ultimately be swallowed up in negation and death. We shall examine these claims by exploring the work of four contemporary theologians: William Hamilton, Paul van Buren, Thomas J. J. Altizer, and Richard L. Rubenstein. These men are the most influential radical theologians in America today. Although there are many differences between them—Rubenstein, for example, is a Jew, while the others are Protestant Christians—several general concerns link them together.

Each of these men has been working through his own dilemma with respect to what he can and should believe and do as a theologian. This crisis was brought on because the once-powerful religious traditions in which they were trained and have worked would no longer fit or speak meaningfully to their personal experience. These traditions share, in particular, an affirmation of the transcendence, omnipotence, and holiness of God. This theological outlook entails, moreover, the assertion that the world is God's loving creation, but that its culture is under his judgment. A man's meaning and glory are found in his faith in, and experience of, the love of God, and his task is to live in conformity to the will of God. For the Christian, the love and will of God are revealed in Jesus Christ. For the Jew, they are made known in God's covenant with Abraham, Moses, and the Israelite people as grounded in the Law. God transcends time and history, and yet he is active in them. His will is sovereign and good, and the shape of history ultimately reflects his loving control.

What leads to the credibility gap between this traditional theological perspective and the experience of the radical theologians? Two factors stand out. First, there are seemingly insurmountable problems and confusions which arise when one tries to reconcile the traditional concept of God with contemporary experience. For example, the strong emphasis on God's transcendence and sovereignty appears at once to remove God from us—except insofar as he chooses to reveal himself—and yet leaves him in control over us. On the one hand, God's fixed nature threatens the reality of our freedom, creativity, and responsibility. Yet this reality, from our perspective, is simply undeniable.

On the other hand, the claim that God's love and will are, in fact, revealed within history gets little corroboration in the facts of contemporary life. Existence is too ambiguous and fragmentary, too full of evil to allow us to discern God very clearly there. Furthermore, if God's judgment occurs anywhere in history, it appears to take on horrible and needlessly wasteful forms of punishment that leave him unworthy of worship. To think of man's plight as the result of God's conscious decision down to the smallest detail leaves men with a sense of tyranny to which rebellion or indifference, not obedient faith, is the most honest response. In a word, contemporary man's thirst for freedom and his immediate experience of ambiguity, evil, and suffering conflict with, and often seem victorious over, faith in the traditional God. One result of this crunch is the claim that God is dead.

Most Americans do not worry about the problems just noted. In fact, no religious or theological concern appears to have much influence on our daily life. Thus the second crucial factor stems from the conviction that men simply find it less and less necessary and significant to speak and think of God at all. Their interest and commitments are directed primarily toward this present world, and that involves little reference to God. Human life has been naturalized and secularized. To speak of the nation as "under God" does not stir many. Even church members often find it difficult to speak of God and to pray or worship in meaningful ways.

A majority find their meaning and their glory, not in God's love, but in the challenges of business, politics, technology, and education, in the pursuit of leisure activities, and in expressions of human concerns. Man sees his task no longer as faithful obedience to the will of God, but simply in the human terms of cultivating and using his talents in the effort to be successful and perhaps to make life more humane. References to God or faith appear to have little influence on these outlooks. Citizens of the secular city seem neither to care about nor to feel much real need for God. If you are a theologian observing and living through experiences such as these, it is not surprising, then, that the provocative and richly ambiguous concept that God is dead presents itself as an idea worth exploring in depth.

Radical theology is a form of self-interrogation. As a result, the writing of these theologians often has a tentative and auto-biographical quality. But they do not take themselves as isolated figures who stand alone in a state of religious crisis. Although each of them identifies strongly with the secular city, each still finds it meaningful to remain connected in some positive way with his religious heritage. On the likelihood that other men share their feelings, this group continues constructive theological work.

Ultimately, then, they do not see themselves as opponents of religious life and tradition. They are interpreters of human experience who aid other secular men in their search for both meaning and identity. They do this by preserving and developing the viable components of religious traditions so that they can still move the human spirit. Although these theologians have much of their careers ahead of them, their work has already had an impact on contemporary theology and life. Yet in what ways is *radical* theology *American* theology?

B. William Hamilton and the New Essence of Christianity

William Hamilton was one of the first American theologians to speak of the death of God. His work has less depth of theological insight than that of the other radical theologians, but his efforts do give focus to some interesting problems. Hamilton wants to restate the core of the Christian faith for secular men who still seek identity as Christians. The context in which this is to be done, however, suggests that the assertions one can make about the essence of Christianity must be tentative and fragmentary. Secular man is characterized more by doubt than by firm religious faith. Theological systems, and the traditional (neo-orthodox) concept of God in particular, no longer speak clearly to him. "We are reduced to fragments, partial vision, broken speech, not because of the unbelieving world 'out there,' but precisely because that unbelieving world has come to rest within ourselves."[1]

If a single dimension of experience stands out as the cause of religious uncertainty and the breakdown of neo-orthodox theology, it is the problem of suffering. The degree of suffering that exists in this world seems incompatible with the traditional image of a sovereign and omnipotent God of love. God appears to be indifferent to suffering or impotent to restructure our existence in order to curtail it. Thus neither nature nor human experience points clearly to the presence of the traditional God. To be a Christian entails standing without God—weak, unprotected, and frightened.

This was Hamilton's initial assessment of the relationship between man and God in the world of the early sixties. He pictured the Christian man as living in the absence of God, feeling the indifference or impotence of God, but waiting with the hope that a renewed experience and conviction of God's power and love might lie ahead. In the interim, however, a Christian could find meaning and support for his hope through identification with Jesus.

Drawing heavily on the work of Dietrich Bonhoeffer, the German theologian accused of sharing in the plot to kill Hitler and who was subsequently executed by the Nazis, Hamilton emphasized the idea that Jesus is the "man for others." He is the one who serves and suffers for other men, working to redeem the world by self-giving love. The Christian man who lives in the time of God's absence is called to stand with Jesus and to give himself in humiliation, patience, and suffering for the sake of others. The essence of Christianity has always revolved around Jesus, but Hamilton speaks about the *new* essence, which interprets the Lordship of Jesus in terms of a call to identify with his suffering and servanthood.

Hamilton did not, however, rest content with this statement for long. His thought moved away from references to the absence of God and the tentative suggestion that God is "somehow dead" (p. 56) to a bolder assertion, and even to the celebration of the

death of God. An important step in this transition was his assertion that there has been a breakdown of the *religious a priori*. For
centuries theologians have maintained that man is by nature a being who needs a positive relationship to God in order to experience meaning and fulfillment. Whether men acknowledge it or not,
the tradition runs, they cannot really get along without God, and
their hearts are restless until they rest in God. Contemporary men,
however, have now come of age. We can "make it" without him.
He is no longer needed either to fulfill our needs or to solve our
problems. "Thus man cannot be said to need God at all; God is
not necessary to man."[2] Even if religious faith is missing, man has
not robbed himself of anything absolutely essential to authentic
existence.

It is easier to talk about the death of God when you are convinced that men have no essential need of such a transcendent being. Having disposed of the religious a priori, Hamilton can speak
more freely and radically about God's "death." The fragmentary
nature of his theology leaves the reader unclear about the details of
his most radical statments, but this much is on record: he believes
"that there once was a God to whom adoration, praise and trust
were appropriate, possible, and even necessary, but that now there
is no such God."[3] The death of God is an event—not merely an
event in human consciousness, but an actual end to God's existence from which there is no return.

Hamilton and Altizer wrote the above statement together, but
Altizer has gone on to develop a theology that explains how God
dies and what happens to him in the process of dying. To date,
Hamilton has not ventured into such metaphysical speculation.
His efforts have been channeled instead toward exploring the event
of God's death as it pertains to human consciousness. In particular, he sees his task as a Christian theologian to interpret the nature of a Christian life-style in a Godless world.

Two elements dominate this interpretation. One is the continued focus on Jesus as a model for authentic existence, and the
other is an emphasis on enthusiastic and optimistic participation
in the affairs of the world. Jesus still stands as the "man for others," whose love for the world leads him both to a life of service
and then to a willingness to suffer and die for men. The Christian

man is the one who assumes a similar relationship to his neighbors. However, like Jesus, he can do so only by entering fully into the joys, problems, and sorrows of worldly existence. He must give himself to the world in order to establish a community of hope and love.

The call to be a Christ to one's neighbor goes hand in hand with a spirit of optimism about what men can do to improve the quality of life. Moreover, this new optimism leads to a celebration of the death of God. The discovery that man does not need God, that he is dead for us, is itself reason for celebration—just because it is accompanied by the awareness that men themselves have the resources they need to make life worthwhile. No longer must we wait for a God who may never act or appear to us. We can shape the world to make existence humane and fulfilling on our own. Optimism about our human world is possible in a way that could not be achieved as long as men groped unsuccessfully for God.

Hamilton's optimism has become the most distinctive mark of his theology. Writing in 1966, he described his "worldly optimism" as a stance that "faces despair not with the conviction that out of it God can bring hope, but with the conviction that the human conditions that created it can be overcome, whether those conditions be poverty, discrimination, or mental illness. It faces death not with the hope for immortality, but with the human confidence that man may befriend death and live with it as a possibility always alongside."[4] In the same essay he asserted: "The sixties may well be the time for play, celebration, delight, and for hope. . . . Pessimism—political, theological, cultural—is coming to an end" (p. 164).

One way to assess Hamilton's contributions is to ask in what sense his theology is distinctively American—and in what sense his predictions have come true. The theme of the death of God in itself has not been a dominant note in American thought. It has its roots primarily in German thought, especially in that of Nietzsche. Furthermore, Hamilton's theological inspiration comes largely from Bonhoeffer, another German. However, he certainly sees his radical theology as American theology. The reason for this is that he thinks contemporary American culture provides the setting to match the proclamation of the death of God. "We are the most profane, the most banal, the most utterly worldly of places."[5] Realization of the death of God is an experience whose time has come in our American lives. Contemporary society reflects—even celebrates—the death of God. The theological task of clarifying this fact and its significance becomes, then, a uniquely American responsibility.

What response should be made to these claims? There can be little doubt that Hamilton has captured a part of our contemporary mood. This nation is not literally, and hardly even symbolically, "under God." For many God is dead. The far-reaching quality of such an experience calls for theological response, and Hamilton's interpretation stands as a possible, but not too helpful, option. Some Americans undoubtedly do live the life-style he describes, and others may opt for it in the future—but what does this lead to theologically?

Hamilton's romantic optimism will not ring true to most contemporary Americans. To be sure, we have usually been optimistic. The loss of this characteristic would rob us of a distinctive and vital quality. But Americans are also realistic and tough-minded, and we are becoming less optimistic. Hamilton's assessment of the sixties, therefore, cannot stand for many. We presently share widespread doubts about our ability to eliminate despair and its causes. If we do "befriend death," it is often an act of hopelessness in itself. This is not to say that dampened optimism is pushing us back toward God and religion. We are in the grips of the problem of evil and suffering, and if God exists he still seems publicly absent.

The "early" Hamilton speaks to us more clearly than the "later." In his optimistic enthusiasm, the "later" Hamilton glosses over the problem of evil, suffering, and negation. It is good to affirm the world, to live in it with enthusiasm and with a willingness to serve and suffer for others, but even after one does so, the negativities of existence still crack the human spirit. If this world is all there is, meaning can exist, but it will always be left in pieces. Celebrations may occur, but they will and should have a melancholy overtone. If despair is partly curtailed and if we face death calmly, hope is still frustrated.

Even if God is dead, men must still live with each other, and there is little reason to suppose that we will cease to act from greedy and selfish motives, or that we will no longer inflict pain and suffering on each other in massive doses. Nor is there much reason to think that many of us will stop sacrificing the future for present desires and goals. This is not to say that positive gains cannot be made. The quality of life can be improved, and there is no reason why some should not be devoted to high ideals. Yet, constructive change is likely to come very slowly, at great cost and subject to constant setbacks. In fact, it will be no surprise if existence remains a mixture of good and evil, one in which men create about as much despair as they alleviate. In such a world, Hamilton's optimism seems hollow, if not naïve.

These claims suggest the need to appraise his treatment of the religious a priori. Hamilton is right: It is not necessarily true that there is a "God-shaped blank within man."[6] But there *is* a *metaphysical blank* in human life, and it takes the form of unanswered questions about the meaning of existence in a world which is an ambiguous mixture of good and evil. Moreover, that blank might show itself to be God-shaped, if theologians could construct concepts of God which both meet the cold facts of our experience and yet speak to our hope that empty silence is not the only content of the blank we feel within ourselves when we reflect on life's significance.

Hamilton helps to underscore the fact that the neo-orthodox concept of God is not fully adequate to secular experience. On the other hand, his particular development of the proclamation that God is dead does not seem especially satisfying. Thus his work might lead to a new realization for numerous Americans that this still is a nation "under God." However, the God we are dealing with is likely to turn out to be quite different from the one we may expect or choose to meet.

Finally, a word about Hamilton's theological method and his emphasis on Jesus. Hamilton takes Jesus as the model for humanity, but he glosses over the fact that there is a metaphysical blank within us and that it is not merely Jesus-shaped. Jesus may fill part of the blank. The story of his life reveals love, and he promises and cultivates new life. But Jesus leaves many issues unclear, if not untouched. Why is life structured as it is? Why its ambiguity? Why

are suffering, pain, and negativity so extensive? Dealing with
Jesus is not enough. We have to interrogate existence more boldly
and fully, and the result we obtain from this metaphysical search
for first principles often goes far toward determining our response
to Jesus himself.

Hamilton's approach is to sift out the fragments of Christianity
which seem compatible with a contemporary mood he accepts as
normative. He takes the pieces of a religious tradition which make
sense to him and puts aside the other parts. All of us do this. There
is really no other way to proceed. But Hamilton's fragments are
little more than that. As a result, his theology appears shallow.
Even if we choose to stand beside Jesus in this world, we can still
ask—or cry out—"Why this world?"

To announce God's death gives us no answer to that question
but only raises it more stridently. Contemporary experience seems,
then, to call for a more philosophical or metaphysical theology
than Hamilton has provided thus far. This means one which begins
by a fresh attempt to answer classic questions in terms of new first
principles. Hamilton's work is not completed, and he may give
such an interpretation of his Christian fragments before he is
through. Until he does so, however, the adequacy of his new essence of Christianity must remain in question.

C. Paul van Buren and Religious Language

Like Hamilton, Paul van Buren believes that men have lost
touch with God. He also agrees with Hamilton in stressing the
importance of Jesus and in directing his theological efforts toward
interpreting the gospel for men who are both secular and Christian.
Van Buren's goal is not to convert nonbelievers but to help Christians understand their faith in a world which is losing all sense of
divine transcendence. Yet, if the thrust of van Buren's work is
similar to that of Hamilton, the two theological methods are very
different. Van Buren's interpretation of the secular meaning of the
gospel is not identical to Hamilton's new essence of Christianity.

Van Buren's guiding question is: "How may a Christian who is
himself a secular man understand the Gospel in a secular way?"[7]
The key to this problem lies in the term *secular*. In van Buren's

view, secular consciousness is dominated by an empirical outlook which entails that propositions are meaningful only to the extent that they are verifiable (capable of being tested empirically). This means that unless we can identify some empirical data or possible experience that would clearly count for or against the truth of a given proposition, it is devoid of meaning.

For van Buren, the most important ramification of this perspective is as follows: statements which purport to be about God are ultimately meaningless. That is, under this empirical criterion, it simply becomes impossible to specify any conditions that would constitute clear evidence for or against propositions about God himself. No contemporary man takes God to be an observable entity within the world. Every attempt to interpret God in this way, or to interpret him as a component of human experience in any sense, results in qualifications. These qualifications are finally so extensive that no specifiable conditions remain which could count clearly for or against claims about God. The result is the realization that talk about God himself simply lacks content. It is without real meaning—at least according to the criterion outlined above.

In a later work, van Buren makes clear that he does not take this empirical perspective as final or as necessarily the best for modern man to assume, but he does stress the fact that most contemporary men see the world in these terms and thus experience the meaninglessness of God-talk.[8] Moreover, his emphasis on the meaninglessness of God-language leads him to differentiate himself from other radical theologians. His aim is not to proclaim the death of God as Hamilton does. Van Buren doubts that the concept of the death of God has any more meaning for secular man than does the concept of God's acting in history. "Today, we cannot even understand the Nietzschian cry that 'God is dead!' for if it were so, how could we know? No, the problem now is that the *word* 'God' is dead."[9]

Secular men cannot speak meaningfully of God, but van Buren is persuaded that men can still make life worth living by appropriating a Christian life-style. In order to see how this can be true, we must pursue van Buren's analysis of language a bit further. If language about God is meaningless because of its inability to fit man's empirical outlook, it does not follow that all *religious* discourse is meaningless. Drawing on the insights of the British philosopher Ludwig Wittgenstein, van Buren notes that language has many varied uses. By seeing how it functions in different circumstances and activities, and by recognizing that its meaning is relative to the context in which it is used, we can understand that much religious language and Christian discourse in particular does in fact have genuine content.

This approach would seem to reopen the possibility that language about God could be meaningful, but van Buren still opts for the conclusion that claims about God should be ruled out of court altogether because they are not verifiable. Even if one takes the position that language about God is really only a way of speaking about man or the world, van Buren maintains that such uses of God-language can only be dangerously misleading and, hence, are best left alone. The crucial issue, then, is to see how religious language—Christian language in particular—functions without God. In doing so, the secular meaning of the gospel will be clarified.

Men do concern themselves with more than statements of fact which can be checked by empirical procedures. Many are not only interested in knowing what the facts are but also take a position with respect to their meaning. Emotions, personal feelings, and hopes have much to say about the way we "take" the objective facts that we encounter. Religious language functions at this level of human life. It is used to express, and perhaps recommend, a basic point of view or fundamental attitude toward existence which makes life significant for an individual or a community. Moreover, this language has genuine meaning because human attitudes manifest themselves in action and in behavior which can be observed. This latter fact, in turn, makes possible a kind of verification process with respect to the fundamental attitude or viewpoint about life which a man may appropriate.

The truth or falsity of a man's outlook or faith can be appraised in terms of his honesty, authenticity, and consistency in fulfilling the life-style implied by his basic attitude. However, this verification process does not allow us to assert that one point of view matches or fails to match reality itself. In fact, religious language should not be interpreted as making verifiable claims about reality in this sense at all. If it is construed as making such claims about ultimate reality or about existence as a whole, it has all the defects and qualities of meaninglessness that permeate God-language. One of the important tasks of the Christian theologian is to clarify and capitalize on all these factors in interpreting Christianity for secular men.

Van Buren stresses the view that Christian faith is man-oriented. It is basically a description and a recommendation of the way we should live in the world, and its content and power to attract human devotion rest in the man Jesus. The salient fact about Jesus is that "he stands out as a remarkably free man" (p. 121). Above all, he was "free for his neighbor" (p. 123). Jesus shows us how to stand above debilitating fear and anxiety. He shows us how to avoid the stifling boundaries of conformity and tradition. His life points toward the creative action and giving for others that make existence humane and meaningful.

Jesus' freedom is "contagious." The significance of his resurrection is that the disciples "apparently found themselves caught up in something like the freedom of Jesus himself, having become men who were free to face even death without fear" (p. 128). Through the testimony of the early Christian community this model of freedom has spread, and it stands as a meaningful and powerful life-style in which men can participate today. To stand in the freedom of Jesus—but without God—and to bring that freedom to life in the world is the invitation contained in *The Secular Meaning of the Gospel.*

Let us ask van Buren the same question that we put to Hamilton: In what sense could this theological perspective be regarded as distinctively American? Van Buren was trained in the neo-orthodoxy of a European theologian, Karl Barth. His thinking has also been shaped largely by dialogue with Bonhoeffer and other German thinkers such as Heidegger and Bultmann and by interest in British philosophy, which concentrates on linguistic analysis. *The Secular Meaning of the Gospel,* then, is not oriented in an obvious way by any American traditions in theology and philosophy, and his book also speaks less directly to American culture than Hamilton's work. In his later writings, however, van Buren has "discovered" American thought and the philosophy of William

James in particular. His recent interest in pragmatism suggests that his original position may contain some elements of American thought, and it also reveals a more flexible attitude toward metaphysics and statements about God.

Van Buren's secular man is a pragmatist in the sense that he believes human claims are meaningless if they point to no distinguishable aspects of human experience. On the other hand, the pragmatism developed by Peirce, James, and Dewey did not take the radical stand of claiming that all discourse about God is meaningless. Dewey argued that talk about God is misleading and full of problems, but he shied away from asserting that it has no meaning at all. Peirce and James certainly felt that meaningful discourse about God was possible and even beneficial in a pragmatic attitude toward life. Van Buren is still reluctant to speak positively about God, but his study of American thought helps make him more open to the possibility of doing so. In particular, he seems attracted to James's conception of a finite God.[10]

James has helped van Buren to see that metaphysical and theological views may be regarded as hypotheses about reality itself which can be explored and evaluated empirically. When men interpret facts and experiences in metaphysical and theological language they may be doing more than merely expressing their own subjective feelings or attitudes. They may, in fact, be making meaningful statements about the structure and content of reality itself. These statements are meaningful at this level because they produce concrete expectations in us which future experience can fulfill or frustrate.

Van Buren has moved toward James's insight that the degree to which a metaphysical or theological view fits with and illuminates our actual experience, expectations, and feeling can constitute real evidence for or against its truth or falsity as a view of reality itself. Like James, van Buren believes that many theories about reality are possible and that no single view can be conclusively demonstrated to the exclusion of all others. A pluralistic strain was present in his thought from the beginning, but now it is further accentuated by the removal of some of the narrow restrictions he adopted initially from certain aspects of British philosophy.

It remains to be seen whether van Buren himself will begin to speak directly and constructively about God. Certainly his later statements make this a possibility, and this fact is of vital importance. "Secular man" has frequently been interpreted as one who has lost either interest or confidence in trying to speak clearly about God and the basic structure of reality itself. There is much truth in this interpretation, but it is not the whole story. We may still be reacting to the excessive claims made by rationalistic philosophers of past centuries, and many do lack faith in the truth of the theologies and religious traditions of their predecessors. In addition, both attention and energy have been turned more fully to the practical, empirical problems and activities of this world. Surprising as it may appear, however, such involvement in the world can actually deepen metaphysical sensitivity. If that is true, the secular city may be precisely the place where a renewal of positive and constructive thought about God can occur.

A secular man still wonders who he is. In fact, secular life places that question before him with a new harshness. If he expected to achieve release and freedom by throwing overboard the theological and metaphysical baggage of previous generations, still he is haunted by the issue of life's meaning in a world of ambiguity. To deny this is to live dishonestly. Some men silence their questions by affirming the absurdity of existence, but that response will not do for most. Man is, after all, a being who hopes for positive meaning and fulfillment. This quality may be a useless passion, but it is real and persistent nonetheless. This hope rarely dies a natural death. Usually to get rid of it you must kill it. With no firm answers for our metaphysical and theological problems ready at hand, every person must be his own interpreter. Any man, however, who devotes himself to philosophy and theology can help by boldly carving out hypotheses which both meet the facts and sustain hope at the same time.

One way to nourish hope is to think about God systematically. That is, you can try to form a theological hypothesis that describes the kind of God who might bring into existence, and then relate to, a world such as ours so that evil, suffering, and death do not stand as the final words. The test for the adequacy of such a hypothesis would be pragmatic: to what degree does it help men understand themselves and their world? To the extent—but only to the extent—

that it does further human understanding, we could trust it and continue to pursue it. That is the only basis on which we can trust our thinking and the only grounds we have for pursuing particular claims. Even if a theory does work this way, it may turn out to be erroneous, but we really have no alternative other than to trust the capacities and the findings we develop.

Some critics are sure to object that such an outlook completely misses the point that we are living in the time of the death of God, or at least in the time when talk about God is meaningless. Silence about God, not new theological statements about him, is most needed. But that criticism begs the question. One possible way to move beyond the death of God, or to show that God-talk is not without power and meaning, is to keep thinking about experience in terms of God. Some Gods are surely dead for us because the very thought of them grates harshly against our experience, but this may not be true of every concept of God we can form. If we try, it may be possible to find God in metaphysical reflection in a day of destruction and basic questioning.

Van Buren's work emphasizes the centrality of Jesus. To speak of finding God in metaphysical reflection, however, may appear to put Jesus on the fringes of theology, if not out of the picture altogether. Such reflection need not ignore Jesus, but it is not likely to take him as the sole authoritative norm in forming a concept of God. Jesus may stand as a crucial figure—especially where hope is concerned—but he does not exhaust experience or clarify all of life's mysteries. Van Buren's theology shows this as much as Hamilton's. The contagious freedom of Jesus—no matter how dramatic and self-giving—does not begin to interpret all of life's problems. Metaphysical thinking does not dissolve every mystery and problem either. Yet the interior dialogue of a man thinking directly about God in terms of his experiences may make important gains of its own and give us a new vision of the meaning of Jesus himself. Ironic as it seems, Christians in our day might benefit by thinking less about Jesus and more directly about God.

The Secular Meaning of the Gospel has much to say about freedom. Without quite intending it, van Buren may point out the possibility and importance of *free theology,* which can be distinctively American if it takes its cue from pragmatism and exhibits speculative boldness and pluralism. It is an open question whether such work would be helpful in renewing religious life in continuity with any of the traditions we have known. Yet the possibility is surely there so long as men are free to think, and so long as ideas of all kinds are allowed a hearing in society.

D. Thomas J. J. Altizer and Christian Atheism

Speculative boldness is the hallmark of Altizer's theology. His version of the death of God is both difficult to comprehend and genuinely radical precisely because he is striving to develop a new concept of God. Altizer believes that God is at work in the world, but his understanding of the nature of God is different from traditional theologies. Thus, the concept of the death of God plays a vital part in his thought. How, then, does he conceive of God and what is the "good news" of Christian atheism?

Altizer shares two convictions held by Hamilton and van Buren. First, we are living in the cultural era of the death of God. Human consciousness has been secularlized. Our attention is focused on the world, and talk about the transcendent God of traditional theology makes little sense. On the other hand, Altizer takes as his task that of interpreting the Christian faith within this secular context. As a result, he also stands with Hamilton and van Buren in affirming the centrality of Jesus. The interpretation he develops of Jesus, however, goes far beyond that of Hamilton and van Buren in the direction of a metaphysical understanding of both existence and God himself. Altizer takes the idea of *incarnation* more seriously that Hamilton or van Buren. The result is a vision of a God who is in process. He is moving in ways strange to us in order to secure identity and peace for himself and the world.

Today the Christian is "called to proclaim . . . the gospel, the good news or the glad tidings, of the death of God."[11] Only the Christian is fully able to experience and proclaim the death of God as *good news,* and it is his loyalty to Jesus as the Christ, the Incarnation of God, which makes this possible. Obviously, however, many Christians have affirmed the Incarnation without speaking of the death of God. In fact, most Christian thought has interpreted Christ as the clearest indication that there is a transcendent

God of love. Altizer's argument, then, depends on a particular understanding of the Incarnation which has been seen by only a few (e. g., Blake and Hegel). He is aware that his notion runs contrary to most traditional interpretations, but believes that his conception captures the essential meaning of Jesus Christ for our times.

For Altizer, a full affirmation of the Incarnation says not only that Jesus is God, but also that God has become flesh in such a way as to have annihilated his own existence as a transcendent being who stands over against the world. "God becomes incarnate in the Word, and he becomes fully incarnate, thereby ceasing to exist or to be present in his primordial form" (p. 44). The Incarnation, then, is both an affirmation of flesh and a negation of transcendent spirit. To become totally immanent in the world, God must negate his own transcendence. Such negation or death occurs—both symbolically and literally—in the Crucifixion. The Resurrection also receives a radical interpretation from this perspective. It is not understood by Altizer as testimony about the eternal reality of the transcendent God of theological tradition. The risen Christ ought not to turn our attention backward to reinstate the God who annihilated himself in the act of incarnation. Instead the Resurrection points toward the continuing process of God's identification with the world, which now is made possible only by the death of the transcendent God.

In the middle sixties, Altizer's writings emphasized that the Christian proclamation of God's death results in a sense of release and in a new birth of freedom for men. If God affirms the world by annihilating his alien transcendence as he becomes flesh, then men are free—indeed they are urged—to respond "by totally embracing the world" (p. 155). Ambiguity permeates this concept, but the thrust of Altizer's thinking includes the idea that we are free to live as secular men. We can be fully engaged in the affairs of the world without experiencing the alienation, guilt, and bondage of standing before the transcendent God of traditional theology. Nevertheless, Altizer's Christian man sees the world very differently from most secular men. Altizer's later work stresses this by accentuating the view that Christian thinking points beyond the present world.

The Christian faith is radically apocalyptic and eschatological. It affirms the end of this world and the conviction that all things will be made new. For Altizer, the self-annihilation of the transcendent God and God's identification with this world are steps toward a radically new creation. Thus, if his earlier statement about man's embracing the world appeared to share the optimism of Hamilton or van Buren, his later work makes clear that this is not the case. He affirms present existence neither because it is fulfilling nor because he is optimistic about its chances for becoming so—rather, because he is convinced that it is a stage which must be passed through on the way to the achievement of a new aeon.

Altizer suggests that we can best grasp God's self-annihilation and identification with the world in terms of a *descent into hell*.[12] The God who becomes flesh does so in a radical sense. As he annihilates himself, the transcendent and holy God becomes fully immanent in the world by assuming flesh in all of its alienation and brokenness. Heaven itself is emptied as God negates himself and immerses himself in the profanity—the hell—of worldly existence. At the same time, however, the affirmation of profane flesh and the self-negation of transcendence are not ends in themselves. The goal of Altizer's dialectic lies elsewhere. God's self-negation and his affirmation of profane existence radically transform both God and the world. All things are being made new, and it is precisely to bring about this new creation—Altizer calls it "a final Totality" (p. 191)—that God must experience and become flesh in all its dimensions and horrors.

Altizer's vision of the final Totality is unclear in its detail, but he does say that it abolishes "all polarities and divisions, including the polarity between God and the world, and the division between humanity and deity" (p. 179). Ultimately, then, the descent into hell, the affirmation of profane existence, culminates in the negation of this world and in a new creation. This final Totality is marked by completeness and wholeness. By working, suffering, and celebrating its way through many diverse forms, by overcoming all alienation, fragmentation, and striving, the process of existence results in a final, everlasting, and blissful peace.

The Christian hastens the coming of this new aeon by announcing the death of God, affirming the world, and proclaiming the eschatological significance of Jesus Christ. God's death and the profanity of existence should not be celebrated in themselves but as signs that the kingdom of God is coming. But it is of special importance to understand that a full awareness of the eschatological significance of Jesus entails the expectation and affirmation of "the loss of all we have known as identity and selfhood" (p. 214) as a prelude to the New Jerusalem. Altizer admits that such a vision "must inevitably appear in the form of madness or chaos to all those who can still find life or hope in an individual center of consciousness" (p. 210). But he stands firm in his conviction that he has discerned the essence of Christianity and that its message can be joyfully affirmed.

The impetus for Altizer's radical theology comes largely from his study of the history of religions and from his analysis of European thinkers such as Hegel, Nietzsche, and Blake. Can a theology which develops out of these sources communicate positively with contemporary Americans? The first point worth noting is that Altizer believes that his radical theology is capable of obtaining a favorable hearing in America because of the extreme secularization of our culture. "America looms large in the thinking of the American radical theologian, not as the literal nation about us, but rather as the place where the public and social expressions of secularization are most advanced in Western European civilization."[13] Secularization and the death of God go hand in hand, he feels. A constructive theology, therefore, which capitalizes on this fact may find a receptive audience here.

In addition, Americans are a people largely detached from the past. The very existence of this nation symbolizes a break with many traditions, and we tend even now to take our orientation more from future possibilities and present problems than from reflection on our own development and heritage. For Altizer this is an encouraging theological situation. In this context one can break out of conformity to archaic religious tradition and speak a new theological word, one which fits the increasingly secular character of all human experience and gives such experience a positive sense of direction. He banks on the ability of his interpretation of the death of God and the eschatological significance of Christ to do both.

Altizer believes that America can be the primary source of theological leadership in the future. His thought also supports the idea that America can be the center of *free theology*. Indeed his efforts are an example of it. Nevertheless, he may have misread American consciousness in thinking that we can respond positively to his work as it stands. Americans wonder increasingly who they are. If what is sought is a meaningful and lasting sense of identity, Altizer's theology does more to make this result impossible than to encourage it.

Elaboration on two themes may illustrate this point. First, although Altizer has taken great pains to describe the form of the process which God and the world are living through together, he has not spoken with sufficient clarity and depth about what grounds this process. Moreover, the little he has said ultimately leaves him trapped in silence. We need, in a word, to know more about the *kind* of God with whom we are dealing. Of particular interest in this regard are our questions about freedom.

Why, for example, does God assume the relationship to us that Altizer has described? Were other options open in creation originally and in God's relations to us now? If not, why is this the case? If a plurality of options were open, why were these particular ones actualized? These questions, in turn, point directly toward the problem of evil. Altizer's concept of God is radical and novel because it suggests that God shares responsibility for evil and experiences it as well. Again, however, he has not given sufficiently specific replies as to why and how this is the case, and in particular what role God's freedom plays in these circumstances.

It is important to try to answer questions such as these. America's future sense of identity may depend on doing so. But Altizer not only neglects these issues; the tone of his most recent writings implies that he must remain mute. In conjunction with his description of the final Totality toward which we are moving, he speculates that there was once an initial, primordial Totality as well. The transcendent God and the world he created are ultimately the result of an original movement within this primordial Totality, one which is best called a Fall.[14] This Fall, however, is a metaphysical dead end. Altizer has very little to say concerning why it occurs or why it takes one form rather than another, and no man is likely to do any better. Certainly no one can say all that needs saying about reality, and Altizer's vision could be correct. But a meaningful sense of identity is not to be found in this primordial Totality and its unexplainable Fall. For that reason, Altizer's theology may have a limited appeal for Americans.

A meaningful sense of identity is not likely to be found in Altizer's final Totality either, which takes us to the second dimension of the difficulty Americans will have in responding positively to his theory. As we have noted, Altizer's sketch of the final Totality is cast largely in terms of the overcoming of the polarities and distinctions we now experience. A crucial point in this vision is Altizer's belief that the emergence of the final Totality comes only via "the annihilation of everything we have known as consciousness and experience" (p. 213). This Totality is described as a state of bliss and complete liberation, but it also seems to entail the ultimate negation of everything we know as human self-hood. In the final analysis, therefore, it is difficult to see that there is any pragmatic difference *for us* between the bliss of Altizer's final Totality and the sheer emptiness of nonbeing.

If the descent into hell is really the ascent toward a Totality in which we disappear as distinguishable, self-conscious beings, many may find their response to Altizer in the words of the song which wonders "if the going up is worth the coming down." Altizer's writing is enigmatic. He may have more in store for the individual than this interpretation suggests, but certainly there is no clear sense of the lasting value of individual identity. This value seems to have been a crucial dimension of American consciousness. Altizer may interpret this fact as evidence of our unwillingness to accept the radical essence of Christianity, but still it is a real obstacle to widespread acceptance of his theology in America.

In another sense, however, Altizer's eschatological vision speaks directly to the heart of any search for identity. He realizes that life in this world does leave us incomplete and fragmented. Clarity about who man is and why he exists will never be more than partial in this existence. If death finally annihilates every man, our world will not be without meaning, but surely it will retain the taint of absurdity forever. It is not clear that Altizer's final Totality does any better for individual men, but he speaks the truth in asserting that this world and life will not leave us fulfilled. Perhaps no form of being in which we participate can do so completely. Such completeness may not be our national lot. But if we can retain a metaphysical boldness such as Altizer's, we may succeed in producing other visions of existence which could provide grounds for the hope that *individuals* will experience more than the limited joys and insights their present lives afford.

E. Richard L. Rubenstein and Religious Life after Auschwitz

Perhaps the most moving expression of radical theology has come from Richard L. Rubenstein. Writing from the perspective of his experience as a Jew, he develops a bold analysis of human existence which clarifies the theological options open in America today. Rubenstein believes that the crucial question for Jewish theology is this: What sense, if any, can be made of the relation between God and man after the Nazi attempt to exterminate the Jewish people? His theology, then, concentrates on the problem of evil, and his goal is to restructure a sense of Jewish identity out of circumstances in which the traditional "images of God, man, and the moral order have been permanently impaired."[15]

The idea that our existence is ultimately under the direction of an omniscient, omnipotent God of history, who is just, good, and loving and who entered into a special relationship with the Jewish people stands at the heart of Jewish religious life and at the center of the Christian faith as well. Yet, if we accept this view of God, how is Auschwitz to be interpreted? Rubenstein believes that the conclusion is clear: If there is a God of history, then "the Nazi slaughter of the Jews was somehow God's will" (p. 53).

This realization deals a death-blow to the concept of any God of history. The horrors of the death camps cannot be denied, and to claim that they are somehow the will of a just, good, and loving God of history—which is the conclusion that the mainstream of Jewish and Christian theology seems to require—creates a credibility gap now beyond repair. Faced by the breakdown of the idea that men are the children of the God of history, a new form of self-understanding must be found. What insights and recommendations, then, does Rubenstein offer?

The first thing to note is that Rubenstein, like Altizer, retains a positive concept of God. Drawing on Jewish mysticism, he speaks of God as the holy, omnipotent *Nothingness* who is the Lord of all creation.[16] To speak of God in this way is not to equate God with an empty void. Instead, Rubenstein takes the holy Nothingness to be the ground and source of all that exists. God is "an indivisible *plenum* so rich that all existence derives from his very essence. God as the *Nothing* is not absence of being but a superfluity of being."[17] The term *Nothingness* (No-thingness) is used to indicate that God cannot be clearly defined. All things emerge out of him and participate in him, but he is "in no sense a thing bearing any resemblance to the finite beings of the empirical world" (p. 185). The holy Nothingness is also the "final destiny of all things" (p. 193). He slays as well as creates, and every finite being ultimately collapses and dissolves within him.

Rubenstein's God is the ground and end of all existence, but our relation to him does little to give life positive meaning in the present world. Our experience is that of being thrown into the world. We exist in a particular time and place as part of some particular culture and history. However, we possess no ultimate account of the reasons for this, and "we stand in a cold, silent, unfeeling cosmos, unaided by any purposeful power beyond our own resources."[18] We must create meaning for ourselves, but at the same time Rubenstein believes we must learn to live without ultimate hope. "We have nothing to hope for beyond what we are capable of creating in the time we have allotted to us" (p. 221). In fact,

. . . eschatology is a sickness with which man conceals from himself the tragic and ultimately hopeless character of his fate. There is only one Messiah who redeems us from the irony, the travail, and the limitations of human existence. Surely he will come. He is the Angel of Death. Death is the true Messiah and the land of the dead the place of God's true Kingdom. Only in death are we redeemed from the vicissitudes of human existence. (p. 198)

With the possible exception of Altizer's later writings, this mood
is rather different from the characteristic expressions of Christian
radical theology. Usually they have stressed the possibility of celebration and joyful affirmation of life in the time of God's death.
Rubenstein will celebrate life joyfully when and where he can,
but his vision retains a more prominent place for the finally tragic
dimensions of existence. He not only lives without eschatological
hope, but also has no naïve optimism about the goodness of men.
He regards "the [death] camps and Nazism as far more than a
sport of history. They revealed the full potentiality of the demonic
as a permanent aspect of human nature" (p. 216). In the light
of these circumstances, we can never escape the quality of melancholy and tragic absurdity in existence.

Somehow, Rubenstein *does* believe that life is worth living. We
lose everything in death, but our lives still allow for creative, joyful,
meaningful activities. We can make existence more humane by
compassionate sharing. In this context he stresses the positive role
man's religious traditions play in making life meaningful. He under-
scores the view that a man's sense of identity depends largely on
his being able to maintain a positive relationship with the past.
Thus, even if Rubenstein no longer can affirm the God of traditional Jewish theology, he makes no move to cut himself off from
Jewish culture and religious practice. He has been thrown into
existence as a Jew, and his life will be fragmented if he cannot
affirm that fact with as much richness as possible.

Moral honesty will not permit Rubenstein to retain every element of the traditional Jewish faith, but religious expression within
the Jewish community remains important to him as a way to share
with others the most profound and abiding realities of life and
death.

. . . I cannot dispense with the institution through which I can
dramatize, make meaningful, and share the decisive moments of my
life. For me that institution is the synagogue. . . . These moments include birth, puberty, marriage, temporary or permanent infirmity, the
marking of time irretrievably past, the rearing of children, the need
to express and find catharsis for feelings of guilt, the need for personal renewal, and the feeling of awe and wonder which overcomes me

when I think about God's nothingness as the ultimate source and the final end. (p. 222)

Following up on his convictions that we can do much to make life more humane and that continuity with religious tradition is important in this context, Rubenstein's later work has been devoted to contemporary moral problems and to a fresh analysis of the Jewish religious heritage with the hope that a meaningful Jewish religious life can be retained even after Auschwitz.[19]

He remains firm in his conviction that the concept of the God of history cannot be revived. Furthermore, he argues that the notion of the Jews being a chosen people is simply detrimental to Jewish well-being, because of the false hopes and morally outrageous conclusions to which it leads and also because of the animosity toward Jews which it produces in other peoples. At the same time, he works to show that the Jewish heritage is full of existential, psychological, and moral truths which all men can appreciate and appropriate in their search for identity and self-understanding.

Rubenstein has said that he writes "as an American theologian, but Europe has had a very great impact on my thinking."[20] This is true not only with respect to Auschwitz. European thinkers such as Nietzsche, Freud, and Heidegger have influenced him extensively. In what sense, then, does Rubenstein's perspective have special significance for theology and life in America?

Three points stand out. The first is the importance of maintaining continuity with the past particularly when one's present identity is unclear and when the future is uncertain. By understanding what we have been and where we have come from, both politically and religiously, we may clarify what in tradition we ought to reject and discern the goals for which we should work. The tendency simply to reject or to flee from the past is often strong, especially when the result of our heritage is ambiguous. The idea that we are a nation "under God" has suffered this fate to a great degree. Perhaps it is justified, but such a conclusion ought not to be reached too quickly, for the concept may still be able to function as a vital part of our national consciousness in a renewed form.

Jews are not the only people who have understood themselves

to be chosen by God. That view is part of the American tradition too. Many of the early settlers of America came here with the vision that they were to establish the New Jerusalem, and religious convictions have never been far removed from feelings about America's national destiny. Some have—and some still do—equate American policy with God's will, or at least believe that God is always "on our side." For most citizens now—and it was surely the case for many of the founding fathers too—such ideas are monstrously misleading. Americans have not directly experienced the horrors of Auschwitz, but our experience has taught us that no clear or simple relation between God and American life can be discerned. This leads many to seek for personal identity in nontheological forms. But another course remains open. Although it is more difficult, it may also prove to be more profound—if we have the courage to try it.

This course is to continue to reflect about America in theological terms, but not simply by trying to reconcile our experience with norms merely taken over from the past. Rather we should think first about our national life together and then discover what concepts of God could be developed to fit such circumstances and hopes. This possibility is not really at odds with radical theology. Most of the work we have explored in this chapter suggests that our experience of the death or absence of God is partly the result of having assumed or looked for the wrong kind of God. By reflecting about God—freely, openly, and honestly—in terms of the experiences we live through now, Americans might find that they can affirm meaningfully the idea that we are a nation "under God." It is not likely that these words will carry a unified content for us, any more than they will have the same meanings they conveyed to our forefathers, but to be able to speak them at all might provide a unifying center.

Rubenstein's second point of special significance for theology and life in America is that we need to reflect on the nature and significance of evil. His reminders of Auschwitz are striking, but we really do not need them in order to become sensitive to the demonic qualities that appear in existence. Vietnam, racial hatred, environmental pollution, and the widespread brokenness of the human spirit in our times are evidence enough.

Americans have tended to think that evil could be virtually eliminated from human life through our own voluntary efforts. That conviction has been part of our optimism. Rubenstein is sure, however, that Americans are coming to share his view more and more. It seems to many that life in this world will never be more than an ambiguous mixture of good and evil. If this is the majority experience today, it raises many questions about ourselves, our world, and God. It forces us to reassess the significance of moral striving. It forces us to reexamine the structures of existence, and it leaves us wondering whether God exists and, if he does, what he is like. To reflect on evil drives some men away from God. For others, God may come to life through such meditation. Radical theology itself shows that this can happen, although the God encountered may be different from the one expected.

Finally, Rubenstein's work challenges us to think about hope. His world is an irreducible mixture of good and evil in which death has the final word. He sees no grounds for assessing existence differently. In fact, to hope that things can or will be otherwise is a form of sickness. On the other hand, Rubenstein admits that "most men simply cannot live in an ultimately meaningless and irrational universe."[21] He senses the centrality of hope in the human spirit, but he has chosen—with some regret—not to heed its yearning for a New Jerusalem either in this world or on the other side of death.

However, it should be clear that Rubenstein's rejection of hope stems largely from his conviction that one particular view of God —the God of history—is not believable, and from his assumption that no viable, empirically honest theological perspective capable of sustaining hope is available. Perhaps no such view is presently in sight, but this does not mean that it is impossible to develop such concepts. The circumstances Rubenstein has described leave another option open, namely, to face the facts of our existence and try to produce a concept of God which can meet them and still keep hope alive.

Rubenstein sees no grounds for the hope that existence is ultimately meaningful and rational, but here he might learn something from American thought and from William James in particular. Hope may create some grounds of its own. It is true that some men experience the death of hope, but we know that hope can exist in the darkest situations, and it may be that the very human efforts that stem from it also create evidence that favors it. We hope that life can be made better on earth, and this hope works its way into action which may in turn effect real changes for the good. At this level, hope can move far to ground itself, although the odor of evil will never be completely removed from this life so long as men suffer and die.

The latter fact pushes us to the issue of eschatological hope. Is Rubenstein correct in saying that "there are . . . absolutely no grounds for eschatological hope"?[22] If hope for the improvement of life can establish some grounds of its own through human action, a similar situation may exist with respect to eschatological hope. By trying consciously to develop a concept of God that meets the facts of existence squarely, one which interprets them to show how negation and death need not stand as the final outcome of existence, some ground for eschatological hope might be established. Further, if a life-style oriented toward such a view should produce genuine illumination and meaningful experience in human lives now, this too could be interpreted as grounds for eschatological hope.

Such theological efforts cannot be expected to produce public agreement, since experience always admits of plural interpretations and more than one theologial framework always remains possible. In the end, one will have to choose what it is possible to hope for, just as Rubenstein has decided to live without eschatological hope. We should point out that, in principle, many alternatives are still open. If among these we have concrete options available to orient hope, that is an important factor for American theology to contribute to the future.

F. American Theology and Religion
   after the Death of God

The death-of-God movement has accomplished one thing beyond question. It guarantees that American theology in the future will be *radically pluralistic*. In this it contributes to a trend toward diverse life-styles which probably will be with us for years to come. Radical theology has shaken many traditional religious ideas to the core. For some men, this will mean the end of faith and constructive theological reflection. For others, the boldness of the radical theologians will reveal new frontiers in theology, especially when we realize that the conclusions these men draw need not be taken as the only ones possible. On the whole, radical theology has opened more theological doors than it has closed. It helps to undermine the authority of tradition, but it has not fundamentally impaired thought about God. This includes the use and reinterpretation of traditional concepts if one wishes to move in that direction. After the "death of God," therefore, American theology should and will increasingly become *free theology*.

There will be relatively little theological unity in the future. Even if current plans for various church mergers succeed, religious life in America is likely to become more—rather than less—pluralistic. When these possibilities are coupled with the realization that the variety of life-styles in America is increasing, a provocative question appears. What might be the most important and distinctive contribution that American theology and religion could make to future existence here? One answer might be put in this way: *they could help to make our pluralism humane and enable men to stand "under God" with hope for the future.*

This answer has two major thrusts. The first emphasizes *social action,* and the second concentrates on *understanding existence* as a whole in a hopeful way. Many disciplines, institutions, and individuals will have to participate in the tasks of improving the quality of life in the future, and a man does not have to be a theologian, a member of a religious body, or even a religiously concerned person to value and strive for a humane pluralism. Religious concern entails moral commitment, but the latter can exist without the former.

Nevertheless, the opportunity is always available for American theologians and religiously active persons and institutions to make important contributions to the solution of certain moral and social problems. If these forces will accept the challenge and the responsibility, they can be a catalyst both for renewing our national conscience and for achieving constructive social changes. They are able to call attention to and act boldly in situations where needs stand largely untouched.

American churches may have difficulty in raising their annual budgets; still, they remain wealthy institutions. Power and wealth go hand in hand. If "church power" at all levels is used boldly and creatively to serve men in the areas of our greatest need—racial reconciliation, rehabilitation of nature, elimination of poverty, genuine peace in the world, to name just a few—much can be done to raise the quality of life and the moral tone of our nation. Moreover, if they can break out of old patterns, if they can learn to give themselves in love for others, American churches may find themselves blessed with a renewal of life and identity. Americans, after all, are by and large a pragmatic people. The improvement of social conditions builds hope. When these factors are the result of religious faith, such commitment can become a live option for many men.

The second thrust may be put in this way: American theology and religion can make distinctive contributions to national life by speaking hopefully to the metaphysical vacuum in human existence. If American theology and religion can provide concepts of God and frameworks for interpreting life so that our experiences of negativity are not the final outcome—so that men can see their lives as related positively to God and as part of a broad context of meaning and personal fulfillment that extends beyond death—a lasting sense of identity, significance, and hopeful expectation may result. These qualities are valuable in themselves. In addition, they release moral energy into the world. They can help to resist the debilitating feelings of despair, desperation, and futility which always threaten social action when it is motivated by a totally secular stance toward existence.

In the future, theology and religion may have an impact on national life which is less direct and overt than it has been in times past. The increasingly pluralistic quality of life seems to assure this. On the other hand, the importance of theology and religion may become all the greater, but only if they can produce and sustain visions of existence that encourage men to trust that their best efforts will have lasting significance and that their highest ideals and hopes are not completely obliterated by the passage of time.

If progress toward these ends is to be made, American theologians and religious leaders must be among the boldest and humblest men of the future. They must be humble in their recognition that theology and religious life are fallible and pluralistic. No single view or program can or should be expected to have exclusive control. Thus, one of the chief tasks of every religiously sensitive person must be to proclaim this essential note of freedom wherever it is under threat. At the same time, American theologians and religious leaders must be bold in facing the facts of life—joy and terror alike—and in their willingness to speak and act creatively in the social sphere and to reflect metaphysically about God.

Whether we will be equal to the tasks required by man's need remains to be seen, but the only way to find out is to try. We are not likely to see the day when all Americans can really affirm that we are one nation under God, but bold theological and religious efforts may take some beyond the death of God and enable them to find meaning and hope in that traditional phrase. If some can do so, we will not only maintain an important link with the nation's past, but may also take an important step toward the achievement of our professed ideal of liberty and justice for all.

However, in order to clarify how American religious life might in fact promote liberty and justice, when often in the past they seem to have done the opposite, we need to understand just now radical theology is indigenously American and in what sense it is not. Insofar as it borrows from European pessimism or nihilism, it is not. Insofar as it pronounces the death of God simply on the basis of a critique of traditional and largely European conceptions of God, it is not, for it has not sought and tested an "American God" sufficiently. On the other hand, insofar as it is based on a radical concept of man's freedom and self-determination, it lies very much in the American tradition and needs only a vision of God clear enough to match it.

The rise of radical theology in America reflects our own disorientation over the adequacy of our early notions of ourselves as a people and what our national destiny should be. It signals the

end of our separation from European experience and the frustration of our hope to be distant and free forever from the troubles
that have plagued man since he fled Eden. The myth of America's
separateness from a scarred world has exploded along with our
simple and naïve enjoyment of religion. Now, all man's collected
sins and all of religion's accumulated difficulties are inescapable
for us too. Our fresh start in a new land and the hope to remain
far from old conflicts, along with the immense benefits of isolation
—all are faded and gone.

Now American theology, in discovering its own unrecognized
and accumulated burden in this country, must face the rising
anxiety and guilt of all mankind. Once we had hoped to be rid of
such a perplexing and haunting inheritance. Instead, what has died
is not so much God as it is the simple American dream of our
ability to achieve isolated perfection. Any God who blessed us in
our isolation is bound to disappear when our involvement in all past
social and religious sins becomes so inescapably clear. *Gods die
when the visions they support disintegrate.* In the very experience
of this basic loss in American life, the crucial question becomes
whether a God can be found who is consistent with the breadth
and depth of our mature national experiences and the revised
hopes still possible. Can a new God call us forth as a freshly
covenanted people from the Egyptian bondage into which we have
driven ourselves?

NOTES

1. William Hamilton, *The New Essence of Christianity* (rev. ed.; New
York: Association Press, 1966), p. 28. This book was first published in
1961.

2. William Hamilton, "Dietrich Bonhoeffer," in Thomas J. J. Altizer and
William Hamilton, *Radical Theology and the Death of God* (Indianapolis:
Bobbs-Merrill Company, 1966), p. 117. This essay was first published in
1965. Hereafter this volume is abbreviated as *Radical Theology.*

3. Preface, in *Radical Theology,* p. x.

4. William Hamilton, "The New Optimism—from Prufrock to Ringo,"
in *Radical Theology,* p. 169.

5. William Hamilton, "Thursday's Child," in *Radical Theology,* p. 87.
This essay was first published in 1964.

6. William Hamilton, "The Death of God Theologies Today," in *Radical Theology*, p. 40. This essay was first published in 1965.

7. Paul van Buren, *The Secular Meaning of the Gospel* (New York: Macmillan Company, 1966), p. xiv. This book was first published in 1963.

8. See Paul van Buren, "Christian Education in a Pragmatic Age," in *Theological Explorations* (New York: Macmillan Company, 1968), pp. 63–65.

9. *The Secular Meaning of the Gospel,* p. 103.

10. See Paul van Buren, "Bonhoeffer's Paradox: Living With God Without God" and "William James and Metaphysical Risk," in *Theological Explorations,* pp. 107–160.

11. Thomas J. J. Altizer, *The Gospel of Christian Atheism* (Philadelphia: Westminster Press, 1966), p. 15.

12. See Thomas J. J. Altizer, *The Descent into Hell* (Philadelphia: J. B. Lippincott Company, 1970).

13. Thomas J. J. Altizer, ed., *Toward a New Christianity: Readings in the Death of God Theology* (New York: Harcourt, Brace & World, 1967), p. 13.

14. See *The Descent into Hell,* pp. 173–214.

15. Richard L. Rubenstein, *After Auschwitz* (Indianapolis: Bobbs-Merrill Company, 1966), p. x.

16. See, for example, *After Auschwitz,* pp. 154, 219–225; also Rubenstein's *The Religious Imagination* (Indianapolis: Bobbs-Merrill Company, 1968), pp. 144–145, and *Morality and Eros* (New York: McGraw-Hill Book Company, 1970), pp. 183–196.

17. *Morality and Eros,* p. 185.

18. *After Auschwitz,* p. 152.

19. See *The Religious Imagination* and *Morality and Eros.*

20. *After Auschwitz,* p. xi.

21. *The Religious Imagination,* p. 177.

22. *After Auschwitz,* p. 258.

VIII

BLACK THEOLOGY

A. America: Sweet Land of Liberty?

The human beings who came to America in the seventeenth century were not exclusively people searching for either religious liberty or a new economic future. Black slaves were among the earliest arrivals. Stolen from their African homes, tortured, separated from family and friends, sold and resold, denied every human dignity and right, these men and women were used to develop some of the early colonies. Slavery flourished in this land of new opportunity, even after we declared our independence in the name of human freedom and equality.

Our talk has always been better than our performance. We extolled liberty, but we compromised with the economic benefits received from the institution of slavery. Our democratic rhetoric had an unmistakably white flavor. At the outset, the Constitution implied that the life of a black slave was worth only three fifths of that of a white man. Later, in the Dred Scott Case of 1857, Chief Justice Taney held that black men of slave origins were not entitled to the rights and privileges of citizenship.

However, it is also true that slavery never existed unopposed. Nat Turner was only one of many slaves who rebelled. Other blacks, such as Frederick Douglass, achieved their freedom and devoted themselves to the liberation of their fellows. Many whites joined in the opposition, too. The Quakers were outspoken critics from the earliest times. The abolitionist movement in the nineteenth century, which included men such as Parker, Thoreau, and John Brown, kept the nation's attention focused on the contradiction between the practice of slavery and announced American ideals.

Still, it must be acknowledged that for many years the opposition was weaker than the combined power of indifference and proslavery interests. If the Southern states had chosen a course less radical than that of secession from the Union, slavery might have continued largely unchecked. It could easily have maintained itself much longer than it did.

America will soon be two hundred years old. For almost 50 percent of that time the country existed half slave and half free. The past hundred years, moreover, do not show a very startling transformation. Instead, they reveal how deeply the experience of slavery has scarred the nation's consciousness and how far from total success we are in this American experiment in democracy. The Emancipation Proclamation, which Abraham Lincoln signed in 1863, did not free black people from every form of slavery, any more than the 1954–55 Supreme Court directives to desegregate public schools with "deliberate speed" completely offset the Dred Scott decision.

Black men and women are no longer sold from the auction block, but in the past century they have encountered new white masters who are more subtle and sometimes more harsh than many slaveholders in the past. Whites have exploited the oppressed blacks by keeping them separate, hence unequal; by continuing to foster the mythology that blacks are racially inferior to whites; and by sharing economic and political power only slowly and with great reluctance.

Of course, there are exceptions to these generalizations. Some white men have acted courageously and sacrificially to see that opportunity, liberty, and justice become facts for blacks as well as for whites. But it does not require a very long look at the record to become convinced that black suffering far outweighs white courage and sacrifice. If real gains have been made, they have come more from the perseverance and initiative of black leadership than from the good will of white society.

American life today is an ambiguous mixture of black and

white. Religion and theology have contributed to these circumstances, and they will have much to say about the outcome. If the nation was founded in the midst of slavery, and if it continues to exist divided by racial tensions, religious life in America has been no different. The slaves who were forced to come to America were not Christians. White leadership debated the issue of whether slaves should be converted, and if so what results would follow.

As every good slaveowner knows, the best slave is a broken man, but the Christian faith seeks to build men up. Assuming, then, that blacks are fully human and in need of the gospel—a point hotly contested in itself—the issue still centered on whether it would be expedient to preach to slaves. A few slaveholders were even concerned about the principle involved: Was slavery really compatible with the Christian faith? As it was in the beginning, is now, and ever shall be, religion and culture reached a compromise. In many areas the plan was: convert slaves, save their souls, but keep religion out of politics. That is, Christianity was interpreted so that it was not only compatible with but supportive of the status quo of slavery.

Two things went wrong with this plan. No compromise between Christianity and culture is ever totally successful, because the former contains elements that evaluate and judge human actions so that every human situation falls short of the kingdom of God. No matter how men try, it is not really possible to make the Christian message compatible with slavery. Many white men knew this and said so. On the other hand, as black men listened to the portion of the Christian message presented or available to them, enough of the Christian themes of liberty and justice and of God's concern for the oppressed came through so that some black men found in Christianity a hope that enabled them to survive and encouraged them to work for freedom. Moreover, when the slaves were allowed to have black preachers and permitted to gather for worship by themselves, these black churches provided a communal experience that helped to cultivate a thirst for freedom and dignity.[1]

Slavery led to the formation of black churches in the South. Yet they were often viewed with suspicion by white men, who knew that they contained a potential for revolution. Thus slaves were often brought into the white churches instead of being permitted to gather among themselves. There was, however, little brotherhood in such meetings. Even in worship, the oppression of separation was the rule of the day. Circumstances in the North were little different from those in the South. Free black men worshiped with whites in some northern cities, but their places were usually assigned to them, and they were excluded from the ecclesiastical power structures.

One result was the formation of more black churches in the North, a move that was often greeted by white hostility because it signaled the black man's refusal to accept the degrading practices of white churchmen. The American churches—pluralistic from the outset—were shattered and splintered by the experience of slavery. Even where divisions occurred because of vehement antislavery feeling, the instances where blacks were welcomed as equals in white communities were the exception. American culture was built on the not-so-hidden premise that democracy was primarily for white people.

The close of the Civil War brought few radical changes in the patterns of religious life. Black churches continued to function in America, not so much by choice as through the necessity imposed by the segregationist intentions of some white churches and the indifference of many others. A few men have criticized the post–Civil War black churches for being too passive and otherworldly. But even if the criticism is partly justified, the fact remains that, from the days of Reconstruction to the present, black churches have provided a communal center that has been indispensable for survival and hope in a nation of segregation and disparagement.

On the other hand, during this time many opportunities have been available for the white churches to transform both themselves and American life by welcoming the black man as an equal. Too often, however, these situations have been passed by, if not rejected with outright scorn. Church and culture have reflected each other too well in the past hundred years of American history, and this fact contributes to the crisis of identity that Americans are living through now. Our awareness has grown. Perhaps more than in other periods, it is now hard to be a Christian and an American at the same time.

Martin Luther King, Jr. analyzed our identity crisis in this way: "Ever since the signing of the Declaration of Independence, America had manifested a schizophrenic personality on the question of race. She has been torn between selves—a self in which she has proudly professed democracy and a self in which she has sadly practiced the antithesis of democracy."[2] Both blacks and whites have to understand themselves and shape their future in the face of this fact. The context, however, in which one faces this dilemma —and the response it elicits—varies considerably depending on whether the person is white or black.

For the past fifteen years, black people in America have been achieving a new and positive sense of identity. From the Montgomery bus boycott in 1956 to the recent emergence of "black studies" centers in colleges and universities, there has been a highly successful movement to cultivate within the black community a sense of the beauty, dignity, and worth of blackness. This movement culminates in concentrated efforts to win freedom, justice, and equality in America without giving up one's blackness in the process. Such efforts have a potential that is—quite literally —explosive.

Black men are overcoming the sense of inferiority and inadequacy which has been the legacy of slavery and segregation. They are achieving the liberating awareness that—as King said—they are *somebody*. This means that black men will not stand still for a continuation of the schizophrenia King pointed to. Black awareness involves the consequence that white men are going to have to "get themselves together." White men must decide which dimension of their divided self will assume control.

The new black awareness is not without its ambiguities. It may involve an uncritical color blindness that results in a too simple equation between goodness and blackness, between evil and whiteness. It may also produce a sense of frustration which will bring on a violent revolution in which everyone will lose. Still, if white men study the developments in black communities, at least some will experience twinges of desire to share in the affirmation black people are making: namely, that one's heritage and community are beautiful.

For many white Americans the trend is quite the other way.

Over the past fifteen years we have been uncovering certain hidden details of our past. The picture is in many ways ugly and unnerving. Some of our ancestors bought and sold slaves; others lynched black men. With few exceptions, most Americans have accepted a segregated society with all its injustice and inhumanity. Not all of us consciously want to contribute to a social order which makes black men second-class citizens, but a man's life and identity include unintentional actions as well as those consciously determined.

Black men are not the only ones who find it difficult to live with whites these days. White men find it difficult to live with each other and with themselves, and one major cause of this phenomenon is a sense of guilt built up over the generations of oppression of blacks. The Confederacy still exists, and the Civil War did not end at Appomattox. It rages inside white Americans every day.

Black men today are moving beyond the psychological destruction of slavery toward a new sense of integrity and identity, but no one can predict precisely what shape or effect this movement will have in the future. Black leaders themselves realize that there is much to be done within their community to overcome the scars of slavery and segregation. Yet in a time when the need for leadership is desperate, there is no single voice that constitutes or determines black policy. Nevertheless, it is clear that self-confidence is emerging in the black community.

On the other hand, precisely the element of self-confidence is now in question in the consciousness of many white men. White Americans are less sure of themselves than they once were, and not so certain they are making—or can make—democracy a reality for all. The inadequacies and destructiveness of many policies in racial matters have been exposed. Many whites feel trapped and baffled by the configuration of a racial conflict they did not choose, but which nevertheless is part of the fabric of everyday life. How often today white men must curse the stupidity and greed of those who first brought black slaves to these shores. But here we are, troubled and more than a little fearful that the "white man's burden" is his own basic inhumanity, for which he may have to atone with his blood.

Recent developments in theology reflect some of the dimensions of this crisis. One result of the movement toward black awareness has been the emergence of *black theology*. As long as there have been black churches, there has been black theology—in the sense that black people have interpreted the Christian faith in terms of their own particular needs and circumstances. Traditionally, however, the black church has relied upon a theology that is primarily preached. That is, it is an oral tradition rather than a developed, systematic, written interpretation. This came about partly because of physical and psychological circumstances. People enslaved or reduced to second-class citizenship through segregation are unlikely to have either the time, the energy, or the resources free from the immediate needs of survival to write theological books.

Fortunately, that situation has changed. Moreover, black men are finding that the written expressions of theology that already exist are inadequate for their needs. The feeling is that American theology has been shaped too much by European sources and is too exclusively white-oriented. If American theology has not actively served the cause of oppression and segregation, it has at least failed to give sufficient attention to the peculiar issue of slavery and racism in America and to the needs and integrity of black people. Black men, therefore, must produce their own theological statements in the interest of carrying forward their distinctively black heritage. It is their special task to bring the liberating message of Christianity to bear on the contemporary struggle for identity, freedom, equality, and justice.

The development of written theological expressions, self-consciously designated as "black," is a new phenomenon on the theological scene. These statements promise, however, to have substantial influence in black circles. Many blacks, it is true, would prefer to divorce the black revolution from Christianity, which they take to be essentially a white man's religion, and also from the traditional black church, which has too often been otherworldly in its emphasis. Thus, the future of specifically "Christian" influence in black religion hangs in the balance, as perhaps it should.

Others, however, recognize that the black church and the Christian faith stand at the core of the black community, and that these resources can add great support to the black struggle. It is also predictable that black theology will have considerable impact on

American theology in general. If theology in the late sixties was dominated by the death-of-God debate, black theology may well become the focal point for the first half of the seventies.

White theologians must respond to black theology. In these circumstances, we have the potential for an authentically American theological revival. Black efforts and white responses can lead to a renewed theological concern to correct the evils of injustice and racism, to develop and defend those ideals and qualities in our national life that are worth preserving. This might help us understand God's relation to what is unique in American culture. "Black theology" will be "American theology" in a significant way, and it may prove to have important insights that could even bring us closer together on new ground.

At this time, any analysis of black theology must consider the work of at least four major spokesmen. The first, Martin Luther King, Jr., is known to virtually every American. King had little to say about the idea of an explicitly black theology, and his views are not dominant in the current movement toward black awareness. Still, his thought is a vital factor in shaping the context out of which black theology now is being developed. Contemporary blacks hold King in the highest esteem, but they are also much more critical of his ideas than most whites would be.

Theologically speaking, then, King's thought provides a perspective that stands in contrast with, and is often rejected in favor of, a more radical religious position. The other men—Joseph R. Washington, Jr., Albert B. Cleage, Jr., and James H. Cone—are less well known to most Americans, but they stand at the center of black theology. In appraising the thought of these men, we should keep the following question in mind: In what sense is black theology also American theology, and how could it set the tone for future theological reflection in this country? In exploring these issues, the themes of pluralism, freedom, evil, and human fulfillment come to the fore.

B. Martin Luther King, Jr. and the American Dream

Martin Luther King, Jr. (1929–1968) was an American dreamer. "I have a dream that one day this nation will rise up and live out the true meaning of its creed: 'We hold these truths to be self-evident: that all men are created equal.' "[3] King worked for this dream in the North and in the South; in Montgomery and Birmingham, in Chicago and Washington, D.C., and in Memphis, where he was killed. No man has ever done more to urge America toward racial health and greatness. Still, by the time of his death the racial scene was shifting, so that more radical and militant voices in the black community were winning an increased audience.

When Stokely Carmichael began to emphasize "black power" in 1966, he received an enthusiastic response from many black people. King knew that the concept of black power provided both a natural and a justifiable reaction to the disappointing performance of white men in response to black need.[4] He also knew that the concept could be psychologically useful in aiding blacks to affirm their manhood. It encourages the use of political and economic resources in new and creative ways to achieve legitimate goals. Yet he was fundamentally distrustful of the idea. It smacked too much of separatism, violence, and defeatism.

King certainly recognized that black men need power, but he was also sure that "there is no salvation for the Negro through isolation" (p. 48). He had firsthand experience of the brutality of white men, but he rejected one crucial implication he saw in black power, namely, that white American society is hopelessly corrupt and can be transformed only by violent revolution. By embracing these ideas, the black man was really condemning his own cause to defeat. Violence would produce no lasting victories. Without a successful appeal to white conscience, little progress would be forthcoming.

Black power is a slogan, not a precise plan of action. It can, therefore, mean different things to different people. King knew that his interpretation might not apply to every version of black power. He believed, however, that the orientation which the concept provided could lead in a direction very different from the philosophy he was urging. As our analysis of recent developments in black theology will illustrate, King's appraisal was fundamentally correct. The black theologies developed by Washington, Cleage, and Cone, which are all sympathetic and supportive responses to black power, diverge sharply from King's position.

Without naming it explicitly, King developed his own version of black theology. This is less "black" than some later statements, and his ideas are often criticized in the circles of black theology today. On the other hand, every contemporary statement in black theology develops in a context permeated by the thought and grandeur of this man. In the future, black theology may reject as much of King's outlook as it accepts, but it is clear that no black theologian can ever ignore him and that King's thinking continues to exert a decisive influence.

King wrote no systematic theology. His insights on God, man, and the Christian faith are found in his sermons and in his books and speeches, which describe and encourage the black man's struggle for justice and equality. In these works, however, several theological themes ring out repeatedly. The first is the dual theme of the fatherhood of God and the interdependence of men. There is little anguish over the absence or death of God in King's perspective, or in any of the black theologies for that matter.

King simply begins with the affirmation that the world and human life are God's loving creation and that God is at work in the world, striving with and for men to achieve a humane community. The fatherhood of God implies the interdependence—the brotherhood—of men. "All men are caught in an inescapable network of mutuality, tied in a single garment of destiny. Whatever affects one directly affects all indirectly. I can never be what I ought to be until you are what you ought to be, and you can never be what you ought to be until I am what I ought to be."[5]

A second theme is the attempt to clarify the nature and meaning of evil within a framework shaped by the idea of God's fatherhood and the interdependence of men. Nothing is more obvious than the presence of evil in the universe, and its chief manifestation in human experience is our own brutalizing tendency to hate and oppress each other, to rob one another of freedom, dignity, and justice. King sees every man's existence as a mixture of, and a struggle between, good and evil. Human life, created in God's image, is good, but it is also stained and shattered by destructive and negative forces.

King does not have a comprehensive theory to explain the presence of evil in human existence, although he does point to man's abuse of freedom as a crucial factor. However, he reflects on some features of the structure of evil, on God's action and man's responsibility for coping with evil in the world. One of King's important theses is that "evil carries the seed of its own destruction" (p. 77). The forces of evil are powerful and stubborn, never voluntarily relinquishing their hold on men. On the other hand, "evil cannot permanently organize itself" (p. 73).

It is the nature of evil to divide, to separate, and to negate. This suggests that there is a sense in which evil is self-destructive. It may not destroy itself completely; there will always be new obstacles to face. But the consuming force of evil powers does not exist unchecked. The forces of evil are internally unstable, and they are also capable of being subdued by the forces of goodness—justice, freedom, and love—which remain alive and powerful, however threatened they may be at times. "Looking back, we see the forces of segregation gradually dying on the seashore" (p. 77). No matter how bleak the circumstances, King was a man who confronted evil with hope and courage. His impact cannot be understood apart from that fact.

What does King's perspective imply about God's action and man's responsibility in coping with evil? King's God is committed to freedom. He *permits* evil as part of the price to be paid for freedom in the world, but King utterly rejects the idea that God *wills* or *causes* evil in any intentional sense. God's commitment to freedom, however, does have some important ramifications for the way in which he permits evil to exist. For it means not only that men can diverge from the course of action that God himself wants them to pursue, but also that trying to discern and follow God's will entails conscious choices.

Further, if divergence from the will of God occurs, he does not use any means necessary to set things right. This is not to deny God's concern for justice. He is committed to it, but within a context of freedom. His purpose for men seems to entail their attempt to establish a community of love through their own creative use of freedom, which includes both controlling the potential for evil in human existence and atoning for evil actions that do occur. "Therefore, God cannot at the same time impose his will upon his children and also maintain his purpose for man" (p. 79). Yet

God will not allow men to make a total shambles of creation. The evil permitted is kept in check to some degree, partly by its very nature. God will not do for us what we can do for ourselves, but when men turn to him in faith, he does renew their strength and courage to attempt what is just and good.

The universe is formed and finally controlled by the love of God. The reality and power of that love are most clearly revealed in the teachings, the life, death, and resurrection of Jesus. Love builds up and transforms life for the good. It also conquers death; the grave is not our end. "Love is the most durable power in the world. This creative force, so beautifully exemplified in the life of our Christ, is the most potent instrument available in mankind's quest for peace and security" (p. 49). King believed that the universe is structured to favor love, if men will give themselves to it. He was also convinced that hate and violence only breed more of the same. Thus, he found himself drawn to the method of nonviolent resistance to evil. It was the best procedure—morally and practically—the black man could use in his struggle to further the cause of love, freedom, justice, and equality.

The power of nonviolent resistance resides in its ability to expose and thwart evil without destroying the persons involved. It is true that suffering may be experienced in the course of it, but such suffering is redemptive. And it is so because it strikes to the core of human conscience and draws out a determined response from men in defense of freedom and justice. It can also lead to repentance in those who cause suffering. Resistance to evil—bold and courageous—is indispensable. The forces of evil must not be allowed to operate business as usual. But only one mode of resistance—nonviolence—saves men instead of annihilating them.

In the final years of his life, King stressed the need for massive civil disobedience much more than he did in his Montgomery and Birmingham experiences.[6] To the end, however, he remained committed to the ultimate moral validity and practical power of nonviolent resistance. His dream was that all Americans—but especially black people—would respond successfully to the challenge set before them by God, namely, to let freedom ring and love prevail by transforming life together through nonviolent resistance to evil.

King's position on nonviolent resistance is the most distinctive quality of his perspective. It is also the factor that separates him from other black theologians, as we shall see later in this chapter. For the moment it is important to reflect on the insights about God that King goes on to develop. Faced by the problem of evil, he opts neither for a death-of-God theology nor for the concept of a finite God. He retains a deep and abiding faith in the goodness and omnipotence of God. In this, as in his assertion that God permits but does not directly intend evil, King is a traditionalist. At the same time, there is a strong emphasis on God's decision to create men with freedom and to respect the integrity and power which that freedom entails.

God gives power to men and then respects it. Such a God takes risks. He recognizes that things may not always function smoothly and that injustices may occur, perhaps even on a massive scale. Such a God also has a high degree of patience and self-control. When things are not going well, he could intervene directly and dramatically. ("Next time the fire.") But if King is correct, God's actions within the world presently are more indirect and subtle. He instills courage when men ask in faith, and he gives renewed strength when men trust him and call upon him to support righteous ends. But the kingdom of God for us is "not yet," and this life remains to the end a scene of struggle and suffering. Improvements, however, are possible. Oppression can be relieved. Freedom and justice can be extended. The evil that God permits is not left free to run unchecked. It is incapable of organizing itself permanently, and in the end—beyond this world—existence will be made new, whole, and perfect.

King sketched a picture of God and the world that fits the American experience in many ways. Life is a struggle, and things often go very wrong. If God is at work in our history, he seems to choose a role which makes him only one power among many, although this by no means excludes the possibility that his power is ultimate and capable of decisive intervention in a radical recreation of the world.

King's description of God entails that every human situation remains open-ended. This outlook not only fits the American emphasis on change and development in existence, but also introduces elements of hope and optimism, always important factors in an American tradition. Death is not the end of life, and therefore men are free to give themselves now for the highest goals and dreams they can perceive and feel. King affirms that nonviolent resistance to evil is one of these. If we dare to practice it extensively, our life together can be dramatically transformed for the better.

The impetus for King's stress on nonviolent resistance came largely from Gandhi, but many of the other themes in his theology are carried forward from American thinkers. He mentions Thoreau, Rauschenbusch, and Reinhold Niebuhr in this regard, and echoes of James and Royce are here as well. At the same time, however, King reflects a common American reluctance to face the problem of evil boldly within a positive theological context. There are exceptions, of course, but the usual American response goes in one of two ways. We either treat God charitably by holding him responsible only for the good, or else we assert that he merely permits but does not directly intend evil in the world.

Of course, we may also reject his existence altogether—pronounce him dead—because the presence of evil is incompatible with what we think he ought to be. In a democracy, however, perhaps we can be more bold and forthright with God and interrogate him more strongly about his direct responsibility for evil in the world. Royce, Rubenstein, and Altizer have theologies that move more in this direction, but each of them has a crucial weakness from an American perspective. Royce's theory is deterministic; Rubenstein's leaves men without ultimate hope; and Altizer's fails to account sufficiently for human individuality.

Black theology should be able to provide a unique perspective for interpreting God's relation to and responsibility for evil, since black people have suffered so severely. But King, as well as the other men we examine, has not broken much new ground in this area of theological discussion. They take the traditional line of stressing God's opposition to the powers of evil. This is an important component of a believable theology, but the problem is to clarify the form of God's opposition. An adequate interpretation of that problem depends, in turn, on our ability to grasp the status of evil powers in the universe. This is a metaphysical issue which can be answered only by bold but tentative speculation.

To meet the facts of our experience, we need a theology which affirms God's ultimate power and love but which also moves between two opposing sides. One of these two poles is the view that God consciously and directly wills from eternity every instance of evil that our world contains. The other is the view that God chooses a world in which he merely permits some evil, but does not cause or directly will any evil to occur. The first of these views is inadequate because it destroys our freedom, but the second is inadequate too. It fails to consider sufficiently the fact that God could have created a world with a structure basically different from this one. To bring this world into existence out of the many that were possible, a conscious choice on God's part is required. Moreover, the choice to bring this world into existence seems to entail a positive commitment to the structures that can and do produce evil, destruction, and suffering.

God may be more wild and daring than we usually give him credit for. He may do more than simply permit evil and suffering. No absolute metaphysical necessity determines the existence of our world. God seems, therefore, to make a conscious choice in favor of structures that, in many cases, produce or lead directly to evil and suffering. The middle way being suggested, then, states frankly that we are faced by a God who consciously and freely chooses a world whose existence is contingent, but in which he knows full well—and even intends and wills—that there will be some suffering, injustice, destruction, and waste.

This does not necessitate that God determines eternally or knows in advance the particular circumstances which will reflect these negative qualities or the degree to which they will characterize our lives. But it does entail that he knows, intends, and wills from the outset that there will be some—perhaps even many—such qualities and circumstances, and that there is also a possibility that they may dominate this world's existence, at least at times. To put the point in a slightly different way, God wills the reality of evil, but he does not determine exhaustively the particular instances, aspects, and degrees of evil that break into our lives. He does, however, accept the instances, aspects, and degrees of evil that occur in the free play of worldly powers, although at the same time he offers a way to overcome and transcend them by a persuading love.

It is not altogether easy to suggest these ideas, especially in the context of the experience of black people. Nevertheless, it is important to consider them. Evil and suffering, after all, have some ultimate source and ground. They do not simply appear in a vacuum. Men are the direct source of a vast amount of suffering and destruction, but the responsibility for the basic structure of the existence into which we are thrown cannot be exclusively human. Some accountability belongs on God's doorstep. Of course, if that is true, questions about the purpose of our existence and our chances for a fulfilling life in this world and beyond are raised with a new intensity.

The future of theology in America depends largely on its ability to cope with such issues in a creative and hopeful fashion. King's theology helps us to see these problems clearly. Its emphasis is on God's decision to respect the freedom of men—even at the cost of momentary defeat—in the hope that they can use it creatively and lovingly to achieve a humane community in spite of severe obstacles and continued suffering.

C. Joseph R. Washington, Jr. and God's Chosen People

"The task of the theologian is to discover what God is doing in the world and to rally around to further his intention."[7] Washington sees God at work in the phenomenon of black power, and he seeks to further God's intention in and for that movement by helping to develop a theology of revolution and violence. To understand the nature of this theological perspective and just how Washington arrived at it, we need to see how his thought developed.

Washington's first book, *Black Religion,* advances the thesis that church separation along racial lines is directly contradictory to the Christian faith. Within this context, however, the book concentrates particularly on the nature, significance, and future role of black religion in America. In pre–Civil War days, black religion was rooted in "racial unity for freedom and equality."[8] Utilizing the elements of the Christian faith communicated to them by whites, black men combined these themes with their thirst for freedom and equality. This developed a "folk religion" which made survival and hope possible, and also kept alive a spirit of rebellion. In the environment of slavery, neither the white nor the black churches could be genuinely Christian, but black people forged a religious perspective out of their condition which frequently resulted in protest and direct action in the name of liberation and justice.

The emancipation of the slaves in 1863 was an important victory, but it did little to bring black and white churches together in any authentic Christian community. In fact, faced by the monumental barriers of segregation, the black churches tended to place less emphasis on direct action to achieve freedom and became increasingly concerned with institutional maintenance, emotional fervor, and otherworldly consolations (p. 95). Such an emphasis characterized much of black religion in America well into the twentieth century.

These themes may have helped black people endure the inhumanities of segregation, but Washington argues that by the late fifties and early sixties such an orientation was no longer viable for black churches. The Civil Rights Movement was under way. A few black churches were in the vanguard, carrying forward or recovering the more militant and authentic folk religion of the pre-Civil War black churches. Most, however, lagged behind. The need was for all black churches to rediscover the original vision of black religion in America and to recognize its radical content.

The goal for the black churches, however, ought not to involve their self-perpetuation. Instead, Washington asserts that black churches and black religion should strive to put themselves out of business. They should work toward an authentic Christian community, sacrificing themselves to transform the white churches in the name of full Christian brotherhood and freedom. "The responsibility of all Negro congregations which exist essentially because of racial ties is to go out of business. . . . It is incumbent upon the Negro now to close his houses of worship and enter the white congregations of his choice en masse" (p. 289).

Two additional points about this early analysis by Washington are worth mentioning. First, he feels that the black churches tend to operate in a theological vacuum. They lack and need clear theological statements that make them come to terms with, and lead them to embrace wholeheartedly, the fact that Christianity means men are children of God who are intended to live as brothers beyond the barriers of segregation and racism. Second, Washington not only believes that black people could play a unique role in creating genuinely Christian communities, but he also implies that blacks are, in fact, being called by God to do so. White men will have to seize the initiative in welcoming black people, but blacks have a missionary responsibility to move out into the white world in order to help redeem whites and blacks together.

Both themes are carried forward in Washington's second book, *The Politics of God,* but set in a different framework. Washington wrote *Black Religion* in the early sixties, a period when it seemed possible that a real transformation in race relations might soon take place. By 1967, when *The Politics of God* appeared, he was less optimistic. His recent studies had led him to explore more fully the nature of color prejudice and racism in America, and he was convinced that this phenomenon was not only irrational but also a vital component in white "folk religion."

White hatred for black men has no rational justification. This has been demonstrated repeatedly, yet the hatred continues largely unchecked. Moreover, Washington argues, this irrational hatred was initially encouraged by and continues to be perpetuated through "the preconscious religion of the white folk."[9] Needless to say, this religion is not authentic Christianity. It is a bastardized version of the Christian faith which interprets the possession of power, wealth, and prestige as signs of God's favor and election.

If we see black men as oppressed outcasts, we consider them as wretched before God and as objects worthy only of hate. Such a doctrine, of course, is not consciously articulated. White folk religion says the correct things as far as the Christian faith is concerned. In practice, however, the situation is very different. White men may make no conscious decision to hate black people. But they do so nonetheless, and thereby produce massive injustices which do not seem to yield to rational argument or protest.

Washington's conclusion, therefore, is that blacks must replace protest with *power*. Social equality is the ultimate goal, and "black prospects are dependent upon gaining what whites have—power" (p. 96).[10] Furthermore, black churches remain the focal point for the masses of black people as far as community life is concerned. This means that these churches must become "centers for concerted action with power" (p. 73). In short, the circumstances are not ripe for a massive exodus from the black churches into the white community. An interim stage must be completed first. Black people must get themselves together to make a determined onslaught against white hatred. Economic and political channels should be given priority, but violence ought not to be ruled out. The objective is a humanely pluralistic society in which men can accept and appreciate each other as persons. However, much hard work and resistance lie ahead before that goal can even be approximated.

If the black churches are to assume leadership in the tasks that lie ahead for black people, a sound theological foundation for their role is indispensable. Washington began to sketch such a theology in *The Politics of God* by stressing the idea that blacks are a people chosen by God for this mission: "to witness to the one humanity of the one God here in the United States where groups reside in divisiveness" (p. 158). This is not the first time that black people have been regarded as a contemporary manifestation of the early Hebrew tribes. Washington, however, adds something to this interpretation by suggesting that black people are chosen to become God's suffering servants. Black people are to carry out the task not only of liberating themselves but also of releasing their white oppressors from the chains of hatred and fear.

Blacks have not selected this role for themselves. They may even be reluctant to accept it once it is clearly set before them. Nevertheless, Washington contends that the suffering of black people should be understood in this way if it is to be meaningful and capable of being channeled in a creative direction. "The Negro's seeming undeserved punishment is his opportunity to release all men from the sin of in-groupness. The 'curse' of being a Negro is really the blessed symbol of God's paradoxical instrument as the means of His grace for all men" (p. 171).

Washington agrees with King in affirming the ultimate unity of humanity and in the belief that God is at work in the world through the redemptive suffering of black people. But there is one crucial difference. The militancy of Washington's suffering servants is not necessarily nonviolent. The obstacles to be overcome are sufficiently irrational so that they may yield only to force. The nonviolent resistance to evil advocated by King presupposes too much rationality in the phenomenon of racial hatred. It assumes that evil, once exposed, will become evil corrected. *However, the results of nonviolent resistance have themselves proved that this assumption must be questioned.*

To restrict black activity to the sphere of nonviolent resistance is seriously to hamper black effectiveness. Moreover, to claim that nonviolent resistance to evil is the only course of action acceptable to God misses the revolutionary thrust of the Christian faith. This faith seeks to make things new. Although it is true that God may not demand bloodshed, he apparently is not above using violence to achieve his purposes. The cross of Jesus Christ reveals this. (In what sense this is violence by Christians, of course, is a crucial question.)

These themes are amplified in Washington's recent statement, *Black and White Power Subreption.* A basic thesis in this book is that black power means revolution. Washington believes that "the task of Black Power is radical change in the society to 'smash racism.' Outside the revolution, there is no Black Power."[11] But it is also clear to Washington that the needed revolution has not yet taken place and that there is even a danger that the movement will be willing to settle for minor, partial victories. The black churches themselves must avoid the error of mitigating the revolutionary thrust of black power and of encouraging black people to rest content with anything less than a full effort to achieve social equality. To prevent the subreption—the suppression or subversion—of the meaning of black power, a black theology (a theology of revolution and violence) is necessary to keep attention focused on the proper goals.

Washington is still convinced that black people have a divine mission, but he plays down the suffering servant image in favor of an emphasis on the cross. The Crucifixion and Resurrection of Jesus signify two major facts. First, they signify God's dominion over the powers of evil and death, and convey a sense of freedom and power which urges man to participate in the liberation of humanity. Second, "the Cross reveals that there are times when no other sacrifice but that of life has the power of defeating evil in the name of new life" (p. 125).

The first point gives man the mandate to engage in revolutionary activity in order to achieve freedom from oppression. Not every revolution needs to be violent, but the second point reveals that violence and death themselves may be necessary to achieve the goals God intends for this earth. This is not, however, a blanket endorsement of violence. It is to be judged and controlled in terms of the end for which it is used: "If suffering takes the form of violence and the sacrifice of life for the good of a whole people and through this people, all people, then it is atonement, in attunement with the Cross. . . . The light in which revolution is judged to be meaningful is the extent to which life is given as a sacrifice to make real the freedom and power the Cross states is the gift of God and his will for all men" (p. 127).

The goal of Washington's revolution is not a black take-over of American society. Even if this were his desire, the power and numbers of the opposition would render it impossible. His view, however, is that militant action—including the use of violence if necessary—against the forces that stand in the way of freedom and justice could bring the nation to a standstill and force it to turn about-face. Violence may be the only thing that will speak to the conscience of the white man with sufficient intensity to create a new climate in which there can be reconciliation and humane communal life for all.

Although developed from different perspectives and with varied shadings, the following themes remain constant in Washington's writings: the need for a theology that speaks specifically to black people; the view that God has chosen to work through black people to help revolutionize and humanize society; and the conviction that this task may necessitate the creative use of violence. At least in certain ways, this is surely an American perspective. Washington is correct: "Blacks have more cause for revolution than those who affirmed, 'Give me liberty or give me death!' " (p. 185). Our forefathers did revolt, and many of them did so with the conviction that it was God's will to secure liberty and human dignity through violent means if necessary. Violence may not be as American as apple pie, but an American theology may have to admit that it can be a step toward a creative change in spite of the waste and negation it brings.

This is not to deny that violent means for combating evil should be tried only as a last resort. Even if it emanates from righteous intentions, the use of violence, once unleashed, is extremely difficult to control and brings everything of value under a serious threat. On the other hand, men are not fully rational animals who always respond positively to rational and righteous protest. Furthermore, oppression has little to recommend it for those who feel its scourge, and human patience with injustice and suffering is finite. If the response to patient and concerted action through "existing channels" and repeated nonviolent protests fails to meet basic human needs, men may have a right to be "unreasonable"—to use violence to force other men to move.

Several additional points must be made immediately. Much depends on what men take to be rightful human needs and how we decide when these needs have, in fact, been met. It is unlikely that we will ever be free of disagreements over these issues. What must be urged and hoped for is that men will try honestly to find a common meeting ground when disagreements occur, so that the waste of violence can be avoided. Black writers are correct in pointing out that whites have treated black men violently for many years in this country, but a premium must still be placed on critical evaluation of circumstances and consequences before more violence is used to root out evil. Even the righteous use of violence can do more harm than good. It may speak to the conscience of the oppressor as Washington hopes; but it may also only entrench oppressive powers, reinforce hatred, and eliminate genuine possibilities for fruitful communal life.

Human life is fragile and finite. Nothing reveals this better than the difficulty of determining how best to respond to the forces that negate humane existence. Moreover, God does not seem to speak or act as clearly as he might to help us in these circumstances. If we are men of religious faith, we may affirm that sufficient guidelines have been revealed or that guidance will come if we ask in faith. Some may even feel that God's intentions are both direct and precise. For most of us, however, including the black theologians, the situation is more ambiguous. Such widespread lack of clarity in our experience suggests some interesting possibilities concerning God which tie in directly wth Washington's perspective.

Washington believes that God has chosen black people for a task of liberation, but also affirms that he has structured human existence so that between birth and death "man alone is responsible for the quality of personal and interpersonal living" (p. 149). If the latter part of this claim is true, it would seem that God interprets human existence at least partly as a test to see what men can accomplish with their freedom. He does not guarantee any victories in this world. On the contrary, he makes the context of human life difficult—more difficult than is absolutely necessary—by giving men wide-ranging powers and potentials and by situating us in a natural environment full of wildness. Such a God leaves us primarily to our own devices. He is largely an observing God.

If the Christian faith is on target, however, God is also more than this. The life-death-resurrection of Jesus adds three things. First, human existence is surrounded and transcended by God's love, which can sustain us in the face of death and negation and will triumph over them. Second, because of this fact, men are urged and enabled to live for freedom and love in their present world. Third, strength, courage, and hope sometimes are given when men seek and ask in faith.

This Christian God is not likely to choose a people directly for a task, but he may allow persons or a group to feel chosen insofar as their desires and goals are in harmony with the aims revealed in the Christian faith. Even so, no victories are promised here, and the best human intentions often produce or result in waste and suffering. This life remains an ambiguous struggle. No one is spared suffering; liberation is never complete. Still, improvements can be made through our efforts, and men have a mandate from God to do all they can to make life worth living for every person.

Would a good God create and relate to a world such as this? The answer depends on the way we interpret goodness. In a democracy, it should be easy to recognize that more than one conception of goodness is possible and legitimate. American theology should try to approach the question of God's goodness from this point of view. We may say that the world is rather different from the one we would establish if we were given full charge. But the issue, then, is whether we can appreciate the fact that God might find our world good enough to warrant establishing and sustaining it instead of any of the other possible worlds open to his original choice. We can do this if we live with the hope that life in this present world is not all there is for us.

If there is nothing other than life in this world, it will be difficult indeed to understand God's choice as good in the sense of that term as we usually use it. Yet are we dealing with a God whose claim is to surround this world with love—who prizes our present existence, our strivings for freedom and love in particular, so much that he will make all things new beyond death? If so, the goodness of God can be made intelligible now in spite of the horror the world contains.

One final word is appropriate in this analysis of Washington's work, and it is a theme to which we shall return later. For the present, God himself does not seem to be a violent revolutionary, although he could become so at any moment he chooses. For now, God's patience with men is more marked than his revolutionary discontent. But his world is certainly one in which men may be revolutionaries—with good reason—and in which there can and should be theologies of revolution.

Washington is correct in stressing the need of black people to have a theology of revolution. Moreover, since this nation emerged out of a revolution steeped in theological concepts, every American theology in the future should reflect on the nature, causes, and meaning of revolution and God's relation to it. Having done this to some degree already, black theology may set the tone for the immediate future of theology. The issue ahead is the meaning of revolution and what form of it the Christian transformation aims to induce.

D. Albert B. Cleage, Jr. and the Black Messiah

As yet, Albert B. Cleage, Jr. has not published a systematic statement of his black theology. Nevertheless, the sermons he has preached from the pulpit of the Shrine of the Black Madonna in

Detroit constitute an important and unique contribution to this
theological movement. Cleage is basically in agreement with Washington's assessment of Martin Luther King, Jr. and the revolutionary nature of black power. He also affirms that blacks are
God's chosen people, and as such are called to use any means
necessary—including violence—to achieve freedom and justice for
black people.

On the other hand, Cleage differs from Washington in important
ways. His writings and concerns are more exclusively directed toward black people. Ultimate reconciliation between blacks and
whites is much less emphasized. The need to unite black people
for the struggle against white oppression is so great, and the forces
of evil to be reckoned with so entrenched, that it is pointless to
waste time now talking about reconciliation. Only when the resistance to white oppression has been intensified dramatically will it
be possible for blacks and whites to achieve the level of equality
from which meaningful discussion of reconciliation can occur. Further, Cleage moves beyond Washington by making the bold assertion that Jesus was literally a black man—the black Messiah for
a black people—and that God himself must also be understood
as black. Needless to say, these claims raise many interesting points.

In a nutshell, Cleage's view is that "Jesus was a revolutionary
black leader, a Zealot, seeking to lead a Black Nation to freedom. . . ."[12] White interpretations notwithstanding, "the Nation
Israel was not at any time a white nation" (p. 40). Instead, during the life of Jesus, the Black Nation Israel was oppressed by
a white nation, Rome. But Jesus came as "a Black Messiah born
to a black woman" (p. 42). His message was not one of universal
love but rather one of revolution—black nationalism. "When he
said, 'Go the second mile, turn the other cheek,' he meant inside
the Black Nation" (p. 98). His task was to bring black people
together and to encourage and free them for a course of self-
determination. If these facts have been missed or ignored in the
development of Christianity, it is because "the white man captured the religion of a Black Nation, the revelations of a Black
God, the teachings of a Black Messiah, and he has used them to
keep black men enslaved" (p. 38).

The theology of Paul, with its emphasis on the individual man and otherworldly concerns, is a primary example of this usurpation and perversion. Cleage rejects, therefore, the Pauline writings and concentrates almost exclusively on the Old Testament and the synoptic gospels—Matthew, Mark, and Luke.

If Jesus is the black Messiah sent from God to and for black people, what does this imply about God himself? One thing is certain: God is not white. However, it does not follow from this that we can think of God as standing aloof from or beyond color. The fact that he identifies with black people through a black Messiah indicates his own identification with blackness. God's election of black people reveals his own essential blackness. Moreover, a similar conclusion about God's black identity can be reached by taking seriously the biblical claim that men are created in the image of God.

Men of varied colors inhabit the earth, but relatively few of them are white. "So if we think of God as a person (and we are taught in the Christian religion to think of God as a person, as a personality capable of love, capable of concern, capable of purpose and of action) then God must be a combination of black, yellow and red with just a little touch of white, and we must think of God as a black God" (pp. 42–43). God does not literally have a black skin, but in Cleage's view the blackness of God is indispensable for understanding who he is.

One purpose of Cleage's stress on the blackness of Jesus and God is to drive home to black people that they are the heirs of the Black Nation Israel and that they are still God's chosen people. What more does this imply about God and men? At this point in Cleage's theology several interesting themes converge, and they lead to considerations that force us to think beyond his analysis. First, Cleage accentuates the idea that God has chosen *a people,* not isolated individuals. God is not unconcerned about the problems and needs of individual men, but his primary concern now, in this time and situation, is with the achievement of freedom and justice for black men as a group. "Understand that God is going to take care of *us,* the Black Nation, because we are God's chosen people. Because of this simple fact, the enemy is not going to destroy us" (p. 54). Cleage warns, however, that it does not follow that every individual's dream and aspiration will be fulfilled here.

Apart from identification with the black nation, God will lend no particular support. Even in the group struggle, there will be suffering and casualties.

Cleage believes that "it is the will of God that black people should be free" (p. 205). At the same time, he not only points out that many individuals may be sacrificed in the process, but also warns black people not to think that this world is structured so that anything right is "bound to triumph and anything that is wrong is bound to fail" (p. 176). The convergence of these themes reveals how ambiguous and tricky is the concept of "the chosen people" in Cleage's theology. Blacks are God's chosen people, but he also emphasizes the nonintervention of God in human affairs. Black men must get themselves together and strive courageously for their own liberation. There seem to be no guarantees, however, that these things will actually take place. God respects human freedom and will not do for us what in theory we can do for ourselves —whether we accomplish it in fact or not.

Cleage's God places stiff demands on black people. Until they make amends for their lack of courage and unity, they "are not fit for a Promised Land" (p. 271). The action to produce this change requires a turning of the will in black people, which God presumably will support but not enact or initiate by himself. Again, no guarantees are forthcoming. Thus it becomes increasingly difficult to specify the "cash value" of being God's chosen people in the context of Cleage's theology.

In spite of what Cleage says, it is not clear that his theology really allows black men to affirm that God underwrites the worldly survival of black people. The most that is guaranteed is that God may give strength, courage, and hope to those who ask in faith. But it is not certain that this strength, courage, and hope will be sufficient to assure victories—or even survival—in our world.

Black theology repeatedly finds itself in a peculiar predicament. Whenever a people are oppressed, identification with the biblical image of the Hebrews as God's chosen people is sure to appear attractive, because at least it can be used as an image to rally the effort needed to throw off oppression. At the same time, however, black theologians recognize that the God we are dealing with is not one who corrects instantly—or even with "deliberate speed"—every evil in the world.

God himself simply does not appear now to be a radical revolutionary in the arena of national and world politics. He may enable men to be political revolutionaries by renewing their individual strength, courage, and hope as each strives for freedom and equality. But his interest seems less in the direction of assuring permanent and lasting victories for us here than in the objective of testing men in harsh circumstances. Evidently he wants to see what we can do with our freedom by way of achieving areas of liberty, justice, and love in the world.

In the final analysis, there are no real winners in this present life. It is forever fringed by the negation of death. The kingdom of God is neither fully of, nor ever completely in, this world; but the prelude to full entry into and joy in that kingdom is dedicated participation in the struggle to make life worth living for men now. The wisest course in present times, however, may not be to single out one's own group or nation as a people specially chosen by God. Every man is chosen by being called into existence and by participating in the promise of strength, courage, hope, love, and life beyond death as revealed in Jesus Christ. But to speak of a contemporary people or nation as being chosen by God is almost certain to produce disappointment in that people, increase hostility between men, and intensify alienation from God—if more is expected from God than he will do.

God may have chosen a people in the past, but if he did so, the intent—Cleage's thesis notwithstanding—was to show that he is the God of *all* men. He grants to some the freedom, power, and responsibility to organize and sustain life, hopefully for humane ends, but this does not come with the guarantee that every wrong will be corrected within this world or that victory here will be the result of every righteous cause. St. Paul is correct: "For freedom Christ has set us free."[13] If that is a mandate never to submit to the yoke of slavery and oppression, it also suggests that there are no more chosen groups or nations. God has grown beyond such particular identification.

This analysis need not pose a serious threat to Cleage's desire to unify black people in a struggle for freedom and justice. His theology already puts the emphasis on human initiative in this pursuit. But the necessity of that initiative may always remain underplayed so long as the mythology of the chosen people is allowed to remain. Such a mythical concept invites false hopes and unrealistic expectations. It can also lead to a dangerous fanaticism that equates a group's actions—no matter how brutal and dehumanizing—with the will of God.

Black people are not the only Americans to think of themselves as a chosen people. The concept still exists in sectors of our society that are not black. Thus, all American theology in the future will have to assess this notion very carefully, but black theology helps to set the context by raising so vividly the idea and its problems.

We must leave the appraisal of Cleage's claims about the color of Jesus' skin to the biblical scholars and historians, but what of his assertion that *God* must be conceived in terms of blackness? Separated from the restrictive and ambiguous concept of the chosen people, symbolizing God as black could have a provocative function in American theology. To do this might help to expose and overcome some of the irrational prejudice and racial hatreds that consume many white Americans. In addition, even without the "chosen people" concept, speaking of God as black could serve a useful function in securing a sense of identity and worth in black men.

The symbol of God as black is valid if it is understood that he is all colors—hence black—but no single one exclusively. Viewed in this way, the blackness of God might speak the word of judgment white Americans need to hear. It can help to spur us to do our part to make life worth living for all peoples. On the other hand, by helping to build black identity, the concept of a black God should stimulate constructive black efforts to reshape life. With movement from both directions, the hope is to disclose a nation refreshed, strengthened, and radically humanized.

A theology which accentuates the blackness of God, but not his specific choosing of any particular group in this present world, and which stresses God's interest in and voluntary respect for human freedom everywhere—this is an option worth exploring in future theological work. Cleage intends his reflections to be predominantly for black people. Nonetheless, his emphasis on human initiative and freedom is something every American can and should appreciate. By being bold enough to suggest that God is black, Cleage opens up a perspective usable in shaping a new and viable sense of identity.

E. James H. Cone and Liberation

The most detailed and systematic black theology to appear thus far has come from James H. Cone, a young professor at Union Theological Seminary in New York City. Cone matches, if he does not exceed, Cleage's hostility for white people, and the theme of revolutionary violence is pronounced in his writings. Cone defines black power as an attitude which affirms and strives for *"complete emancipation of black people from white oppression by whatever means black people deem necessary."*[14] Working within this context he seeks to state what the Christian faith is saying to black people.

His view is that "Christian theology is a theology of liberation."[15] The Christian gospel begins and ends with Jesus Christ. The message preached by Jesus, as well as that revealed by his life-death-resurrection, is one that proclaims good news to the poor and release to the captives.[16] Jesus Christ liberates those who are oppressed. The uniqueness of Christian theology is that it studies God's reality from the perspective of this gospel of liberation which is proclaimed in and for the community of the oppressed. Moreover, insofar as theology fails to emerge out of such a community, it ceases to be Christian.[17]

The fact that Christ is the liberator of the oppressed provides a key for understanding the contemporary black struggle to reach freedom and justice. Wherever the struggle for liberation from oppression is under way, the spirit and power of Christ are present. Thus, for contemporary Americans—black and white—"the message of Black Power is the message of Christ himself."[18] The task of black theology is to drive these points home, to participate in the process of liberation by clarifying the hopeful message that God is "the God of the oppressed, involved in their history, liberating them from human bondage."[19]

Cone recognizes, however, that the proclamation of this message is no simple matter. He is aware that the history and present condition of black people raise difficult questions about the nature of God's liberating activity in the world. As a result, he wrestles with many dimensions of the problem of evil in a more complete fashion than any of the other black theologians we have mentioned. His approach to these issues produces theological claims that are both bold and problematic.

Cone is a militant man, and this militancy shows in his reflections about God. Instead of asking the question, "What *could* God be like in light of the experience of black people?" his approach is more to assert that God *must* have particular qualities and attributes if he is to be the God of black men. Either approach places a premium on facing honestly the brute facts of experience, but the second tends to move more in the direction of confronting God with nonnegotiable demands. As we shall see, if God meets these demands at all, it is perhaps in a far more subtle fashion than Cone desires or may be willing to accept.

Before exploring this thesis in detail, let us consider one important general implication it contains. Black theology promises to be one of the more provocative approaches to God we now possess. If, however, its thrust is to dictate what God *must be* like rather than to explore what he *could be* like in the light of black experience, black theology may follow the path of the sixties and end in the proclamation that God is dead. Since American thought has already been through that experience, it is to be hoped that black theology can sustain different conclusions. But that depends in part on what assumptions about God's nature black theology takes to be necessary in order to do constructive theological work.

Now, let us develop and analyze some of the crucial assumptions in Cone's theology. We can begin with the following claim from *A Black Theology of Liberation:* ". . . Black Theology cannot accept any view of God that even *indirectly* places divine approval on human suffering" (p. 149). On several occasions, Cone makes it clear that black theology cannot accept either a God who directly wills the suffering of black people or any view which claims that slavery and oppression for blacks are a metaphysical necessity.[20] The statement that we have selected here, however, is more radical and interesting. Unless we are dealing with a God who is finite and impotent, candor produces the conclusion that we may very well be confronting a God who, *at least indirectly,* has placed approval on human suffering.

This is not an easy thing to say, and it certainly does not imply that men ought to condone or become passive in the face of the horrors this world can conjure up. But if we are honest about the facts of our existence, and if we think in terms of a God who has the power claimed for him in the Christian faith, then it is surely the case that God could transform this world radically. Further, the fact that our life remains an ambiguous mixture of good and evil implies a decision on God's part to allow it to have this quality. It does not follow that God finds the present state of affairs to be the best situation possible. On the other hand, knowing and permitting something to exist when one does have the power to change it surely can be construed as a form of indirect approval.

Cone's God is not deficient in power. His hope for liberation banks on the faith that—as King would say—God is able. But God's relation to this world of ambiguity is complex. Given his original choice and his few attempts at direct intervention, he seems to have higher priorities than the simple elimination of evil and suffering by any means necessary. Precisely because he has the power to set things right now and to use any means necessary if he wishes, the implication is that he accepts a high degree of evil and suffering in this world when he does not have to do so. In that sense, he approves indirectly.

Now consider this question: If God accepts—at least indirectly approves—the high degree of evil and suffering in this world, why does he do so, and what more can be said about the nature of this acceptance? Only God himself can give a complete and final account with respect to this question, but one piece of the answer is that the God of this world seems to be more a democrat than a dictator. That is, the beings and the powers called into existence are allowed to exercise their freedom before God, and God's particular interests simply appeal to and compete with all others in an encounter largely open and undecided. If this is true, it suggests that God's first consideration is to create a world of power and freedom. He then watches to see whether it can be shaped—largely through its own self-determination—into a community where power and freedom are tempered and controlled by justice and love.

God's creation is a challenge both to himself and for us. His commitment to the freedom and power of his creation voluntarily restricts him to less direct and dramatic means of influence than he might use. It is true that the life-death-resurrection of Jesus has power and influence that often are spectacular. Yet even there the effect is to lure and persuade men to take the initiative for justice and love. This is done by instilling the hope that all existence is finally surrounded by a care and a power which will not let us be destroyed ultimately by negation and death.

God will not do for us what we can do for ourselves. In addition, where the struggle between good and evil is concerned, he makes the odds steeper than they absolutely need to be. The world surely could have been structured so as to be a little less wild and destructive, but God seems to desire no easy victories, either for himself or for us. His acceptance of evil and suffering, however, is not passive. If there is a sense in which God chooses evil and suffering for our world, it is also true that he does oppose them. But his opposition is measured; he does not employ any means necessary to win, and he may suffer defeat for a time. The opposition he adopts is more subtle and indirect. It seeks to overcome stiff odds by the power of persuading love, not coercive force.

For now at least, God seems to be less interested in the total transformation of existence at any single moment of time than in the ongoing struggle. To date, this struggle has been largely characterized by a mixture of finite victories and defeats. This world could be better than it is, but God himself seems in no great hurry to transform its basic structure, which produces a perpetually ambiguous combination of good and evil. For the time being, God favors a form of democratic rule for existence, and he continues to be concerned to see what it can accomplish. Such a situation may not always exist. Experiments in democracy do not last forever, and certainly it is basic to the Christian promise that all things are to be made new. For the present, however, God savors the struggle itself more than the taste of ultimate triumph.

If there is any validity in this interpretation, it raises some important issues about another of Cone's views: "We will not accept a God who is on everybody's side—which means that he loves everybody in spite of who they are. . . ."[21] Cone accentuates the idea that blacks are God's chosen people. God is on the side of black people and against whites insofar as they deny the beauty, worth, and power of black people. We have already explored the ambiguities of the chosen people concept, and it is sufficient to note that Cone does little better in facing them than do Washington and Cleage. The new element introduced by the statement above is the relation between the love, justice, and wrath of God.

When Cone says that black theology cannot accept a God who is on everyone's side and who loves everyone in spite of who they are, he is declaring that God stands with some men—the oppressed —and against others—the oppressors. Unless God's judgment and wrath fall on the oppressors, it cannot be affirmed that God is just. Moreover, if it can be affirmed at all that God loves men universally, it must be the case that the form of God's love for some men is righteous wrath, which may come in the form of a black revolutionary power that uproots the original white violence of slavery, oppression, and racism.

Yet is this in fact the way that God's love functions in the world? A candid look at our situation does not present a convincing picture of divine love such that it be seen chiefly in either the successful liberation of oppressed peoples or in vengeance against the destructive forces that brutalize men. Forces of evil succeed too frequently, and the humanizing powers in our world are harshly rebuffed too often for such a simple equation to hold.

In our present circumstances, the most obvious manifestation of God's love may be neither in his direct support of the oppressed nor in his righteous vengeance against oppressors. Rather, it is found in his patience with men. Love as patience in an ambiguous world of good and evil is a strange phenomenon. What can be said to clarify such an idea? We can start with this point: If God's acceptance of evil is blended with opposition to evil, it is also true that his patience is not infinite. It has limits. The question is, where and when does he draw a line not otherwise fixed?

God loves all men in the sense that he respects their freedom and power. He is willing to let this manifest itself in a self-determinative manner and compete for its place in the world. Much needless waste results from such a nondirective process. Lives are often snuffed out before they have a chance to develop, and innocent persons suffer. He could have chosen more efficient routes.

Some checks are built into the structure. For example, men are created rebellious. They occasionally act to overthrow tyranny and oppression and to relieve suffering, when they might all have been created eunuchs and made to be entirely docile. Moreover, the forces of evil themselves have some self-destructive tendencies. They can create massive havoc, and we never seem to lack for new manifestations of evil power. On the other hand, there is a self-divisiveness in these powers which prevents a total and lasting take-over. Oppressive agencies split. They turn against one another and spend much of their potentially destructive power uselessly. Still, these factors are not sufficient to negate the impression that God is allowing the world to develop largely on its own terms. God chooses to play only a supporting role by renewing hope, courage, and strength—yet not so much so that victory is automatic—in those men who seek to live for justice and love.

God may be on everybody's side much more than Cone would like to admit. This is not to say that God condones white racism or that he desires the suffering and oppression of black people. Nor is it to say that men ought to rest content with the status quo because it is God's will. Oppression is not good for any of us—oppressed or oppressors—and we ought to be rid of it. But God expects men to take the initiative in the struggle. As Cone himself emphasizes, he gives no guarantees of victory. Perhaps the reason is because of his love for all men, not just those who are on the side of righteousness. That is a strange phenomenon, too. How is it to be understood?

God does not love sin, but according to the New Testament he does love men and seeks to save them even if they are sinners. In a world shaped by a struggle between forces of good and evil, this is a difficult and delicate stand to take if you are a God committed voluntarily to respect the freedom of men. Human judgments and efforts to correct evil often result in the destruction of persons. In addition to allowing men to take this corrective action at times, God could work in this way himself if he chose to do so. In point of fact, however, his role is more restrained.

Men are free to be violent revolutionaries, but God's way is more to lure and to persuade. Christ did drive the money changers out of the temple, but his more dominating images are different: drawing men to himself by hanging on a cross and urging men to follow him by knocking on their doors and by calling their names. God has great power, but he uses it cautiously and with self-control in dealing with men—precisely because his goal is to save rather than to annihilate.

Men are less patient than God, and hence less loving. These characteristics are a part of our nature as men. This fact entails both that we can do violence to each other and that revolutions against evil and suffering may take place. If God exists, virtually anything is permitted on this earth. But this ought not to make us think too easily that the particular course of action we take— even in struggling with evil—is the vehicle of God's direct inter- vention in the world. Our decisions and actions are just that—they are ours. If God is at work in them, it is only in the supporting role of renewing strength, courage, and hope when men ask direction and strive honestly.

Cone's theology of liberation ends on an eschatological note. He wants a God who vindicates the oppressed in this world and who achieves a definite and visible triumph over the forces of op- pression. On the other hand, he plays down the concept of win- ning now in favor of the idea that the crucial thing is the black man's affirmation of his worth and his willingness to give every- thing for liberty. This implies that it is only beyond death that things are fully set right. The resurrection of Jesus Christ points to this reality and keeps hope alive—both for the future and in the present. Just because the future is alive beyond death, men are en- abled to give all for liberty now. They literally have nothing to lose.

A hope lying on the horizon of the future intensifies man's impatience with present conditions. It is as if God lures us into action with the future. But this question remains: How will things be when they are all made new? Only God can tell, and perhaps his decision on this may itself lie in the future. The biblical images, however, are suggestive. They point toward a true community of love. There in some recognizable form we exist together and with God, with knowledge and appreciation of him and our fellow men. The significance of all existence is underwritten, and there is meaningful work to do; freedom, power, and justice are harmonized.

For all of us—and especially for those now caught up in extreme forms of behavior—this transformation will entail a harsh judgment by God. Our human lives will be found wanting. We will feel this and know it. But such judgment, like death itself, ultimately will heal us—or at least that is the Christian hope. For every man, God will offer liberation from oppression. "He will wipe away every tear from their eyes, and death shall be no more, neither shall there be mourning nor crying nor pain any more, for the former things have passed away."[22]

God's patience with men does not make it easy to have a hope such as this, for a patient God often seems little different from a God who is absent or dead. Moreover, if God is either absent from us, dead, or nonexistent, then the present world is very likely all there is for us, and hope will die. There are no ultimate winners in this existence. Every individual passes away. All flesh is like the grass.

On the other hand, perhaps a patient God is likely to save us and, finally, make us new. A patient God is one with power, one who creates out of love, one who respects the power and freedom he gives. A patient God may create a world of wildness, and risk momentary defeat to see what men can do. Yet he can be confident that—even if we are driven to doubt—whatever is of value can be rescued from destruction. Paradoxically, it may even be a patient God who is most effective in spurring us to action for justice and love. Patience, too, may bring a renewal of American life, if only we reflect on such a God's motives and learn from him.

Cone's version of black theology is an important American theological statement. It raises virtually every crucial issue about the nature of God and man with direct reference to the basic issues of American life. More than some of the figures we have met in this book, Cone takes the American experience with deadly seriousness. It knows God as alive and far from dead.

We founded a nation in the name of liberty, but from the very beginning men here have been in need of liberation too. No American feels this fact more deeply than Cone, and few are as aware of the price we may have to pay in order to make even small gains toward this oft-stated ideal. As it stands, Cone's theology is a long way from being free of serious theological problems, but it can have an impact on the black community and on America's religious life. His work should force every creative theologian to reflect more deeply on the American experience, God's relation to it, and what God may be trying to say to us through such a medium.

F. Black Theology and Pluralism

Black theology produces provocative insights about the pluralism present in American life and theology. In the first place, it indicates that our present form of pluralism is not humane, and it gives us clues about what our various levels of life ought to entail as a whole. Freedom to pursue and develop the interests and life-styles that attract individuals or groups may be a sufficient condition for pluralism, but it does not assure that the resulting pluralism will be humane. Since a humane pluralism must have something additional, it is much more profound and difficult to achieve. It includes an attitude of appreciation and respect for the things done by other people and different groups. This, in turn, implies that the actions and projects undertaken by any individual or group are themselves worthy of respect and appreciation—or at least we have to stand ready to admit that they might be.

Beyond that, a humane pluralism provides a setting in which men encourage each other in their self-determination and help one another to achieve their goals—not by giving up their own individual identities and concerns but by utilizing them to build a community of variety, excellence, and harmony. A humane pluralism, then, exists fully only where every person has meaningful, freely chosen tasks to perform which also contribute to the up-building of the total community. It exists fully only if every person can accept and appreciate the contributions of others while appropriating and retaining the best in the social patterns and group ties his own existence thrusts upon him.

On the other hand, pluralism is not fully humane where it entails only the existence of a variety of power centers, each striving for its "share of the pie" with little mutual respect or esteem. A mere balance of powers is one form of pluralism, but it ought not to be the kind that satisfies Americans. Our goal should be more the achievement of a variety of life-styles that still are mutually upbuilding. It should include racial awareness and appreciation, but not hatred and racism. It ought to involve the continued cultivation of the cultural and religious backgrounds from which we have come, but not bigotry and intolerance. Openness without loss of personal and group identities, equality without mediocrity—these might still form the components of an American dream.

Black theology shows us that we are a long way from these goals and that they are extremely difficult to achieve. The very existence of black theology reflects the fact that the American government and the attitudes of most Americans have both been deficient in their response to the needs of black people. This indictment hits at American churches and theology, too, in a most severe way. Black theology's critique of white Christianity in America probably is exaggerated. Nevertheless, there is no escape from the fact that the racial split of the American churches, at least as it has existed in our history, has no place in a humane pluralism. White churches have fumbled the ball time and time again as far as a movement toward reconciliation and brotherhood is concerned.

The record of American theologians may be somewhat better than that of our white churches, but it is not without fault. In every generation there have been voices urging us to take our own tradition more seriously, but we have not always immersed ourselves in the American experience as deeply and as honestly as we could and should. Too often we have let European thinkers do our basic theological and metaphysical work for us. Even black theologians do this to a large extent. Nevertheless, black theology is encouraging because it does accept the American experience as distinctive—although in its more unfortunate respects. It uses that experience as a vital theological base. This pushes our theology in a more "American" direction, and that in itself is an exciting prospect.

Still another dimension of the relationship between black theology and pluralism is worth noting in conclusion. We have argued in this book that pluralism is one of the distinctive characteristics of American theology. Multiple theological views have existed here from the beginning. Americans gradually found this variety desirable and moved to encourage even greater diversity of opinion. Black theology fits this pattern. It may have emerged more as a necessity than as something whose existence would have been consciously chosen at the outset. But it does bring novel and original insights to the American theological scene. Moreover, its tone emphasizes a pluralistic thrust, just because many black theologians consider their theology to be primarily for black people.[23] In fact, it is claimed that authentic appropriation of the message of black theology by white men is dependent on "the blackness of their existence in the world" (p. 12). This means: there cannot be one theology; there must be many, since not all experience can fit that pattern.

If this orientation is a fundamental factor in the strength of black theology, still it should be pointed out that crucial problems lurk here as well. There is a latent theme in much black theology—especially present in Cone's work—to the effect that disagreement with or criticism of black theology by white people may be a not-so-disguised manifestation of white racism. (See, for example, pp. 32–34.) In addition, Cone suggests that a genuinely Christian theology can emerge only from an oppressed community (p. 17), which in Cone's view means primarily the black community.

Several points are worth making in response. First, Cone is correct in saying that some disagreements with and criticisms of black theology are manifestations of racism. He is also careful to clarify that white men can be "black" theologians by identifying themselves with the goal of liberation for the oppressed and wretched of the earth. Nevertheless, a word of caution must be spoken. Cone's theology is not without a dogmatic quality. It runs the risk, therefore, of being antipluralistic and of establishing agreement or disagreement with its own particular views as the norm for determining whether the response of any white man is "black" or racist. Unless that tendency is kept in check, Cone's version of black theology will in the long run lose much of its effectiveness. It will deny Christian openness by becoming another exclusive theory claiming truth for itself.

Religion and theology in America have had an ambiguous career vis-à-vis relations between blacks and whites. But the fact remains that religious and theological motivations may still be the strongest base from which progress can be achieved toward making America a humanely pluralistic society. Advance along those lines, however, is not likely to come without a theological openness which allows, takes account of, and even encourages the fact that there can be a plurality of legitimate Christian theologies developed out of varied contexts and situations. This is not to say that a theology which condones, advocates, or does nothing to combat oppression and racism is one of these. Cone is absolutely correct in denouncing every view that has such dehumanizing qualities. On the other hand, any stronger tendency to restrict theological pluralism will move us further away from the humane society many of us seek.

In these days of racial tension and conflict we should demand theological variety and openness more than ever. We do not need "white theology," i. e., theology that seeks to condone, advocate, or do nothing to combat oppression and racism. We do need thoughtful, critical, and humane theologies from varied sources aimed for white and black and all people alike. We need black theologies, written by black men primarily for black people, but we also must encourage creative responses to them from both white and black communities.

Let us also solicit bold, original statements from white theologians who will take the American experience seriously and honestly and seek to interpret God's relation to it and his intention for it. All of these efforts must focus on the ambiguous life we share, and each should enable us to move toward a more creative society. If they are brought into contact with each other in the spirit of a willingness to listen and learn from everyone, each could play a part in making this nation a land of liberty.

One hopeful sign for the future of America stems from the fact that we live in a time when theological pluralism will inevitably increase. We may find ourselves—partly as a result of this very phenomenon—moving in the direction of a renewed, revitalized, and even radically restructured sense of unity and identity as Americans. Although we appear to be moving further apart, the very pluralism of our theological views—if we can remain open to each other—could be one catalyst that sets the nation on a path true to her original ideals. On the other hand, there is no guarantee that this will occur. Like every human situation, our theological context is both ambiguous and precarious.

In the late twentieth century, we have arrived back in Old Testament times. Ours is again a "pre-Christian" era when some men want a God of vengeance, one who identifies with them and destroys their enemies. We are also back in the era of early and formative Christianity, a day when we thought God's promise had come, but only to some one group. Peter's "second conversion" (see Acts 10) awaits us again, the radical and difficult and baffling discovery that now we are to announce his promise as available to *all*. Can't we understand? Christian liberty really means the release from *every* restriction of race or class, not the pre-Christian notion of God's partiality to one group.

Black theology has returned us to the question that faced primitive Christianity: Is God's message for some special group or is it the amazing message of our deliverance from bondage to all tribal laws, our new freedom from *all* racial attachments? The argument between Paul and Peter returns: What is Christianity if it is not just another religious sect? Did Jesus come simply to promote some special group, or to align himself with the causes (however just) of one sect? If, like the disciples on the day after Jesus' crucifixion, we are disappointed because our own jealous causes seem not triumphant, we may yet discover our hopes fulfilled as God's own action moves in some unexpected direction. Black theology sets us up to be disappointed all over again when our cause cannot win the day completely, but it also raises questions which may open us again to the universality of the Christian gospel.

Perhaps, if we are to achieve something significant we must begin by demanding what is impossible. Martin Luther King, Jr. says in his dedication of *Where Do We Go from Here?* that he feels assured "brotherhood will be the condition of man, not the dream of man." Blacks are and have been oppressed in ways which leave us far from such brotherhood. This oppression we can and should stop, as men have been saying thousands of times over since the union of American colonies was formed. Yet, even without ghetto discrimination, is it at all clear that whites have achieved brotherhood to the degree blacks have under oppression? If we think the removal of one artificial restraint will in itself create an ideal life, this may be because we do not understand the human condition, and thus we simply open ourselves to greater final disappointment.

In recent years, King tells us, "the Negro stood up and confronted his oppressor."[24] That was a significant event in American history, and we live in that new era. The Negro became the active organ of change. He understands today what most Americans once knew: "Freedom is not won by a passive acceptance of suffering. Freedom is won by a struggle *against* suffering" (p. 20). Blacks today repeat our early colonial experience, except that the clash comes as intensified face-to-face combat between fellow citizens and not at a distance over vast oceans. Yet the enormity of the need may involve a frustration in accomplishment and a certain blunt "either/or" kind of thinking. ". . . Disappointment produces despair and despair produces bitterness, and . . . one thing certain about bitterness is its blindness. Bitterness has not the capacity to make distinctions between some and *all*" (p. 26). When the ideals are high, the resulting disillusion can be unbearable too.

"The emergence of the militant Negro, insisting upon his rights as a human being and equality as a citizen, is the great, new fact of this half of the American twentieth century," Joseph Washington, Jr. tells us.[25] But he also reports a weakness in Negro religion which makes their churches unable to cope with the situation. If so, that really puts blacks and whites in the same vulnerable religious situation. A strong black "folk religion" actually exists, Washington goes on to say, but this is different from a strong black church structure. Similarly, whites now find that their ecclesiastical organization is a questionable instrument. If so, both blacks and whites are thrown back more upon themselves. They must locate internally the source of the religious strength they need, if it is not available to them formally in a useful way through organized churches.

James H. Cone speaks of the black man's loss of identity and self-hatred.[26] This is fascinating to consider in light of the fact that a similar mood also appears today among young white Americans. Thus, whatever new sense of identity Americans can achieve might be worked out by black and white together, although Cone does not see it that way.

Cone proposes a theology of revolution, and he sees Jesus' work as essentially one of liberation (p. 35). Unquestionably that is right, but the dilemma that perplexed the early disciples—and perplexes us still—is what *form* this liberation can take and how and when it will come or is to come. Black power may be God's new way of acting in America (p. 61), but the trick here is that God often does not behave in the way we expect, nor does he always realize for us what we want when we want it.

NOTES

1. Almost all of the books cited in the footnotes for this chapter contain important information about the history of the black churches in America and about the significance of religious life in black communities. Three other books are worth mentioning in this context: Major J. Jones, *Black Awareness: A Theology of Hope* (Nashville: Abingdon Press, 1971); Benjamin E. Mays, *The Negro's God* (New York: Atheneum, 1968); Henry H. Mitchell, *Black Preaching* (Philadelphia: J. B. Lippincott Company, 1970). Mays' book was first published in 1938.

2. Martin Luther King, Jr., *Stride Toward Freedom* (New York: Harper & Row, 1964), p. 167. This book was first published in 1958.

3. Quoted from King's "I Have a Dream" as reprinted in C. Eric Lincoln, ed., *Is Anybody Listening to Black America?* (New York: Seabury Press, 1968), p. 65.

4. See Martin Luther King, Jr., *Where Do We Go From Here: Chaos or Community?* (Boston: Beacon Press, 1968), especially pp. 23–66.

5. Martin Luther King, Jr., *Strength to Love* (New York: Pocket Books, 1964), pp. 65–66.

6. See Martin Luther King, Jr., *The Trumpet of Conscience* (New York: Harper & Row, 1968), especially pp. 51–64.

7. Joseph R. Washington, Jr., *Black and White Power Subreption* (Boston: Beacon Press, 1969), p. 122.

8. Joseph R. Washington, Jr., *Black Religion* (Boston: Beacon Press, 1964), p. 31.

9. Joseph R. Washington, Jr., *The Politics of God* (Boston: Beacon Press, 1967), p. 104.

10. In a more recent book, *Marriage in Black and White* (Boston:

Beacon Press, 1970), Washington has interpreted social equality as entailing a cultural disposition that accepts fully—even welcomes—racial inter-marriage as something desirable. If these circumstances come to exist, our society will be virtually free of racism, and only if they exist will our society exemplify as it should the qualities of humane pluralism to which our best American ideals commit us. It is obvious that we are very far from actualizing the conditions Washington has in mind.

11. *Black and White Power Subreption,* p. 118.

12. Albert B. Cleage, Jr., *The Black Messiah* (New York: Sheed & Ward, 1968), p. 4. Similar themes can be found in the work of an earlier black writer, Marcus Garvey.

13. Galatians 5:1.

14. James H. Cone, *Black Theology and Black Power* (New York: Seabury Press, 1969), p. 6.

15. James H. Cone, *A Black Theology of Liberation* (Philadelphia: J. B. Lippincott Company, 1970), p. 17.

16. See Luke 4:16–21.

17. See *A Black Theology of Liberation,* p. 17.

18. *Black Theology and Black Power,* p. 37.

19. *A Black Theology of Liberation,* p. 19.

20. See, for example, *Black Theology and Black Power,* pp. 124–125.

21. *A Black Theology of Liberation,* p. 131.

22. Revelation 21:4.

23. *A Black Theology of Liberation,* p. 12.

24. *Where Do We Go From Here?,* p. 15.

25. *Black Religion,* p. 1.

26. *Black Theology and Black Power,* p. 18.

IX

CONTEMPORARY CULTURE
AND THE FUTURE OF THEOLOGY

A. The Present as an Expression of the Past

The natural human tendency is to take our present experience as an expression of itself alone, or perhaps as a forecast of the future. In fact, no present event can be understood by itself. St. Augustine taught us that both past and future are necessarily involved in the present moment. The present is only a thin line drawn between them, a razor's edge. To understand what is happening to us at any time, we must recognize what parts of our past history are still active, and we also must become skilled at deciphering the novelty of the future that is beginning to break in upon us.

Particularly in a time of uncertainty, rebellion, and revolution we are not allowed to take the preservation of the past for granted. Everything goes rigid with age. Even a good judicial system becomes overburdened and outmoded unless revised. When radical disruption threatens, the trick is to open the door to reform without destroying the valid elements of the past. Of course, the problem is that this is easier said than done. In the heat of protest and under pressure of change, it is just quicker to reject all that is past.

Americans should not want to adopt an entirely historical approach to self-understanding, however. In our present situation, the future should provide the key as much as the past. But it is still true that we must discern just how the present unfolds as an ex-

pression of the past—both for good and for ill—so that even justified rebellion need not cut all our ties and leave us rootless. In the
rush to usher in the future, we have to be sure its vital connections
are sufficient to sustain its new life.

In this regard it is interesting to note that, perhaps for the first
time in our history, Americans now look more to either the past
or the present than to the future. This is a crucial change in attitude, since we have rarely been historically oriented. In fact, our
original driving principle had been to cut all our ties to the past in
the hope of escaping the world's accumulated ills and creating a
better future here. Perhaps, then, the greatest cause of upheaval today is no single issue—neither war nor poverty. Instead, present
turmoil results from the painful sense that the future we waited for
so long is now here, but that it is not very different from the situation of other men all over the globe. Endless opportunities and a
completely open future no longer are quite so much a part of the
American experience.

If the American dream is now realized, it has too many aspects
of a nightmare for comfort. In spite of the positive accomplishments, then, any new sense of the future today is going to have
to come from somewhere other than our past dreams. Blocked
materially and geographically, we may have to discover a "spiritual
future" for ourselves. To move in that direction would skip over
the industrial nineteenth century and return to original American
immigrant ideals. Of course, some early arrivals came here primarily to satisfy material ambitions, but others came to escape
oppression and to worship freely. These groups expected to be
able to live, but their dreams were neither of nineteenth-century
industrialization nor of twentieth-century abundance. They could
not have foreseen those developments. Yet, now that such progress
and abundance no longer satisfy all of us, we may have to return
to seek spiritual freedom again—as once we did. To do this is to
see the present turmoil as one expression of our past.

If we remember that no single racial or religious group settled
America and that no one colony conquered the others in order to
rule all, we may grasp both the source of American strength and
the reason for our constant turmoil. If we could endorse one theory
or one religion, we might have peace. But as long as there is

diversity of thought and background, there will be controversy and lack of unanimity. Overcome by our new material success and power, we forgot this for a time, and the rude awakening to accept a past fact is painful. We have been momentarily lulled to sleep with the thought that, if we all (or most of us) enjoyed material plenty, then everyone would agree. Instead, we have rediscovered the fact that pluralism is the first principle of American life and thought. This situation makes us politically unique. Unfortunately, it also subjects us to constant dissent, and this unceasing argument is jarring to our newly sophisticated nervous system.

Instead of warring among the colonies to see who should rule, we decided to try a union of diverse elements—a brave experiment. Tolerance was not originally an ideal among all the colonists, any more than it is today. It did emerge as the necessary condition if the states were to unite; but to achieve compromise and toler- ance is still hard work in any time of disagreement. If the present is always to a degree an expression of the past, what is rejected when some turn against the American past? Clearly, it is no one thing and so cannot be cast out as a whole. Most important, we may in fact be reacting against elements in American society that resulted from industrialization, rather than against an earlier in- digenous strain. In a nontotalitarian country, to reject the past can only mean to recover one of the previous strands which at the time seems more genuine.

In a day when so much appears changed from colonial days, we have to plot the future by first recovering some of the past. We ask, is it possible to be born and to live here and not carry over some of the past? The future is always what is not yet and cannot be lived in; the present, on the other hand, is a knife-edge and does not provide us with enough room. The meaning of the present and the future depends on our ability to carry forward and to reject aspects of the past which now are either acceptable as ideals or unacceptable as inauthentic. Where pluralism is the first principle, this fine process of discrimination cannot be avoided. In fact, it must go on continually.

If our past is not one thing, our future can never be handed to us automatically. This is an interesting but unsettling fact which cannot be said of many countries of the globe. Uncertainty and instability are an infuriating part of our nature. Americans have been preoccupied with freedom and fulfillment, it is true. But, if we have no single formula for them, then pluralism involves a constant discussion—sometimes a quarrel—over the means. Although the original settlers probably never thought every man could be raised to middle-class enjoyment, that optimistic note did take over for a while. Now that such uniformity of enjoyment seems no longer either possible or desirable, we are back to more somber economic forecasts, and this forces us to accept a variety of social goals. The hope of uniformity was a late American notion. Dissent and plurality are more authentic—if we can see our present turmoil as an expression of our past.

If we seek a religious understanding of our present political and economic turmoil and uncertainty, we should remember at least three things: (1) Neither the early colonists nor any human group have ever been all "religious men." Religious motivation is an inescapable part of the American spirit, but many came here out of greed or adventure or simple human wants—and so it still is today. (2) Our religious situation has now changed permanently, and religion will never again be so closely identified with national aims as once it was. With a wealthy and powerful nation, this must be so, and religion is now better off not being identified with the mistakes a giant is bound to make in his awkward movements. (3) Quakers, Mormons, Christian Scientists, Judaism, and Pentecostal groups—all are as much a part of the American religious scene as Puritanism, Presbyterianism and Catholicism.

The presence and strength of these groups testify to the American principle of religious diversity. Moreover, their orientation is often more practical than intellectual. They arose out of religious needs and not from quarrels among theologians. Thus, American religious life never has been either "orthodox" or unified. Everyone did not have to be religious to be accepted at first, although for a time religion came close to being identified with middle-class goals of success. Mormons celebrate the pioneer spirit. They are Latter-Day Saints in a new world, but they still have ancient ties. If Christian Science offers a science of health for body and spirit, the religious market place also teems with a thousand other offerings—some not so pure and calm and healthy.

Unfortunately, this means that the American religious spirit can never find either rest or full satisfaction. To reach such fulfillment, one must follow one certified road, and our founding decisions deny us that comfort. We launched on a more perilous religious odyssey. Religiously we can never feel really at home without constant challenge. We are strangers in a strange land, not assured aristocrats and landholders of the spirit. We have a large country to roam in, and lately the world has been our path, as Americans—perhaps more than any other people—have wandered about the globe. With so many resources at home, we still have no spiritual security, and thus our spirits are condemned to wander religiously homeless.

Just for a moment, we seemed to achieve stability in the golden age of the 1950s. Neatly dressed, we appeared around the world certain that we had finally produced a culture (or at least a vast economy) and escaped our unseemly past. But that proved to be a unity falsely based. Our original raw quarrels and lack of agreement emerged as more fundamental in the national spirit. It is, as it always was, still possible to achieve spiritual peace and to produce beauty, but this must be individually accomplished without demanding prior national agreement or even support. Technology unified a great land into a highly sophisticated and interlocking complex. But the machine cast the man out to wander the land on a continued spiritual odyssey—just as if he had never accomplished a thing.

In every era there is a tendency to take what is visible at the moment as characteristic of what is available. This seems particularly true in a time of crisis, when it is hard to remember what the past has been—and when ironically the future reaches out to draw on ideas not readily available. Thus it is important to see what aspects of our past intellectual tradition can be pulled into the present, and a review of the history of specifically American philosophy reveals a depth and variety too easily forgotten. As appears in other aspects of American life, the peculiar and pervasive characteristic of American philosophy is its pluralism.[1] Contrast this with either the clear line of English philosophy or the fascinating German dialectical movements, and it becomes all the more noticeable how unorganized American philosophers are.

A pragmatic strain has been widespread, with its confidence and optimism in the ability of knowledge to solve the problems of men. The Puritans hoped to found a new Zion. They were intolerant of dissent and heresy, but they did not carry the day or shape the mood of the future. Congregational churches contained the seeds of a wider democracy which was to win. However, the now traditional notions of liberty, equality, and natural rights have been under attack from the beginning. The Southern aristocracy never really accepted these as fundamental goals in America, a fact which became obvious in the Civil War. Our present problems are not recent but primordial.

Transcendentalism, as it developed in the nineteenth century in American literature and philosophy, was a distinctive note and placed us at odds with a strict British empirical or a Continental scientific concept of philosophy. Subjective and mystical insight is acceptable to transcendentalism, for instance. Intuition and sentiment are important, but at the same time its moral idealism supports civil disobedience, if society contradicts the individual moral conscience. The abolition of slavery and the establishment of utopian communities were a common aim, which gives today's communes their source in the past. Naturalism did have a revival here,[2] but its aim to establish the empirical methods of science as *the* valid procedure for establishing cognitive claims works against some of the assertions of traditional religion. Yet this never became the exclusive route for all American thought—not even among pragmatists.

For one thing, waves of immigration have continually given American philosophy new life and new direction,[3] just as has been true of the social and political scene. Thus we have the slight comfort of knowing that our past is fully as confused as our present. We cannot fit into the German historian's model for systematic development. *We grow by remaining the same in diversity and lack of reconciliation.* In religion, this means a failure of authoritarianism.

. . . What was in Europe primarily a revolt of the middle classes against ecclesiastical privilege became in America a positive basis for the founding of independent political communities in which the clergy gradually lost their power and kept their prestige only to the extent that they themselves adopted the "lay" point of view. (p. 7)

Yet European ecclesiasticism did reassert itself when pietism and evangelicalism migrated to America and swept the populace off its balance in the "Great Awakening." We are not now, religiously, a group of democratically run and individually administered churches as we might have been. We brought old structures over too, such as slavery, so that struggles between free and slave, religious independence vs. ecclesiastical control, still go on. We did develop a democratic religious tradition. However, it never became completely dominant and so is forced to exist alongside every ancient ecclesiastical structure and imported spiritual form.

While England's landed aristocracy settled in Virginia bringing with them orthodoxy and conservative views patterned on British nobility, the Plymouth Colony represented the lower strata of English society—a fact we should remember when we speak of New England as the home of American aristocracy. The Dutch in New York were primarily merchants and only secondarily church members. Religious persecution might easily have gone further here than it did if necessity had not forced tolerance on the settlers. Calvinism was also imported as a theology at the same time that the problem of freedom held a conspicuous place in intellectual and political discussion. This made a simple transplant of religious orthodoxy impossible. Popular needs moved the philosophy of the early years in a variety of directions simultaneously.

Morris R. Cohen suggests that American thought has been "very largely a province of British thought—despite the Declaration of Independence and two wars."[4] This widely held assumption needs careful examination and qualification where the interests of this book are concerned. That is, if we are to understand our present situation as an expression of the past, it is important to come to terms with the exact role that British thought has played. In philosophy, our dependence on it is clear in certain schools of thought during certain eras. But America does have theories not British in their derivation. Over the years, every other tradition has come to be represented too—in spite of the fact that there are times in philosophy of a nearly complete dominance by British-derived theories.

The Continent has tended to call the tune for American theology, at least until recently, and where religious life is concerned, every conceivable variety flourishes. Since religious life should reflect the needs of the people, this is to be expected. Even the temporary dominance of Puritan modes of thought should be examined carefully, since this certainly was not "establishment" religion in England at the time of its import. Far from it. And as American theology has developed, it retains only certain strains of Puritan thought. Immigrants sought America as an escape from oppression of caste and persecution, so that this element in our religious life and thought is inescapable—even where it was realized only negatively among the blacks. The clergy were the first to challenge the prestige of the commercially successful early colonists. Thus social criticism in America also has religious roots. In the recent alliance of economic success and institutional religion, this fact was temporarily lost from sight—until a sector of the clergy arose again as a challenge to political and economic success.

Cohen is convinced that "the prevailing temper of American life remains pronouncedly anti-intellectual" (pp. 36–37). This may be true, but his hidden assumption is that this is bad. On the contrary, it is perhaps the best part of the American tradition that it remains a little suspicious of the intellectual. Every mode of life should be allowed its expression, and perhaps intellectualism flourishes better as a minority enterprise.

In addition, Cohen also believes that the distinctive feature of American thought for three centuries was the conviction that the American way of life is so clearly preferable to any other that an immigrant will be turned into a useful American citizen in only a few years (p. 61). Certainly this assumption now has vanished for many, which brings us as a society to our middle age. We look back to a youth now clearly gone and are no longer so confident that the expected glorious future will in fact arrive. A profound reorganization in American thought is under way as now we are forced to accept the fact that the goal we sought in our youth may not be reached. Moreover, it may be unobtainable in principle. If so, the issue is whether we will settle for less—as much as we can achieve—or turn away and destroy the whole enterprise in the frustrated rage of a child whose toy won't work.

Does this change now make America a backward-looking nation rather than a people primarily future-oriented as we have been? Emerson and Walt Whitman advised men to turn their backs on the past and their faces to the future. We may still be future-oriented. The future, however, is not turning out quite the way many of us thought it would. Thus we must reassess the past in order to make the adjustments required by this new awareness. We are not, on the whole, a people given to the historical approach, but by this time we have lived at least long enough to make a record we can study. And we must appraise the past critically to find out where we went wrong and adjust our calculations accordingly. Religion particularly requires some looking back to past events, and our religious life may be smaller in size but healthier if it is cut loose from unrealizable future visions.

John E. Smith thinks that American thought has often focused on the themes of experience, purpose, and community.[5] Thus social categories play an important part in American thought, which opens it to a religious interpretation. We are by nature purposive in our outlook. As John Dewey did, we view thought not as independent but as governed by a purpose beyond itself, and that purpose cannot be a matter of theory alone (p. 13). This may smack of American "anti-intellectualism," but that is far from being all bad. For a time this idea may have become identified with an evolutionary notion of thought and life. Yet, once we see that evolutionary patterns may not govern us in the social realm, we can recover the purposive notion of thought as being directed beyond itself and still admit that such direction is not always one of improvement.

American philosophy has constantly appealed to experience as a norm, as our book's title suggests. Paul Tillich once remarked that when he first came to New York he could not understand the constant use of this term, until finally he realized that Americans used "experience" just as "being" had once been used, to refer to "the totality of all that is." Moreover, as long as religious experience can be included as a primary mode (as William James did), this concrete orientation for thought is conducive to religion, since it can stress religion's practice and active role as a crucial dimension of experience.

"Irrelevant" thinking has always been a cardinal sin in American philosophy, and the most damning complaint against a thinker is that his ideas have no concrete consequences.[6] Such a tradition has often tended to dampen speculative theology at the same time that it accepted the ethical and social sides of religious life. However, as old visions are lost, as our dreams of both political harmony and an ideal religious life fade, free speculative thought and a metaphysical examination of first principles receive a new impetus. In fact, if a basic adjustment of American social and religious aims must take place, and if this involves questioning some very primitive assumptions, speculation begins to take on a practical urgency as the only way to open up a future which otherwise is closed— just because it is clear that past dreams will not now develop automatically. We may once have been voluntaristic and noncontemplative (p. xiv), but today we are forced to a vast reassessment and to a reflection on our past.

Smith accepts as part of the spirit of American philosophy that *"the earth can be civilized* and obstacles to progress overcome by the application of knowledge" (p. 188). Somewhat unfortunately, this kind of optimism stands severely shaken in America, perhaps even beyond recovery. If so, American religious thought has a basic readjustment to make, just to the degree that it has identified with this optimism. We need not go to the other extreme and cry that thought and effort can accomplish nothing, but the blanket optimism of the nineteenth and early twentieth centuries is surely under challenge. We are back to the less certain days when the colonists faced a threatening wilderness, rather than living on in the expansive mood of industrialization.

If action still remains the justification of all thought in America (p. 192), even Smith's appeal for a recovery of faith in reason (pp. 209–210) may not really be our best route into the future. As Smith himself helps us to see, the age of strict rationalism is over. We are no longer confident that reason of itself delivers us to any one best solution. We now view reason as finite and fallible. One result is that our belief in its saving power may also have been shattered beyond recovery. Ultimate trust in reason involves an optimistic humanism and the conviction that man can control his own future successfully. These assumptions are now in question. They clash with a religious spirit of accepting at least some degree of dependence on God. Yet if religiously we are ready to abandon humanism, this is not a betrayal of all American thought but only of certain more recent forms. Our illusion of unity is gone again. The land looks raw once more, this time as the result of our own work, and now we must find a way to unite divergent purposes and work to tame the land we have made wild.

Robert J. Roth, S.J., tells us that religion came to be "identified with the American dream of a good life,"[7] and this is perhaps one source of the religious perplexity of the late twentieth century. That American dream in its detail was a product of nineteenth-century industrialism and evolutionary concepts, not colonial ideals, and it must be radically rethought today. We may not make it. In fact, it is rather clear that such a goal is not really achievable. Those who refuse to rethink national aims will insist that religion continue to support their own social image. Those who think the nation's values must be reappraised will either try to remake religion into an instrument of radical reform or turn away from it.

Liberal Christianity in this country capitulated to naturalistic philosophy, thinking that its assumptions were inescapable. Today that philosophical outlook is under wide attack, and the liberal religion identified with it is thrown into confusion, the more so because it took its position to be inevitable for modern man. And so it was—except that "modern man" has been made obsolete by the upsurge of fantastic nonrational forces. Somehow we thought to become "concerned with this world" (p. 9) was a new discovery. Most men's concerns have always been predominantly secular. Against this reaction, some few who are religiously interested have tended to withdraw from the world, but they are always a minority. The bulk of religiously disposed men must live in two worlds simultaneously, which is a more difficult feat to accomplish. Naturalism as a philosophical outlook (that is, stressing man's continuity with nature) is an easy expression of certain American goals. Its suitability as a religious base, however, is yet to be determined.

In examining the rapid religious growth and expansion of the churches which occurred in the 1950s, William McLoughlin and Robert Bellah termed this another "Great Awakening" and thought the whole society was reoriented by this religious turn.[8] In looking back now, however, we see that growth as due partly to the happy union of (1) the national ideal to provide a comfortable future for all and (2) religious institutional support of this aim. When these goals came under question, and when the country became locked in debate over its actions, both internal and external, the church went into numerical decline because religion was thrown into confusion too. The mood before was of hope, excitement, and exhilaration (p. xi), but these are questionable religious attitudes when they are tied to the success of some national or economic aim.

As a nation, we are and have been both highly materialistic and deeply religious at the same time, although not always in the same ways. Evidently the two can go side by side—the mistake is to identify the two goals. Fruitfulness may lie, not in religious and secular unity, but in their corrective opposition to one another. American church leaders are and have been (in varying degrees at various times) deeply involved in both social reform movements and business organizational techniques. Thus, our fear that religion may become irrelevant can only be because we demand such a high degree of relevance—perhaps more than religion can ever have to secular goals. And this split becomes all the more pronounced as we become increasingly and predominantly secular as a society.

Politically speaking, religion had been a kind of national faith, because many Americans felt an obligation to carry out God's will on earth. The "civil religion" of the founding fathers provided a role for God, and the equation of America with Israel in the notion of an American Israel was not infrequent.[9] First we gave religious connotations to the event of the Revolution, then the Civil War, and today Black Liberation and the Vietnam war raise religious issues for all sides. Death, sacrifice, and rebirth became national themes in the profound unsettling caused by the Civil War, and they appear again as major themes today, after the close of the period of the Great Opulence.

The French were anticlerical in their revolution, but America has tended to see its revolutions in positive religious terms. Perhaps this is because our religion has tended to be activist, moralistic, and social rather than contemplative. However, the end of the notion of achieving completely the American dream seems now to have opened us to the inner or spiritual dimension of religion (especially among the young) to a degree not imaginable by either the advocates of religion as social concern or those who saw it as a corollary to national success. Clearly our notion of God drops into chaos as the country falls into confusion, because the two were so closely linked in what Bellah calls our civil religion. Thus the interesting fact is that a new, and perhaps more profound, notion of God may appear as one positive result from this era of national turmoil and destruction.

"Spirituality" as a term was abandoned by academic religionists in the first two thirds of the twentieth century. "Transcendence" seemed to disappear too.[10] Why, then, has the search for transcendence, by drugs if necessary, recently burst in upon the scene so disruptively? Because, if society's goals become unachievable or its culture intolerable, the human spirit can no longer identify with it as the naturalists had hoped. Spirit bursts out, seeking release, so that religion in a time of social revolution is forced to reexamine new possibilities for the development of the spiritual side of man. A disillusioned American becomes either rigid in his defense of former goals or cynical and defeatist—or he amazes a blatantly secular culture by his intense exploration of long-dormant spiritual dimensions.

Harvey Cox saw a "New Breed" of laymen and minister arising in the fifties whose symbol was the socially activist clergyman.[11] Of course, this is not a new breed at all in American life, but simply the reemergence of the social gospel after an era of extraordinary religious contentment with society. To say that churches now take the leadership in social change, however, is probably to overestimate what the institutional church can do on this broad front. Its laymen may not allow it to accept this role, since we are largely democratic in our church structure and not clergy-dominated. To press the church in this direction can also lead to an equal disillusionment in religion, if certain social goals of reform are not accomplished or prove impossible. Ironically, the reformer—along with the conservative—endangers religion by placing it too close to secular society, whether positively or negatively.

Knowing our past and seeing its expression in varying forms in the present, can we discern and shape various "alternative futures" for our religious life?[12] Something new has appeared. Because the present has become so unsettled, and in ways we did not expect, our past seems unclear too, and in apocalytpic ages attention shifts toward the future. This resurgence of interest in predicting the future, and a decline in historical study, comes naturally when expected goals either do not materialize or taste not so sweet because material abundance makes us jaded. Institutional religion is on the wane, but must that trend continue? We are foolish if we predict the future only by extending present trends. Life is exciting just because it undergoes major and unexpected changes of direction.

For instance, an increase in knowledge largely meant, for the rationalists and the sons of the Enlightenment, a disappearance of mystery. Instead, we may be witnessing an upsurge of appreciation for mystery precisely while knowledge increases. As Socrates tried to point out, at its best to learn is to come to appreciate what is beyond your knowledge. Intellectual sophistication does not necessarily lead to complete rationalism. The ways of learning are strange. The curve of knowledge is curious and does not extend itself indefinitely upward. Sometimes it turns back upon itself to open the learned mind to what is beyond itself—which may explain the sense of the mysterious sweeping over America on the heels of the world's greatest effort at education and rapid cultural sophistication. Our educational burst has succeeded, but not in producing the clear rationalistic generation we expected.

What seemed once to lead away from metaphysics—as not being theologically important because universal enlightenment and the spread of science would make it obsolete—now strangely brings us to a metaphysical mood and to a need for depth exploration and reconstruction of alternative first principles. The extension of naturalistic, scientific, and blatantly secular assumptions has led to their spiritual exhaustion, and thus the turn back to the primitive and to a search for new first principles. Harvey Cox, who has stressed and celebrated so much in secular culture, now forecasts that "this inward journey also gives our time its characteristic tone."[13] Material abundance and unwilling involvement in human destruction have plunged most of the nation into an unexpected spiritual wandering, an inner odyssey.

Cox says: "Theologies grip us today only if they have the power to change our inner and outer worlds, to make them more worthy of human habitation" (p. 47). If so, clearly *the era of religion as primarily an intellectual enterprise is over.* Americans have always worn the veneer of intellectualism rather thin anyway. Our attempt to imitate "high culture" was short-lived. A more chaotic, loud, and violent life has erupted again, as it often has in our past, so that this amazing change is best seen as only the resurgence of a wild past we thought lost. *What is amazing, to a generation which took the rationalism of modern man as its unquestioned standard, is that the test of religion now is not so much intellectual plausibility as its vitality to produce changed lives* (p. 48). If today's world is committed to the incredible, the vast effort to make Christianity credible has been wasted.

Prophecy and ecstatic vision have replaced the reverence for reason (p. 49), and this is an atmosphere much more conducive to religious growth, even if painful for hard-core rationalism to accept. Evangelism does not trim off religion's irrational edges; it exploits them. And perhaps just because of this change, the problem of God is profound and serious in our culture. This is not represented by the death-of-God theologies, since their God dies because he is too rational and eternal. Still, once that God-of-reason-alone is removed, the door is open to other experiences of God, primarily because transcendence is no longer outlawed. Contemporary experience reaches toward it. The "modern" form of Western culture is dissolving, Michael Novak tells us.[14]

Religion no longer can celebrate contemporary culture. It must look further. The future has a different aspect. It will not be modeled on progress but more on apocalypse.[15] In just such a time as this, mysticism traditionally becomes viable and transcendence is expected. This fact, so upsetting to the fixed rationality of the modern mind, is not a sudden novelty but a return to our origins. It is best understood as an expression of the past reappearing in the present. A stress on feeling and change and action need not be reported by churches to some un-American Religious Activities Committee. It is an attitude fully consistent with our past. Some Americans hoped to leave enthusiasm behind, never to be reminded of it in our modern city sophistication. Fortunately for the vitality of religion, the shattering we hear is only our past breaking through to mock us.

B. The Return to Transcendence

Chaim Potok's novel *The Chosen* centers around two boys, each just as American as Tom Sawyer. The story is set in the Jewish section of Brooklyn, and one of the pair of hero-friends is the American-born son of a Reformed Jewish scholar. The boy, too, follows the traditional Jewish scholarly route to become a rabbi. The other boy is the son of a Hasidic rabbi whose community is new to America, having been dislocated from Europe by Nazi persecution and destruction and then resettled in Brooklyn. In the reverse of what we think of as the normal immigrant pattern, the Hasidic community draws tightly in upon itself and resists the adoption of American ways—except for baseball, which is what brings the two boys together.

As the novel proceeds, the average American will be shocked at the harshness of the Hasidic life, repelled by its refusal to accommodate and change. What is most extreme of all, the reader discovers, is that the Hasidic rabbi, in the mystical tradition that characterizes his sect, raises his son in *silence*. True, father and son speak when they meet to discuss the boy's religious studies hour on end, but no casual personal conversation is allowed between father and son in the pattern we take to be normal. The boy is thrust back upon himself and his own inner resources by his father's strict use of silence. One would expect such harsh treatment to be reported in disapproval, but this is not quite the case.

In spite of the pain involved in this strange relationship, the Hasidic boy tells his friend somewhat in surprise: "You can listen to silence, Reuven. I've begun to realize that you can listen to silence and learn from it. It has a quality and a dimension all its own. It talks to me sometimes. I feel myself alive in it. It talks. And I can hear it."[16] And, in partial justification for his harsh methods, the father explains: "One learns the pain of others by suffering one's own pain" (p. 265). ". . . I did not want him to grow up a mind without a soul" (p. 266). "He suffered and learned to listen to the suffering of others" (p. 267).

In the bright days of the twenties or the fifties, this is not quite how we thought of American life. Actually, it is as much a part of America as apple pie. Silence and suffering and compassion have always been here, along with lavish Texas hospitality and high-pitched cocktail-party talk. A mystical note and inner exploration are not something we left behind, an experience foreign to these shores. Nor have we moved beyond it in evolutionary fashion. Rather, inner silence stays as a pervasive theme and emerges again from time to time when suffering becomes visible and seems to demand it. In Potok's novel, the Reformed Jewish scholar explains to his outraged son that such harsh methods kept the Hasidic Jews alive in the midst of unbelievable persecutions in Europe. So we should be cautious about rejecting these techniques in the name of rationalism and the Enlightenment.

Such a press to transcendence is neither new nor passé. In fact, after any period of materialism and public vulgarity, it will reappear on many fronts. Disillusion and the failure of dreams also induce an urge to discover within what eludes us without. *The crush, the violence, the noise and the harshness of contemporary American life will renew the press for transcendence in ways no strict empiricist could predict or be happy to see.* What we have to ask is whether the quest for spiritual transcendence is somehow natural in such an American setting. If so, it is probably not what popular opinion would have thought. But a style of life blatantly opposed to religion on its surface may prove to be just what is needed to drive us to an inner search.

If Europe is the home of empiricism and modern rationalism, why is it any more natural for an American setting to reject these confines? Potok's Hasidic rabbi wants his son to have a compassionate soul, not just a brilliant mind, and so uses methods Descartes could not approve, if man really is essentially a "thinking substance." In Chapter I we pointed out that many of religion's early functions in this country have been secularized and taken over by others (e. g., education and welfare). What function will religion serve in America in the future, if others have absorbed many of its former concerns? One answer now is that the development of the inner life of the spirit and the search for transcendence may take on more religious centrality than a social activist could ever have predicted in our economically expansive eras.

Transcendence is not really a new theme.[17] Some have thought that the emergence of a technological culture would mean the dissolution of a viable sense of transcendence. But a little reflection beyond the surface should cause us to realize that, just as the disappearance of transcendence was enforced by the dominance of technology, the reaction against technological control induces a search to escape its electronic confines. For instance, Herbert Richardson points out that an underground of books exists in American universities. Students passively accept their official studies, but the books that circulate and attract their attention privately are those "related to the urge to move from ordinary dimensions of action and consciousness to extraordinary dimensions of life" (p. ix).

Professors lag as much as a generation behind their students. While philosophy departments still tend to banish all transcendence, and religion departments often support a bland demythologized form of scientifically acceptable religion, in the underground the current student generation educates itself on transcendence and finds the nonempirical not only meaningful but increasingly necessary. This is not true of all the younger generation, of course, but it is a movement too large and significant to be ignored—and it may have the sign of the future on it. Why? Because transcendence seems to many what alone makes a meaningful future conceivable.

"Pragmatic America does have her own mystical tradition traceable from the Puritans through Emerson and the Transcendentalists to the many metaphysical religions of today" (p. xiii). Michael Murphy of the Esalen Institute tells us that "in America today there is a widespread and growing interest in various psychophysical disciplines which evoke transcendent experience."[18] The popularity of Zen training or transcendental meditation provides only two illustrations. These learned routines focus attention on the unfamiliar aspects or possibilities of one's inner world—which in a sense is the opposite of the direction of empiricism. "Common to the practitioners of all of them is the sense that a fuller reality has made itself known, that something more has entered one's being, that a grace has been bestowed" (p. 18).

Sam Keen wants us to yield to the rhythm-induced ecstasy of the dance. And if the crush and enthusiasm at rock festivals is any indication, a large number of the young agree. ". . . Dionysius is again issuing an invitation to the dance, to ecstasy, enthusiasm, and a touch of divine madness."[19] In the festival setting, you do not focus on the self in Cartesian or even Kantian fashion. You seek to escape it. If we have lost the capacity for transcending the present, as Harvey Cox suggests,[20] certainly there is a vast effort under way to overcome this limitation. Feeling is what the young want to explore and develop. Certainly this offers a different approach to religion than rationalism or empiricism, and feeling is by nature more open to transcendence than pure thought.

In the search for transcendence, American youth has developed a considerable interest in classical mysticism, much of which takes the form of a turn to Eastern religions. This movement, which seeks its sources outside the Western tradition, probably comes about because it is assumed that the sole available source for mysticism is Eastern. Actually, it is only in very recent years, in the rush of industrialization and scientific expansion, that the West has seemed so bare of mystical sources and so hostile to such interests. The Western world in general, and America in particular, have a mystical tradition of their own, which if explored could be much more compatible with American minds than borrowed Eastern forms. We have simply forgotten that it exists and that it is just as much a part of the American past as the social gospel.

What is important is not that mysticism in the new world is so vastly different from other forms, but that it is available locally and in native dress. Although Americans have shown a persistent interest in mysticism, it may now be rising to a peak.[21] Possibly we have reached the stage where our physical boundaries are fixed, so that further exploration must take an inner direction. And certainly mysticism is directed inward; there is seldom mention of objects in the outer world (p. 3). It centers on experience rather than thought alone, and such experience is selfless, direct, and transcendent. Strong emotion characterizes its description, so that strict rationalism is offended.

Americans have been thought of as being blunt, direct, highly verbal, and graphic. But perhaps that is only a recent picture and not quite valid. Mystical experience is usually imageless and soundless (p. 7), which provides a new picture of American experience and a needed corrective. James and Perry and Santayana all considered such experience valid and a prime object of interest, so that the whole of the pragmatic movement was not antimystical by any means.

In addition to the continual philosophical investigation of mysticism present from the early years, we often forget that Quakerism has represented the mystical inner light in this country since our inception. Their approach makes it a group phenomenon and less individualistic than some patterns of mysticism, although Quakers impose no one fixed form. Yet this path is not pursued for its own sake but for its results. "The individual who has true mystical experience undergoes transformation of character" (p. 33). Thus, interestingly enough, in spite of its apparent opposition to what we consider the American stress on action, mysticism fits our pattern, since its aim is *personal change.* Suffering is often a theme in mystical experience, which made it seem antithetical to an aggressive and confident American optimism. Jewish mysticism, too, has always been present beneath the American scene. Today a tragic sense of life is not so far away.

Psychedelic experience and the widespread use of consciousness-changing drugs are an unprecedented phenomenon in America (p. 131). In our own time we have to ask: Can chemical agents induce mystical experience? Probably we cannot yet answer that question fully. Certainly the experiences are sometimes similar, and what is even more clear is that youth often use drugs with this intent. On the other hand, the results of traditional mystical experience have been characterized as *unselfish, constructive, and loving,* and it is not at all clear that drug use—even if religiously motivated—leads in this direction. One reason we are so little aware of mysticism in America at times is because it is so difficult and requires so much work and preparation. By its nature, it must be rare and quiet. It is unlikely that it can be fully duplicated simply by paying the price for certain drugs.

Alan Watts stands as a good symbol of American interest in Zen, since he is himself both an American and one of its greatest publicizers. His book of the early fifties is typical of many.[22] His more recent work, *Does It Matter?*, works against the prevailing notions of materialism,[23] and his critique is now on the lips of many of the younger generation. Thomas Merton represents the continued presence of a Roman Catholic mystical tradition, and his popularization of the contemplative life surprised many in its attractiveness. *Thoughts in Solitude*, for instance, is his report of a time spent in continual silence,[24] and this setting is different from our usual picture of American life.

Until recently American mystical writing has been a kind of underground effort. Roman Catholic circles, for instance, are full of authors unknown to outsiders who continually write about the mystical life, although their work seldom penetrates the walls that surround their community. Today such divisions are falling, and what once was underground literature now seems quite respectable. Catholics have turned away from any exclusive stress on withdrawal and have become more secular. The old barriers have broken, but at the same time those interested in mystical thought now appear on a much wider front. A mounting nihilism also leads to the search for a new ecstatic consciousness.

"One's life and work," Robert H. Bellah remarks, "are an effort to find a form which will reconcile inner needs and outer pressures."[25] Americans have been thought to be primarily outer-directed, although the persistent strains of mysticism and the early role of religion in the birth of the nation prove this to be a false impression. For a time, American economic affluence hid the rising need for an inner search to offset the outer pressures of our technological age. Our affluence, however, has not fulfilled every need. "The contemporary religious consciousness certainly has a strong note of innerness" (p. 224). Our world is just as alive with religious possibility as any age. We have not passed beyond religious awakening. We simply have to discover what new form it will take.

Traditionally, we have thought of the sociologist as being primarily empirically oriented, and such a stress is at least slightly antithetical to religion. "Transcendence" is not likely to be the sociologist's favorite category. A concentration on the empirical and the immediate undoubtedly still attracts many. Yet recently at least some sociologists have rediscovered the supernatural.[26] Most men had agreed that the supernatural had taken leave of the modern world never to return. A majority appeared to celebrate this departure, but now we are not so sure about the finality of the separation.

Is there, Berger finds himself asking, *"an other reality"* (p. 2) which transcends that within which our everyday experience unfolds? In deciding our response to this question, we ought first to understand that, in point of fact, primitive man was just as much dominated by pragmatic and utilitarian concerns as we are. "The preoccupation with 'natural' consciousness is not at all peculiar to the modern age" (p. 3). Probably most men always have been oriented this way. However, with the decline of churchly religiosity in America, what we find is an increased turning to explore whether there are genuine religious forces alive outside the traditional framework. This raises the question of the supernatural and its availability once again.

What we find is that those who begin to discern such a nonempirical reality will have to accept the status of being a minority group, but this is not bad unless you assume the automatic rightness of the majority—which our political forefathers did not do in creating a system of balances designed to protect minority opinion, opposition, and protest. Thus "pockets of supernaturalist religion are likely to survive in the larger society" (p. 26). However, Berger does not foresee this as sparking any impressive rediscovery of the supernatural on the dimensions of a mass phenomenon. It will be interesting to see whether his forecast holds, especially since some shift toward rediscovering the supernatural has already taken place.

In order to control human experience, we have reduced its scope, but Peter Berger thinks such a shrinkage in the confines of experience may not last (p. 75). Since he accepts a "modern" framework, Berger is not sure whether transcendence can reappear decisively, though he senses signs of it that create "rumors." Nevertheless, he knows what it would be like: "A rediscovery of the supernatural will be, above all, a regaining of openness in our perception of reality" (p. 95), and surely we see such an openness appearing on many fronts as the twentieth century mounts toward a climax.

Berger seems convinced that secularization will continue to shape religion decisively.[27] Yet he also senses a "revolutionary transformation of consciousness" (p. 80) on the horizon. Thus it is possible that the sociological analysis he accepts as characterizing the situation of religion might actually change dramatically, depending on the results of the present protest against culture and the outcome of the projected revolution.

C. Revolution Renewed and Protest Continued

We are living through the shock waves produced by an upsurge of energy aimed at capturing individual freedom once again. This jarring of our security causes consternation only because for a time we settled into a happy pattern and—as is natural—took that form of life to be what freedom meant. Since freedom actually involves no set form, to reject one pattern of life is not to reject freedom but to continue the search for it. However, in the burst of power necessary to break out of one mold, we are likely to drop into the opposite sin of those who take their own revolutionary vision as the only viable way. Or, in the name of freedom, we make the mistake of labeling every experiment "good," when the fact is that freedom can involve the release of the destructive as well as the creative.

In the press to preserve freedom in America, we do tend to forget that all societies are not free, that freedom has belonged to few men in the earth's history, and that normally, once we have it, we probably cannot really appreciate it until it is lost. It is hard to make anyone value what he simply inherits, educationally, politically, or religiously. Freedom involves the risk of loss which itself —unless we fall beyond recovery—induces the energy to repossess liberty. There is no safe path to the preservation of freedom. America's notorious sense of insecurity and uncertainty cannot be overcome. Only totalitarian and aristocratic societies have the self-assurance we so admire. We stay alive by accepting, and then struggling to overcome, the blunders and anxieties that freedom so often produces.

We thought advancing years and power would bring America sophistication. Now we are sad to see that the revitalization of our liberty requires us to be perpetual adolescents. A few may learn how to order vintage wine and collect art. Nevertheless, the bursts of wild experimentation that freedom must allow do not permit the country as a whole to acquire the mellow culture we admire in Europeans and thought—at last!—would become ours. It is embarrassing to find that freedom requires the constant vitality of youth, and that like Peter Pan we can never grow up but must continually dream of the maturity that escapes us.

We support art, literature, and music, not by venerating them or making them part of American peasant life, but only by allowing them to develop along with a vast array of noncultural activities. America will have no Paris of the high Middle Ages, no Florence of the Italian Renaissance. We will create, and already have produced, much of artistic value, but continued freedom means that all needs and tastes are offered expression, not just the best. We can only encourage the distinguished by not cutting off the vulgar. When openness is fostered, limits may be set, but they are hard to arrive at and maintain, and always subject to challenge by peasant revolt. Taste is difficult to cultivate in such circumstances. Freedom encourages experimenting with the new, but the question always arises whether this requires the death of the old. America may die, but it simply never will become an "old culture."

Size and affluence and age do present new challenges. We wonder whether our political machinery has developed to such self-sufficiency that it is no longer responsive to the people. Of course, in a nondemocracy this is not so much a problem, since an authoritarian society may not intend to reflect mass needs. However, a revolutionary first principle such as ours should tell us that the American system cannot be fixed, although it may require continual pressure and the accompanying risk of upheaval in order to insure renewed responsiveness. To be sensitive to needs is never automatic in men, and routines will take over if pressure is relaxed for a moment. This applies individually as well as nationally, spiritually as well as politically—and the danger is greater if the only authority we can recognize rests in negotiated agreement and enforced compromise. Neither religiously nor politically will we ever agree to focus authority exclusively in any one man or group, although to do so is very convenient and conducive to serenity. Thus, even our political life inevitably has a spiritual quality, since it must find its locus in nothing tangible.

When at times we identify religious interests with national goals, we are not entirely wrong. A central part of America's aim is religious in nature and origin. To forget or to lose this is to slip into a violent orgy of consumption. What we have temporarily forgotten is that America never was and never will be one thing. Thus, when plural aspects break out which are questionable, religion is needlessly dragged into conflict because we have repressed the fact that America is a bawdy mixture and that no person or church could—or should want to—identify with or control all its aspects. In happy days, we wrongly characterize America by only her good sides; this makes it painful when frustration brings out our other less pleasant personal qualities.

Hannah Arendt is a typical American in that she was born in Germany but later came to this country to teach and write. Her *On Revolution* is as important to the American religious spirit as to our political understanding. If wars and revolutions have determined the political physiognomy of the twentieth century,[28] they have also decisively shaped the religious sphere. The problem is that many Americans came to feel they were largely immune to this—that their political life could be isolated and their religious life established independently. War is an ancient happening, but revolution is a product of the modern age. Still, it is hard to remember that America is a modern nation just because it is revolutionary in origin.

Religiously, we can argue without distortion that Jesus preached at least an inner revolution, a freeing of the individual from dulling restraints. In that sense American political ideals are an external parallel to an ancient religious hope, and this aim of social renewal might be left unsupported if its religious connection—although never uniform—is ignored. Hannah Arendt thinks revolution as a political instrument is here to stay (p. 8), which means the stability we once thought we might achieve cannot be found. And since violence is just as much a part of revolution as of war, we need to reexamine in what sense we can be a peaceful nation and stay free, and in what sense our religious life must be subject to constant upheaval too.

Violence was our beginning, and no fresh start could be brought about without violence. Yet, since we have agreed to try not to impose a fixed pattern or to admit any single authority, neither our political nor our religious life can escape the threat of violence, just because we do not move or evolve beyond our beginning point, and originally we had no desire to do so. The hope to forget our past came later, once economic success and military power made us yearn to ignore our plebeian roots and strive for another form of respect. ". . . Revolutions are the only political events which confront us directly and inevitably with the problem of beginning" (p. 13), which means we never should grow beyond either 1776 or Jesus' breaking of encrusted ritual to free the spirit.

Religious revolutions of course are a little less visible, and are better observed only after the fact through the changes they produce in individuals. They show themselves on the surface in the struggle against current religious practices which no longer serve to free the spirit. Religious revolutions are externally peaceful but inwardly violent, because what is unformed within seeks a form without but finds no frictionless way to do so. Politically, violence must be held short of total destruction. Religiously, the self tends toward madness in violence against itself if its internal search finds no coherent meaning.

Poverty, according to Hannah Arendt, is part of the source of revolutionary upsurge, because we began to doubt that poverty was really necessary (p. 15). As long as we accepted our generally given framework, we worked within it. Now we are not sure that what we formerly took as necessary has to be, and we are willing to rise against the basic conditions of life itself. America became the symbol of a society without poverty, but if our revolution sparked that hope, it must be rethought again today (see our next chapter). We did spark the revolution against poverty, and it almost succeeded. But if the reform program is not moving to completion, what form will the American revolution take next? We became a refuge, an asylum, a meeting ground for the poor. If we are this no longer, what can be our new role?

We learned that it was just as important to change the fabric of society as to change the structure of the political realm (p. 17). And if we agree with Condorcet that the term 'revolution' should only be applied where freedom is the aim, then the crucial question is how to change society's fabric to meet that aim? In keeping society open to freedom, what role can religion now play? We have learned that material success has enslaved us to routines and styles of life that cannot be easily escaped—in spite of our adolescent desire to be innocent and loved once more. Religion, however, can or should release the spirit from bondage to itself and to material wealth. *Perhaps the only way a wealthy nation or a powerful person can escape self-enslavement and experience freedom as still alive is by increased religious sensitivity.*

Revolution gives us the experience of man's capacity to begin something new (p. 27). What in 1776 was new in America no longer is, so that novelty now must come on other fronts—social, artistic, and religious. We should turn the revolution, the experience of creating something new, into these avenues. In the religious life this involves the experience of God creating something new unexpectedly where life has seemed to go out. In an American setting it may also involve greater emphasis on the basic equality of men. The idea that every person is born an equal is so radical a notion that we ought to remember its recent political origin. However, it was present in Christianity long before that. If political equality remains as much dream as fact, it requires constant religious reference to keep progress toward it alive.

Revolution originally meant "restoring." Thus, once our early revolutionary days are gone, the task is to restore that creative moment continually. To retrieve man's ancient liberties was the original intent in striking out for America—it only became revolutionary by inadvertence (p. 37). So today, every time we seek to restore ancient rights (e. g., for blacks), we verge on revolution if basic change is a necessity. The French Revolution ended in disaster, while the American Revolution remained quietly successful. If that is so, and if today the success of America's first revolt seems in question, what part can religion play (as it once did) to return us to those original events? Or is the loss of religion really a serious matter for the success of the revolution?

If the happiness of the people (as against freedom) becomes our god, or if abundance becomes the goal of revolution, the scene is quite changed. Abundance and happiness did slip in to become our goals, whereas the original revolution aimed primarily at freedom. *If we are disillusioned with abundance and the good life as spiritual goals, it is time to return to the original American revolutionary aim: freedom.* We tried to promote abundance on a world-wide basis and failed (except for the Marshall Plan in Europe and the revival of Japan). Perhaps we might be better as promoters of freedom—which is how the nation began.

Compassion for the poor and those who suffer was not the original aim of the American Revolution. The conservative's position on that issue probably is right. However, once a free society is formed, the only new goal for revolution would seem to be a spread of that kind of compassion. And it may very well be that such a rise of compassion for suffering is one form our contemporary revolution must take, and precisely this difference from our early American aims (even in religion) makes its emergence as a social goal the cause of so much upheaval. What is urged upon us today by the new vanguard is not identical with early American aims. *But can compassion—should it—be established as the new American revolution?* If so, religion has a great part to play in undergirding it, since sustained compassion is hardly possible apart from religious conversion. The irony is that precisely as we grow most secular, the goals urged on us require the prior converting power of religion if they are to be widely accepted.

Yet compassion for suffering is not calm or well suited to negotiation and compromise. In that sense, the early American Revolution was easier to manage than the swift, direct action which compassion seems to demand, often verging on violence. Pity, as a spring for virtue, unfortunately has a greater capacity for cruelty than cruelty itself (p. 85). It may be just this unusual phenomenon that we are experiencing today, and it is one our early revolutionaries did not have to face. "The direction of the American Revolution remained committed to the foundation of freedom and the establishment of lasting institutions" (p. 87). Thus the aim of the Revolution was to build a new civil law. On the other hand, compassion easily slips into lawlessness to achieve its purposes.

The French Revolution was shaped more by the immediacy of suffering. Its lawlessness sprang from the boundlessness of sentiment over the immensity of the people's misery, which unleashed a stream of limitless violence in Paris. Thus those who see present civil disobedience as a simple continuation of the American Revolution are not quite accurate. Since it springs from sympathy over black injustice and opposes the suffering in Vietnam, today's atmosphere is more like the French Revolution in spirit than the institution-founding early American revolt. The current struggle is between those who feel American protest must be consistent with the preservation of law and institution (historically they are correct) and those whose pain and sympathy with misery and their desire to relieve it make them unable to be moderate in their actions.

We can see important religious implications in this struggle. Since Christianity was central to the ideals of the American Revolution, it also has a stake in this quite different turn of our continued revolution. Religion usually has great concern for the relief of suffering and misery. Today it is this aspect that comes into play to support a new revolution, and not so much the desire to found free institutions, as it was originally. Important as it was and is that men be free to worship according to their choice, the success of religion does not really require release from persecution. The survival of the early Christians and Jews indicates this. The question of compassion and suffering actually is closer to the heart of religious concern, but this time their link to political rage and violence makes the union of church and state more questionable than our forefathers could have foreseen. They separated them to prevent oppression; we separate them to relieve support for violence.

Originally we sought to keep church and state apart so that individuals could worship freely without coercion. Now the question is more complicated and revolves around the use of political acts to achieve religious goals, that is, the release from suffering and oppression. We developed a political religion of a type in America, but today's problems represent a turn in a new direction.

These issues are also less easily resolved, since it can never be said that religion must not use a political instrument to achieve its goals. Yet it is fatal to the spiritual life if politics becomes the only avenue for religion to act out its goals.

The French Revolution accepted the role of mass opinion, but the American Revolution never did, and instead considered public opinion a form of tyranny (p. 89). Today, this is an issue as it was not in our first revolution. When the government is not immediately responsive to public opinion, some cry that democracy fails. Yet the government was not designed to be so, and there are times when it is fortunate that it does not act immediately in response to some passing fancy or fashion. When the cause seems more urgent and meritorious (e. g., stopping the war in Vietnam), it is less easy to accept the negative side of the government's un-immediate response to popular sentiment.

Precisely as in eighteenth-century France, the war of the young today is against "hypocrisy," which is a very different goal from the first American revolution. But as Hannah Arendt remarks of the scene in France, "After hypocrisy had been unmasked and suffering been exposed, it was rage and not virtue that appeared" (p. 106). Suffering, once it is transformed into rage, releases overwhelming forces, but these sent the French Revolution to its doom. "No revolution has ever solved the 'social question' and liberated men from the predicament of want" (p. 108). The attempt to do so leads to terror, and it is terror that consigns revolutions to failure. This factor was almost absent from the first American revolution, but *the appearance of terror today makes the outcome of change almost more in doubt than it was in 1776.*

Religiously this issue is crucial. Political motives and religious aims could support one another at the origin of America, because freedom was the prize and religion stood only to gain from independence. Our new goal of release from suffering is closer to the heart of religion's concerns, but it is also less clear that an attempt to achieve this goal politically is the church's best means of expression. Not that all churches supported the first revolution. Politics played a part in keeping some Anglicans loyal to England. Still, the church's more spiritual way to accomplish the release of suffering, and its questionable association with the rage that so easily explodes into terror when a moral goal cannot be accomplished simply by political means—all this places religion in a fascinating and tense and precarious position, one where deep inner reflection should become a necessity.

This issue, of course, goes to the heart of the question of the religious use of militancy as against the usual association of Christianity with peaceful means. In studying the life of Christ and his own reaction to suffering, it is clear that he chose a route other than militancy and political rebellion. The fact that he did so disappointed some of his followers who wanted a political leader to press on to political release. Thus, rage and terror and revolution do not appear as the results recorded on the pages of the New Testament. If there was a revolution—and there probably was—it took a less overt, less expected avenue, and thus its form is more difficult to make out even to this day.

To anyone who has eyes, it is clear that a "counter culture" has been developing in America. This involves more than the appearance of long hair and eccentric dress, or even the widespread use of drugs and the development of a communal style of living. We would be wrong, of course, to think this fashion will increase and continue to expand along a single line. Some new modes disappear as fast as they come. Yet the change in the life-style of the young is so significant that we are forced to acknowledge a rising counter culture, even if it eventually takes a shape different from any of its present forms. Religion ought not simply to reflect cultural moods. Yet in the recent past, religion in America has been so closely identified with a particular mode of life that any change in that sphere is bound to have important religious significance, even if it involves only the divorce of religion from its previous cultural attachments.

Religion on the American frontier, in immigrant and revival days, followed the people—as it should—and reflected their background. We had hoped to have outgrown this immigrant heterogeneity, but instead we are back with it again. Religion will have to desert respectability and follow the wanderings of the young, not necessarily endorsing every new mode as good, but learning to minister to genuine need regardless of the life-style. And it may prove that those who make themselves social outcasts will become best able to appreciate religion's message of the healing available for the sufferer. In any case, a counter culture offers good reason to reassess religion's cultural role in America.

Theodore Roszak describes the making of a "counter culture" and, as others do, traces it to the rise of "technocracy" and the youth rebellion against the conformity it requires.[29] The values we thought fixed by the scientific revolution are now gone, and this shows us the shortsightedness of adjusting Christianity to any cultural norm, since the science we thought had to dominate theology now itself is under challenge as a cultural determinant. However, this also means that the values of the counter culture should not shape religion entirely either, unless we want to court obsolescence with the next shift. We had thought the scientific framework would be ultimate and beyond change—that is the important difference. The development of a counter culture should not make religion accommodate to it, but rather force it to pull back from any exclusive cultural identification and simply try to speak to all the people in a variety of tongues.

An industrial complex requires social engineering, and it is against all such rule by experts that the young now rebel. Technology made us feel we were near the fulfillment of our needs. We dreamed of being technical gods—and did not realize it was a dream and not reality. What the counter culture tries to tell us is that no such ideal engineering is possible. Psychic reality is in the ascendant over social reality among the young, and this opens many doors formerly closed to religion. "The unprecedented penchant for the occult, for magic, and for exotic ritual" (p. 124) marks the counter culture as different from the modern man who previously wanted to censure religion precisely because it reflected these qualities. "The cry is not for a revolution, but for an apocalypse: a descent of divine fire" (p. 126).

If this continues to be true, it makes any demythologizing tendency in theology almost laughable in its rush to purge religion of what the scientific mind could not accept, when now the challenge is out against any continued dominance by scientific standards. Psychedelic experience is widespread and gives evidence of the desire to explore levels of consciousness beyond the rational.

The reformulation of personality is its aim (p. 156), and it is amazing how close that is to religion's classic promise. *The issue is
drugs and a radical life-style vs. religious involvement as the means.*
Utopian yearnings return again, and the early Christian visions of
a new order no longer seem so absurd. The issue is God's involvement in this as against man's reordering of his own style of life.
Religious groups originally formed as small separate communities,
too, and that is something utopian dreamers understand better than
an established and culturally oriented church.

Kierkegaard's stress upon the need to concentrate on the subjective aspect of life is now widely followed, as opposed to modern
science and modern philosophy's cry for objectivity (p. 215). The
objective mode of consciousness is accepted too, but now the
pressure is on to explore the other ways in which we can know
the world (p. 233), and that opens doors for religious experience
as legitimate again. The visionary experience, so long explained
away, once more is a conscious goal. These eyes see the world
not in rational objectivity but as transformed into a new heaven
and a new earth, much as the New Testament book of Revelation
reports. The interest in magic prepares the way for the possibility
of religious miracle.

"It is a strange brand of radicalism we have here that turns to
prehistoric precedent for its inspiration," Roszak says (p. 265).
Thus the inevitability and the supposed nonreversibility of the
modern scientific outlook is denied. For many the primitive seems
preferable, and mystery is accepted as natural. We live in an age
of protest we did not expect to see, since it is directed against the
modern culture we thought invulnerable—one which could only
be welcomed by all enlightened minds. Instead, the strange phenomenon is that the rising level of intellectual sophistication has
brought about revolt rather than conformity. This, however, is
merely to return to an earlier condition in America, and it denies
nothing but recent notions of progress.

"Protest is an inherent part of human experience. . . . In a
democracy, there is not only a right of protest, but a duty to
protest. . . . By its very nature, democracy encourages conflict
and dissent."[30] For religion, the only problem involved is that, for
a time, churches identified with a "smooth" notion of society.

Then, achieving affluence, we could not understand why anyone would want anything else. Now the American right to variety has inserted itself again into both culture and religion. The problem is that so many people shout so loudly that this makes it hard to separate out the legitimate protest. Further, the political and cultural forms of overt protest are not always a possible religious path; but it is very hard to say just what form specifically religious protest should take.

Possibly, since religion aims to relieve human suffering, in addition to working to alleviate misery it must also protest its sources. Possibly, since religion (like early American thought) seeks freedom, release, and individual fulfillment, in pursuing these goals it must protest whenever it sees individual life cut off or thwarted. In this sense, Herbert Marcuse's book *One-Dimensional Man* is a religious protest, and it has been treated as such. It paints—perhaps in extreme terms—the dangers to individual liberty and free expression that come from the growth of an industrial society. Our very success and efficiency threaten to flatten men to a single dimension.

Marcuse wants to label such a society "irrational."[31] This is because the technical social order tends to muffle protest and stifle change. He thinks it possible that forces exist which can break this containment and explode society (p. xv). Quite probably what we are witnessing is this phenomenon and not the containment of change he so fears. For he is afraid that what is comfortable and smooth will lead us to accept unfreedom (p. 1). Freedom can only mean, for him, freedom *from* our present technological society, and this notion causes difficulties because modern society reflects on its own advantages and cannot understand that anyone would want anything else. Marcuse wants "inner freedom" (p. 10) where man can remain himself, but he thinks technology invades privacy. If so, we see why there is today a turn away from civilized ways and a veneration of the primitive. Privacy may be obtainable only outside the structure.

Religiously, the greatest question Marcuse raises is that of material domination. That is, an industrial society does have great control over its products, but do the material needs of society and their control completely determine the freedom of the individual?

Does the issue of freedom really revolve around the production of consumer goods? If the life of the spirit can be somewhat independent of material means or their mode of production, then control in that area need not destroy human freedom. Of course, among those who are economically deprived, this line is harder to draw. However, in a technologically advanced society, freedom's battle ought to be fought on a front other than that of goods and services. Let them be in the grip of technology; that neither hinders nor enhances spiritual freedom.

Marx excluded religion as no longer being necessary after a certain stage in the liberation of the economically exploited masses. Perhaps religion's present return as a necessity, at a certain stage of sophisticated development, is one of the means by which the spirit gains release from a highly structured society. Of course, if it identifies totally with any social norm of the day, religion cannot serve this liberating purpose for a highly educated people. But if it stands aloof and issues a call to a world apart, it might. This need not mean to turn away from worldly concerns, as religion's critics claim. But it does mean not to turn so totally to the secular (as some advocate) that it becomes unclear that religion does offer release from secular conformity.

If Christianity is *in* the world but not *of* the world, it can offer the "place apart" where one who shares its life may stand in independence of society's pressure. Perhaps it was in turning religion to secular goals that we lost the depth of the spirit, and not as a specific result of industrialization. Recovering the dimension of the spirit need not mean escape, but simply the achievement of a separate base from which to meet society's demands—and rewards—without accepting its norms. If culture has become flat and oppressive in its conformity, the life of religion can dance to different tunes. Even the artist does not meet natural demands in the religious sphere. Perhaps its release from confinement to the secular is one reason why religious art has been able to be great. Marcuse deplores "the total mobilization of all media for the defense of the established reality" (p. 68), but religion inevitably involves a solitary life, and so may teach its followers to stand alone.

Marcuse is afraid that solitude has become technically impossible (p. 71). But if religion is precisely connected to solitude, moments of silence in religious worship might be one of our few remaining means of escape from domination. Religion has traditionally cultivated both silence and solitude, and in a technological society perhaps this becomes a crucial function. Communication starves for the production of genuine meaning as all words are reduced to clichés, Marcuse laments (p. 87). However, religion has traditionally concentrated on the power of the *word*. Even if religious discourse has gone flat in modern society too, it still may offer the best hope for a revival of depth in individual communication.

Christianity traditionally recognizes no temporal authority, which may qualify it as one means of escape from the authoritarian character of every industrial civilization, as Marcuse sees this threat (p. 102). Contrary to the notions of rationalism and some evolutionary theories, all religious need does not disappear as we pass beyond primitive societies. Religious need does not evaporate. It actually deepens and goes underground as men seek to avoid a growing conformity to the technological machine they have created. This may not be obvious at any given moment, because formal religion usually lags behind its people's needs. Today, for example, many theologians and religious leaders are still trying to accommodate religion to the secular city, when *its only viable future appeal may be in offering a way to transcend such programmed conformity*.

Christianity was launched on its way around the world by Paul's experience of release from the detail of the Mosaic law. His experience of Christ gave him freedom. That fundamental religious note is worth emphasizing in the late twentieth century, when the creations of our own genius threaten our liberty from many sides.

The early American colonists linked their political freedom to their love of religious liberty, but they could not foresee how a then sparsely inhabited land would close in on their descendants. Although some men try physical migration again as an escape, there may be little such room left. This calls on religion in America to discover the sense in which it offers release from the oppressive social conformity technology forces on us. The outdated Mosaic law which fetters our spirits today may lie in the storage unit of a gigantic IBM machine. Is the only escape to refuse to play the conventional game (p. 257)? Not if religion offers more than one dimension to the spirit and thus to freedom.

Charles A. Reich also predicts a coming revolution,[32] although his is happier and more evolutionary in character. What he pictures is more like a return to conventional utopian Marxism, where a golden land inevitably emerges. It evolves from the revolutionary process artificially stimulated by the truly enlightened. Again the current stress on apocalypse, radical transformation, and a coming utopia comes out clearly, and these are notions very sympathetic to traditional Christianity. The argument centers around the means and the route. Specifically: Does God play a role in this transformation, or is it all of man and nature and already on the horizon at the present time?

America has heard forecasts of doom, but we have had more than our share of optimistic predictions of a happy future too. In an uncertain land, built on compromise and plurality, either could probably come true. Americans need constant philosophical redefinition, since no specific life-style or set of beliefs is absolutely required of us all. We have no single ethnic or religious background, and presently we are developing an even wider diversity of styles. We are united if at all, strangely, by the slim thread of theory. We cannot take American goals and assumptions for granted, since no physical fact makes us one—if we do not find a theoretical base and some agreed goals in spite of such heterodoxy.

Charles Reich has come up with a new and optimistic prediction of what America will become, and it is based on a particular notion of evolution. This projection has religious importance, as all proposals for a new direction for America have, due to the involvement of religion in the founding notions and because Reich's proposal amounts to a way of life in itself. This is particularly true because he bases his "new life" on the inevitable coming of a revolution in life-style (p. 2). If this should come about, religion must reassess its role in such a new age, or else offer a critique of the assumptions of Reich's proposals. We all seem to agree that certain profound changes are at work in American life. The issue hinges on their direction and supposed irreversibility.

Reich predicts the emergence of "a higher reason, a more human community, and a new and liberated individual" (p. 2). Religiously, the truth of his prediction is quite important, since in certain ways this is the same goal religion has worked toward, although perhaps in different ways. Something has gone wrong in America and the American dream must be reconsidered, but Reich's specific pinpointing of the difficulty centers on the loss of control of American society (p. 3). To say this is somewhat ironic, coming on the heels of a high technology which offers perfect control through its superior means. But disorder and corruption and loss of self are pointed out as the sign of this deterioration.

In considering all the ills of the nation that Reich points to, it is clear that the Devil has been rediscovered in the 1970s. The issue becomes, however, whether this is a new phenomenon or only appears so because we have passed through an era in which we took all such ills to be once and for all behind us. Reich underlines a spreading sense of man's powerlessness (p. 6), and in raw numbers this is probably true as the optimism level shifts from age to age. Is this the result of an overestimation in our immediate past of just how much power we did possess or could control? We may be in the inevitable stage of disillusion and readjustment following an overly romantic hope. Control is always precarious and difficult to maintain, and it is hard to see why we ever thought we had it made.

Bureaucracy, organization, and technology do dominate America today. This is new since 1776, and it does alter our fundamental situation. However, as much good comes from these forces as evil, because of the new possibilities they offer. We can only be disappointed if we expect these developments to be all good in their results; but we are wrong if we see them as all bad or as the ultimate source of evil in human affairs. Even a dumb animal makes a better scapegoat than a machine. There is a discrepancy between the realities of our society and our beliefs about them— but our ideals were very high to start with. We are hypersensitive to our lack of performance largely because we lived in a daydream for a while that American goals were about to be realized by all. Reich's answer to this is the emergence of "Consciousness III."

Consciousness I he identifies with the farmer and the small businessman in the nineteenth century, and Consciousness II is the organizational society of the first half of the twentieth century. He is right that America has ceased to be a country of agriculture and small business, and the first half of this century did see the vast growth of technological organization. Further, it is clear that an almost unified direction and life-style settled on the land from, say, 1945 to 1970, and now the rush is away from organization, conformity, and machine patterns. What it is interesting to note is that this merely returns us to the consciousness prior to Reich's Consciousness I. We have turned back to the basic diversity out of which the Union first emerged: Consciousness Zero.

Our size, our military and industrial power, our science and technology are all very different. But this may only fool us into missing the fact that as a nation we have moved right back to where we started. Must we force conformity and one direction on all the people and struggle until one side wins? Or, without abandoning the values and ways of any group, can we still unite plurality and find some union of purpose? Freedom and individual fulfillment were the original common aims that made us willing to tolerate diversity, and it is striking how similar our goals and arguments are today to those that brought the pilgrims here and eventually encouraged union.

Americans can still do better in union than apart, in spite of our inability to agree on any pattern of conformity. No Consciousness III has emerged as the result of some inevitable evolutionary cycle. But, unexpectedly, we have returned to the primitive state of our origins as a people and must fight out again the questions of diversity and union, individual freedom and common purpose. The new consciousness is not so much higher or transcendent as it is primitive and original. It just seems novel because we thought our rude origins were behind us, forgotten forever.

Reich's proposal of a new ideal state is not the first. Utopian surges have arisen constantly as one way to try to recapture a dream in time of chaos. We are beyond our state of innocence, it is true, and it will never return. In that sense, we cannot go back again. We are not the first to find that the Devil is a constant threat and that his followers tear us apart as fast as we can build. In our original innocence we thought Satan might remain across the sea and leave us free of disintegrating forces. The fact is that no exclusive cycle holds, and all three forms of consciousness have been and are in America, plus others, although one or another may be in the public eye and more dominant at any time. However, none will be left behind forever.

Reich's evolutionary assumption of necessary successive phases is his most questionable piece of metaphysics. Men today are alienated from their own function and needs, but is this something that appeared with industrialization or is it a common human problem for each man to work out, one which will remain with us in any form of consciousness? In a real sense, Reich follows the Marxian model and holds economic considerations as basic. It may be that they are not quite so exclusively important in determining consciousness—or if they are for some, they are not for all. Reich echoes the current cry against the "expert," but is this really more than discovering (in the face of all that experts and technology can achieve) that the soul of man has other needs?

We seem on the verge of mass paranoia, where everyone feels he is being manipulated by the expert—by some bureaucracy, technology, or American corporation. These gigantic creations are the genius of American success, but corporate structure does have its difficult sides. However, is it not always hard to think for yourself and to be independent? If so, the forces that threaten to control us are not new; the modern forms are just different. We talk of "mass men" dominated by machinery, but was the mass of men not in even more dire straits before? And isn't the role of the vast majority bound to be dreary—except for individual resourcefulness? Ironically, about as much variety and opportunity are open here today as anywhere, but we still protest because every man is not beautiful and free.

Some men use terms in strange ways and name every requirement of regularity and imposed order "repression" or "violence." This is an extremely important issue, because no society or family can long endure without order. The issue is our original one. Must each man demand only his own way, or can we allow liberty and diversity and yet stay within a constitutional framework? If all imposed order is to be called repression or violence, then we do have severe problems—perhaps even unresolvable short of anarchy. Our popular will may not always be immediately translated into political effect, but was the intention of this constitutional machinery ever simply to reflect the popular will of the moment? If not, the issue is whether we can accept a political instrument with built in checks and balances and learn to make it work, even if it blocks us at important junctures.

We need to ask all advocates of "power to the people": Would the immediate reflection of mass interest really direct the state best? There is much to make us cautious about such an assumption, and it is not without religious import. Religious sentiment depends on a willingness to locate an authority external to the person. Although Christianity has wrongly been identified with monarchical forms, it also suffers when it refuses to locate any authority above the people, be it law or the good of society or whatever.

The man in the chic office is not given to reflection or originality, but perhaps we are wrong to seek in commerce what we should find in philosophers, artists, or religious men. Most men are victims, not innovators, but is the discovery very new that few and not all men are really free? Most of the current critique of society rests on a high and uncompromising idealism. We want to make true for every last human being what traditionally religion has reserved for the "saved man."

There is nothing wrong with extreme idealism. It is very close to religious sentiment. It follows on the heels of a period of contentment mixed with cynicism about change, and thus seems radical, whereas it is only more traditionally American. However, the problem the next chapter will explore for the future is whether our basic situation has changed. Are we caught with demands for complete human fulfillment at just the time when we are first beginning to doubt the real possibility for final enactment of the American dream?

Reich tells us that the corporate state has separated man from his sources of meaning and truth, and he calls a society "mad" unless it is guided only by what makes men healthier and happier. These are tricky points to handle, for the corporate state does provide our social context today. But the issue is whether men are not always, and under any condition, at some distance from their sources of meaning and truth? Does such protest rest on a false assumption that there was once an idyllic day when this distance did not exist, or that there will be a day in the future when we do not have to struggle to overcome this handicap? We are engulfed by these myths of the primitive, but we ought to learn that no situation in this world—neither corporate, nor agrarian, nor utopian—offers us value and meaning without constant struggle over alienation.

Reich is convinced that the self is lost today (pp. 141–170). All we can ask in reply is whether there ever was a time—or could be—when selves were found except by being made through struggle? Of course, our recent period of national affluence and optimism temporarily blinded us to this human fact. However, now that we are in tune with the realities of human nature, let us not blame our times but simply accuse all men always. Like others, Reich uses "violence" in a strange way. He calls an academic examination or test a form of violence, but to do so assumes a goal of such total isolation of the individual from pressure as to be unreal where men must live in community and evaluate one another. The trick is not to reject outside tests but to learn to submit while maintaining inner control.

If Spinoza is right and "all things excellent are as difficult as they are rare," then we have an enormous job before us if we want the best life for everyone equally. The majority have always led a dull, sheeplike existence and, ironically, this has been alleviated as much in American life as anywhere. Why, in a time when more men have freed themselves than in any era of the past, are we so disturbed because everyone doesn't have the best? Were there no faults in an agrarian culture that made farm boys desert it in droves? Why did they flee to the city if rural life was so idyllic? To say this is not to excuse faults or to say that much does not need a correcting that is long overdue. It is simply to point out that we must be careful of any overharsh denunciation which rests simply on the objection that the situation is less than ideal.

Freedom may have come to mean consumer comfort in America recently, and there is a needed revolution under way to return us to a more primitive and perhaps better American concept of freedom. We have lost our feeling of community and the traditional notion that all should work for the common good. This affects our religious health just as much as it harms secular society.

Youthful disillusion is traditional, but in our time it may be building toward a revolution in attitude rather than resignation. If so, the religious spirit only stands to gain, since its struggle is made of the same stuff. And it is perhaps the Vietnam war that has forced this collective break of consciousness, both social and religious.

It is Reich's prediction of the coming of Consciousness III that is both the most controversial and of greatest religious significance. This is because what he describes is somewhat like the kingdom of God, a blissful state in which the present is radically transcended. When and how will this come? Is it already among us, unseen but within certain individuals? Will it come in a process of time, or will what is now only partially possible not come to full fruition unless the natural order is broken to release it? Reich thinks the radically new is destined to arrive by natural evolution, but that is an assumption as romantic as it is dangerous, given our past history. Should we expect the future to be different, unless some transcendent power reaches in to break up the present structure?

Our young seek such a transformed life; that is true and very fortunate. However, if it does not come in nature's course, we have a generation set up either to hear Christianity's message for an offer of divine release, or to break up in disillusion as dreams prove unobtainable within nature's structure—our own alterations of it notwithstanding. Reich thinks there is less guilt and anxiety today (p. 235), but we wonder if that is true. He posits a sense of betrayal as being behind the current mood (p. 236). That is a profoundly religious theme, too, though the solution he proposes is social and not religious. Thus the issue is whether reconciliation is possible by a natural route. Reich describes the desired change as conversion (p. 240), and so the issue becomes: *What power can cause and sustain such a transformation of nature?*

"Liberation" is the foundation and goal of his Consciousness III, and this involves a return to early American ideals. He postulates the absolute worth of every human being (p. 242), but that may be an assumption which requires religious underwriting just because it is not sustained by political facts. His new consciousness follows the biblical injunction to "judge not" (p. 243). It is egalitarian and hates all distinctions; but, again, this may be more a matter of transcendental religious assertion than the way any society can be run in fact. Reich asserts that a world-wide community is forming, just as Christianity claims, but is this a fact or an eschatological ideal which requires a divine breaking up of our order? It must either be religiously based or it will be lost, if the transformation does not come by natural evolution as Reich expects.

The ideal community Reich describes, without authority or command, leads to small Christian communities but hardly to a national state. Will the young who seek this ideal agree to live in two worlds simultaneously, if they cannot have just the one they want? There is a return to the earthy and the sensual and the primitive, but the question is whether this outer form is enough to produce the inner freedom they seek. A monk wears clothes that indicate his chosen life, too, but he knows that this is the bare beginning of inner change. The problem is, if Consciousness III people are anticompetitive and unaware of rank, there are plenty of others who are ready to take their place, and then society's struggle goes on. The top positions will never go begging. The revolution would have to be universal to accomplish this, and America should not—and probably will not—produce such uniformity.

Experimentation in small community forms is very much on the increase, just as the small Christian communities first formed and monastic communities still exist. Such experiments are extraordinarily healthy. They offer society a contrast and perhaps a corrective, but seldom a possible model. Rationality, too, comes in for criticism by Reich, which marks his attitude as more sympathetic to religion than some recent views. Like a religious cult, Reich's Consciousness III seeks to expand awareness and claims to possess "new knowledge" very akin to revelation. Yet to date this is a youth movement, and the past should make us cautious about asserting its automatic extension into middle age. Should this not happen, a religious revolution, one based on these same changes which now are expected naturally, becomes a real possibility.

The cry is to be reborn, just as it is among Pentecostal groups, and the issue is whether such restoration comes by human or divine power. Nonmaterial—or spiritual—values come to be uppermost, and given these circumstances religion has not had such an open door in America since the rise of affluence pushed spirituality into the background. Reich chides society for not promoting nonmaterial goals, but has that ever been society's task, or even possibility? Religion guarded spiritual aims in the early days of America, and we created a strict separation of church and state to protect this function. Either religion rises to call for the primacy of spiritual values again or the state is foiled in achieving the people's aims, since it cannot itself serve the function of religion here.

Reich's description of the "new man" is so ethereal that it constitutes a new religion. The question is, what does it take to sustain such a perfect life (e. g., no hostility) as he outlines it? Religion has always called for a life of service and withdrawal from society. In such a missionary spirit of conversion, people must be reached, but it is a question whether society could ever reflect such a reform as a whole. Like St. Paul, Reich is sure that nothing can hold down the liberated man, and his description of the new state reads somewhat like the New Testament book of Revelation in its description of radical transformation. But can it be done without God, and does the church have a role to play in spreading such a gospel?

Reich believes in the immense power available to change one's life, but again the question of human *vs.* divine transformation is the issue. All we can do is wait and see whether such radical alteration can be accomplished by human effort. Must it come from outside or else be incomplete and partial? Reich senses the similarity of the life he describes to that of the Christian, but suggests that Christianity has failed. He wants a better life now; the question is whether his wanting can make it so. He also perhaps treats Christianity as something too overt. Thus, because he does not readily see its accomplished transformations, he assumes their nonexistence. Like the Marxist, he is convinced of the inevitable coming of his new state, but whether this hope is justified is precisely the question.

Reich is right: the power of transcending has been missing in America. It was present, however, in our early years and we could recover it. Reich seeks a new age of man; our only fear should be that the years ahead will fail to live up to his fantastic expectations. Perhaps he still seeks its presence in a little too overt and literal a manner, although he reasserts the existence of nonmaterial values. Perhaps, in attaching this new life to certain manifestations of dress and life-style, he is still too superficial in his associations. If so, the new age may be already here and accessible (although perhaps not in the sense he expects—such that all natural life is transformed now).

Reich is convinced that his Consciousness III is not reversible (p. 427), but given the vast and unexpected changes we have witnessed, this seems a not very safe assumption. He ignores the power of evil, and unfortunately all is not working with him in this world to achieve his lofty spiritual goals. Forces are as ready to tear down and destroy as they are to build up. The struggle is never won.

Reich draws a romantic picture of a college dining hall (p. 421), as if it represented the dawn of the next age, and this is perhaps typical of his overconfidence. College dining halls have always been carefree. They are not the world but a protected and special place—as they ought to be. Not what happens in the college dining hall but what transpires after students leave—that is the crucial test.

Reich assumes that there are no real enemies (p. 428). How can he do that—since, if true, it makes ludicrous the vast struggle of men to date to create and preserve any achievement of value? His mistake is to assume that everyone wants Consciousness III, when there is little reason to believe it. The Mafia is always willing to take over. To be ignorant of evil and of the opposing forces in any movement is to be destroyed by their backlash. It may take stronger stuff than his Consciousness III to return us to Eden. It may even require the strength of the same God who drove us out of paradise. We also may have to settle for less than having everybody on our side; and perhaps no political state can be exactly like Reich's vision.

It is fascinating to read some of the records of the young revolutionary movement.[33] They have the passion and the zeal for a new world of an old-fashioned camp revival meeting. It would take only a small move to transform this into a new wave of American religious revivalism. The young in assembly already look like an American frontier town. And they will not be limited to the mind alone. Soul is important. Their view of education, for example, has largely returned to the ideal of the small Christian college: to educate soul and body as well as mind. All that has changed since the founding of Christian colleges is the puritanical notion of how this ought to be achieved. Recently, in the name of freedom we rejected every attempt to educate the spirit. Now the cycle has come round again, and that is exactly what we seek.

The new Americans which Mitchell Goodman sees as emerging from the revolution (p. vi) are, of course, very similar to preindustrial Americans. The movement admittedly has a religious impulse, and so the issue in America is the same as that of other religious Great Awakenings: how to take the spirit and results of this movement and infuse them into the life of the structural church so that it reflects such enthusiasm. The present anti-intellectual mood is a return to primitive culture, or really to the American mentality before the expansion of the arts and higher education, an era which was suspicious of the intellect. Today we are ready to pursue spiritual values rather than simply "religious concerns."

A preoccupation with the transcendent (p. ix) pervades the young revolutionary spirit. This fact is crucial for the future of religion. For years it has had to fight the idea that all transcendence was forbidden to the modern mind. But the revolution has "blown" the modern mind and opened a way for traditional religious concerns, whether accepted as yet or not. Freedom, revolution, and liberation pop the cork of imagination, just let it out. Young Americans reach back and quote Thorton Wilder (p. 79): "It is difficult to be an American because there is as yet no code, grammar, decalogue by which to orient oneself" (from *Towards an American Language*).

Thus the problem of how to find unity out of an original plurality still exists. If youth is now the pivotal class within the United States (p. 84), this fact poses difficulties. It seems clear to them, for instance, that man's natural being and his instincts are to be trusted and followed (p. 108), but the question is whether this has not been traditionally truer for the young and less possible for older groups. If so, the philosophical assumptions of youth cannot be carried across to state or church, attractive as they may be. Of course, the new breed think they have a way to preserve the spirit of youth eternally, but that is precisely the great political and religious question of the future.

D. New American Theology

One haunting question is present through this entire exposition: Can theology—should theology—be "American"? It might be argued that theology, along with science, has been universalized, that culture too has been made universal and that national boundaries are no longer important. To meet this question fully involves a lengthy analysis, but some light can be shed by examining some recent theological statements by Americans to see whether they display anything of indigenous origin. This approach does not imply that local ideas cannot be expanded and extended to cross national borders in their application. Our own view is quite the opposite. But perhaps theology does operate best when it grows from provincial and powerful and unique experience to produce insights that lift it from its regional sources.

Herbert Richardson has suggested that we should build an American theology.[34] His suggestion, however, looks not so much to American philosophical and theological tradition as to the prominent features of American culture as it has recently developed—professional management, electric technology, etc. (p. ix). Our matrix of accepted common meaning and purpose has broken down—he is right in this. The issue is how many of our new constructive materials will come by reaching over the recent past to an earlier and perhaps more authentic American heritage. Richardson agrees that the modern period of history is coming to an end, but it is a question whether the future really will be dominated by sociology, economics, and political science as he thinks. This is not in fact a new theme, but an old hope.

He is right, as other contemporaries will argue—God has lost his reality for modern man. Yet two questions are involved here: Is "modern man" himself passing into history, and is any sense of a new (or old but revived) God appearing on the scene as viable in place of a nonvital deity? Atheism, he explains, is not a purely modern phenomenon. Thus there is nothing evolutionary or inevitable or irreversible in its presence. We know how fast human dispositions can change, once the supporting walls begin to crumble. Public atheism may simply mark the coming of a new concept of God. Cultural disintegration often begins with or includes an attack on religion, so that any violence against God may indicate more about society's transition than it does about the supposed untenability of religious belief (pp. 4–8).

Protest is a phenomenon in religion as well as politics, and protest comes when the available religious or political forms do not seem adequate or able to express the people's mood and will. Richardson suggests that "sociotechnics" (a new knowledge whereby man exercises technical control over society) is the source of many religious problems (p. 20). This is probably true, but the contemporary mood may increasingly rebel against precisely such technical control. Richardson thinks that "theology must develop a conception of God which can undergird the primary realities of the cybernetic world, viz., systems" (p. 23). He wants to adjust us "to live in harmony with the new impersonal mechanisms of mass society" (p. 25). But he is a generation behind the times. This is what the younger generation protests against, and certainly a sociotechnical God would be even less appealing as a model today than the military-industrial complex.

Harvey Cox's theology involves similar problems. He says, for example: "In our day the secular metropolis stands as both the pattern of our life together and the symbol of our view of the world."[35] To read this even a few years later is to experience a shock at the rapidity of change, since urban decay and our despair over ever keeping ahead of deterioration have made the city the opposite of attractive. The turn is already toward the rural, the primitive, and the isolated. This trend may be no more lasting than our brief veneration of city life, but it most certainly tells us that a theology courts disaster—or at least very brief popularity— if it identifies closely with any secular model of life.

We have been thoroughly secularized, as much by modern churchmen as by salesmen. But Arthur Miller's *The Death of a Salesman* testifies to our disenchantment with this style of life, and perhaps even the drug culture does the same. To give a nontheistic interpretation of biblical concepts to this generation (as some death-of-God theologians propose) is to offer ashes when

it is ready to handle fire. If secularization turns our attention away
from other worlds and toward this one, as Cox says (p. 17), our
present revulsion for the world (now that modern visions of beautiful new cities have faded) turns religious interest back to ask
whether there are worlds to explore other than city streets. The
"urban secular man" (p. 45) now is hardly the model for anyone
under thirty, and the religious ideals he exemplifies are not likely
to be very effective in the near future, if they ever were.

We are highly mobile, but instead of catering to this, the appeal
of religion might lie in offering again a lost stability. And if secular
man "relies on himself and his colleagues for answers" (p. 81), it
is just this individual self-assurance and confidence that has been
swept away overnight. That loss may produce a more religiously
receptive generation than secular independence ever could. Cox is
sure that "the organization is here to stay" (p. 173) and that this
is an ultimate fact to which religion must accommodate. However,
quicker than the eye can wink, the rebellion and protest of the
younger generation move precisely against all "organization." It is
not because the church lacks this aspect that the young are hesi-
tant about formal religion, but because the church embodies it.

Cox ends by admitting that we must be able to speak of God
meaningfully in the secular city, and that if we cannot, then all he
has said about "secularization as the work of God for man is nonsense and the whole thesis of this book is erroneous" (p. 241).
Unfortunately, his suggestions in this area are his weakest, and
thus the issue of how God is to be discerned and described is left
open. Cox tends to reject metaphysics (which covers a lot of
ground, since metaphysics is a vast variety of doctrines) and suggests that we use a political idiom (p. 249). He thinks that politics
"brings unity and meaning to human life and thought" (p. 254),
but observation hardly bears this out. If we must see a "politician-
God" at work in our cities, as Cox suggests (p. 255), it is likely
that we will never find God again. Where is God at work?—that is
our question. But it may not be in secularism.

God might manifest himself to us "in and through secular
events" (p. 266), and perhaps he always has. The issue arises
over whether he is contained in these events and is to be described
in their terms, or whether he breaks them open and demands non-

secular categories for their understanding. We always start with a secular context, it is true, but are we driven to transcend it? Is the transcendent acceptable to a postmodern man? Cox suggests that we may have to do without the name of God for a while, but even silence on the part of the divine can speak to those religiously attuned to hear the sound of silence.

Langdon Gilkey takes up the question of our ability to name God today and ties this to the traditional notion of God's voice in the whirlwind.[36] Interestingly enough, Cox also resorts to biblical notions and imagery when he wants to describe God. This might lead us to suspect that speaking about God is not more difficult than ever before, and that we have not progressed to a new secular era beyond the reach of primitive metaphor. Our relationship to the great theological systems of the recent past has shifted, Gilkey is right (p. 7). The question is whether these were more doubtful in their assumptions than we thought, in which case something not so novel behind them in our tradition could fill the breach. The church is experiencing doubts, but this may only mean that her former certainty was a questionable religious attitude.

However, Gilkey wants to limit his age to the concrete. He is suspicious of the speculative, but this may come just at a time when the speculative has become no longer so objectionable. He should not tie religion's future to the confining assumptions of the "modern mind," when the rejection of empiricism and narrow rationalism may have rendered impotent any view of God based on those assumptions. Gilkey, amazingly, accepts as his fundamental thesis that the secular spirit "represents the cultural *Geist* of our time" (p. 34). He proposes to become radically this-worldly just when the self-imposed limits of the modern world are bursting open—but then, the best students are and should be a generation ahead of most of their teachers.

Contingency, relativity, transience, and autonomy may well be general elements in the contemporary spirit, but this does not necessarily mean that our only alternative is that man must "create by his own powers whatever meaning his life on earth may achieve" (p. 62). God may break in, or man break out, of such a framework just as easily as to stay within it. As Gilkey puts it, the question is: "How *does* one speak of God in such a cultural

mood?" (p. 71). Yet that only pushes us back to ask just what
the cultural mood is, and are we simply moving backward if we
take a present dominant trend as indicative of the future? Perhaps
(as we will suggest in the next section and the next chapter) new
and quite different moods are forming which are not so unsympa-
thetic to God.

In discussing the sources of radical theology, Gilkey concludes:
"Any theological answer to this revolt against God must incorpo-
rate . . . modern sensitivity to evil at its deepest point and never
relinquish it" (p. 145). Thus, if evil is a major religious factor in
our time, any new American theology must reflect it. This is "un-
American" only if we take as American what is a comparatively
recent romantic and optimistic view. The early settlers were all-
too-aware of the presence and power of destructive forces, so that
to build a theology around evil is simply to return to a colonial
theme.

Gilkey's conclusion seems to be that meaningful "God language," although difficult in our day, is not impossible—but has
this not been the basic situation in every era to a significant degree? Since God is never an immediate object, and secular concerns are always more real and often more attractive, it takes
constant effort moving against the current to form a meaningful
picture of God. Gilkey's point is that our day is more difficult
than some. That may be true, but is it the case that most earlier
periods have been God-prone and only ours secular? Moreover,
secularism blatantly carried to its extreme has often bred a reverse
phenomenon: revivalism. It is possible that a rapid reversal of
religious disposition is ahead of us once more—although it cannot
and should not be that God will become instantly alive and concrete for all.

Following Tillich, Gilkey locates an element of transcendence
and mystery within the finite realm. By focusing on this aspect,
we gain a ground for religious language (p. 307). Yet his aim is
to give only the prolegomena to a new description of God and not
to explain God anew (p. 413). As such, that prologue is important, but the need of the day still remains to describe God in terms
both adequate to our experience and not inconsistent with our past.
However, Gilkey also follows Tillich in believing that religious

language is not direct talk about God (p. 465). In fact, since it is always symbolic, "our direct referent is *not* the divine as it is in itself" (p. 466). Evidently, if we are to describe God concretely, we will have to look for a base or source of experience other than the one Gilkey's theology provides.

Michael Novak is a young Catholic theologian with a radical flavor who illustrates the growing community between Protestant and Catholic writers today, a new experience in America. In an early book, he says that "America has known neither . . . nihilism nor the need for renaissance."[37] This statement merits reflection, given the whirlwind events of our last years. Now many are at the brink of nihilism and the need for renaissance is widely admitted. But perhaps such a situation actually is more conducive to renewed religious understanding and belief than the earlier one Novak described. He ties the search for God to reflection upon oneself (p. 76), and certainly we find an abundance of that all around us. Yet the force of events may also carry us outside ourselves in a violent era.

In America, Novak is convinced, "the tide of philosophy and the social sciences runs against belief in God" (p. 186). But this may be a temporary phenomenon, already in the process of a quick shift. In a later book, he opens this possibility himself in commenting on the growing revolution in the quality of human life.[38] The revolution is a struggle for human freedom, and "when the spirit of man is suppressed, God begins to die" (p. 17). Thus, as the change in American life spreads, a new experience of God may result as freedom is uncovered—or at least that is a possibility. In addition, the young have experienced a profound sense of their own complicity in evil (p. 23), so that the contemporary reality of God may also spring from an encounter with evil.

There is an Emersonian transcendentalism recurrent in the New Left (p. 39), which involves a revival of earlier American forms of thought and an abandonment of the confines of strict naturalism. Immediate feeling and action become important criteria. These are standards much more sympathetic to religion than complete rationalism. The trust is gone that some form of evolution will bring us out at the right spot. A fundamental change in direction is necessary (p. 70), which brings us back to the indigenous American notion of revolution. When such drastic changes are a political model, the idea of religious conversion becomes credible in a way it never could have been to naturalism or rationalism. An empiricist trust in the rightness of the majority is swept away.

A revolution in consciousness is essentially a religious task (p. 92). Recent conventional America may have been hostile to the openness required for an experience of God, but that closed quality of American life has been blown wide open. An acute sense of loneliness among the young predisposes them to find religious concepts attractive (p. 103). The younger generation, as a consequence, flirts with madness (p. 122). Dangerous as that is, it is also very close to religious sensitivity. As Americans, we have come to experience "nothingness" to a depth probably not felt since the pain of the Civil War. We have come to wonder whether the American notion of progress and fulfillment is wrong.[39]

Now we meet boredom, helplessness, and the collapse of values head on (p. 7). The effect of widespread drug experience is having an impact we are only beginning to comprehend. We trusted universal higher education to enlighten the young and to lead them —and all of us—only to good things. But education has not proved to be a road to any particular set of values, and it is just as able to lead us to revolt as to an accepted role in society. Scientific and technological progress, now no longer trusted, did not form our original confidence. It represents an optimism that developed comparatively late. Tradition, rationalism, and humanism (p. 53) are under question as they have not been in this century. To question these phases of our life is to introduce the experience of nothingness into American awareness.

In this new American sense of nothingness and the void, Novak recognizes the seeds of the traditional mystic's experience (p. 116). If his vision is sound, then the development of "inner solitude" becomes important and perhaps even the basis for an American religious attitude. Flamboyant and endlessly optimistic Americans will think this a strange attitude and even a betrayal of American goals. However, it has its roots deep in early American experience and is much less a nationalistic religion than was our mood earlier in the century. It involves a return to the strict separation of church and state, where the inner life of the person must be developed independently from the current economic and social situation.

In his early work, Novak acknowledged his debt to Bernard Lonergan, a Canadian.[40] Most younger Roman Catholic thinkers have been affected by Lonergan's detailed and systematic analysis of the functioning of human understanding as it produces insight. If we extend "American" to include "North American" (as we shall for Leslie Dewart, also a Canadian), Lonergan's influence on American thought is considerable. However, as a basis for constructing systematic theology it has not yet been developed, and its assumptions for exploring the limits of the understanding are so similar to Kant's that it may not provide a very adequate base to explain the later and more explosive experiences of Novak and others. The confines of the understanding that Lonergan accepts and explores may have been broken. The kind of metaphysics Lonergan proposes is developed altogether from an analysis of the rational side of understanding, and thus may not fit the upsurge of stress upon emotion, transcendence, and evil. The rational structure has blown apart.

Leslie Dewart writes on the future of belief, but he too reverts to lamenting the "incongruity between Christianity and the contemporary world."[41] First, we have to ask if he is up to date on "experience" and whether the gap now is all that wide? Second, even if the scene has shifted, is Christianity—or should it ever be —congruent with generalized experience? Is religion by nature something uncommon rather than common? This remains true even if we are passing through an uncommon and therefore religiously conducive time.

We may face a day of differing conceptions of God (p. 14), but that is unfortunate only to one who has accepted the modern notion that we must have universal agreement. In an age of violent change, such variety is likely to increase. However, if we examine our assumptions, we need not consider this a bad situation. Of course, Roman Catholics have further to go to adjust to it than Protestants, but they are fast diverging from uniformity of thought. We do need some new, unifying concepts of God to emerge out of this, but it is quite possible that the confusion of conflicting variety is our only fertile source. We ought to show how God can be present to human experience, Dewart feels (p. 170), and it may be that postmodern man's experience is open enough to do this.

Dewart seems ready to abandon the traditional notions of God as person, as omnipotent (pp. 185–194), and as nontemporal and authoritarian (pp. 194–206). But these proposals need careful study. Rather than rejecting such concepts, we may find that they require only reinterpretation and a new context. He is convinced that the supernatural has lost its usefulness to Christianity (p. 209); yet that judgment, too, may be a little hasty. The supernatural may yet have its day, or rather its new day, if both its meaning and what we call experience are radicalized. Silence is important in any thought about God (p. 214), and today silence may make its own sounds heard.

In a newer book, Dewart goes into greater detail on the philosophical basis for belief, but here he takes a world-culture approach.[42] He thinks that religious integration must come eventually. This is a questionable assumption, as to both desirability and possibility. Such unification may be theoretically beyond the power of what the intellect can achieve, and the necessity for the roots of religion to be in native soil may make a universal religion ineffectual, even if such a theology could be formed. Religion as a way of life draws too heavily on particular experiences which cannot always be universalized. Possibly one reason Dewart believes in such a union of religions is that he accepts a basic evolutionary framework (p. 24). If man's history is evolutionary, that could lead us out of our past diversity. Yet if it is not (except perhaps biologically), then we may have to deal with a future not unlike the past.

Dewart thinks that the "latest revolution" is man's becoming aware of "historicity" (p. 25). This is a strange thought, since history is more the category of the eighteenth and nineteenth centuries and is precisely what the late twentieth century has rejected. We are no longer sure that history follows evolutionary patterns. Dewart takes the reshaping of the future to be the other side of the analysis of the past (p. 43), but, in spite of the assumptions of historically oriented interpreters, no such symmetry may exist. *The future can be novel and difficult to forecast precisely because it conforms to no such predictable pattern.* Certainly our present experience in America is unlike what anyone might have thought it would be from analyzing our past a mere twenty years ago.

Dewart shares the arrogance which holds that somehow an evolutionary process has brought us to a place where we now have a superior outlook (an arrogance that colored the thought of Hegel and Marx). Others failed for centuries or else understood only in part, but now we have overcome our previous blindness by ferreting out the evolutionary cycle (p. 58). That was the nineteenth-century's fantastic confidence, which carried the day in America too through the first two thirds of the twentieth century. But it is precisely this optimism that has suddenly crumbled. If we can understand that no position is universal or in all ways superior to every one that has gone before, then our present religious situation becomes radically primitive too. We may develop new and fruitful concepts, adequate to our time and needs, but we have not advanced so far beyond the basic human starting point.

Dewart gives us his analysis of Greek thought, but we must stop and ask: Should a current view be based upon the correctness of an historical analysis, so that somehow, if the author understands the Greeks, then his current proposal is legitimated? This was, of course, the assumption of historical analysis, but suddenly we feel cut off from an historical sequence and continuity. To propose that man understand himself in such a developmental and evolutionary framework seems somewhat unreal. The world has spun too fast. It has skipped its developmental and sequential track and brought us around to where man first began.

When Dewart turns to the reconstruction of theistic belief, he still proceeds on a premise of the "historical, evolutionary nature of consciousness in general" (p. 357). As he admits, this is Hegel's assumption, but if it is no longer acceptable today, then much of his suggestion for theism is left suspended in mid-air. He does see atheism as the possible source for a new insight into God (p. 364), and recognizes that some reinterpretation of transcendence as well as immanence in God is crucial. Dewart does believe in historical progress, and thus religion for him must reflect this evolutionary change too (p. 472). Still, if consciousness has not grown or changed shape in these ways, then our religious situation is not as he describes it. It may, for example, be open to a wider variety of alternatives, including primitive and classical notions.

Whereas Roman Catholic philosophy has been alive and widely read for some time, it is only recently that Catholic theology has broken out of its own closed circle. Very quickly, however, Protestant and Catholic thought have interpenetrated. This is not to deny a still existing difference, but only to note that for the first time in American existence, our religious experience seems to stem from common sources and to respond to similar goals. George Lindbeck tells us that the conciliar documents of Vatican II "reflect a genuinely new vision of the world."[43] If so, one interesting side effect is that this view may be much more compatible with a peculiarly American experience of the world, whereas earlier Catholic thought on the whole took its cue from pre-American sources.

If the old issues of the Reformation are passing away, then Protestant and Catholic traditions can realign and perhaps draw on common sources. This is certainly true regarding their use of American history. For instance, both the new sense of the church and the vision of a world renewed fit into the early idea of America as a pilgrim country seeking a new order as God's people. The idea of a pilgrim church is very compatible with American notions and strikes a familiar chord. We are now prepared to understand that kind of church. Biblical eschatology comes to the forefront in Vatican II, and that was present early in the American experience. Then it reappeared in the Civil War, and it is striking us with full force again today.

A world headed toward redemption by radical eschatological means (p. 25) is a theme which should be acceptable to many in America. We once were, and have become again, a pilgrim people wandering in search of a new land and a new home. In the first part of this century we thought we had passed that stage, but now we are back in the mood. This is also the mood of the scriptures, and there is an increasing tendency among Catholic theologians to stress scripture as a theological source (pp. 97–98). In the Middle Ages and post-Reformation period, the atmosphere was not biblical, but now there is a greater sense of return in the air. The high plane of rationalism is gone and the eschatological mood of scripture is upon us.

In Roman Catholic reform there is a mixture of the old with the new, "but it is the new which is likely to shape the future" (p. 117). However, the "new" here is in some sense really the old or the primal. It is new only as opposed to recent strict rationalism or evolutionary or historical views that dominated theology until the cultural crisis broke their hold on our imagination. Roman Catholic theology has up until now been very little affected by its American experience, and thus has not been free to draw on it to shape its theology. In an ecumenical era, both Catholics and Protestants alike are open to explore this background for its possible resources. Now that Catholic thought has accepted the traditional American notion of pluralism in expression, it can appropriate American material in ways never allowed by its centuries of stress on unity and certainty.

*   *   *

> I know the plans I have in mind for you—it is Yahweh who speaks—plans for peace, not disaster, reserving a future full of hope for you.
> —Jeremiah 29:11 (The Jerusalem Bible)

Our analysis of the roots and trends in American theology moves at least toward this conclusion regarding a new American theology: The future of theology in America depends largely on our willingness and ability to produce *free theology,* one which looks at the scope of the American experience seriously and honestly and which concentrates on the concept of a *democratic God.* Free theology is characterized by a pluralism of opinion, an openness, and a metaphysical boldness. It capitalizes on one of the chief insights of the American experience, namely, that men can encounter and know God in many different ways and that no single way is sufficient to rule every other out of court. It encourages every man to develop his own theological perspective, but it also urges the cultivation of a sensitivity for the experiences and ideas of others. Free theology, therefore, also draws on another basic ideal and hope of American life, namely, that variety need not be finally divisive—that instead it can help to build up a spirit of unity and even a sense of identity.

Free theology can take scripture and religious tradition as normative, but only by choosing to regard them in this fashion. However, its emphasis should fall first on a critical and imaginative grappling with human experience. The object is to try to understand human existence and, if possible, to give ourselves a sense of the future by reflecting on God. Many of the people who have contributed most to America's best achievements could be called *free theologians*. They sought to understand themselves and their circumstances by thinking creatively about God, and the result was new vision for the future and a hope, kindled by that vision, out of which a sense of identity could emerge. Theological reflection helped to bring separate groups together as a nation in the first place, even though such a union was not the primary intention of early American leadership. In our present state of division and uncertainty, theology might play a role almost as important once again. Yet this can happen only if our theological efforts choose such a task as a self-conscious goal.

An emphasis on free theology, plus the American ideal of variety in life, precludes the possibility that Americans will or should agree on any particular philosophical or theological view. Rather, what we hope is that, by encouraging free thinking and expression about God, Americans may rediscover and build upon the values and ideals which are indispensable if we are to have lives that are humane and meaningful. This is a risky road to follow. There are no guarantees that such an objective can be achieved, because, wherever variety is encouraged, the seeds are also sown for the destruction of communal life.

Still, the Union was founded in the face of such risks, and its genius rests precisely on the insight that the richest form of community is achieved, not when men come together in spite of diversity, but rather when they unite in order to preserve and to cultivate a variety of talents and life-styles. An American community of freedom is still alive, but the struggle for its existence also continues, as well as the challenge of its possible destruction.

This nation's life is largely a success story—but not completely so. The American dream is at least a bit dimmer than it used to be, if not tarnished beyond recognition. Yet enough has been accomplished so that America is still a symbol of hope and promise for many persons. The tasks that face us now are those of renewal and rebirth. If either dimension of the precarious balance that constitutes our country—individual freedom and variety on the one hand and communal cooperation and unity on the other—is undermined much further, the Union will exist in name only. By interpreting the broad framework of existence into which God casts our lives; by stressing man's need for and God's relation to love, justice, and freedom; and by underscoring the theme that death, evil, and negation are not the final scenes of life's drama, American theology might open renewal, promise, and national rebirth.

Today life in America is a maze of political, social, and moral crises. Unfortunately, our resources for coping with them often run dry. Communal concern frequently dissipates into a consuming selfishness which brings more emptiness and despair than most of us care to think about. Many Americans are tired and frustrated. Such a situation, however, is tailor-made for creative theological work. A religious message can speak most clearly and profoundly to men who face severe problems and who need encouragement, and it does this through a promise for the future. We are not witnessing a massive religious revival at the present time. Yet the times could hardly be more exciting or promising for creative theological work. The volatile nature of our circumstances ought in itself to be the challenge we need to achieve a renaissance of American theology.

An emphasis on free theology means that many theologies are possible and that many ought to be developed simultaneously. On the other hand, our analysis of the roots and trends of American theology indicates that, given the mood of the hour, some options are likely to speak more forcefully and meaningfully than others. The idea of a "democratic God" provides one viable alternative from which many significant theological views emerge. In fact, the very concept of free theology implies the existence of a democratic God. Such a God is one who recognizes and accepts the fact that his relation to human life can be regarded in various ways—not all of which are flattering. Such a God understands and accepts the fact that some men may ignore, reject, or curse him, and deny his reality altogether.

This God, while being the source, ground, and goal of all that is, shares and respects freedom and power. His reality is not the most obvious fact about this world, any more than the existence of some single American ideology is the most obvious fact about this nation. The God implied by a free theology is a God who stays largely in the background of the world. He has power and may ultimately be omnipotent, but his present involvement or interference is subdued.

One reason for a restrained use of power on God's part is that he is vitally interested to observe what emerges from the free play of the present configuration of life. With special reference to human existence, God's concern is to see whether men can establish a humane community in which power and freedom are controlled by love and justice. God's hopes and expectations are high, even though the circumstances into which he thrusts men are not the most conducive to their success. Apparently, such a God wants no automatic victories. The wildness and harshness of nature make our lives fragile. Our lack of both immediate insight and innate charity and love for other men makes it difficult for us to temper power and freedom with love and justice.

Saddled with the burden of the faults of our ancestors and often trapped by our own guilt, we sometimes seem faced by insurmountable obstacles. The world did not have to be this way. But even if we are partly responsible for its jagged shape, God is directly implicated too. Human life in this world, then, is a test against severe odds. It is a test to see what we can accomplish in the way of establishing a community of freedom, justice, and love in spite of the odds that God sets and in spite of the obstacles we create for ourselves. Some men play more dramatic parts than others. But every individual plays a dual role, and he possesses the freedom to shape these in varied ways. Each man is at once one who is tested and one who figures in the context that tests others. Every man casts his own unique vote, but is in turn influenced by the votes cast by everyone else.

God plays a similar dual role. He both cares about this wild world and is influenced by it. He casts at least one unique vote in the form of a man hanged on a cross. Raised from death to life, this person reveals the power, meaning, and cost of love. He provides a future and a hope which allow us to have courage now to do the best we can for the ideals of humane communal life. But God does not guarantee worldly victories for any of us. This means that, like all of us, he can suffer by seeing his expectations and hopes for this world crushed, just as he may experience joy whenever love and justice win out.

One crucial difference remains, however, between God and man. God retains ultimate control of existence, and this control will be characterized, finally, by a sustaining and victorious love—or at least, it is the Christian's faith that this is or will become true. If such a love is not the ultimate backdrop for our world, life is merely a struggle in which everyone ultimately loses. However, given the hope promised by the report of divine love, the future remains at least open-ended. Meaningful striving within this life and fulfillment beyond this world might be our destiny.

This world is not the best of all possible worlds, but it may be God's experiment in democracy. If so, some of us will experience great difficulty when we try to achieve a positive religious relationship with such a bold and democratic God. On the other hand, many Americans ought to be able to understand this kind of God. They should, in turn, be capable of using their reflection about him as a means to revive and renew their mutual life.

Every man dies, and so does every nation. America will not exist forever. Since our time is limited, we ought to make the best of it. Free theologies which capitalize on the idea that our present existence is largely a test—involving multiple centers of power and freedom but also projected toward God's love—could become indispensable for encouraging and accomplishing self-renewal. The future of America and the future of theology in America may turn out to be very closely related. Can American theologians speak to the current situation in a way that combines honest and critical judgments on the facts of our lives with direct appeals to what is best in the religious, political, and social heritage of Americans?

Such a responsibility will tax theological ingenuity. Yet even if sound views are produced, they alone will not be sufficient to guarantee a wholly successful outcome. Theological insights are effective, after all, only as they are appropriated and used by people. On the other hand, it is clear that, if we fail to develop theologies that are uniquely and self-consciously American, we will only contribute to the erosion of confidence.

This nation could exist without contemporary theologies distinctively American, but we are unlikely to actualize our full potential if we do not develop and appropriate such statements in the next decades of this century. If America has in any sense been a land of opportunity and hope in the past, and if she continues to have this glow even as we struggle with a multitude of crises, theology has played a part in making it so. The future will not be different in this respect. The quality of future life in America will depend at least partly on our ability to formulate and use theologies which take our peculiar experience seriously and honestly. Each should focus on the concept of a democratic God, a God who is both obscure and harsh, yet possibly also present and loving, a God who gives and respects power and freedom, but who also has his own ultimate plans: "plans for peace, not disaster, reserving a future full of hope for you."

NOTES

1. Paul Kurtz, ed., *American Thought Before 1900* (New York: Macmillan Company, 1966), p. 15.

2. Paul Kurtz, ed., *American Philosophy in the Twentieth Century* (New York: Macmillan Company, 1966), p. 27.

3. Herbert W. Schneider, *A History of American Philosophy* (New York: Columbia University Press, 1946), p. vii.

4. Morris R. Cohen, *American Thought* (New York: Collier Books, 1962), p. 27.

5. See John E. Smith, *Themes in American Philosophy* (New York: Harper Torchbooks, 1970).

6. John E. Smith, *The Spirit of American Philosophy* (New York: Oxford University Press, 1966), p. xi.

7. Robert J. Roth, S.J., *American Religious Philosophy* (New York: Harcourt, Brace & World, 1967), p. 3.

8. William McLoughlin and Robert Bellah, eds., *Religion in America* (Boston: Beacon Press, 1968), p. x.

9. Robert Bellah, "Civil Religion in America," in *Religion in America*, p. 9.

10. See Martin E. Marty, "The Spirit's Holy Errand: The Search for a Spiritual Style in Secular America," in *Religion in America*, pp. 167–183.

11. Harvey Cox, "The 'New Breed' in American Churches: Sources of Social Activism in American Religion," in *Religion in America*, p. 370.

12. See Thomas F. O'Meara and Donald M. Weisser, eds., *Projections: Shaping an American Theology for the Future* (Garden City, N.Y.: Doubleday & Company, 1970).

13. Harvey Cox, "Political Theology for the United States," in *Projections: Shaping an American Theology for the Future*, p. 44.

14. Michael Novak, "Social Concreteness in American Theology," in *Projections: Shaping an American Theology for the Future*, p. 73.

15. Thomas F. O'Meara and Donald M. Weisser, "Afterword: The End of Theology?" in *Projections: Shaping an American Theology for the Future*, p. 217.

16. Chaim Potok, *The Chosen* (Greenwich, Conn.: Fawcett Publications, 1967), p. 249.

17. See Herbert W. Richardson and Donald R. Cutler, eds., *Transcendence* (Boston: Beacon Press, 1969).

18. Michael Murphy, "Education for Transcendence," in *Transcendence*, p. 18.

19. Sam Keen, "Manifesto for a Dionysian Theology," in *Transcendence*, p. 31.

20. Harvey Cox, "Feasibility and Fantasy: Sources of Social Transcendence," in *Transcendence*, p. 53.

21. Hal Bridges, *American Mysticism* (New York: Harper & Row, 1970), p. 1.

22. See Alan Watts, *The Wisdom of Insecurity* (New York: Pantheon, 1951).

23. See Alan Watts, *Does It Matter?* (New York: Vintage Books, Random House, 1971).

24. See Thomas Merton, *Thoughts in Solitude* (Garden City, N.Y.: Doubleday Image Books, 1968).

25. Robert Bellah, *Beyond Belief* (New York: Harper & Row, 1970), p. xviii.

26. See Peter L. Berger, *A Rumor of Angels* (Garden City, N.Y.: Doubleday Anchor Books, 1970).

27. Peter L. Berger, *The Sacred Canopy* (Garden City, N.Y.: Doubleday Anchor Books, 1969), p. 171.

28. Hannah Arendt, *On Revolution* (New York: Viking Press, 1965), p. 1.

29. See Theodore Roszak, *The Making of a Counter Culture* (Garden City, N.Y.: Doubleday Anchor Books, 1969).

30. Gregory Armstrong, ed., *Protest: Man Against Society* (New York: Bantam Books, 1969), p. 2.

31. Herbert Marcuse, *One-Dimensional Man* (Boston: Beacon Press, 1964), p. ix.

32. See Charles A. Reich, *The Greening of America* (New York: Bantam Books, 1971).

33. See, for example, Mitchell Goodman, ed., *The Movement Toward a*

New America: The Beginnings of a Long Revolution (New York: Alfred A. Knopf, 1970).

34. See Herbert W. Richardson, *Toward an American Theology* (New York: Harper & Row, 1967).

35. Harvey Cox, *The Secular City* (London: SCM Press, 1965), p. 1. Cox revised the book in 1966, but his revisions did not substantially alter the basic theses that we are examining in the following paragraphs.

36. See Langdon Gilkey, *Naming the Whirlwind: The Renewal of God Language* (Indianapolis: Bobbs-Merrill Company, 1969). See Job 40:6–7, from which Gilkey takes this title.

37. Michael Novak, *Belief and Unbelief* (London: Darton, Longman & Todd, 1966), p. 37.

38. See Michael Novak, *A Theology for Radical Politics* (New York: Herder & Herder, 1969).

39. See Michael Novak, *The Experience of Nothingness* (New York: Harper & Row, 1970).

40. See Bernard Lonergan, *Insight: A Study of Human Understanding* (London: Longmans, Green & Company, 1958).

41. Leslie Dewart, *The Future of Belief* (New York: Herder & Herder, 1966), p. 7.

42. Leslie Dewart, *The Foundations of Belief* (New York: Herder & Herder, 1969), p. 14.

43. George Lindbeck, *The Future of Roman Catholic Theology* (Philadelphia: Fortress Press, 1970), p. 1.

X

THE NEW SENSE
OF THE FUTURE

A. Tower of Babel West

> "Come," they said, "let us build ourselves a city and a tower
> with its top in the heavens, and make a name for ourselves; or
> we shall be dispersed all over the earth."
> —Genesis 11:4 (New English Bible)

The basic problem of Charles Reich's vision of an America become green again is that it never was all green in the first place.
His description of Consciousness III is an eschatological vision, a
world transformed just as it is pictured in the New Testament book
of Revelation. However, the religious question is whether this can
be done by man, or whether God's power must intervene to produce such a basic revision. Nor does Reich allow for the power
of evil continuing right down to Judgment Day. He wants all men
to be selfless Christians, more concerned for others than themselves, more interested in outgoing love than their own self-interest.
Such people have never been a majority, in spite of our wishing
it were so, and there is little evidence that good ever will control
the earth unopposed.

Those who do change their personal orientation are a minority.
In this fact, all Christians join all blacks as part of the loyal opposition, but minorities can contribute great things which often flow
precisely from their feeling of isolation. As a people, Americans

have been as generous toward others as any nation, but it is too much to expect every individual to give up being selfish. We have always had men who will destroy others—and sometimes themselves—in order to achieve their goals. Somehow America kept an image in which this frightening type never represented us in a national self-portrait. Controlling wealth and power as we now do, we are bound to see criminal and destructive men increase. The issue is whether a better minority can again capture the leadership, in church or state.

We tried to build a Tower of Babel in the West, and almost made it. Our modern construction methods make those employed in the biblical story (see Genesis 11) pale by comparison. First we had the vision of a new life for the early colonists, and the land could support that, since their requests were modest. As the waves of immigrants came, it seemed possible to extend the dream indefinitely. There still was room for all. After industrialization and the technological revolutions of science, our horizons again expanded seemingly without end. We really thought it possible to do for all what earlier we had done for a comparative few of the hordes of men born to this globe. In the late twentieth century, suddenly, the ceiling has fallen in. We know it is not possible to extend a full life to everyone in the world, and we are not even sure it is feasible to do for every American what once seemed so easy.

Even if our watermark is far higher than any left before, we failed to storm the gates of heaven successfully. This experience, coupled with a realization of the limits of both human and natural resources, can bring about a profound religious sensitivity—even if our pain of disappointment is too great to allow us to realize fully the benefits involved. This does not mean that the fading American dream forces anyone to be religious in reacting against it. Some will be bitter. They will rage against themselves and the economic and political dream they once believed in. Some, hopefully, will work to accomplish all that remains possible. Others, when they are limited materially in the natural goals they can achieve, will enter the basic experience necessary if God is to be encountered.

The biblical tower builders hardly got to first base compared to the way we almost lifted men to heaven—or at least to the moon.

Yet the resulting experience for many is one of spiritual emptiness. Even the best record does not seem good enough. Like the children Americans are, we want all or nothing. If we do not get all we want, we tend to ignore what has been accomplished, and concentrate on what we do not have or lament where we went wrong. By providing one generation with more material comfort and security than possibly man has ever known, we found that "man does not live by cake alone." In recent days we have, in fact, produced a youth rebellion against success, and in the process launched a massive spiritual quest (see Postscript).

In trying to comprehend this phenomenon, plus religion's role in a changed situation, we must resist the common temptation simply to extend a present trend on into the future. Charles Reich foresees a life-style developing in the most unreal atmosphere of the college dining hall, and expects it to grow and take over. But in actuality we know that developments, however good, do not extend themselves so easily. The crucial test comes when the opposition counterattacks. This is neither to say that significant changes cannot come about nor to deny that we are already in the midst of one. It is simply to point out that to discern the hidden but emerging factors is most difficult. Of course, it may be that the exact shape of the future remains never fully determined and thus constantly subject to change.

If the practice of slavery endangered the Union, and if our most bitter battles then and now come over equality and opportunity, native blacks may provide us with a significant clue to the future of religion in America (as spelled out in Chapter IX). If the white colonists came here for religious freedom (and many for adventure and economic gain as well), *it would be a neat twist of fate befitting the action of a free God if the saving note in American religious life came back to us from the men we brought here in bondage.* Of course this has happened before, when God chose to liberate the oppressed Israelites in Egypt and use them as a minority instrument. As was probably the case then, every thought and word of a people seeking to be free will not be religious—far from it. But along with the turbulence, the key to gaining release for the spirit may also lie in the prior experience of oppression.

If we castigate America for perpetuating forms of human bondage down to the present day, we must lift our sights beyond our own struggle and remember that the coming of slaves to America was simply a minor example—and not so odious by some comparisons—of the colonial expansion going on all over the world. We did not get the idea of slavery all by ourselves. The subjugation of native peoples by whites was increasing around the globe at a fantastic pace at the time, and for years America prided herself on not reaching out to seize great colonial empires. This does not make slavery right, but the forces that brought the practice here originally were far from uniquely American.

Richard Wright comments on this world-wide phenomenon in his *White Man Listen!* The wave of colonial suppression drew America into its net too, although the majority of men came here for other purposes. The South, however, was settled on the European colonial pattern, often by those more closely allied with aristocracy than was true in the North. Thus, expansion and exploitation extended their grip to America. Of course, the early colonists spoke in different terms, and the founding fathers tried to modify or eliminate this aspect. Nevertheless, exploitation and power and expansion were part of America from the beginning. The settlers escaped some problems by fleeing Europe. Others they imported with them while not quite realizing the future reverberations.

On the whole, as far as religion is concerned, the Puritans and Quakers will do as an illustration of the small sects who came seeking religious freedom (among other things). We often turn to them in drawing our model of religion in America, but *the new tone of religion in America may come from a black source, from men not brought here as Christians or even as new Americans.* Richard Wright left his Mississippi home and went to Paris to live and write, and he learned that problems of race "are not confined to the United States."[1] The issue is white vs. nonwhite all over the world. Our ability to solve our race problem religiously and politically is merely part of a world-wide struggle from which we are not as isolated as we once hoped.

Of course, the literature of social critique is not new in America. Theodore Dreiser, Upton Sinclair, and Sinclair Lewis all caused sensations in their time by pointing to aspects of emptiness in

American life. That a meaningful life is accomplished with great effort and by only a few—this comes as a shock only to a people who thought they had escaped from previous human limitations to build a new Tower of Babel in the West. Of course, whenever our speech and goals have been united in America (just as the biblical story reports), we have been nearly invincible. Now, whether through God's action or our own, common aims seem uncertain and our own voices many. Richard Wright wrote to plead for the elimination of man's gross inhumanity to man, and that also is a religious goal. The issue is what role this motive should play in American religious life in the future.

Wright describes his state in Paris as being lonely. He is a rootless man when detached from Mississippi, and yet he cannot go back. In the battle for human dignity he recognizes the role religion should play to show each person that he is still a human being, in spite of the forces that try to dehumanize him (p. 24). A sense of dignity is the common human need. If black religion can show us how that can be achieved under severe conditions, the black man in America may teach the white man a lesson. The function of giving dignity to the downtrodden human spirit largely disappeared from white religion in the time of national success, but the need to know that you are human and loved as such has now returned in fury upon whites as well as blacks.

Richard Wright's *Native Son* is an American classic. It is a gripping drama of the soul, and yet, Wright says, it came straight out of a myriad of experiences that pressed in upon him as a black man in search of dignity. Wright tells us that one reason Bigger Thomas (the hero of the novel) revolts is that "he had become estranged from the religion and the folk culture of his race."[2] Ironically, exactly the same situation has turned up for many white Americans today, and in a way no one could have predicted.

Thus, we must all either revolt from society and religion or else find a way to renew their function in quite different circumstances. But, as we suggest, times such as ours may be favorable to religion and thus make it possible to accomplish a revival of its ancient humanizing function. Wright's character, Bigger, revolts because of a wild and intense longing to belong, and Wright recognizes that what he uncovered in his novel now applies to white Americans too

(p. xiv). Wright sees a complex struggle for life going on in his country. In such a situation, religious solutions may be rejected, but they certainly are not meaningless.

Can an America of the future offer spiritual sustenance to its own dispossessed and disinherited men? Once we offered a material home to some who were dislocated in their own native land. What we did economically for those who came from afar we must now do spiritually for all Americans born here. "The springs of religion are here, and also the origins of rebellion" (p. xxv). In the Negro, Wright is convinced, we have "the embodiment of a past tragic enough to appease the spiritual hunger of even a [Henry] James" (p. xxxiv). If suffering and tragedy, not success, are necessary for the flowering of a religious spirit, Americans need no longer wander abroad in search of soul. We have much to contemplate in our own native sons. Of course, in the novel Bigger Thomas rejects his mother's traditional religion. Thus the definition of the role religion can play in appeasing spiritual hunger must still be tested. It cannot simply take past forms.

In *David Walker's Appeal* we have a document from 1829 that helped to trigger resistance to the enslavement and degradation of blacks.[3] One hundred and fifty years later the battle is still on. The black writer of the book cries out against hypocrisy and injustice—a classic religious theme—but the question today is whether whites have finally lived through enough of this so that now we can really learn from the black experience. Walker's plea was to throw off slavery because it corrupts and destroys the soul. That demand still pertains to the unresolved social and political needs of black people, but the white man today also feels an urgent need for release from human degradation and for restoration of a soul torn to pieces. Israel was born as a religious nation when it marched free of slavery under God's guidance. *Black Americans might lead white Americans out of the material bondage into which our souls have become locked.*

Martin Luther King's famous "Letter from Birmingham Jail" is an intensely religious document; it is addressed to his fellow clergymen and takes its place in a long line of Christian prison literature.[4] King presents himself as a missionary carrying the gospel of freedom beyond his own home town (p. 98), and Christianity has only been fully alive when it had a missionary message to lift it out of its own self-concern. The American church is under judgment, and the record of the church to date has been rather poor where justice is concerned. The church is tied to ancient practices of segregation. Thus renewal in American church life depends on a prior soul-searching of considerable magnitude.

James Baldwin is another black novelist who has written magnificently out of the black experience. His *Another Country* tells us how difficult life and love are in this land for both whites and blacks. At least we know that, for many, the American success story can never come true. As one character in the story says, "I suppose that one replaces a dream with reality."[5] In the long run, that is the only basis on which Christianity can be built. Women dreaming and men under illusions of progress cannot really be reached spiritually. We have to learn, as Baldwin reports, that the most difficult thing can also be the most rewarding,[6] and certainly to be born a Negro is to face that lesson.

If the power of revelation is the business of the novelist (p. 15), it may be that contemporary Christian revelation comes alive again on the pages of black literature. The black had to learn forbearance (p. 17), and so must every religious man. Baldwin's *The Fire Next Time* is drawn from the story of Noah and God's threat that, if men make a mess of human society again, he will have to intervene with more than a flood. Perhaps one can only know God by living under such a threat. The black knows the world to be loveless, but still we have lived on in a dream of accommodating religion to society and in the thought that the structure of the society we built would in fact reflect love. Now we are all learning the religious lesson the black is born with. To find love is always hard, and no social structure alone can provide it, although some forms block its expression more than others.

James Baldwin pleads with his nephew, to whom he writes, to accept the white man in love because whites are trapped in a history they do not understand. ". . . We can make America what America must become."[7] In part this optimism over the black source for future progress means that we must all find freedom together or not at all—just as the early American colonists learned. Baldwin reports being driven to religion at the age of fourteen, but at first it produced only blindness, loneliness, and terror rather than faith, hope, or love. Yet the church was exciting to him in its drama and music. And this is a needed experience, as Baldwin comments: "Something very sinister happens to the people of a country when they begin to distrust their own reactions as deeply as they do here, and become as joyless as they have become" (p. 57).

Baldwin's comment that "one can give freedom only by setting someone free" (p. 100) is certainly central to the Christian commandment to go into the world to spread the gospel and minister to the needy. *The solution to the problem of black freedom could be at once the solution to the problem of white freedom and our joint discovery of the meaning of the Christian gospel, if it is only in ministering to the needs of others that man can find the means of release.* To create one nation has proved to be a hideously difficult task because we did not remove the sources of division at the beginning. Even to create one Christian community has now turned out to be more formidable than any early American colonist ever dreamed.

The American Negro might lead us all back to an original vision just in the day when our long-held dreams are tumbling, because the black "has the great advantage of having never believed that collection of myths to which white Americans cling" (p. 115). Thus, our education in political as well as religious reality today might have its best source in black America. If Richard Wright's Bigger Thomas is not our only native son, it is still true that we cannot understand our spiritual situation until he is placed alongside Elmer Gantry and Tom Sawyer.

The rage we see boiling to the surface in black literature appears as a strange phenomenon to some citizens, but it is an American phenomenon nevertheless. Rage is not an emotion we have thought much about in religion recently, but perhaps this is what lies behind America's present religious indifference. If we want to understand this emotion, *Black Rage* should be our model.[8] These explorations by two black psychiatrists were not carried out for their religious significance. Nevertheless, they explore the basic condition of the man whom Americans may have to use as their religious test case—the black. The inner suffering of the black is caused by the hostility he faces. Oppression and capricious cruelty are the sources of his rage. The story of Bertha, which the authors present, is that of one who feels so unworthy of love, so filled with self-depreciation, that she cannot accept love simply. It is to this condition that Christian ministers must bring love so that emotional barriers are broken—or else God's love cannot come to anyone in America.

Doctors Grier and Cobbs go on to describe the present strange relationship of blacks to religion in *The Jesus Bag*. Religion helped blacks to develop an attitude of resignation that enabled them to survive oppression (that is "the Jesus bag"). But the passivity and sense of inferiority connected with this idea of resignation are precisely what must be overcome in the black quest for political freedom and social equality. Thus the issue in black religion is whether, for these new goals, blacks can derive strength from the same religious convictions that once sustained them in a different way. If they can, this might serve to reform the nation and, possibly, the world. This represents an old-fashioned evangelism, but if that enthusiasm is ever again to permeate the American religious spirit—just when we thought it had departed forever, replaced by a new-found sophistication—its most likely source lies in the black American religious experience.

Yet because blacks have had to reject the white community's code of behavior in order to survive, any spirit captured there will not spring from patriotic fervor [9] Considering the lengths to which we originally went to separate church and state, and the difficulties we experience today because our religious goals have become accommodated to society's norms, this may be a valuable detachment for religion in America to learn. The black learned to adopt a passive attitude as a life-saving shield against whites, and religion was a broader means of maintaining his balance. The strictures of religion haunt blacks today. If today white pressure is directed against the restrictions of society, black tension opposes religion's restraints too.

In recent days in America, we have thought that the human spirit must be lighthearted and optimistic in order to be religious. Now, as our vast dreams are on the wane, religion is in trouble just because, for many, it is tied to that hardly tenable attitude in the face of a vast antipathy. But spiritual manuals have really always known better and understood that the spirit must experience degradation and worthlessness before it can be exalted. A black man's religious spirit is forced to spring from that level or not grow at all. Since his basic experience cannot be lighthearted, it is always close to genuine religious insight.

Massive violence is a part of this country's way of life, unfortunately, which means that any God we discover must know the meaning of violence and experience the suppressed ambition from which violence usually comes. Once Jonathan Edwards roused religious fervor by describing sinners in the hands of an angry God. In our borrowed Continental rationalism, we forgot about such a picture of God and put it behind us as primitive. Yet, whatever we may discover about love—whether divine or human—anger is perhaps the level from which religious emotion originally stirs. Thus the neoprimitivism we see manifesting itself when the young gather together is not far from the origins of religion. ". . . Blacks are angry and . . . they hold their rage in check by monumental self-control" (p. 41). Thus late twentieth-century Americans may learn the origins of a religious spirit by being held in the hands of an angry black God.

At the same time, *bitterness is the spirit which must be avoided now, no matter how deserved, and that is what a new religious spirit must fight against if it is to establish a gospel of love and forgiveness.* If the black man were able to learn to forgive the white without asking whether or not he deserves it, America could hardly ask for a more striking example of the ability of God's action to transform hate into love, and thus the white (or black) sinner into a man saved from his own self-destruction. That is a future religious revival to encourage. But economic affluence alone will not bring about such religious generosity.

Grier and Cobbs tell us the story of Melba the schoolteacher. Her problems were manifold but little of her own making. Yet, as health arrived, it came primarily through a spirit of forgiveness. "There was no changing the past but she could now forgive" (p. 154). Christianity need not make a man passive and submissive—whether he is black or white—but its central message still is forgiveness. Americans have found a new religious model. If white America can be forgiven—by God and by black—for its toleration of slavery, then there may be new hope in the land. However, such magnanimous strength in the black soul may not be possible against so terrible a record. The black soul struggles between religion and violence, and all await the outcome.

Christianity does recommend humility, but what we need to get straight is that this attitude is to be before God and precisely *not* before men, if the religious aim of the restoration of all life is at stake. Religion should not be imposed to enslave. That is its perversion. This fact, however, points America toward a classic question: In what sense does the religious spirit offer freedom and release, if it does not always do this politically and socially? "Soul is the toughness born of hard times" (p. 167), and white Americans cannot find much "soul" today because they have lived through too easy a time in recent years. If soul means graceful survival under impossible conditions, and compassion is something we must learn from an oppressed people before we can exhibit it, then America has much to borrow from her black native sons.

It is a miracle that blacks endured under the conditions imposed, but so also is it a miracle that Jews have survived and kept their faith alive when one would have thought it had to be abandoned. Ghettos are not an American invention. Minorities have tended to inherit them since the early exile from Eden, and the capacity of dismal confines to generate a religious faith that goes beyond a superficial level is amazing. Yet many Americans now feel locked in a ghetto; we are estranged from other lands by our own—perhaps sometimes well-intentioned—action. We first wanted isolation from Europe. Then we wanted idolization. Now we feel confined to this land by some undeserved hostility, moderated by moments of idolization still. In this new great American ghetto we all inhabit, God may be discovered again.

"Blacks must learn to live with the immediate prospect of death, to face death every day" (p. 171). Like Jesus, Martin Luther King may have been condemned to death from the beginning. Americans have usually hidden death, but in the destruction of life in Vietnam we have seemed to feel death more than in the heroic sacrifices of World War II. Christianity means faith in renewed life in spite of death. If this is America's most needed religious lesson, perhaps blacks can teach some of it to us. A renewed religion means to become unafraid to die, "willing to die for principles we hold dearer than life" (p. 172). Such an attitude requires a deeply religious spirit, but it is an original American spirit. If whites have lost it, perhaps we can only find American zeal again by appropriating the black experience.

Grier and Cobbs are not sure that the new black spirit has much to do with Christianity. "It is rather the creative response of a tortured, driven people" (p. 179). But that is precisely where Christianity began, however it has been transformed into a success story since. Thus, the black response, if it can be generous and bountiful, might lead us back to the primitive Christian experience. Forgiveness and love are its fruits; and, as always, that is the way —and the only way—Christianity's presence can be discerned. Spiritual riches often come precisely from what once entrapped us, after the lock is sprung. If one feels the action of God in gaining release, then that experience is religious—and this is what the early pilgrims thought they had established once and for all. If one does not feel divine action, the struggle for release becomes primarily a human endeavor which relies on its own strength and on man's power.

B. The Vanishing American Middle Class

The traditional middle-class American is an endangered species. In fact, we may need to establish reservations for its protection, so that schoolchildren may visit specimens of it to see what life in America used to be like. *The Music Man,* which documents the antics of a small town in Iowa, may represent its recorded memory. Of course, as Mr. Doolittle says in *My Fair Lady,* not everyone is "saddled with middle-class morality." In point of fact, there have always been a variety of life-styles here, but it is amazing how uniformly and for how long we accepted the *ideal* that everyone should enter the middle class and share those values. So, if the fact never quite existed, at least the ideal is vanishing of eventually having everyone in the middle class.

If such a shift is in process, it has profound consequences for the future of American religious life. Since immigrant days, when the churches followed the flow of new settlers, we have known a good deal about how to adapt in order to minister to people in varied situations and with diverse needs. But in the age of affluence, the American church drifted to an identification with the ideal of the middle class, and it will not be easy to break that pattern and reach out to minister to those groups who now reject it. We developed an "aristocracy of the middle class" with all its accompanying disdain for any who did not share its good values. Instead, today we are moving toward a proletarian openness to every form and mode of life. This is not to say that middle-class virtue is bad. It may be a great American strength, but the Christian gospel in the future will have to move in greater independence of these particular values.

Arthur Miller's *Death of a Salesman* probably is the best illustration of the fading American dream of "making it" in the middle class. Hermann Hesse's *Steppenwolf* is popular among the American young because it shows the perplexity of a man caught in the box of middle-class virtue. Its strictures are inhibiting even if rewarding. It does require conformity to convention. It is extremely difficult to be free, impulsive, expressive, and creative—and at the same time middle-class. Yet middle-class conventions do bring their reward of stability, so that the objection is not that they do not have value but that they are inhibiting.

If Christianity means a freedom from the outer observance of ceremonial law and the acceptance of all as equals, it should be able to survive the shock of separation after its happy years of marriage to American middle-class success. Not that the middle-class man does not deserve religion too—he perhaps needs it more just because he is not liberated externally. In fact, the odds are, as usual, that the greatest stability and financial support for religion will continue to come from this sector. The American "dollar aristocracy" may be less willing to be church-involved in the future, once they feel the impact of the new separation of church and state and the resulting threat to the status quo. The issue in America, then, is not so much the abandonment of middle-class patterns of religious life as it is a preservation of these forms while at the same time opening religious institutions to serve an increasing variety of people. If our religious life once tended to follow the ideal image of American middle-class life, the problem now becomes: Can we orient ourselves religiously in the future by a less idyllic model?

If America had an aristocracy which could set a pattern of taste for us all, or even if we had one church form, that would make our situation easier to deal with. For a while we thought the middle class could serve as this unifying ideal, both socially and religiously. To reject this, as many of the young have now done, is not really un-American but just a return to the harder times of frontier vulgarity and of admitting no single standard for all. Of course the Salvation Army and revival and Pentecostal groups helped to keep these old ways alive. And they see themselves vindicated as gospel tunes and informal style once again become popular. We Americans originally went to Europe to escape vulgarity and to find sophisticated and cultivated ways. When the return to the primitive becomes fashionable, we need no longer flee. We are beginning to like our peasant ways and to envy aristocrats less.

Sinclair Lewis parodied the foibles of the rural and provincial middle class in his *Main Street*. The interesting fact is that we have changed a great deal since that time. We are no longer Mark Twain's *Tom Sawyer*. The truth is that we are becoming all of these at once, and more. We came near to achieving a one-class society because we agreed on the values it should embody—or at least the underground press was not aboveground at that point. Now we are more segregated by life-style and values than ever before, and it remains to be seen how churches can adapt to serve such a wide variety of needs. Actually, the needs may still be very human and common, but the approaches to them will have to cover a broad spectrum.

If we had been able to keep an agreement to use the middle-class model, we might have kept unanimity, but it is exactly the uniformity implied in this that youth now rejects as a price too high to pay for harmony. The problem is the original one of the colonies, except that our degree of diversity far exceeds what had to be reconciled in 1776. Can such divergent people create a nation without demanding a single goal? Religiously, this issue was first resolved by a separation of church and state, and now the accumulated identification between the two must be set aside once again. The White House is not a temple for religious services, even if we hope a religious man will occupy it from time to time. As before, this new separation need not mean a lack of national support for religion in general. It should not imply hostility toward the government on the part of churches, but it must at least mean the tolerance of both a wide diversity of religions and the social critique that comes with diversity.

If our future experience is to include an even wider separation between social classes, this possibility again presses religion to minister to all without distinction or identification—to be *in* the United States but not *of* the United States. If we are true to our past, no one group will "win" the current revolution, but a greater variety of life-styles will emerge. Close as we came to it for a time, we will not speak one language in the future. A revolt brings greater separation if all styles remain and none are driven out. Those who control the financial and political centers of power will not give them up, and others will be in line to take their place; Consciousness III shall not enter here. If this proves true, religion must play a mediating role once again.

People have either derided or been embarrassed by Los Angeles and its proverbial jungle of religious variety. However, since the move to homogenize religion has failed, Los Angeles may turn out to be the Rome of America, its "holy city." The spurious is there along with the genuine, the vulgar along with the sophisticated, revivalism and faith healing and speaking in tongues along with new cultural centers. Los Angeles is as blatantly pagan as Sodom and Gomorrah. But if we grant that the goal is not to include the majority in churches but only those who want to join, then religion flourishes in multiplicity as well as in conformity. When the dance has gone on to exhaustion, the spirit develops just as many needs as the body, and perhaps at last the spirit's cries can be heard above the music.

Religion's hope is always to become part of what is ongoing. At the same time, not every new development ultimately enshrines itself or is later taken as characteristic of the age. Some religious movements are fruitful and grow and multiply, but others develop no such sustaining power because they identify too closely with a cultural pattern that passes away. The effect of a religion is seen in the lives of the men it changes. But the goal is permanent revival, not temporary alteration which washes off when the excitement is gone. Unfortunately, effective forms of change are few. Many experiments are tried—we seek new classical patterns by frantic novelty—but only a few have lasting beneficial results.

Contemporary America also includes a new leisure class. Some use their new freedom productively and to their satisfaction. Other spirits wither in leisure for lack of meaningful things to do. We want to reject the Protestant "work ethic," but when work is not our goal it is clear that psychologically this often produces intolerable pressures and anxieties. Work is a simple, obvious goal, so that if the clear, industrious values of the middle class are not to prevail, we are forced to fight the battle of the spirit, where victory is much less clear-cut. Identity becomes harder to grasp when it is created more from within and is determined less by obvious work requirements and standards. Without intending it, our achievement of more leisure has left us more vulnerable. It has launched us on a spiritual quest, and our survival hangs in the balance.

The renewed movement toward communal living and utopian communities is another contemporary phenomenon which has spiritual significance. The increasing mass society, produced by both technology and the expanding middle class, has induced a reaction in the form of a search for simpler and, in a human sense, more intimate and less harassed forms of living. This search has religious overtones. On the other hand, no simple identification will do here. The religious life cannot be equated with any particular external style, but it ought to affect the individual who is touched by it. This should show itself in the way he lives, of which utopian communities can be one expression. Some communal forms are more conducive to religious commitment than others; but no particular one can guarantee the presence of a religious spirit.

B. F. Skinner's vision of *Walden Two* is now amazingly passé. The principal character in his novel rejects nineteenth-century American utopias and uses modern social science as his theoretical base instead. Problems are solved by a scientific technology of human conduct, he asserts. Contemporary values are surpassed. He also shares the willingness of current utopians to experiment with something that matters, to *"experiment with your own life!"*[10] Such an attitude, whether itself religious or not, is consonant with Christianity, since it involves action and does not hold objective detachment as an unbreakable norm. However, securing "economic self-sufficiency with the help of modern technology" and "behavioral engineering" (p. 14) is not at all the present utopian goal. Amazingly enough, today we are much closer again to Thoreau and Walden Pond. Our progress is not inevitably toward Walden II but back to Walden I.

No matter what its benefits, at least one segment of society today revolts against the idea of "engineering" human beings. Such a return to nature and land and simplicity works against the transformation that scientific control requires. To say this is to decide in favor of neither group, but simply to realize that the clock does not always run forward. The elemental and the primitive are always with us, at least in America, and they stay barely beneath the surface. In religious life this demands the involvement of emotion. American churches, rather fortunately, will never have much luck as theological debating societies or as aesthetic centers of elaborate ritual. They must reflect the lives and emotional needs of the people—with all the perils this involves—or else they fail.

Of course, one irony in the rejection of social engineering is that this conflicts with the other god of our time, that is, the relief of the plight of "the wretched of the earth." Frantz Fanon is not American, but his book by that title helps us to remember that the rise of the blacks is not an American phenomenon but a world movement.[11] We sometimes forget this, because our awareness of our own record of slavery focuses attention primarily on our own past. In the history of the enslavement of the world, however, ours is a rather mild chapter. The "Third World" must be a factor in the churches' future life, and a new form of missionary service to it may need to emerge if we are to learn to reach outside ourselves. Elsewhere blacks seek national liberation. Here black and white are tied irretrievably together in an American spiritual renaissance.

Ferdinand Lundberg writes about the contrast of poverty and plenty that still exists in America and thus constantly rises to plague us.[12] As long as we dreamed that this inequality would eventually disappear, organized religion could take a different and more temperate attitude toward it. Now that it seems clear that such an ideal solution is not forthcoming, the role of religion in relation to the wretched of the land becomes an agonizing, permanent problem. Americans had not wanted to believe Jesus' saying that the poor would be always with us. The irony is that some social regimentation and loss of personal freedom is the only way to deal with poverty on a mass scale, and this Americans resist almost as much as being poor.

If one fundamental problem of political philosophy is "how the moral autonomy of the individual can be made compatible with the legitimate authority of the state,"[13] Americans are now caught in that dilemma—in both church and state—in ways they did not expect to see again. We believed that the vast bureaucratic structure initiated by the New Deal could handle almost every human problem. As Charles Reich and others inveigh against such mammoth organizations, we realize that individual liberty and the solution of social problems on a national scale are two goals that are constantly in conflict.

We have had anarchists in America in the past—which is not strange, given our heavy emphasis on human freedom. In a day of exasperation over social methods of control, it is not surprising to see anarchy grow again. This tendency also affects both college and church, since both require some subordination of the individual to community good, and that is precisely what many are unwilling to accept now. Thus the political crisis in America over individual rights has its counterpart in religion. The anarchist will accept no authority of one man over another as legitimate, and such an attitude carried over to the life of the church makes the individual's acceptance of a community role difficult if not impossible. While some of us treat all governments as nonlegitimate bodies whose commands must be evaluated in each instance before they are obeyed, the anarchist in religion has trouble binding himself to any command at all. But some obedience is essential if one is to acquire the religious spirit, which few men inherit naturally.

The agreement to accept majority rule is under attack today, as much from the right as from the radical left, both of which are extremely individualistic in different ways. Many black men, too, are prepared to follow Malcolm X's cry to reject any government which blacks do not control.[14] Further, the withdrawal from formal religion is as significant as the disaffection with government. Rebellions against constitutional decision and majority rule crop out everywhere. At times, we may think a solution can be found which will resolve these tensions and satisfy all. However, that idyllic result now seems unobtainable. American life-style is destined to produce turmoil. If we stay together, it will be because we learn to cope with this reality.

If there is a growing renaissance of Indian culture,[15] this too takes us back to the original situation in this country, rather than to the Westernized and assimilated Indians we had happily supposed would result. Indian tribal religion can highlight our own white tribal rituals by contrast. The Indian's struggle between his own inherited religion and the new Christianity is like the early days of Christianity in a Jewish context. Christianity must learn to speak to those with other gods by trying once again to convince pagans of the appearance of a new and powerful act of God. The middle class accepts religion too easily as a part of its acculturation and civilizing process. With the dispersion of the middle class and the proliferation of new values beyond number, religion is forced out on its own. The rebel demands something more radical from religion than that it make him "good." Such a minor transformation is not enough.

C. The Lovely Americans

If religion in America can no longer be identified with middle-class ideals, because the middle class is dissolving out from under it, it does not follow that religion here should be anti-middle-class, any more than it should be antiestablishment. That is too easy an alternative. The conservative spirit needs to worship, too. What we are brought back to in religion is its lack of class identification, so that all may be served equally.

Nevertheless, for a time at least, the break with traditional middle-class patterns is likely to increase in religious circles. Uniformity of dress in religious services may be the first outer sign to go, just as uniformity in the wedding ritual has already gone. In such experimentation, mistakes are bound to be made. Classical forms are safer, but we are back to the days of frontier chaos. The challenges are similar to those from which the original forms first emerged and then proved to have more than passing value.

Theologically speaking, any idea of God that goes along with experimentation must revise the notion of divine completeness. Emphases on plurality, diversity, and freedom, on the other hand, do not always produce good religion. Lots of nonsense will be preached—in Los Angeles and elsewhere—without any check on the purity of the message. Proletarian religion will be mixed with many questionable ties, so that we must get over our notion that all freedom is good. We must recognize that independence is worth having, but it often leads us down blind alleys and to a religious life without much content. However, such venturing is preferred now to a safer orthodoxy—in fact, we have no choice but to risk it. It is no wonder we face an identity crisis over being American. It doesn't mean any one thing easily, but rather involves a constant choice in order ever to become or to remain anything in particular.

We are back at the beginning again and have not really progressed much. However, this experience of return to native America may produce some lovely Americans to replace the ugly Americans so many have found embarrassing, ranging the globe as our national representatives. The ugly Americans were a product of our assumed superiority and inevitable triumph. With the loss of that confidence, we may go back to being just a home for the wretched and the poor, the hungry masses struggling to be free. Once that description applied to foreigners who passed the Statue of Liberty as they came from abroad. Now it applies to Americans at home trying to pick up the pieces of broken dreams.

Black religion might prove a liberating force here. Black theology never surrendered belief in radical evil. Black men have felt this evil and so could share no white optimism. Yet, interestingly enough, many of them also clung to God's omnipotence and thus the responsibility of his promise to heal human wounds. Blacks did not limit his power as some white theologians tended to do. Calvin and Augustine had reconciled evil by making God's actions necessary. However, black religious experience was much more likely to see him in terms of will and emotion and personal qualties, and this may fit the American religious situation more than most European descriptions of God. The black religious experience is free of "modern" hang-ups. It is elemental in its emotions and thus more traditional in its affirmation. Black religious inspiration may help to produce some lovely Americans.

What has surprised the recently affluent American is the speed with which many of the next generation rejected some of the material advantages that made us the envy of the world—and at the same time ugly and unloved. One seldom loves a person who carelessly possesses what others desperately need or want. It is a well-known fact that the spurning of material values comes not so much from the have-nots as from the haves. Since he who represents power and wealth cannot be loved, the widespread youthful return to the primitive is in part an attempt to be loved by being more desirable. This search is largely spiritual, and like the ancient religious hermit, young Americans have learned that both the world's values and surplus possessions must be surrendered before the human spirit can make much progress.

Thus, in exactly the opposite of our usual caricature, Americans are changing image and becoming inner-directed. The hearty, jovial, extroverted American may disappear along with the Model T—each a vintage product of its day. The proverbial national characteristics will become more inward, more difficult to detect, and thus perhaps more spiritual. That certainly is possible as a byproduct of the attempt to move away from the expansionist and outer-directed national image. Today we do not try to create an image by becoming supercultivated and slickly cultured in the arts and literature—once our only apparent avenue of escape from provincialism. The cocktail party with its sophisticated chatter is not a model for many of the young. More satisfaction may have to come from within and less from without. If any nation has explored the benefits of material possessions, we have, but it does not seem to satisfy the American soul.

America is a material culture now turned in upon itself, and the clash is all the more intense because our pride is strong and our power great. The ongoing struggle should be enormous, the crush gigantic, and the results both partially destructive and religiously significant. *The sometimes violent attempt of the materially unlovely to become spiritually beautiful is a fascinating plot to watch unfold.* "Rage" will appear—and has appeared—in white Americans as well as black. Blacks felt imprisoned by whites, but whites have reason to be even more outraged to find that they have only succeeded in imprisoning their own souls. Rage needs to focus on an object (whether real or imaginary) in order to gather itself, and in this respect blacks are conveniently situated; at least they have a visible object to focus on (whites), and the justification is there, even if oversimplified. We poor whites have no easy target but ourselves, and to see a man turn in upon himself can create a sight terrible to behold. It is also, religiously, the only way to go.

White American rage stems from the failure to achieve our goals or to find that they satisfy, and we can only turn it back upon ourselves. Our cultural failure is now as destructive to whites as black inferiority was to that group. But perhaps, according to the ancient religious message, we must destroy our old self to find new life, and the destruction of a former self is certainly a risk many of the young are taking—and succeeding in—these days. In spite of what we once hoped (and Charles Reich still promises), we face the unavoidable presence of violence in our future. The lack of singleness of goal, and our refusal now to accept material accomplishment as the test of loveliness, force the rage of an inner-directed spirit frequently to burst out in violence. As Americans we are not yet skilled in handling this inward quest. Since spirits cannot be rounded up like cattle, a stampede or a shooting match is bound to break out from time to time.

If we are uncertain as to the beauty of American material accomplishments—which are considerable, perhaps even a world's record—where is our beauty likely to be found in the future? Of course, in the past the generosity of Americans with their material wealth itself is a story of beauty, but that already has faded away, as our many resources prove unable to save the world from want. We have learned the old story that nobody loves even a generous wealthy man. Power only breeds envy. Thus the proverbial American desire to be loved and to be lovely is forced into different channels, strange ones for eyes so long oriented to the beauty of external affluence. We began this country religiously in part, but other more fascinating pursuits soon took over. Now we are back to the Pilgrims' quest for a place to worship God in freedom, but we have little acquired skill for this subtle spiritual game.

Into the midst of our notion of calm rural America, Norman O.

Brown has introduced *Love's Body*.[16] An unholy madness breaks loose, and the aphoristic style heralds a note of the transcendence of rationality. Apocalypse is the mood, and imagery is the medium much more than clear thought. This excites the spirit without drawing clear confines around it. In its untamed quality, it launches an American spiritual counterpart of Wild West expansion. It is a violent hurling of the spirit into the air. It batters the soul with meanings, just as the roar of traffic makes New York City constantly unquiet.

Probably nowhere else in the world have "free" churches known or embodied quite the measure of freedom which the expansion of America provided.[17] Along with this, we have in the past thought of ourselves as valuing the active over the contemplative life, but this balance may now be shifting. In the future, "activism" will exist amid a wide variety of values and styles and cease to be an accepted single model. In the same way, the main-line Protestant denominations will not go out of existence; and instead of forming one large common body, Christianity in America may have to put up with even greater variety and diversity.

Americans tried for a time to be very intellectual about their religion, but this did not work. We attempted to follow British and Continental theological trends. As with the pure intellectual life, a few Americans do follow such imported theories, but except perhaps for Barth's thought these trends have never passed over from the seminaries to shape the religious life of the whole people as the work of Augustine and Luther once did. Academic and scholarly theology simply cannot take root here among the masses in spite of all its discussion in seminaries. This is not to say that it does not have an educational value, but we have tried to mass-produce intellectuals in American colleges and universities, and the attempt did not take. To be effective here, a theology must speak to more than the intellect.

From the religious perspective, one difficulty we face in transforming ourselves into "lovely Americans" is the growing radical movement, plus the fact that as a nation we will never be all one thing. And the growth of variety involves at least some violence. The revolutionary can use "truth" to suit his own, perhaps good, humanitarian purposes. In the name of this goal of change, he adopts and pretends to accept certain roles on a provisional basis, depending on how they support his purposes. Yet religion and Christianity in particular have never used hidden means to accomplish a goal of transformation. In this sense there may be a similarity in aims to transform the present into a better world and men into better human beings, but the role of religion never takes the hidden route—unless of course its practice is outlawed, which is not the case in the United States.

If we want to look at the culture we are trying to transform, Tom Wolfe gives us some good verbal pictures.[18] Los Angeles is a picture of inevitable religious heterodoxy, but he takes Las Vegas to be a fundamental symbol of American life. In prosperity, massive amounts of money were pumped into every level of society. "Suddenly classes of people whose styles of life had been practically invisible had the money to build monuments to their own styles" (p. xiii). Some have lamented that we do not produce enough classical opera. Yet, whatever we do create in the arts (and in has its chance to flower profusely only amidst a great vulgar variety), the people as a whole will develop different art forms. Wolfe sees this reflected in the custom-car obsession. Las Vegas, he says, is the Versailles of America (p. xv).

Americans have had enough money for the common people (the "proles") to build monuments to their style of life "completely outside the art history tradition of the design schools of the Eastern universities" (p. xvi). This does not prevent the possibility of new styles and works of art emerging which may in time take their place among the classics; but this can only happen in America along with a fantastic, varied production of the blatant and the bawdy. The saloons of our Wild West era have simply reemerged in new forms, and this fact is of considerable importance to the secular desire to become lovely Americans and the religious desire to transform human lives. All this must be done in a Las Vegas style setting, it seems, or not at all.

Harvey Cox wants us to celebrate life, to capitalize on its potential for irrepressible festivity and its constant invitation to fantasy.[19] These suggestions are influential in young religious circles today, and they are important in the notion of developing a generation of lovely Americans. But the issue for American religious life is how this attitude can be assimilated. Cox thinks world-changers can be reconciled with celebrators of life in the "festive radical" (p. viii). The saint-revolutionary is the new style born of the re-birth of the spirit of festivity and fantasy—for fantasy can be social criticism as it unmasks the pretense of the powerful (p. 5).

This, of course, has always been a part of religion: to stand apart and not to accept society's estimate of value. If we have lost our own soul while gaining the whole world of commerce, as Cox claims (p. 7), can we become lovely and recapture religion by so easy a route as festivity and fantasy? Cox believes that festive revelry and an ability to fantasize are a way for man to grasp his divine origin (p. 10), and he is undoubtedly right insofar as such a spirit breaks open the confines of the modern rational attitude. We may need to put more verve and feeling into our parties, and religious practice may be much in need of a little evangelical spirit, but is this really enough to bring American religious centers to life and power again?

"The potency has drained from the religious symbols that once kept us in touch with our forebears," Cox says (p. 15). He is largely right again, but the issue is whether festivity and fantasy have enough religious significance to stem this tide. We do need to celebrate, but *first we need to find something worth celebrating.* Just to force ourselves to celebrate in the hope of uncovering a reason for it—this is a rather hollow affair and subject to dis-appointment. Christianity once engaged in religious worship to celebrate God's action. It is hard to remain Christian, ignore God, and simply celebrate man in pagan revelry. Moreover, we have been doing the latter in secular America for some time. It isn't new, and it doesn't seem worth very much fuss unless we learn *why* we celebrate.

Harvey Cox senses the restless American religious quest and the need to release the spirit. Yet from a religious standpoint he has little to say about God, and in fact seems to recommend that we not worry much about that consideration. But if we are tired of celebrating man (and perhaps that is why we've lost our capac-ity to celebrate), and if the religious response of joy is primarily a discovery of God and his action, then the American religious spirit can only be satisfied and given cause to celebrate if in its tribulations it discovers God in new ways. Christians celebrate a feast, as Jews do, and our "feasting" may be more somber and less joyous than it should be. This can change, not by forcing ourselves to celebrate, but by uncovering God and experiencing a movement of change in human life that gives us cause to feast in joy.

The search for a lovely American is very close to a religious quest, and it can become one if, in its course, we discover what God seems to be like now. The role of religion, in this American quest for release from an ugly or staid image, is an attempt to state religion's power to transform once again. The American quest for joy and release and loveliness of spirit is one with the religious desire to be born again. Thus many Americans, looking first at their past dreams, then at their creeping middle age, and finally at their uncertain accomplishments, ask, "Can a man be born again?" If religion ever recovers its traditional explanation of God's power and its unusual avenues to accomplish this rebirth, it could meet a ready acceptance on Main Street.

D. Beyond Marxism

Marxism grew out of the industrial age and came to dominate its later years, either by positive acceptance or negative rejection. Once radical thought was considered to be a thing of the past in America. It was something intellectuals had toyed with in times of economic depression but which now had been outgrown. Suddenly, on campus and in church, we are faced with a radical critique of American society and religion, and this time it stems as much from social and spiritual dissatisfaction as it does from economic disproportion. As far as Marxism is concerned, the question is whether we have grown beyond it—whether its "materialism" is really the opposite of the spiritually based revolution welling up inside the young.

For instance, ours is no longer an industrial age in simple Marxist terms, but an electronic age. Marxism vaunts itself as being "scientific," and that was a noble goal which offered rich prizes in Marx's day. Now we have tasted the fruits of scientific investigation until, like the sorcerer's apprentice, we cry for someone to turn off the flood of its engulfing benefits. To be scientific is no longer enough. We now see a scientific attitude as a monster which can enslave, pollute, and crush life in its machine, unless we are careful to keep it subservient to humane, nonscientific ends. The cry today is for release from the domination of sterile techniques.

The Marxist analyses of the control of economic forces by scientific understanding can no longer be accepted as the single solution for our problems—at least not in the form of dogmatic adherence which Marxism demands. We seem to cry for pluralism and a chance to explore endless variety, but Marxism is internally constructed intent upon rejecting any competing theory. It is born of the era in which salvation was thought to depend on the discovery of *the* scientific way. We are more prone to believe that no such simple avenue is available to any of us. We are saddled with a pluralism of "good ways," and must learn to live with that fact rather than try to convert everyone to one view, whether by persuasion or revolution or science.

Perhaps, then, a new American Religious Mission is being born, comparable to but different from the original colonial quest. Americans have felt, at times, like a people chosen by God for special things, and yet perhaps our present religious task grows precisely out of our shattered Tower of Babel and the realization that all has not turned out as we planned. Religious openness and hope spring only from a sense of common failure, not from a romantic humanism which trusts its own powers and goals implicitly. God could raise America up again out of the depths of black slavery—our original sin—and use the people for more interesting and vital purposes than our recent sense of power and wealth could have imagined. Our problem is to receive a new religious assignment arising out of the collapse of the American dream of a good life for all in isolation from man's ancient self-inflicted woes.

For instance, do America's private colleges, and her churches, still have a goal—admittedly a new one—of molding life in certain ways? In the rush to reject the old patterns of religious and educational indoctrination, a student generation rebelled against the idea of anyone else assuming responsibility for shaping his educational or spiritual direction. Nevertheless, that rebellion may stem more from our rejection of an old and now unsatisfactory notion of intellectual and educational formation than it does from a conviction that no direction is necessary during formative periods of growth. To discover what form this shaping might take depends on our ability to see a new religious mission for America. This is not to assume, of course, that every citizen would share in it, but only that it would arise in some out of their American religious experience.

In considering this question, we need to ask: What explains our behavior as Americans, if it is not a theory of economic determinism such as Marx offers? From the religious perspective (as we will try to state in the Postscript), the answer may lie in recognizing Americans as being still a pilgrim people, blasted off once more on a spiritual odyssey, an adventure of the soul in inner space. We might begin this inquiry by asking how those whom we have exploited, even in the process of achieving new corporate heights, are to be repaid. Since any lasting religious sense springs from a personal and communal sense of guilt, we now have an abundance of material for self-incrimination. We perhaps even go far beyond what we deserve in the severity of our self-denunciation.

Yet anyone who falls from virtue seldom is remembered later for his good deeds—unless he can be born again from his fall. Thus our problem is to turn self-incrimination into depth of religious feeling and personal healing. We thought we experienced God at the height of our success and in our many virtuous deeds, but now that America is like a fallen woman, the question is whether we can discover God in the strange phenomenon of a partial self-destruction, partially self-induced. As is traditional, the sinner accuses himself loudly and will not accept the consolation of remembering what he has done right. America's current mood, and her future course, fit amazingly into the ancient experience of fall and a search for new birth.

As we consider the age beyond Marx's vision, we have to ask what happens to a country once it achieves industrialization—and now electronic technology—in the way America has done to an astounding degree. Of course, Marx stressed one theory of economic control which he thought would bring us out to a new golden age. In practice, Marx's analysis, so amazing in his day, seems to have become incapable of grasping the explosions of succeeding years—uncanny as it was in its prophecy regarding rising industrial nations. The issue may still center on how the means of production are to be controlled, but the point is that the search today is to fill a spiritual thirst first, and this means that material forces are not the controlling factor of the day.

Marx banished God as detrimental to accomplishing the goal of material control and the conversion of national resources. Given the radical change in our situation since he wrote—and considering his strict dependence on a particular theory of historical development—the question is whether God has returned from exile with a new role to play. Marx attacked a view of God that is and probably always was unsatisfactory, but our question is whether our recent experience provides grounds to draw a new picture of God.

Since the classical Judeo-Christian religious experience of God comes through slavery and suffering and release, if Americans could find a release from their present spiritual suffering and stumble onto a balm for their bruised souls, they might yet become a people of God in ways they never expected. Then they could announce a God to the world who is capable of relating to a postmodern, postindustrial future. The role of American religious experience—and her various religious institutions—in this quest is crucial to the future, just as the variety of the religious experiences of the colonists poured in to shape the original American dream. The difference is that then we were largely new and pure, while now we are suddenly aged and scarred and not so clean in our record.

As Marshall McLuhan tells us, "Any technology tends to create a new human environment."[20] Thus, our day is as far into the electronic age as Marx's era was into the industrial age, and we experience the same confusion he did in being forced to live simultaneously in two contrasting forms of society and experience. Only one foot now remains in the world which Marx explored so profoundly. Major new factors have been set loose in the past hundred and fifty years that drive us—and soon Russia and China—beyond the world he knew. Amazingly, the electronic (vs. the technological) age allows us to identify with oral modes of communication again —as opposed to the German ideal of a perfect scholarly piece of printed research.

What is fascinating is that all this takes us, not beyond biblical times, but back to the age when we understood the impact and the way of an oral tradition. The "electric or post-literate time," as McLuhan calls it (p. 11), is amazingly primitive in form even if vastly sophisticated in its means. All of our faculties must become collectively conscious again—not just the mind, as in Descartes' model. This new orientation really fits our nonintellectual strain in America more comfortably than the Marxist notion that history is shaped by an inevitable dialectic. It suggests, too, that the individual as a whole can again become the center of the theory and replace the dominance of machines.

"Innumerable confusions and a profound feeling of despair invariably emerge in periods of great technological and cultural transitions."[21] We feel this in leaving Marx's industrial age, just as he felt—and responded so prophetically—when he entered it. "By now Communism is something that lies more than a century behind us, and we are deep into the new age of tribal involvement."[22] McLuhan thinks, moreover, that the arts have the power "to anticipate future social and technological developments, by a generation and more."[23] Whether true or not, religion has traditionally had a prophetic function, and if it is to be useful in the future before us it should recover that voice.

McLuhan views the Western world as now extending its consciousness to a global embrace, just as the mechanical age first extended bodies in space (p. 19). A nervous system now technologically expanded to involve the whole of mankind—that idea bursts the old limits of rationalism and opens us to transcendence. "The aspiration of our time for wholeness, empathy and depth of awareness is a natural adjunct of electric technology" (p. 21). And it also marks a return to the classical expression of the spiritual quest which is a part of all religions. Imagine—electronics reintroduces religious sensitivity and a spiritual desire! Electric circuitry has made our need for sensory awareness more acute.[24] Thus, it opens us to religious sensitivity rather than cutting us off as the machine age did.

Television is now the machine through which the American (and increasingly all) people are reached, Robert MacNeil points out, and this fact has caused a radical change in political communication.[25] As a people, we can be instantly informed, and yet this benefit also poses the threat of controlling us. Today we are in revolt against the domination of machines. We want not so much to control industrialization and the means of production as to free the human spirit from the threat of bondage to electronic devices. This means, however, that the spirit must be rediscovered as a reality different from the physical, or there will be no escape from the explosions of science that surround us.

We do not yet see clearly the shape of the age to come, the future in which we are destined to live. All we know is that it does not look like the early projections of the expanding age of science. The world is spinning backward from that point, and all we feel at present is the wrench of being torn loose from familiar moorings. The clean, closed, smooth, rational scientific world which once forced God out is itself today breaking open, and our experience is that of beginning again with the primitive. Now we know how it felt on the day before creation, when God's hand had only begun to stir and move against chaos. In some ways, no previous religious form available to us can quite express this experience. Yet we feel a kinship to every religious ritual and spiritual awakening.

In such a disturbing time, when our promised methods of complete control are failing, we are open to understand prophecy and miracle, because the future does not feel like a mere extension of the past, and because we know in our own experience what it means to feel the natural order violated and broken in upon. Religion, at least in the West, is built around prophecy and a concentration on the future. At the same time, these qualities usually are closely related to an appraisal of the meaning of the past.

Most Americans have never been particularly historical-minded. Like the Greeks, their spiritual brothers, they are too busy quarreling among themselves and planning the future to use such a complicated mode of understanding. The first Americans were future-oriented. They had no past here to think about. Nevertheless, we now have a record to contemplate, and the upheaval of inbreaking revolution demands that we reflect on it at the same time that we turn inward to draw knowledge from our anguished souls. The hope is to recover a new, prophetic vision of the future.

NOTES

1. Richard Wright, *White Man Listen!* (Garden City, N.Y.: Doubleday Anchor Books, 1964), p. ix. This book was originally published in 1957.

2. Richard Wright, *Native Son* (New York: Harper & Row, 1966), p. xiii. This book was originally published in 1940.

3. See Charles M. Wiltsie, ed., *David Walker's Appeal* (New York: Hill & Wang, 1965).

4. See Martin Luther King, Jr., "Letter from Birmingham Jail," as reprinted in *Protest: Man Against Society*, ed. Gregory Armstrong (New York: Bantam Books, 1969), pp. 97–113.

5. James Baldwin, *Another Country* (New York: Dell Publishing Company, 1960), p. 301.

6. James Baldwin, *Notes of a Native Son* (Boston: Beacon Press, 1955), p. 5.

7. James Baldwin, *The Fire Next Time* (New York: Delta Books, 1964), p. 24.

8. See William H. Grier and Price M. Cobbs, *Black Rage* (New York: Bantam Books, 1969).

9. William H. Grier and Price M. Cobbs, *The Jesus Bag* (New York: McGraw-Hill Book Company, 1971), p. 1.

10. B. F. Skinner, *Walden Two* (New York: Macmillan Company, 1962), p. 9. This book was originally published in 1948.

11. See Frantz Fanon, *The Wretched of the Earth*, trans. Constance Farrington (New York: Grove Press, 1968). The book was originally published in 1961.

12. See Ferdinand Lundberg, *The Rich and the Super-Rich* (New York: Bantam Books, 1969).

13. Robert Paul Wolff, *In Defense of Anarchism* (New York: Harper Torchbooks, 1970), p. vii.

14. See *Malcolm X Speaks* (New York: Grove Press, 1966).

15. See Stan Steiner, *The New Indians* (New York: Delta Books, 1968).

16. See Norman O. Brown, *Love's Body* (New York: Vintage Books, Random House, 1966).

17. James Ward Smith and A. Leland Jamison, eds., *The Shaping of American Religion* (Princeton, N.J.: Princeton University Press, 1961), p. 11.

18. See Tom Wolfe, *The Kandy-Kolored Tangerine-Flake Streamline Baby* (New York: Noonday Press, 1970).

19. See Harvey Cox, *The Feast of Fools* (New York: Harper & Row, 1969).

20. Marshall McLuhan, *The Gutenberg Galaxy* (New York: New American Library, 1969), p. 7.

21. Marshall McLuhan and Quentin Fiore, *The Medium is the Massage* (New York: Bantam Books, 1967), p. 8.

22. Marshall McLuhan and Quentin Fiore, *War and Peace in the Global Village* (New York: Bantam Books, 1968), p. 5.

23. Marshall McLuhan, *Understanding Media* (New York: New American Library, 1964), p. xi.

24. Marshall McLuhan and Harley Parker, *Through the Vanishing Point* (New York: Harper & Row, 1969), p. xxiii.

25. Robert MacNeil, *The People Machine* (New York: Harper & Row, 1968), pp. ix, xiii.

POSTSCRIPT

2001: A SPIRITUAL ODYSSEY

My soul, your voyages have
been your native land!
—Nikos Kazantzakis, *The Odyssey: A Modern Sequel*[1]

America has started off on a new trip. Fasten your seat belts. The
journey will be rough. Taming the wilderness, conquering space, developing marvels of technology—all will prove to have been smooth
paths compared to this one. Now our task is not so much to bring
law and order to the Wild West—although shoot-outs in the
streets are here again—or even to industrialize a continent. Instead, the adventure that grips many Americans today is essentially
a *spiritual* quest, and that makes it difficult to plan just because
we are unused to traveling inward. The landmarks are unclear
in this uneasy territory, and success is difficult to discern.

"Odyssey" is a concept given its meaning by Homer, a Greek
poet who saw very clearly what life is all about. The word
comes from his long epic poem recounting the adventures of Odysseus on his way home from the siege of Troy. More popularly, we
use it to mean a long wandering, referring again to Odysseus's
series of adventures or journeys in the course of his attempt to get
home, marked as it was by many changes of fortune. You start out
on a fishing trip feeling pleasure and high anticipation; but an
odyssey is a journey of frequently unwilling adventurers who have

to pursue a course not entirely of their own choosing. Such factors add up to a strange tale. Yet, like it or not—and it runs counter to the happy image we have had of ourselves—Americans have just been shoved off on an extensive intellectual/spiritual wandering or quest of just this kind.

We are unwilling adventurers in this new land of the spirit, because we were not ready to leave the paradise of a rural and virtuous America. Yet we can hardly wait to have someone write up our spiritual wanderings into an epic poem. It hurts so much to live through all this, that to put it all in poetic form might make the torment seem beautiful, just as blacks write magnificent literature today out of their suffering spirit.

Unfortunately, the results of our odyssey cannot yet be written up. The wanderings have just begun. The year 2001 is not now. The countdown has been completed. The blast-off has occurred. But the long journey is barely under way. The sufferings and the torments of renowned Odysseus are about to have an American sequel, and the only hope of deliverance seems to be to pass through all the stages of our contemporary anxieties and to pursue even the most daring hopes.

This modern struggle offers us a greater adventure than opening the frontier. It starts off by responding to the call of freedom, flinging back necessity's firm yoke. As Kazantzakis puts it:

> *Learn, lads, that Time has cycles and that Fate has wheels*
> *and that the mind of man sits high and twirls them round;*
> *come quick, let's spin the world about and send it tumbling!* (p. 1)

> *Snatch prudence from me, God, burst my brows wide, fling far*
> *the trap doors of my mind, let the world breathe awhile.* (p. 2)

Into such a spiritual odyssey we Americans have reluctantly been pushed, and it will make the Crusades of the Middle Ages look like child's play, because this time the battle will be fought more within than without. In such a situation, we can be sure that religion will not serve as a source of national unity. That is, it cannot unless we all forget our ancient quarrels and join the high adventure.

Our generation has lived through a space odyssey. That is a unique experience which men who lived before us cannot claim. It raises, however, more issues than it solves. For example, the movie version of *2001: A Space Odyssey* shows man's development, coming first from out of a silent planet, then unfolding to future fantastic space exploits and transformations.[2] It ends with man on his way to Venus, whereas Odysseus's adventures bring him home again. The end of space-man is his own self-transformation into a higher being, his spiritual rebirth, his divinization through man's own creative vision. The movie ends once again in silence, just as it began among the speechless apes. Yet today we have lost all such confidence that man can transform himself. We are not at all sure that man's adventures in space will in any way alter his spiritual condition for the better.

Then, is the great odyssey from now until the year 2001 really to take place in space? Yes—but more in inner space than outer. Let us agree to stop and reflect again when we reach that first year in the twenty-first century. Then we'll look back and see on what fronts the great American exploration has taken place. If we are blasted off onto a spiritual odyssey, and if we are to reach into the future, what will it be like? Science fiction is popular, but there is no reason why there should not be a booming business in spiritual fiction too—and what if some of our soul's predicted adventures and exploits should come true? Americans now wander the earth incessantly. No other people do or ever have traveled as much as we. It seems that our souls must be very restless. Other people with money do not spend it in that way. Could it be that what Americans are really searching for through incessant travel is their spiritual home and the route back to their native land?

We wander the face of the globe further than Odysseus could have thought of going. Without our knowing it, perhaps our soul's voyages are our native land. That is, we really are unsure what it means to be an American now or how to live on our own native soil, and we are even less sure just how the American dream is turning out. Some men run from this uncertainty. The real adventure, however, is to accept the wanderlust of our spirit and push on with this strange voyage in the hope that it will bring us home in due time. Our travels would appear to take us to Katmandu and to Fiji. In reality, they are spiritual and just as much an exploration of our mother country as the expedition of Lewis and Clark into the great Northwest. We must not be fooled by so superficial a fact as that our wanderings take us first to strange lands. It is still our native land that we explore and seek to understand from afar.

Theodore Dreiser's *An American Tragedy* is the story of a boy who begins as a street evangelist but rebels against his family's obsession with religion, only later to forfeit his life in desperate pursuit of success.[3] The novel is also a portrayal of the American society that shapes his tawdry ambitions and seals his fate. In half a century we have come a long way from Dreiser's commercial Midwest. We no longer start with revivalist street-corner religion and then reject it to pursue secular pleasures. Today we more likely start in the midst of Las Vegas-style fleshpots and ask if this wild life is necessary or whether the spirit can rebel a second time and find its way home.

If, a short time ago, we used to laugh at street-corner revivalism, owing to our new-found intellectual and artistic instant-culture, how can Judy Collins create a popular folk hit by singing an old revival tune, "Amazing Grace"? The words are simple and emotional in their appeal, hardly Bach or electronic rock. Listen to the verse:

> Amazing grace—how sweet the sound—
> That saved a wretch like me!
> I once was lost, but now am found,
> Was blind, but now I see.

The theme of lostness and of spiritual seeking haunts the refrain, and that tells it like it is where America is concerned today.

Ralph Ellison's novel, *Invisible Man,* chronicles the experience of what it is like to be black in a white society.[4] The major character wants the reader to see the world through his eyes, to understand what it means to be treated as if you didn't even exist. Today all Americans seem a little invisible. We do not quite know how to "see" one another. Our outer dress and manner are sometimes strange, so much so that we are sure that nothing visible any longer defines the man. If we are to see Americans again, if we are to become visible to each other, we may have to learn what "the eyes of the spirit" mean. They enable us to look inside each other, and that is not as easy as to play baseball or eat a hamburger. The visible, distinguishing marks of Americans are rapidly fading. We will have to discover other less overt signs if we are ever to see each other again.

Of course, what we see most vividly in America today we often do not like. We cannot escape seeing the Black Panthers and Huey Newton on trial for killing an Oakland policeman.[5] On the surface, the trial probably was a fair one. Underneath, forces move larger than any individual: both sides are blinded by myths and images, moved by rage and fear. We need not go to Greece any more. We have all of the classic ingredients for high tragedy right here in our own homeland. Watching such events, we feel like people in a nightmare. Panthers and police—unable to see each other as human and American—both contribute to the doomed collision. We all stand alert in limbo, American but barely so, American but divided and poised to attack each other.

Blacks in this country have found their tongue and pen (as well as their sword). The literature is beautiful and powerful and tragic and also very spiritual—full of "soul." Some of us still prefer the Horatio Alger story of the very–American struggle for success. But *The Autobiography of Malcolm X* is also an American (underground) success story[6]—at the moment a story probably more influential than that of Tom Sawyer. Yet Malcolm X rejects Christianity and arouses fear and hatred in the white man by his struggle. Malcolm X constantly walked in danger, and he lived in ways we have not been used to picturing as American life. He is also a doomed figure, a man of mission, a powerful personality who purged himself of all the ills that afflict the depressed Negro mass: drugs, alcohol, tobacco, not to speak of criminal pursuits. He achieved a form of human redemption, and he called others to do likewise, even by violence.

Yet, amazing to realize, the afflictions of the Negro mass—it makes us shudder to read the list—are not too far from those that now threaten to place white America in bondage. We whites are like Malcolm X; we just have a wider number in need of personal redemption, restoration, and return from a lost condition—with the homecoming veterans of Vietnam heading the list. On the other hand,

Peter L. Berger in his *Noise of Solemn Assemblies* describes the state of mind of the churches in America as "a sort of Christian malaise."[7] He is convinced that an erosion of genuine Christian content has taken place. If true, this leaves us ill prepared at a time when we are forced off on a spiritual odyssey—protesting all the way that we would rather watch football on television. Can the American church be born again to meet this new and more difficult challenge?

In spite of all this, Berger goes on to conclude that "America represents the future more than any other society" (p. 18). Why? Simply because all the forces we have to meet and overcome—just as Odysseus must triumph in the trials and tribulations of his journey before he can return home—all these are present in their most advanced form in America. Industrialization, technology, vast bureaucracy, pollution, enormous education, high science, instant communication, noise, decaying cities, and above all, the problem of how slave and master can discover freedom and release together.

Such a challenge in the future involves high adventure, but the battle will not be fought on the sea or on the land or in the air. This country is already explored and now even crowded. The venture into which we are unwillingly plunged is a spiritual odyssey. It should lead us back to 1620 and 1776, and beyond to 2001. Our soul's forced voyage is its native land, spiritual wanderers that we have become. At last, as the twenty-first century approaches, present-day Americans can discover what it means to be a pilgrim.

NOTES

1. Nikos Kazantzakis, *The Odyssey: A Modern Sequel,* trans. Kimon Friar (New York: Simon & Schuster, 1969), p. 509.

2. See also Arthur C. Clarke, *2001: A Space Odyssey* (New York: New American Library, 1968). This novel is based on the screenplay of the film, written by Stanley Kubrick and Arthur C. Clarke.

3. See Theodore Dreiser, *An American Tragedy* (New York: New American Library, 1964). This novel was originally published in 1925.

4. See Ralph Ellison, *Invisible Man* (New York: Random House, 1952).

5. See the account of Gilbert Moore, *A Special Rage* (New York: Harper & Row, 1971).

6. See *The Autobiography of Malcolm X* (New York: Grove Press, 1966). Written with Alex Haley.

7. Peter L. Berger, *The Noise of Solemn Assemblies* (Garden City, N.Y.: Doubleday & Company, 1961), p. 9.

SELECTED BIBLIOGRAPHY

Adams, John. *The Political Writings of John Adams.* Edited by George A. Peek, Jr., New York: Liberal Arts Press, 1954.

Altizer, Thomas J. J., and Hamilton, William. *Radical Theology and the Death of God.* Indianapolis: Bobbs-Merrill Company, 1966.

Altizer, Thomas J. J. *The Descent into Hell.* Philadelphia: J. B. Lippincott Company, 1970.

————. *The Gospel of Christian Atheism.* Philadelphia: Westminster Press, 1966.

————, ed. *Toward a New Christianity: Readings in the Death of God Theology.* New York: Harcourt, Brace & World, 1967.

Arendt, Hannah. *On Revolution.* New York: Viking Press, 1965.

Armstrong, Gregory, ed. *Protest: Man Against Society.* New York: Bantam Books, 1969.

Baird, Robert. *Religion in America.* New York: Harper & Row, 1970.

Baldwin, James. *Another Country.* New York: Dell Publishing Company, 1960.

————. *The Fire Next Time.* New York: Delta Books, 1964.

————. *Notes of a Native Son.* Boston: Beacon Press, 1955.

Bellah, Robert H. *Beyond Belief.* New York: Harper & Row, 1970.

Berger, Peter L. *The Noise of Solemn Assemblies.* Garden City, N.Y.: Doubleday & Company, 1961.

————. *A Rumor of Angels.* Garden City, N.Y.: Doubleday Anchor Books, 1970.

————. *The Sacred Canopy.* Garden City, N.Y.: Doubleday Anchor Books, 1969.

Brauer, Jerald C. *Protestantism in America.* Philadelphia: Westminster Press, 1953.

Bridges, Hal. *American Mysticism.* New York: Harper & Row, 1970.

Brown, Norman O. *Love's Body.* New York: Vintage Books, Random House, 1966.

Burke, Edmund. *Reflections on the Revolution in France.* Edited by Thomas H. D. Mahoney. New York: Liberal Arts Press, 1955.

Bushnell, Horace. *Horace Bushnell.* Edited by H. Shelton Smith. New York: Oxford University Press, 1965.

Channing, William Ellery. *Unitarian Christianity and Other Essays.* Edited by Irving H. Bartlett. Indianapolis: Bobbs-Merrill Company, 1957.

Clarke, Arthur C. *2001: A Space Odyssey.* New York: New American Library, 1968.

Cleage, Albert B., Jr. *The Black Messiah.* New York: Sheed & Ward, 1968.

Clebsch, William A. *From Sacred to Profane America.* New York: Harper & Row, 1968.

Cobb, John B., Jr. *A Christian Natural Theology.* Philadelphia: Westminster Press, 1965.

Cohen, Morris R. *American Thought.* New York: Collier Books, 1962.

Cone, James H. *Black Theology and Black Power.* New York: Seabury Press, 1969.

————. *A Black Theology of Liberation.* Philadelphia: J. B. Lippincott Company, 1970.

Cox, Harvey. *The Feast of Fools.* New York: Harper & Row, 1969.

————. *The Secular City.* New York: London: SCM Press, 1965.

Dewart, Leslie. *The Foundations of Belief.* New York: Herder & Herder, 1969.

————. *The Future of Belief.* New York: Herder & Herder, 1966.

Dewey, John. *A Common Faith.* New Haven: Yale University Press, 1964.

————. *Experience and Nature.* New York: Dover Publications, 1958.

Dreiser, Theodore. *An American Tragedy.* New York: New American Library, 1964.

Edwards, Jonathan. *Freedom of the Will.* Edited by Paul Ramsey. New Haven: Yale University Press, 1957.

————. *The Nature of True Virtue.* Ann Arbor: University of Michigan Press, 1960.

————. *Religious Affections.* Edited by John E. Smith. New Haven: Yale University Press, 1959.

————. *Selections.* Edited by Clarence H. Faust and Thomas H. Johnson. New York: American Book Company, 1935.

Ellison, Ralph. *Invisible Man.* New York: Random House, 1952.

Emerson, Ralph Waldo. *The Selected Writings of Ralph Waldo Emerson.* Edited by Brooks Atkinson. New York: Modern Library, 1950.

Fanon, Frantz. *The Wretched of the Earth.* Trans. by Constance Farrington. New York: Grove Press, 1968.

Franklin, Benjamin. *The Autobiography and Selections.* Edited by Herbert W. Schneider. New York: Liberal Arts Press, 1952.

Friedrich, C. J., and McCloskey, Robert G., eds. *From the Declaration of Independence to the Constitution.* New York: Liberal Arts Press, 1954.

Gabriel, Ralph H., ed. *Hamilton, Madison and Jay on the Constitution: Selections from the Federalist Papers.* New York: Liberal Arts Press, 1954.

Gilkey, Langdon. *Naming the Whirlwind: The Renewal of God Language.* Indianapolis: Bobbs-Merrill Company, 1969.

Gilson, Etienne. *Being and Some Philosophers.* Toronto: Pontifical Institute of Medieval Studies, 1949.

————. *God and Philosophy.* New Haven: Yale University Press, 1941.

Goodman, Mitchell, ed. *The Movement Toward a New America: The Beginnings of a Long Revolution.* New York: Alfred A. Knopf, 1970.

Grier, William H., and Cobbs, Price M. *Black Rage.* New York: Bantam Books, 1969.

————. *The Jesus Bag.* New York: McGraw-Hill Book Company, 1971.

Hamilton, William. *The New Essence of Christianity.* Rev. ed. New York: Association Press, 1966.

Hartshorne, Charles. *The Divine Relativity.* New Haven: Yale University Press, 1948.

————. *Man's Vision of God.* New York: Harper & Brothers, 1941.

Hocking, William Ernest. *Living Religions and a World Faith.* London: George Allen & Unwin, 1940.

————. *The Meaning of God in Human Experience.* New Haven: Yale University Press, 1912.

James, William. *The Moral Equivalent of War and Other Essays.* Edited by John K. Roth. New York: Harper & Row, 1971.

————. *The Moral Philosophy of William James.* Edited by John K. Roth. New York: Thomas Y. Crowell Company, 1969.

————. *A Pluralistic Universe.* New York: Longmans, Green, & Company, 1909.

————. *Pragmatism.* New York: Longmans, Green, & Company, 1907.

————. *The Principles of Psychology.* 2 vols. New York: Henry Holt & Company, 1890.

————. *Some Problems of Philosophy.* Edited by Henry James, Jr. New York: Longmans, Green, & Company, 1911.

————. *The Varieties of Religious Experience.* New York: Modern Library, 1955.

————. *The Will to Believe and Other Essays in Popular Philosophy.* New York: Longmans, Green, & Company, 1897.

Jefferson, Thomas. *The Political Writings of Thomas Jefferson.* Edited by Edward Dumbauld. New York: Liberal Arts Press, 1955.

Jones, Major J. *Black Awareness: A Theology of Hope.* Nashville: Abingdon Press, 1971.

Kazantzakis, Nikos. *The Odyssey: A Modern Sequel.* Trans. by Kimon Friar. New York: Simon & Schuster, 1969.

King, Martin Luther, Jr. *Strength to Love.* New York: Pocket Books, 1964.

————. *Stride Toward Freedom.* New York: Harper & Row, 1964.

————. *The Trumpet of Conscience.* New York: Harper & Row, 1968.

————. *Where Do We Go From Here: Chaos or Community?* Boston: Beacon Press, 1968.

Kurtz, Paul, ed. *American Philosophy in the Twentieth Century.* New York: Macmillan Company, 1966.

————, ed. *American Thought Before 1900.* New York: Macmillan Company, 1966.

Lincoln, C. Eric, ed. *Is Anybody Listening to Black America?* New York: Seabury Press, 1968.

Lindbeck, George. *The Future of Roman Catholic Theology.* Philadelphia: Fortress Press, 1970.

Lonergan, Bernard. *Insight: A Study of Human Understanding.* London: Longmans, Green, & Company, 1958.

Lundberg, Ferdinand. *The Rich and the Super-Rich.* New York: Bantam Books, 1968.

Malcolm X. *Malcolm X Speaks.* New York: Grove Press, 1966.

————, with Alex Haley. *The Autobiography of Malcolm X.* New York: Grove Press, 1966.

Marcuse, Herbert. *One-Dimensional Man.* Boston: Beacon Press, 1964.

Maritain, Jacques. *Approaches to God.* New York: Collier Books, 1962.

————. *Existence and the Existent.* Trans. by Lewis Galantiere and Gerald B. Phelan. New York: Pantheon, 1948.

Mather, Cotton. *Selections.* Edited by Kenneth B. Murdock. New York: Hafner Publishing Company, 1926.

Mays, Benjamin E. *The Negro's God.* New York: Atheneum Press, 1968.

McLoughlin, William, and Bellah, Robert, eds. *Religion in America.* Boston: Beacon Press, 1968.

McLuhan, Marshall. *The Gutenberg Galaxy.* New York: New American Library, 1969.

————. *Understanding Media.* New York: New American Library, 1964.

McLuhan, Marshall, and Fiore, Quentin. *The Medium is the Massage.* New York: Bantam Books, 1967.

————. *War and Peace in the Global Village.* New York: Bantam Books, 1968.

McLuhan, Marshall, and Parker, Harley. *Through the Vanishing Point.* New York: Harper & Row, 1969.

MacNeil, Robert. *The People Machine.* New York: Harper & Row, 1968.

Merton, Thomas. *Thoughts in Solitude.* Garden City, N.Y.: Doubleday Image Books, 1968.

Miller, Perry, and Johnson, Thomas, eds. *The Puritans: A Source Book of Their Writings.* 2 vols. New York: Harper & Row, 1963.

Mitchell, Henry H. *Black Preaching.* Philadelphia: J. B. Lippincott Company, 1970.

Moore, Gilbert. *A Special Rage.* New York: Harper & Row, 1971.

Niebuhr, H. Richard. *The Kingdom of God in America.* New York: Harper & Brothers, 1937.

———. *The Meaning of Revelation.* New York: Macmillan Company, 1946.

Niebuhr, Reinhold. *An Interpretation of Christian Ethics.* New York: Harper & Brothers, 1935.

———. *The Nature and Destiny of Man.* 2 vols. New York: Charles Scribner's Sons, 1947.

Novak, Michael. *Belief and Unbelief.* London: Darton, Longman & Todd, 1966.

———. *The Experience of Nothingness.* New York: Harper & Row, 1970.

———. *A Theology for Radical Politics.* New York: Herder & Herder, 1969.

Ogden, Shubert M. *The Reality of God.* New York: Harper & Row, 1966.

Olmstead, Clifton E. *History of Religion in the United States.* Englewood Cliffs, N.J.: Prentice-Hall, 1960.

O'Meara, Thomas F., and Weisser, Donald M., eds. *Projections: Shaping an American Theology for the Future.* Garden City: Doubleday & Company, 1970.

Paine, Thomas. *The Age of Reason.* Edited by Alburey Castell. New York: Liberal Arts Press, 1948.

———. *Common Sense and Other Political Writings.* Edited by Nelson F. Adkins. New York: Liberal Arts Press, 1953.

Parker, Theodore. *Theism, Atheism and the Popular Theology.* Edited by Charles W. Wendte. Boston: American Unitarian Association, 1907.

———. *Theodore Parker: An Anthology.* Edited by Henry Steele Commager. Boston: Beacon Press, 1960.

Peirce, Charles S. *Charles S. Peirce: Selected Writings.* Edited by Philip P. Wiener. New York: Dover Publications, 1966.

———. *Philosophical Writings of Peirce.* Edited by Justus Buchler. New York: Dover Publications, 1955.

Potok, Chaim. *The Chosen.* Greenwich, Conn.: Fawcett Publications, 1967.

Rauschenbusch, Walter. *Christianity and the Social Crisis.* Edited by Robert D. Cross. New York: Harper & Row, 1964.

Reich, Charles A. *The Greening of America.* New York: Bantam Books, 1971.

Richardson, Herbert W. *Toward an American Theology.* New York: Harper & Row, 1967.

Richardson, Herbert W., and Cutler, Donald R., eds. *Transcendence.* Boston: Beacon Press, 1969.

Roszak, Theodore. *The Making of a Counter Culture.* Garden City, N.Y.: Doubleday Anchor Books, 1968.

Roth, Robert J., S.J. *American Religious Philosophy.* New York: Harcourt, Brace & World, 1967.

Royce, Josiah. *The Philosophy of Josiah Royce.* Edited by John K. Roth. New York: Thomas Y. Crowell Company, 1971.

————. *The Problem of Christianity.* 2 vols. New York: Macmillan Company, 1913.

————. *Studies of Good and Evil: A Series of Essays upon Life and Philosophy.* New York: Appleton, 1898.

————. *The World and the Individual.* 2 vols. New York: Macmillan Company, 1899, 1901.

Rubenstein, Richard L. *After Auschwitz.* Indianapolis: Bobbs-Merrill Company, 1966.

————. *Morality and Eros.* New York: McGraw-Hill Book Company, 1970.

————. *The Religious Imagination.* Indianapolis: Bobbs-Merrill Company, 1968.

Santayana, George. *The Genteel Tradition: Nine Essays by George Santayana.* Edited by Douglas L. Wilson. Cambridge: Harvard University Press, 1967.

————. *The Life of Reason.* Vol. 3. *Reason in Religion.* New York: Collier Books, 1962.

Schneider, Herbert W. *A History of American Philosophy.* New York: Columbia University Press, 1946.

————. *The Puritan Mind.* Ann Arbor: University of Michigan Press, 1958.

Skinner, B. F. *Walden Two.* New York: Macmillan Company, 1962.

Smith, John E. *The Spirit of American Philosophy.* New York: Oxford University Press, 1966.

————. *Themes in American Philosophy.* New York: Harper Torchbooks, 1970.

Smith, James Ward, and Jamison, A. Leland, eds. *The Shaping of Religion in America.* Princeton: Princeton University Press, 1961.

Steiner, Stan. *The New Indians.* New York: Delta Books, 1968.

Thoreau, Henry David. *The Portable Thoreau.* Edited by Carl Bode. New York: Viking Press, 1964.

Tillich, Paul. *The Courage to Be.* New Haven: Yale University Press, 1952.

————. *Love, Power, and Justice.* New York: Oxford University Press, 1954.

————. *Systematic Theology.* Vol. 1. Chicago: University of Chicago Press, 1951.

————. *Theology of Culture.* New York: Oxford University Press, 1959.

Tocqueville, Alexis de. *Democracy in America.* Trans. by Henry Reeve. Chicago: Henry Regnery Company, 1951.

Van Buren, Paul. *The Secular Meaning of the Gospel.* New York: Macmillan Company, 1966.

————. *Theological Explorations.* New York: Macmillan Company, 1968.

Washington, Joseph R., Jr. *Black Religion.* Boston: Beacon Press, 1964.

————. *Black and White Power Subreption.* Boston: Beacon Press, 1969.

————. *Marriage in Black and White.* Boston: Beacon Press, 1970.

————. *The Politics of God.* Boston: Beacon Press, 1967.

Watts, Alan. *Does It Matter?* New York: Vintage Books, Random House, 1971.

————. *The Wisdom of Insecurity.* New York: Pantheon, 1951.

Weiss, Paul. *The God We Seek.* Carbondale, Ill.: Southern Illinois University Press, 1964.

————. *Modes of Being.* Carbondale: Southern Illinois University Press, 1958.

————. *Religion and Art.* Milwaukee: Marquette University Press, 1963.

Whitehead, Alfred N. *Process and Reality.* New York: Social Science Bookstore, 1941.

————. *Religion in the Making.* New York: Macmillan Company, 1926.

————. *Science and the Modern World.* New York: Macmillan Company, 1925.

Wieman, Henry Nelson. *Man's Ultimate Commitment.* Carbondale, Ill.: Southern Illinois University Press, 1958.

————. *The Source of Human Good.* Carbondale, Ill.: Southern Illinois University Press, 1946.

Williams, Daniel Day. *The Spirit and the Forms of Love.* New York: Harper & Row, 1968.

Wiltsie, Charles M., ed. *David Walker's Appeal.* New York: Hill & Wang, 1965.

Wolfe, Tom. *The Kandy–Kolored Tangerine–Flake Streamline Baby.* New York: Noonday Press, 1970.

Wolff, Robert Paul. *In Defense of Anarchism.* New York: Harper Torchbooks, 1970.

Wright, Richard. *Native Son.* New York: Harper & Row, 1966.

———. *White Man Listen!* Garden City, N.Y.: Doubleday Anchor Books, 1964.

INDEX